Peace and the
Public Purse

**CENTER ON
INTERNATIONAL
COOPERATION**

Studies in Multilateralism

Peace and the Public Purse

Economic Policies for Postwar Statebuilding

edited by
James K. Boyce
Madalene O'Donnell

LYNNE
RIENNER
PUBLISHERS

BOULDER
LONDON

Published in the United States of America in 2007 by
Lynne Rienner Publishers, Inc.
1800 30th Street, Boulder, Colorado 80301
www.rienner.com

and in the United Kingdom by
Lynne Rienner Publishers, Inc.
3 Henrietta Street, Covent Garden, London WC2E 8LU

Library of Congress Cataloging-in-Publication Data
Peace and the public purse : economic policies for postwar statebuilding /
James K. Boyce and Madalene O'Donnell, editors.
    p.   cm. — (Center on international cooperation studies in
multilateralism)
   Includes bibliographical references and index.
   ISBN 978-1-58826-540-1 (hardcover : alk. paper) — ISBN 978-1-58826-516-6
(pbk. : alk. paper)
    1. Economic assistance—International cooperation.   2. Postwar
reconstruction—Case studies.   3. Nation-building—Case studies.
4. Finance, public.   I. Boyce, James K.   II. O'Donnell, Madalene.
   HC60.P3536 2006
   338.9—dc22

                                                        2006101894

British Cataloguing in Publication Data
A Cataloguing in Publication record for this book
is available from the British Library.

Printed and bound in the United States of America

The paper used in this publication meets the requirements
of the American National Standard for Permanence of
Paper for Printed Library Materials Z39.48-1992.

5   4   3   2   1

Contents

Acknowledgments

This book is the outcome of the Project on Public Finance in Postconflict Statebuilding, a truly collaborative effort hosted by New York University's Center on International Cooperation. In its course we have incurred many debts of gratitude. First and foremost, we thank the center's codirectors, Shepard Forman and Bruce Jones, and research director, Barnett Rubin, whose enthusiasm and support were crucial in making the book a reality.

We also thank the members of the project's Advisory Board for their generous guidance and suggestions: Jean Arnault, Ian Bannon, David Biggs, Sarah Cliffe, William Dorotinsky, Ashraf Ghani, James Jonah, Mbuyuma Matungulu, Larry McDonald, Duncan Overfield, Rathin Roy, Steven Symansky, Gebreselassie Yosief Tesfamichael, and Simon Lee.

We are grateful to others who participated in one or both of the conferences where earlier versions of the chapters in this book were discussed: Gilles Alfandari, Charles Call, Jonathan di John, Ibrahim Elbadawi, Abda El-Mahdi, Scott Gilmore, Antoine Heuty, Stephen Jackson, Beatrice Kiraso, Nicolas Manning, Barbara Nunberg, Nicola Smithers, John Toye, Sheetal Vyas, Susan Woodward, and Benaiah Yongo-Bure.

We also benefited from feedback given by participants in seminars at Cornell University's Einaudi Center for International Studies, the United Nations Department of Peacekeeping Operations, the UK Department for International Development, the London School of Economics, the World Bank, and the Center for Global Development.

We thank Laura Sitea, Margy Elliott, and Sue Holmberg for excellent research and logistical assistance.

For their financial support of the project, we thank the Carnegie Corporation of New York, the government of Norway, the UK Department for International Development, and the William and Flora Hewlett Foundation.

Finally, we thank Shena Redmond of Lynne Rienner Publishers and Libby Barstow for their superb editorial assistance.

None of the above-named individuals or institutions will agree with all views expressed in this book, which are those of the authors alone. We hope, however, that all will find somewhere in these pages the imprint of their contributions to our thinking on the complex issues at the intersection of public finance, peacebuilding, and statebuilding.

—James K. Boyce and Madalene O'Donnell

1

Peace and the Public Purse: An Introduction

James K. Boyce and Madalene O'Donnell

In the wake of a civil war, building a durable peace requires building a state with the ability to collect and manage public resources. To implement peace accords and to provide public services, the government must be able to collect revenue, allocate resources, and manage expenditures. To collect revenues, the state must be seen as legitimate in the eyes of its citizens; at the same time, to secure legitimacy the state must allocate resources and manage expenditures effectively.

The importance of building legitimate and effective states is now widely recognized. The "Principles for Good International Engagement in Fragile States," agreed upon by the development ministers and aid agency heads of the major donor countries in March 2005, identified "state-building as the central objective."[1] This is a marked contrast to the prevailing wisdom in the final decades of the twentieth century, when the state was widely seen as the problem. Today the state has been rediscovered: it is now seen as the solution. The rhetoric of policy has changed from downsizing the state to building the state.

Yet little systematic work has been done on how the international community can help strengthen the economic core of states—the capacity to mobilize, allocate, and spend public resources—in postwar environments. There is a substantial literature on public finance in developing countries, but not much on how to tailor public finance policies to the circumstances of countries emerging from violent conflict. And there is a growing literature on postconflict peacebuilding, but little treatment of public finance issues within it. This book seeks to redress this gap.

In the course of internationally assisted peacebuilding operations, widely divergent views have emerged among policymakers and practitioners as to the implications of the symbiotic relationship between peace and the public purse. One view holds that the politics of peace and the economics of the public purse should not be allowed to interfere with each other: they should be pursued along parallel tracks. A second view accords primacy to the former, asserting that economic policies must be recast in light of the political dynamics of war and peace. A third view takes the opposite stance: the political and security dimensions of peace processes ought to be realigned to reflect the realities of public finance.

This book makes a compelling case for reshaping *both* economic policies and peacebuilding assistance in light of their mutual interdependence. The authors suggest that economic policies for managing the public purse can and must do more to meet the political and security challenges of war-to-peace transitions. At the same time, they suggest that external assistance for peacebuilding must do more to address the fiscal challenges of statebuilding. The task is complicated by the division of labor among international actors, in which the international financial institutions (IFIs) specialize in economic matters while the United Nations and other providers of peacebuilding assistance address political and security issues. Building a legitimate state and forging a durable peace require new thinking on both fronts: a fundamental reappraisal of what constitutes "sound" public finance and equally profound changes from "business as usual" in the policies and practices of international peacebuilding efforts.

The book presents six case studies plus two topical chapters, all of which explore the relationship of public finance to the dynamics of peacebuilding and statebuilding. The case studies—Uganda, Cambodia, Guatemala, Timor-Leste, Afghanistan, and Palestine—were chosen to reflect diverse initial conditions, varying lengths of time since beginning peacebuilding assistance, and different relationships to the international geopolitical environment. These studies focus on the core issues of revenue mobilization, budget allocation, and expenditure management. The two topical chapters focus on closely related issues: postwar monetary policy, drawing in particular on experiences in Afghanistan, Bosnia, and Kosovo; and postwar external debt management, drawing on experiences in Uganda, Mozambique, and Democratic Republic of Congo.

Postwar Environments

This book is premised on the belief that postwar countries often share important features in common—notably a mismatch between fiscal capacities and needs as well as ongoing societal tensions that could precipitate the renewal of violent conflict. Yet there is also a great deal of diversity in postwar environments, and it is important to consider the differences among them in formulating public finance policies. One lesson of the experiences reviewed in this book is that even though knowledge of other postwar experiences is a great asset, off-the-shelf solutions cannot be imported from one setting and simply grafted intact into another. Among the key axes of differences in postwar environments are the following:

- The *type of transition and the resulting balance of power* among contending parties: A winner-take-all victory as in Uganda or a successful independence struggle as in Timor-Leste presents different postwar political dynamics than a negotiated settlement that leads to power-sharing arrangements, as in Cambodia.
- The *level of economic development:* Some countries embark on postwar peacebuilding with extremely low per capita income and human development indicators, low levels of macroeconomic stability, or very low ratios of revenue and expenditure to gross domestic product (GDP); others start from a more favorable economic position in one or more respects.
- The scale of *external assistance:* In some cases, as in Timor-Leste and Afghanistan, postwar aid inflows are massive in relation to the local economy, particularly the "formal sector" of the economy; in others, as in Guatemala, aid is modest relative to both national income and the government budget.
- The role of *natural resource extraction and narcotics:* If natural resources or illicit narcotics—such as timber in Cambodia or opium in Afghanistan—are important as sources of financing for armed groups, this poses special problems at the interface between security and public finance.
- The *fault lines of conflict:* When differences along lines of ethnicity, race, religion, region, language, or class correspond to the axes of violent conflict, a key challenge in statebuilding and peacebuilding is to ease these tensions by promoting political and economic inclusion. Such tensions figured prominently in the wars in Uganda, Guatemala, and Afghanistan but were less central in Cambodia's civil war and in the Palestine and Timor-Leste conflicts that mainly pitted the population against an external enemy.
- The *neighborhood:* The characteristics and interests of neighboring countries can have significant impacts on peacebuilding and statebuilding processes. Regional conflicts have figured dramatically in the political economy in Uganda, Timor-Leste, Afghanistan, and Palestine; they have been somewhat less central in Cambodia and Guatemala.
- The presence of an *agreement on final status:* A comprehensive peace settlement helps to remove key political issues from further contention. Where fundamental final-status questions have not been resolved, as in Palestine and Kosovo, or where some parties were excluded from the settlement and armed conflict continues, as in Afghanistan, the line between conflict resolution and postconflict peacebuilding is blurred and the political foundations for statebuilding are less firm.

- The *history of relations with aid donors:* Where international aid agencies have a long history of engagement, their past alliances with individuals and parties within the country can be both an asset to build upon and a constraint on their room to maneuver. In countries where the aid agencies have not been active in recent years, they face the challenge of forging new alliances.

Of course, no set of case studies can hope to capture the full diversity of postwar environments.[2] In choosing the ones for this volume, we have been guided by two objectives. First, we aimed for a set of countries that vary along the dimensions sketched above. Second, recognizing that different issues come to the fore over time, we selected cases that vary in the length of time that has elapsed since the beginning of postwar assistance: more than a decade in Uganda and Cambodia; medium-term experiences in Guatemala and Timor-Leste; and recent cases (where violent conflict has yet to reach a definitive end) in Afghanistan and Palestine. We also enlisted authors with a variety of professional experiences: expatriates as well as nationals of the countries whose experiences they recount; political scientists as well as economists; university-based scholars as well as individuals who work for national and international agencies.

Table 1.1 presents basic comparative data that illustrate some of the similarities and differences among our case study countries. GDP per capita, for example, varies by an order of magnitude between Afghanistan and Guatemala. The human development index (HDI), a broader measure of economic well-being that is based on education and life expectancy as well as income, is lowest in Afghanistan and highest in Palestine. The ratio of government revenue to GDP—a measure of what sometimes is called the "degree of the state"[3]—ranges from 4.5 percent in Afghanistan to 18 percent in Timor-Leste and Palestine. Public perceptions of "voice and accountability" and of government effectiveness (based on survey data on a 0–100 scale) are lowest in Afghanistan and highest in Timor-Leste in the case of voice and accountability and in Uganda in the case of government effectiveness.

As further indicators of initial conditions, Table 1.2 presents comparative data on foreign aid and inflation in the immediate postwar years. Aid ranges from 1.4 percent of national income in postwar Guatemala to almost 60 percent in Timor-Leste. Inflation rates show great variation, too, from 7 percent in Guatemala to nearly 100 percent in Cambodia.

A comparison of the revenue figures in Table 1.1 to the aid figures in Table 1.2 provides an indication of what may be termed the "degree of sovereignty" of the postwar governments: where the ratio of domestic revenue to external assistance is high, as in Guatemala, the country can be said to possess a high degree of sovereignty; a low ratio, as in Afghanistan, suggests a lower

Table 1.1   Recent Indicators for Six Countries

	GDP/Capita 2004 (US$)	HDI 2003	Revenue/ GDP 2004 (%)	Perceptions of Governance (0–100) 2004	
				Voice and Accountability[a]	Government Effectiveness[b]
Afghanistan	228	0.346[c]	4.5	11.2	9.1
Cambodia	346	0.571	11	24.8	18.8
Guatemala	1,941	0.663	10	36.4	18.8
Timor-Leste	369	0.513	18	52.9	10.1
Uganda	263	0.508	12	30.6	38.5
West Bank/Gaza	1,110[d]	0.729	18	12.1	12.5

Sources: GDP/capita: International Monetary Fund, *World Economic Outlook Database*, September 2005 (available at http://www.imf.org/external/pubs/ft/weo/2005/02/data/index/htm). West Bank/Gaza figure is from World Bank, *World Development Indicators 2005*, Table 1.1 (available at http://devdata.worldbank.org/wdi2005/Section1.htm). Human Development Index: United Nations Development Programme, *Human Development Report 2005* (New York: Oxford University Press, 2004). Afghanistan figure is from *Afghanistan: National Human Development Report 2004* (Kabul: United Nations Development Programme, 2005). Revenue/GDP: International Monetary Fund Country Reports (Afghanistan, Cambodia, Timor-Leste, West Bank and Gaza), the Economist Intelligence Unit and World Development Indicators (Guatemala, Uganda). Perceptions of Governance: D. Kaufmann, A. Kraay, and M. Mastruzzi, *Governance Matters IV: Governance Indicators for 1996–2004*, 2005 (available at http://www.worldbank.org/wbi/governance/pdf/GovMatters_IV_main.pdf).

Notes: a. Voice and accountability measures civil liberties, political and human rights, and the extent to which citizens of a country are able to participate in the selection of governments.

b. Government effectiveness measures perceptions of variables such as the quality of public service provision, the competence of civil servants, their independence from political pressures, and the credibility of the government's commitment to policies.

c. Afghanistan figure for HDI is for 2002.

d. West Bank/Gaza figure for GDP/Capita is for 2003.

Table 1.2   Postwar Aid and Inflation in Six Countries

	Aid[a] (% national income)	Inflation (% per year)
Afghanistan (2001–2003)	19.6[b]	14.4
Cambodia (1992–1994)	11.7	98.5
Timor-Leste (1999–2001)	58.9	47.7
Guatemala (1997–1999)	1.4	7.1
Uganda (1988–1990)	9.5	29.1
West Bank/Gaza (1994–2003)	18.1	11.9

Sources: Aid: From Organization for Economic Cooperation and Development, Development Assistance Committee, International Development Statistics Online (available at http://www.oecd.org/dataoecd/50/17/5037721.htm). Refers to total disbursements of official development assistance (in 2003 US$ million). Inflation: Economist Intelligence Unit Country Reports.

Notes: a. The Aid figures refer to total disbursements of official development assistance (in 2003 US$ million).

b. Afghanistan's gross national income (GNI) figure is estimated based on the United Nations Children's Fund's 2003 GNI per capita estimate of $250 and population of 28.7 million. An alternative estimate in the World Bank's World Development Indicators dataset puts the aid/GDP ratio at 33 percent.

degree of sovereignty. Among other things, this can have implications for the international community's ability to influence the outcome of peacebuilding efforts.

Key Issues in Postwar Public Finance

Weak state capacities are a common feature of many countries emerging from violent conflict. The size of public revenue and expenditure relative to national income reflects the quantity, if not the quality, of state capacity. By this measure, some postwar governments start from near zero—as in Timor-Leste and Afghanistan—although never from a "blank slate" in terms of institutional legacies, as the case studies in this volume emphasize. Many others start from a very modest base. Today Cambodia, Timor-Leste, and Afghanistan have the lowest revenue-to-GDP ratios in Asia; Guatemala has the lowest ratio among the Spanish-speaking countries of Latin America; and Haiti has the lowest in the Western Hemisphere.

The capacity to mobilize, allocate, and spend domestic resources is crucial for the success of peacebuilding efforts for three reasons. First, governments must be able to ensure *sustainable funding* for new democratic institutions and social programs that ease tensions and redress grievances. In the early postwar years, countries often receive a substantial influx of external assistance that can temporarily address some of these needs. But aid usually diminishes over time, and so domestic resources are necessary to sustain institutions and programs. A key issue explored in this book is how external resources can be used to "crowd in" domestic resources and capacities—as opposed to crowding them out.

Second, fiscal capacities are needed in order to build a *legitimate state*. Democratic elections do not, in and of themselves, ensure state legitimacy. Neither do "quick impact projects" in which international agencies address needs unmet by the state. Legitimacy comes from government delivery of services that people need and want. This is a question not only of supply but also of effective demand, that is, state responsiveness to the citizenry. Elections are a way to express demand and to make the government accountable for its performance. There is a two-way relationship between the revenue and expenditure sides of fiscal capacity: governments need revenue in order to provide services, but they must provide services in order for people to be willing to pay taxes.

Third, in some cases there is a need to curtail extralegal taxation by warlords and armed groups, so as to *enhance security*. This has been a key challenge in Afghanistan, for example, where control of border customs outposts quickly emerged as both a fiscal issue and a security issue. It has also been important in Cambodia, where control over revenues from natural resource extraction, particularly logging, often has bypassed the state.

The case studies in this book vividly show that building the fiscal basis for an effective state and a durable peace is not just a matter of economics. It is also a matter of politics. It is a question not only of *what* should be the tax structure, expenditure priorities, and so on, but also a question of *how* these decisions should be made. For war-to-peace transitions and the democratic transitions that are often part and parcel of the peace settlement, the process of public finance decisionmaking—including issues of transparency, accountability, and participation—can be as crucial as the policies themselves.

Revenue Mobilization

On the revenue side of fiscal policy, the conventional criterion for assessing the "soundness" of public finance is efficiency. Taxation and nontax revenue collection (such as fees or earnings from state-owned enterprises) should be efficient both from an administrative standpoint, taking into account administrative costs, and from the standpoint of minimizing distortions in economic activity. The latter, for example, is the main rationale for the shift from tariffs to value-added taxes that has been a centerpiece of policy advice from the international financial institutions in recent years.

In war-torn societies, "soundness" must be reassessed in light of the goals of conflict prevention, conflict resolution, and postconflict peacebuilding. Given the enormous human, social, and economic costs imposed by violent conflict, these goals can be understood as part of a broader, more robust notion of efficiency, rather than as a departure from the efficiency objective. The studies in this book shed light on what it would mean to translate this broader notion of efficiency into practice in the field.

As we have noted, in postwar settings efforts typically must be undertaken to increase the size of revenue. There is room for debate as to what is the "efficient" size of the state relative to the economy, as measured by the revenue/GDP ratio. In the United States, the ratio currently is 33 percent; in the euro area, the average ratio is 45 percent; among the member countries of the Organization for Economic Cooperation and Development (OECD), it ranges from 31 percent in Korea to 60 percent in Norway.[4] Whatever one's opinions as to how high a ratio is "too high," there can be no doubt that the ratios in postwar countries are often too low. Indeed, the British government's Department for International Development regards a tax/GDP ratio of less than 15 percent to be an indicator of "state fragility."[5]

Where the need for additional revenue is great and administrative capacities are low, types of taxes that might be considered "distortionary" in other settings may well turn out to be the most efficient available options. Notwithstanding the conventional case for trade liberalization on efficiency grounds, for example, trade taxes that can be collected at a relatively small number of border crossing points are attractive from an administrative standpoint.

Looking at revenue policies through the conflict lens also brings out the need for serious attention to distributional impacts on both "vertical" and "horizontal" equity. Vertical equity—the dimension most familiar to economists—refers to distributional impacts across the population stratified from rich to poor: taxes that fall more heavily on the rich than on the poor (as a percentage of their incomes) are termed "progressive," whereas those that fall more heavily on the poor are termed "regressive." Horizontal equity refers to distributional impacts across regions or population subgroups defined in terms of ethnicity, race, religion, caste, or language—divisions that can correspond to the social fault lines of conflict.

It is sometimes argued—mostly by economists with graduate-level training in public finance—that distributional issues ought to be addressed exclusively on the expenditure side of fiscal policy, leaving revenue policies to be set so as to maximize efficiency and minimize distortions. Three points can be made in rebuttal to this argument.

First, this stance rests on an "optimal planner" model that assumes that the government aims to achieve a target that defines the optimal income distribution after taxes and transfers. This assumes, in turn, that the government is both omniscient and omnipotent; that is, the government knows the distributional effects of everything it does, and indeed of all else that is happening in the economy, and it has the power to hit the target, subject only to random differences between actual and expected outcomes. But such optimal planners exist nowhere except in the writings of public finance theorists. It would be fanciful to imagine that they inhabit postwar governments.

Second, even if policymakers choose to pursue distributional objectives mainly via the expenditure side of fiscal policy, they need to take into account the distributional impacts of revenue collection in setting these objectives. In other words, the conventional textbook wisdom does not logically imply that the distributional incidence of revenue policies can or should be ignored. On the contrary, this is essential information for policymaking.

Finally, no matter what public finance theorists believe, most members of the public simply will not accept the claim that the distributional impacts of taxation and other revenue policies "do not matter" because everything is being optimally adjusted on the expenditure side. This is true even in high-income, industrialized societies, where tax reform proposals routinely are subjected to exhaustive scrutiny on distributional grounds. It is even truer in war-torn societies where mistrust of the government generally is more widespread. Regardless of what economic theory tells us, political theory tells us that if enough people think something matters, it does.

In recent years, growing recognition of the interplay between economic policies and conflict dynamics has prompted efforts to introduce "conflict impact assessment" into decisionmaking at official development assistance agencies. Much as environmental impact assessments are intended to take into account "negative externalities" in the form of pollution and natural resource depletion, conflict impact assessment aims to incorporate impacts on social tensions and risks of violent conflict into policy formulation and project appraisal. As on the environmental front, it will take serious commitments of time and effort to develop capacities to conduct such assessments and integrate them into decisionmaking processes. As of this writing, the application of conflict impact assessment to revenue policies is still in its infancy.

Budget Allocation and Expenditure Management

On the expenditure side, as on the revenue side, the "soundness" of public finance is often defined in terms of efficiency, tempered perhaps by concerns for "optimal distribution." Budget allocation and expenditure management, in this view, should aim to maximize social returns, so as to get the most "bang for the buck." Once again, in war-torn societies the soundness of expenditure policies can be judged only by a broader standard of efficiency that encompasses conflict dynamics. In effect, expenditure policies must also be devised with an eye on getting the most "nonbang" for the buck.

In all societies, government expenditures are needed to provide public goods and services, things that cannot be efficiently produced and distributed by private-sector markets. These include not only physical infrastructure, such as roads and electricity grids, but also the institutional infrastructure for providing education, health care, public safety, and the rule of law. War-torn societies are likely to face large shortfalls in these types of infrastructure. They also often need substantial investments in what can be called the *social infrastructure of peace:* expenditures that redress the horizontal and vertical inequalities that are implicated in violent conflict. In addition to measures to redress historic disparities, such investment could encompass assistance to demobilized ex-combatants and to the communities that will support their reintegration into civilian life.

The expenditure side of public finance has two distinct stages. The first is the framing of the budget, allocating scarce public resources among competing uses, in the course of which expenditure priorities are determined. The second is expenditure management, implementing the decisions taken in framing the budget. At both stages, policymakers must face issues of participation, transparency, and accountability as well as efficiency. Answers to the process question of *how,* as well as the outcome question of *what,* can strongly affect public attitudes toward the state and the depth and breadth of public support for peace. They also have a strong effect on the willingness of the public to pay taxes: revenue is needed to fund expenditure, but at the same time effective expenditure that responds to the needs of the people legitimizes revenue collection.

A key problem in public expenditure—one that may be particularly acute in war-torn societies—is the set of phenomena that are commonly lumped together under the label "corruption." A distinction is sometimes drawn between "grand corruption," in which policy decisions (such as budget allocation) are manipulated to benefit powerful interests at the expense of the public interest, and "petty corruption," which involves the payment of bribes for government services or kickbacks on government contracts. Both kinds of corruption can squander scarce resources, undermine state legitimacy, exacerbate inequality, and deter private investment.

There is a gray line between corruption driven by personal greed and corruption driven by the desire to sustain political alliances and lubricate political networks. The latter—sometimes referred to as "patronage," a term with somewhat less negative connotations—can have similar corrosive effects on economic performance and state legitimacy, but against the costs must be weighed the benefits of the political cohesion that patronage can buy. And the latter may be more important in war-torn countries than in settings where political contests are resolved peacefully. Here the challenge is not only to strike a balance between the costs and benefits but also to devise strategies that ease the trade-offs posed by patronage-based political systems. Accommodating patronage in the name of short-term political stability—as happened in the Palestinian Authority during the Arafat era—not only stunts the effectiveness and legitimacy of state institutions but also turns out to be a less-than-sure recipe for building a durable peace.

External Assistance and Fiscal Capacity: "Crowding In" or "Crowding Out"?

In the wake of violent conflict, countries often receive an "aid bonanza." The influx of humanitarian assistance, reconstruction aid, and international support for peace implementation brings large-scale external resources into the country, at times dwarfing the domestic resources mobilized by the government.

Although postwar aid can play a valuable role in meeting pressing needs, it poses the risk of crowding out local efforts to lay the fiscal foundations for an effective and legitimate state. The ready availability of external resources can reduce the incentive for the government to raise domestic revenues: it is easier to rely on foreign aid than to collect taxes. On the expenditure side, the influx of aid can overwhelm the state's limited capacity to disburse funds in a timely and transparent fashion. But if much of the aid is routed through private contractors and nongovernmental organizations, bypassing the state, this can undermine efforts to build state capacities in budget allocation and expenditure management.

The potentially adverse impact of external assistance on domestic fiscal capacity is one dimension of a broader dilemma that confronts international efforts to promote statebuilding. Just as external resources can crowd out domestic resources, so the government's quest for external legitimacy can undermine its legitimacy at home—particularly if the motivations for donor assistance differ markedly from local needs and aspirations. In the security sector, external military assistance can similarly undermine efforts to build financially sustainable and locally accountable military and police forces.[6] In each of these dimensions—fiscal, legitimacy, and security—the challenge is to make external assistance a long-term catalyst for statebuilding rather than a short-term substitute for the state.

In the fiscal arena, this does not mean that all aid can or should be routed through governments, or that aid to governments should be provided with no strings attached. Where state capacities are severely limited, and the immediate need for public goods and services is great, the advantages of bypassing governmental institutions may outweigh the costs. And it would be disingenuous, as well as potentially costly, for donors to abdicate responsibility for how aid channeled through the government is used. Once we recognize that the aim of postwar assistance is not only to deliver goods and services but also to build state capacities, however, we need to strike a balance between service delivery and capacity building. And once again, there is a need to devise strategies that could ease this trade-off by using external resources to crowd in domestic fiscal capacities. As illustrated in the Afghanistan case study, the international community is beginning to experiment with new ways to address this problem.

Organization of This Book

The next six chapters present the country case studies, in roughly chronological order based on the date at which their peacebuilding processes began. The two topical chapters—on monetary policy and external debt management, respectively—follow. The concluding chapter draws together some of the most important lessons that emerge from this review of past experiences.

In Chapter 2, Léonce Ndikumana and Justine Nannyonjo discuss Uganda, a country that is often cited as a "success story" of postconflict statebuilding in Africa. The authors find a mixed record. In the two decades since President Yoweri Museveni's forces took control in 1986—winning a peace without an international peace operation—Uganda has been a favorite of aid donors and a testing ground for internationally promoted innovations in public expenditure management. Yet progress on the revenue side has been slow, resulting in continued aid dependency. Deep horizontal inequalities, persistent conflict in the north, and a deficit in democratic accountability raise further concerns for the country's stability and sustainability.

In Chapter 3, Paul Smoke and Rob Taliercio diagnose public finance weaknesses in Cambodia that persist fifteen years after the tripartite Paris peace accords of 1991. Initially, postwar Cambodia was administered by the UN Transitional Authority in Cambodia, the largest UN peace operation ever mounted at the time. Following the transition to an elected coalition government in 1993, external assistance mostly bypassed the government budget, a pattern that continued after the Cambodian People's Party consolidated its grip on power in 1997. Meanwhile substantial revenues from the forestry sector have remained outside treasury control, funding what has been termed a "parallel military budget." Smoke and Taliercio suggest that the international focus on short-term "peace and security" has come at the expense of building the fiscal capacities needed for an effective state and a durable peace.

In Chapter 4, Pablo Rodas-Martini reviews efforts to strengthen public finance in Guatemala since the 1996 Peace Accords that brought an end to more than three decades of civil war. A unique feature of the Guatemalan accords is that they included specific commitments on taxation and public expenditure: revenue as a fraction of GDP was to rise by 50 percent in a four-year period and to be "globally progressive" in its distributional incidence; spending on education, health, and housing was to increase by the same percentage. These explicit provisions reflected the recognition that building a durable peace would require sustainable funding for new democratic institutions and efforts to reduce the severe economic inequalities and political exclusion that were seen as root causes of the conflict. Efforts to increase revenue have foundered, however, hampered not only by opposition from the private sector but also by public perceptions of widespread corruption in government expenditure.

In Chapter 5, Emilia Pires and Michael Francino find that the UN transitional administration for Timor-Leste, which administered the country from the end of the Indonesian occupation in 1999 until the birth of an independent state in 2002, missed opportunities to build fiscal capacities and to use the postwar aid bonanza to stimulate local economic development. They argue that even though a period of international administration was necessary, since the Timorese were unprepared to take charge immediately, a smaller international presence more focused on knowledge transfer could have been more successful in building an effective state. The legacies of this crowding-out process have been weak institutions, an inadequate revenue base (for which future oil revenues are the only rescue in sight), and vulnerability to increasing corruption.

In Chapter 6, Ashraf Ghani and his colleagues describe efforts undertaken in Afghanistan, since the international intervention in 2001, to rebuild the country's public finance system, including issuing a new currency and reform of revenue collection and expenditure management. As finance minister from mid-2002 until the end of 2004, Ghani put particular emphasis on trying to make the government's budget a central instrument of statebuilding. The chapter illuminates the obstacles to this aim that were posed by the decisions of international aid agencies to route much of their assistance through private contractors and nongovernmental organizations, bypassing the state and creating a "dual public sector." Ongoing conflict and security problems have further complicated efforts to lay the fiscal foundations for a sustainable state.

In Chapter 7, Rex Brynen describes the post-Oslo efforts in Palestine to establish the Palestinian Authority as the foundation for a future state, pending a final settlement with Israel. Renewed upsurges of conflict periodically prompted the Israeli government to withhold customs revenues and impose "closures" that resulted in rising unemployment and falling incomes in the West Bank and Gaza. Meanwhile, neopatrimonial governance, rising public employment, and donor-driven public investments with high operation and maintenance costs pushed up expenditures. The resulting fiscal squeeze has been both a symptom and a cause of weaknesses that have beset the effort to build an effective Palestinian quasi-state.

In Chapter 8, on monetary policy, Warren Coats draws on his past experience with the International Monetary Fund to discuss the challenges of choosing a currency, rebuilding a central bank, and establishing a payments system—issues at the interface between monetary policy and public finance. At first blush these may appear to be technical matters, but his review of experiences in Afghanistan, Bosnia, and Kosovo makes it clear that they have far-reaching political ramifications, too. For example, the choice and design of a national currency can have enormous symbolic importance. In a similar manner, the independence of the central bank has political as well as economic implications. Coats maintains that in these three cases, monetary policies responded reasonably to the political demands of statebuilding and helped to move statebuilding processes forward.

In Chapter 9, concerning external debt management, Patricia Alvarez-Plata and Tilman Brück discuss the problems posed by debts accumulated prior to and during violent conflicts that are then inherited by successor governments. To resume lending operations, the international financial institutions require that arrears be cleared, a task often accomplished by bridge loans that in effect pass the accumulated debt to the new government. Debt-service payments on these and other past loans divert scarce public resources from other uses. Drawing in particular on experiences in Uganda, Mozambique, and Democratic Republic of Congo, the authors explore the case for special treatment for postwar countries, including the scope for invoking the doctrine of "odious debt" as a means to reduce debt-service burdens.

Finally, Chapter 10 draws lessons for how public finance can be better integrated with statebuilding and peacebuilding operations. Some of these lessons—for example, the need for more "conflict-sensitive" revenue and expenditure policies —involve reshaping public finance decisionmaking in light of the political dynamics of the peace process. Others—for example, the need to develop dual-control systems for expenditure management as opposed to creating dual public sectors—involve reshaping peacebuilding assistance in light of public finance and statebuilding imperatives. In the public finance arena, as elsewhere, greater policy coherence is both difficult and necessary.

Notes

1. Draft principles accepted by the High Level Meeting of the Development Assistance Committee (DAC) of the Organization for Economic Cooperation and Development, Paris, March 3, 2005. Available at http://www.oecd.org/dataoecd/59/55/34700989.pdf.

2. On these and other differences among postwar circumstances, see Call (forthcoming); Stedman, Rothchild, and Cousens (2002); and Doyle and Sambanis (2000).

3. The "degree of the state" refers to its capacity to mobilize resources and to generate basic public goods, whereas the "kind of state" refers to the relationship between the state and the society; for discussion in relation to peacebuilding, see Barnett et al. (2007).

4. Data on general government total tax and nontax receipts are from OECD *Economic Outlook* no. 79, Annex Tables, May 2006. Available at http://www.oecd.org/statisticsdata/0,2643,en_2649_34597_1_119656_1_1_1,00.html.

5. For discussion of this and other donors' classifications of "fragile" countries, see Picciotto et al. (2005).

6. See Rubin (2005) for discussion of the dilemmas of "extroverted state formation."

2

From Failed State to Good Performer? The Case of Uganda

Léonce Ndikumana and Justine Nannyonjo

You can see that when our country borrows, we are committing a sin. We are devaluing ourselves . . . . Make sure that we engage in production and we make our country a country of lenders, not of borrowers.
—*President Yoweri Museveni of Uganda, The New Vision*[1]

When Yoweri Museveni's victorious National Resistance Army (NRA) marched in the streets of Kampala in January 1986, Uganda's new leaders faced the urgent task of rebuilding the economy and mending a social fabric torn by decades of violent conflict under despotic regimes. This chapter examines the role that public finance has played in advancing reconstruction, development, and statebuilding. Two decades having elapsed since the end of the war, it is now possible to observe the medium- to long-term consequences of early policy choices made by Uganda's postwar government.

In this postwar period, Uganda has experienced an unusual degree of continuity in its political leadership, commitment to pro-growth economic policies, and relationships with aid donors. At the same time, Uganda offers the opportunity to examine public finance in the context of macroeconomic reform. The government's commitment to a series of structural adjustments, liberalization, and tax reforms, which generated strong support from the donor community, gives us an opportunity to examine how these reforms have affected the government's ability to mobilize revenue and manage expenditures.

Postconflict public finance faces divergent demands from various constituencies. The government must increase tax revenues without frustrating private investment and trade. It must reverse the wartime deterioration in services and living standards experienced by the bulk of the citizenry. Finally, it must tap external assistance to help meet these vast needs without undermining macroeconomic sustainability. The success with which the government meets these challenges determines not only its effectiveness but also its legitimacy. Public finance goes beyond the technical dimensions of collecting taxes and allocating expenditures: it is a core element of economic development and statebuilding.

With these considerations in mind, we examine Uganda's experience in public finance since 1986 under the National Resistance Movement (NRM) regime. Our discussion includes the historical background, economic performance, and resource mobilization from both domestic and external sources. Next we turn to the budgetary process and expenditure management, including a discussion of the impact of external resource flows on fiscal policy and macroeconomic management. We then discuss the continuing insecurity in northern Uganda and neighboring countries, and the implications for public finance. We conclude with a summary of key findings and some policy implications.

Conflict Background

The Colonial Administration and the Politics of Ethnicity and Civil War

The Ugandan population comprises more than forty distinct ethnic communities, commonly classified into two main linguistic groups: the Bantu-speaking cluster and the Nilo-Sudanese-language-speaking cluster (Byrnes 1992). These ethnic clusters are geographically demarcated, with the Nilo-Sudanese groups located in the north and the Bantu groups found predominantly in the center and the south (see Figure 2.1).

Demographically, none of the ethnic communities is large enough to be dominant. The Bantu-speaking Baganda, the largest group, constitutes only about 17 percent of the population (see Table 2.1). This is an important difference between Uganda and neighboring Burundi and Rwanda, which have a large demographic imbalance between two main ethnic groups. As in the case of Burundi and Rwanda, however, ethnic antagonism in Uganda is a legacy of the policies of the colonial administration, perpetuated by regimes that came to power after independence.

The colonial administration sowed the seeds of ethnic antagonism through three main channels (Mutibwa 1992; Matovu and Stewart 2001; International Crisis Group 2004). First, as a means of consolidating their control, the British found it convenient to rule the country as a conglomerate of independent and ethnically demarcated territories. The British administration conceded substantial autonomy to the Buganda kingdom, which it sought to use as a collaborator in the administration of the colony. This created antagonisms between the Baganda and other groups who viewed them as an arm of the oppressor.

Second, like the Belgians in Burundi and Rwanda, the British promoted the racial theory that some African populations were more intelligent and fit to

Figure 2.1 Major Ethnic Groups in Uganda

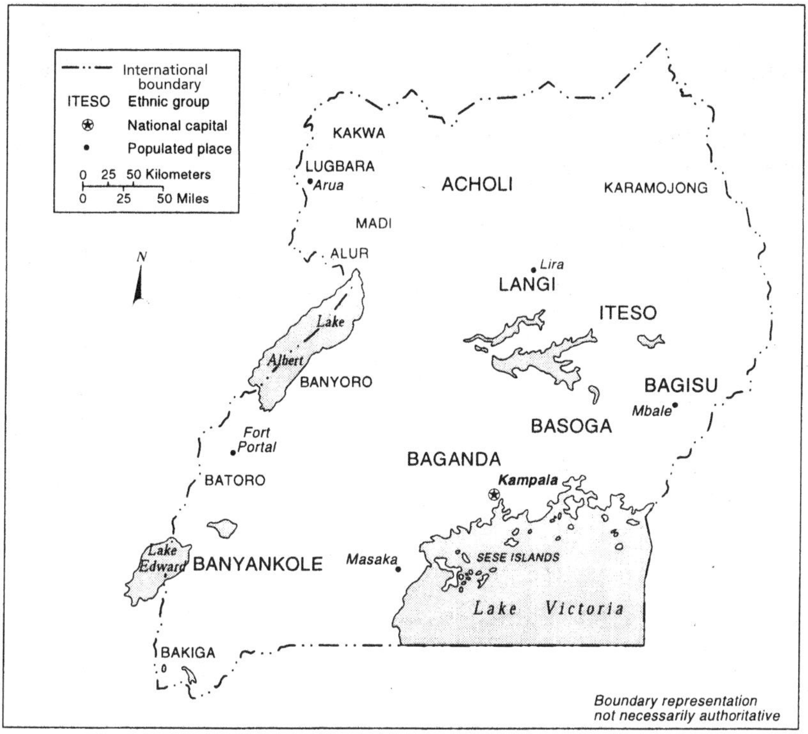

Source: Byrnes (1992).

rule than others. They argued that the Baganda had superior intelligence and leadership talents in order to justify the privileges accorded to them.

Third, the British colonial economic policies concentrated development investments in the south and neglected the north. As the anticolonial movement started to develop after World War II, most of the leaders were intellectuals from the south. In an attempt to rebalance power between the south and the north and to combat the anticolonial movement, the British started to concentrate military power in the hands of the northerners. The opposing regional imbalances in economic development and in the military became a further source of antagonism along ethnic lines.

These antagonisms were the outcomes of a colonial system of political control that transformed ethnicity from a latent factor into a primordial determinant of access to power and economic advancement. This has clear implications for postconflict reconstruction. It suggests that success is contingent on the government's ability to promote economic and political integration and

Table 2.1 Major Ethnic Groups in Uganda

Major Ethnic/Language Cluster	Largest Ethnic Group in the Cluster	Region and Traditional Organization	Size (% of population)	Main Traditional Activities
Eastern Lacustrine Bantu	Baganda	Buganda organized in centralized kingdom under the *Kabaka*	16.7	farming minor role of cattle (herded by hired herders from the North)
	Basoga	Southeastern region organized in small independent kingdoms	8	subsistence farming
	Bagisu	Eastern region	5	farming high population density; high pressure on land
Western Lacustrine Bantu	Banyoro	Western region organized in one kingdom under the *Omukama*	3	farmers (the Iru) cattle herding (prestigious among the Hima; cattle = symbol of high class/status)
	Bataro	Western region. Toro kingdom (under *Omukama*) = breakaway segment of the Bunyoro Kingdom	3.2	farming
Eastern Nilotic	Banyankole	Southwestern	N.A.	Two groups: Hima pastoralists; Iru farmers
	Karamonjong cluster	Northeast	Eastern Nilotic = 12	pastoralists
	Iteso	Eastern	8.1	farming
	Kakwa	Extreme northwest	1	farming; some cattle herding
Western Nilotic (15% of population)	Langi and Acholi	North-central region	4 (Acholi) + 2 (Langi)	pastoralists
	Alur	Chiefdoms not united under kingdom	N.A.	pastoralists; marginalized under colonial rule; source of migrant labor
Central Sudanic (6% of population)	Lugbara	Northwest (highlands)	3.8	cattle; also farming
	Madi	Northwest (lowlands)	1.2	farming

Source: Byrnes (1992).
Notes: N.A. = not available. "Major" ethnic groups account for only about 78 percent of the population.

equitable treatment of all ethnic groups and regions. Although improvements to infrastructure and sustained economic growth are critical for the success of reconstruction, political stability will require that this growth be shared among all the regions and ethnic communities in the country.

Violence Under the Postindependence Regimes

From independence in 1962 until 1986, Uganda experienced chronic instability under monolithic regimes that sought to consolidate power through repression, exclusion, and extortion. These regimes perpetuated practices inherited from the colonial administration that undermined the country's chances for national unification and political stability (Matovu and Stewart 2001; Mutibwa 1992). Leaders advanced their own interests, and those of their ethnic and regional groups, while repressing the rights of the people from other groups and regions.

The first regime of Milton Obote (1962–1971) built its control of power with two main instruments: first, discriminating against the Buganda region, as a means of shifting the balance of power in favor of the north; second, increasing the power of the military while consolidating domination of the army by northerners. Obote's reign inaugurated an era of state-sponsored terrorism during which the army systematically killed political opponents and their civilian supporters. The most notorious case of state-sponsored crime was the attack on the palace of the king of Buganda in 1965, in which many innocent civilians were massacred. Obote's first regime was responsible for more than 2,000 deaths at the hands of the government's troops (see Table 2.2).

When army officer Idi Amin overthrew Obote in January 1971, the Ugandan people breathed a sigh of relief, hoping he would bring an end to social and economic chaos. The new ruler initially attempted to accommodate the Buganda region. Amin also won early approval from the Western world as he rejected Obote's policy of nonalignment. Shortly thereafter, however, the Idi Amin regime turned into a brutal machine of repression, targeting especially the people of Buganda and members of the army from Obote's ethnic groups (the Acholi and Langi). In Amin's drive to gain control over the country's economy, he nationalized foreign-owned businesses, drove the prosperous Asian business community out of the country, and redistributed their assets among members of his own entourage. The social climate deteriorated, and the economy descended into chaos.

In 1979, Amin was overthrown by the Ugandan National Liberation Army (UNLA) of the Uganda National Liberation Front (UNLF), with the support of the Tanzanian army. The UNLF transitional government proved to be as sectarian and brutal as its predecessor. The army orchestrated revenge raids against Amin's kinship group (the Kakwa) in his native region of the Western Nile. The failure of the transitional government paved the way to the return of Obote in 1980.

Table 2.2 Political Regimes in Uganda

Period and Regime	Regional Bias	Ethnic and Religious Bias	Ideology and Mode of Government	Violence and Conflict
Colonial era	economic development in the south; military predominantly northern	favors to Baganda; Christianity	no nation/state formation	
Obote I (1962–1971)	Obote is Langi northerners in control; hostility against Baganda	discrimination against Bantu groups	military dictatorship; nonalignment ideology	1965 attacks against Buganda king; 2,000 people killed
Idi Amin (1971–1979)	Amin is a Kakwa from West Nile support from Sudanese rebels	early attempts to accommodate Baganda revenge attacks against Obote's groups	military dictatorship; reject nonalignment ideology	massacres of civilians and Acholi and Langi soldiers, estimated more than 300,000 people killed
UNLF[a] transition government (1979–1980)	dominated by northerners; revenge killings in Amin's region (West Nile)			massacres in West Nile
Obote II (1980–1985)	Obote is Langi northerners in control; hostility against Baganda	discrimination against Bantu groups	military dictatorship	300,000 people killed; 500,000 people displaced
Transition Okello government (1985–1986)	Okello is an Acholi (from the north)	Acholi dominance of the army	no clear national policy	
Museveni (NRA/NRM) (1986–present)	initially broad-based government balance in favor of the west and central	broad-based, inclusive	nation building is priority; economic reconstruction and development	opposition from West Nile, northeast, and north (Idi Amin and Obote supporters)

Sources: Matovu and Stewart (2001); Byrnes (1992).
Note: a. UNLF = Uganda National Liberation Front.

Obote's second regime proved to be even more brutal than his first. Discriminatory practices further widened the social divide between his ethnic group (the Langi) and other ethnic clusters, especially the Baganda. Between 1981 and 1985, civil war and army repression took a heavy toll. More than 300,000 people were killed, and another half million were displaced from their homes.

By 1985, Obote had alienated even those who had initially supported him. In particular, members of the military from the Acholi ethnic group resented Obote's favoritism toward the Langi in the military. He was eventually forced out of power by UNLA Acholi commanders, and a transitional government led by Tito Okello (an Acholi) took over in July 1985. This event brought little change, however, as the new government had no clear policy apart from self-preservation and consolidation of the domination of the army.

In protest against irregularities in the elections that brought Obote back to power, Yoweri Museveni, a former member of the Military Commission, formed the NRA and NRM in 1981 and started the "bush war" to overthrow Obote. The NRA quickly gained military strength and popular support, particularly in central and western Buganda and the western regions of Ankole and Bunyoro. The repression against civilians by Obote's government (in an attempt to punish NRA supporters) further alienated the population and increased support to the NRA. With backing from Tanzania, the NRA finally defeated Obote's army in January 1986. Museveni, as president, began the monumental task of rebuilding a country that had been ravaged by civil war and military repression.[2]

Conflict in Northern Uganda

The NRM's coming to power was soon clouded by the outbreak of a new conflict in the north, which continues to the present day. The genesis of this conflict springs from two main elements. First, it epitomizes the north-south divide fostered in the colonial era and perpetuated by the postcolonial regimes. The NRA victory displaced the Acholi from power and shifted military dominance from north to south, upsetting the old balance between the northern control over the military and the southern control over the economy. The failure of the NRA to integrate former officers and fighters from the Acholi ethnic group further deepened the north-south divide. The second element in this conflict is the intranorthern antagonism created by the breakdown of the Acholi-Langi alliance, after Okello (an Acholi) overthrew Obote (a Langi) in 1985.

In August 1986, deposed Acholi officers created a new force called the Uganda People's Defense Army (UPDA) and promoted the notion that armed struggle was the only means for the northerners in general and the Acholi in particular to regain power. The northern insurrection was energized the following year by the creation of the Holy Spirit Mobile Forces (HSMF), which injected a religious dimension to the movement under the leadership of Alice Auma, who claimed to have received a divine call from a spirit called Lakwena (messenger) to defend the Acholiland from "foreign" invasion (International Crisis Group 2004). The HSMF was defeated quickly by the NRA, but Joseph Kony, claiming to have inherited the spiritual powers of Lakwena from Alice Auma, then launched his own movement, drawing support from UPDA deserters (International Crisis Group 2004). Kony's military force was first called the Lord's Salvation Army, then the United Democratic Christian Force, finally becoming the Lord's Resistance Army (LRA) in 1994.

The LRA presents itself as a defender of the Acholi and uses regional and ethnic grievances as mobilizing tools in gathering support. The conflict in the north also has a broader regional dimension. The International Crisis Group (2004, 24) described the LRA as Khartoum's "proxy militia." For a long time, the rebel movement helped the government of Sudan to fight the Sudan People's Liberation Army (SPLA) while stretching the Ugandan government's military and reducing its own capacity to support the SPLA. The Sudanese conflict gave leverage to the LRA, which received military equipment, staging ground for attacks, and hideouts when on the run. The recent signing of a peace settlement in Sudan on January 9, 2005, therefore marks a critical turn of events for the conflict in northern Uganda, one that could inject new life into the peace negotiation process between the LRA and the government.

The conflict in the north has caused widespread economic and social devastation, including massacres and gross violations of human rights. The war has internally displaced more than 1.3 million people (about 8 percent of the Ugandan population), who are forced to live in overcrowded camps.[3] The delivery of health care is constrained by an inadequate supply of drugs, health workers, food supplements, medical equipment, and infrastructure. Education is severely affected by the destruction of school buildings and targeted killings and abduction of teachers and children by the LRA.

Not surprisingly, the north lags behind the rest of the country in terms of human development. The Human Development Index for northern Uganda in 2001 was 0.35, compared to 0.55 for the central region and 0.45 for the country as a whole. The northern region has the highest incidence of poverty at 63.3 percent in 2002–2003, compared to the national average of 37.7 percent (Uganda Bureau of Statistics, 2003). Meanwhile, the abuse and trauma inflicted on children are sowing the seeds of hatred, raising the risk for further conflict.

Instability in Karamoja

A second ongoing regional conflict is taking place in the "Karamoja cluster," which includes the pastoral and agro-pastoral ethnic groups of northern Uganda, northwestern Kenya, southeastern Sudan, and southwestern Ethiopia. The instability in Karamoja includes conflict within the cluster as well as conflict with outside groups, spanning national boundaries. Historically, conflict revolved around cattle raids and the struggle for grazing space and water that is accentuated by the region's high exposure to drought. The culture in the region traditionally has not only tolerated but also encouraged cattle raids as a means to acquire wealth and restock herds, making it hard to eradicate the practice.

An important contributing factor to the chronic instability in Karamoja is the marginalization and neglect of the region by the central authorities since the colonial era. From the declaration of Uganda as a British protectorate in 1890, two decades went by before the colonial administration appointed the first district commissioner in Karamoja in 1912. The British colonial policy of territorial autonomy in this case amounted to territorial neglect: the British decided to leave Karamoja to its own fate, mainly because it had no natural resources worth exploiting (NGO Forum 2002). Karamoja thus lagged behind other regions in terms of economic and social development and infrastructure.

Two events ultimately prompted greater British attention to the region. The first was the region's booming ivory trade, which attracted Arab, Greek, British, and US traders. At one point, ivory accounted for as much as 10 percent of total exports of the colony (NGO Forum 2002). Second, in exchange for ivory, the Karamojong began to acquire modern weapons. The British intervened in an effort to prevent entry of guns and their reexport to neighboring regions. Unable to control the arms trade, the colonial administration opted to simply ban the ivory trade altogether, leaving cattle trade as the only source of monetary income in the region.

The trade bans and lack of any meaningful development program in the region, along with military repression, created antagonism between the state and the Karamojong people, whose feeling of alienation still persists. Yet the conflict in Karamoja has never taken the form of a rebellion of the people against the state. In fact, some northerners argue that the state has allowed the Karamojong to prey on other ethnic groups, such as the Acholi and Teso, who are perceived to be opposed to the government (US Agency for International Development 2002, 45).

Since 1986, the Karamoja conflict has evolved in two important ways. First, the level and severity of violence has increased dramatically (US Agency for International Development 2002). The lack of economic opportunities creates incentives for expropriation and theft, and this has been exacerbated by the proliferation of modern weapons. Second, the nature of the conflict has mutated. Traditionally, the casualties of violence were limited to cattle and male warriors, but today the conflict affects the ordinary civilians, including women and children. In addition to traditional cattle raids, the region has experienced an increase in roadside banditry and commercial cattle raids. These changes have raised the level of animosity among ethnic groups, but at the same time they may erode the cultural acceptance of cattle raids and perhaps encourage local support for conflict resolution.

Postwar Economic Performance: Successes and Challenges

When Museveni's NRM took over power, it inherited "a corrupt society, empty coffers, and an external debt running into billions of dollars" (Mutibwa 1992, 190). The challenge to the new government was to deliver on both the security front and the economic front. Economic success is critical to constructing and sustaining a stable state in the postconflict era. It ultimately determines the ability of the government to win the heart of the people by demonstrating through economic outcomes that the era of irresponsible governance is over.

A Strong Overall Macroeconomic Record

Uganda has accumulated an impressive macroeconomic record since 1986, with solid economic growth and stabilization of inflation. From 1986 to 2003, the country registered an average real gross domestic product (GDP) growth rate of 6 percent per annum, or 2.9 percent in per capita terms. Growth has been unbalanced, however, with agriculture lagging behind. The share of agriculture in Uganda's GDP fell from 74 percent in 1978 to only 33 percent in 2003; meanwhile the share of services rose from 20 to 45 percent (World Bank 2004g).

Inflation has declined dramatically from the triple-digit levels in the 1980s to low single digits since 1993 (Figure 2.2). The improvement in the

Figure 2.2   Uganda: GDP Growth and Inflation, 1983–2003

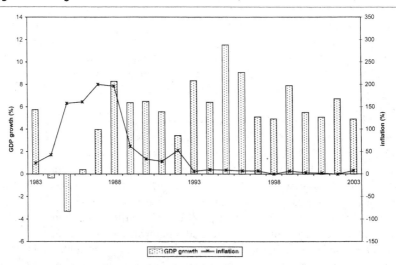

Source: World Bank (2004g).

Note: Average GDP growth: 6.07 percent (1986–1995), 6.14 percent (1996–2003). Average inflation: 75.7 percent (1986–1995), 4.1 percent (1996–2003).

macroeconomic environment was followed by substantial private investment response, as illustrated by the increase in gross capital formation and foreign direct investment (Figure 2.3). Uganda has been successful in attracting repatriation of capital by the Indian business class that was exiled under the Idi Amin regime as well as remittances from nonresident nationals.

Macroeconomic Challenges

These impressive achievements conceal important weaknesses at both the macroeconomic and microeconomic level. The country remains highly vulnerable to shocks, owing to its concentrated structure of production and its dependence on primary commodity exports, which represented 92 percent of merchandise exports in 2002 (World Bank 2004g). When the NRM took power, it recognized the need for the country to "break away from the colonial structures and institutions on which both the colonial and post-colonial economy of Uganda was based, characterized as it was by emphasis on the production of such crops as cotton and coffee that were required in the metropolitan states" (Mutibwa 1992, 191). After two decades in power, the government is still struggling to diversify the country's economy.

Figure 2.3 Gross Capital Formation (% of GDP) and Foreign Direct Investment (% of gross capital formation) in Uganda: Pre- and Post-1985

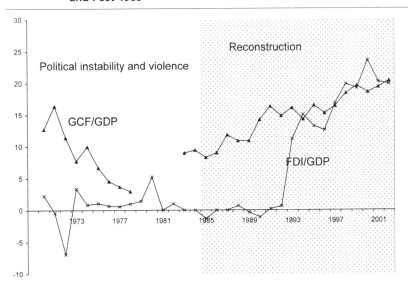

Sources: World Bank (2004g); International Monetary Fund (2004).
Notes: GCF = gross capital formation. FDI = foreign direct investment. No GCF/GDP data available for 1979–1981.

A second macroeconomic challenge is the high level of budget deficits, due to low revenue performance and rising government expenditures driven by the needs for reconstruction and growth promotion (see Figure 2.4). In 2002, the deficit stood at 4 percent of GDP if grants are included in revenues, and 11 percent exclusive of grants (World Bank 2004g). From a meager 4 percent of GDP in 1988, government revenue rose to 11 percent by 2002, but this is still low by developing countries' standards.

Third, the sustainability of vigorous growth is compromised by a widening trade imbalance (Figure 2.5). The country's terms of trade index (with 1995 as base year) dropped from 150 in 1986 to 57 in 1999. In other words, relative to its imports, the country's exports lost almost two-thirds of their value.

Fourth, and related to all of these, the sustainability of the country's macroeconomic performance is compromised by its heavy dependence on foreign aid. The availability of large-scale aid is in part a consequence of the government's strong commitment to economic reform and its success in gaining donor confidence.[4] But it also reflects the failure to raise domestic revenue, a topic to which we return below.

Social Development Challenges

Uganda has registered some visible improvements in social development. Investments in health and education have translated into greater access to safe

Figure 2.4   Uganda's Budget Performance: Expenditures and Revenues

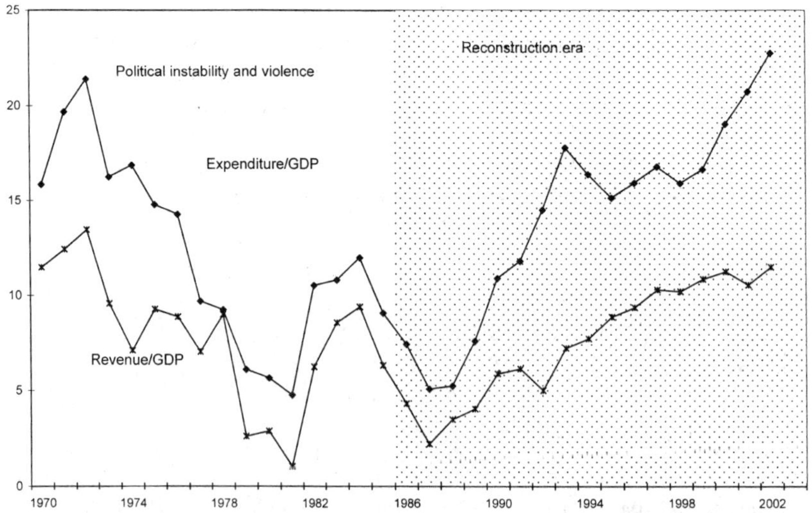

Source: International Monetary Fund (2004).

Figure 2.5 Trade Balance (US$ million), 1993–2003

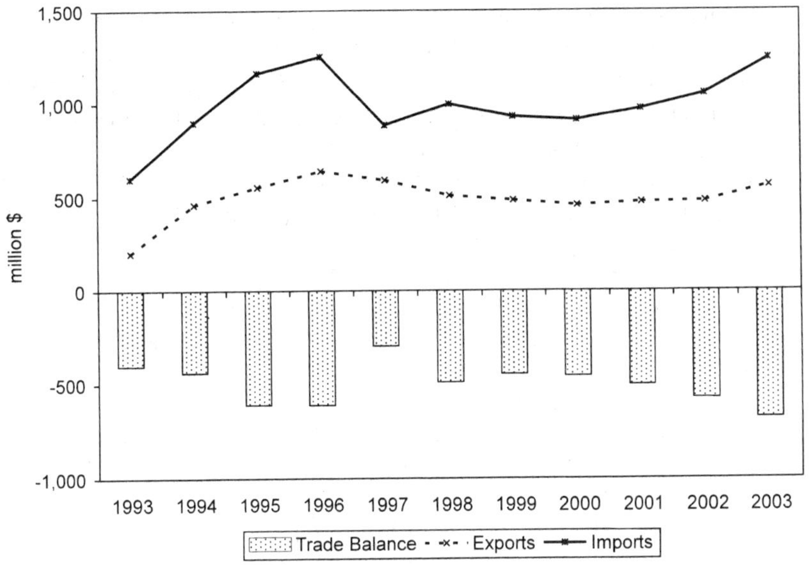

Sources: Bank of Uganda, *Quarterly Report,* annual editions.

water and sanitation and increases in educational attainment (see Table 2.3). Most important, the end of chronic political crises (except in the north and Karamoja) has allowed the country to regain its historical self-sufficiency in food supply, with accompanying improvements in nutritional status.

Three key social challenges nevertheless cast a shadow over the country's postwar macroeconomic performance. The first is high inequality at the national level as well as across regions. Economic growth has benefited dispro-

Table 2.3 Some Indicators of Social Development

Indicator	Basis of Comparison (Year)	Latest Outcome
Human development index	0.395 (1985)	0.493 (2002)
Access to safe water (%)	45 (1990)	52 (2000)
Undernourished people (% of total population)	23 (1990–1992)	19 (1999–2001)
Infant mortality rate (per 1,000 live births)	100 (1970)	82 (2002)
Youth literacy rate (% ages 15–24)	70 (1990)	80 (2002)
Poverty head count	55.7 (1992–1993)	37.7 (2002–2003)

Sources: United Nations Development Programme (2003); Uganda Bureau of Statistics (2003).

portionately the wealthier class of the population. The Gini coefficient rose from 0.35 in 1997 to 0.43 in 2003 (see Table 2.4). In 1999, only 5 percent of national income went to the poorest 20 percent of the population, whereas the richest 20 percent of the population received about half of the country's income (World Bank 2004g). This increase in income inequality is partly due to the deterioration of the terms of trade of agriculture, which depressed the purchasing power of the rural population (Appleton 2001).

Second, the regional imbalances inherited from the colonial era, which deepened under the regimes from 1962 to 1986, continue to be an important economic and political challenge. Not only does the northern region fare much worse than the other regions, but the disparity appears to be widening: from 1992 to 2000, the north saw a decline in poverty headcount of only 10 percent, compared to a national decline of 37 percent (see Table 2.4; see also Appleton 2003).

Third, even though the government has undertaken major efforts to invest in social services and infrastructure, this has not translated into commensurate improvement in the availability and quality of services. This lack of improvement is due to the chronic disparities between budgetary allocations and effective expenditures (Ablo and Reinikka 1998), leakages in the flow of funds, and inefficiencies in service delivery (Reinikka and Svensson 2004). These development challenges imply pressure on public finance to improve the quality as well as the quantity of public expenditures.

Table 2.4   Regional Inequality Indicators

Indicator	Year	National	Central	Eastern	Western	Northern
Consumption expenditure (in 2002 $/month)	1999	84	119	72	83	44
	2002	85	124	72	79	47
Maximum education in household (years)	1999	7.1	8.0	7.1	7.1	5.5
	2002	8.0	9.1	7.7	8.1	6.5
Assets (in 2002 $)	1999	1,445	2,336	1,047	1,547	361
	2002	1,528	1,867	1,327	1,825	836
Female-headed households (%)	1999	25.2	27.6	21.6	20.4	32.2
	2002	24.5	27.1	21.3	20.4	30.2
Poverty head count (%)	1992–1993	55.7	45.6	58.8	53.1	72.2
	1997	45.0	27.9	54.3	42.8	60.9
	1999–2000	33.8	19.7	35.0	26.2	63.6
	2002–2003	37.7	22.3	46.0	31.4	63.3
Gini coefficient	1992–1993	0.36	0.40	0.33	0.32	0.34
	1997	0.35	0.36	0.33	0.28	0.31
	1999–2000	0.40	0.42	0.35	0.32	0.34
	2002–2003	0.43	0.46	0.36	0.36	0.34

Sources: Deininger and Mpuga (2005), and Okidi et al. (2004), both of which are based on National Household Survey data.

Resource Mobilization

Tax Reforms

The tax system inherited by the NRM government was structurally ineffective and vastly distortionary (Uganda Revenue Authority 2004; Chen, Matovu, and Reinikka 2001; Ayoki, Obwana, and Ogwapus 2005). The system was handicapped by a narrow tax base, owing to the fact that the economy was dominated by the public sector, whereas the private sector comprised a large informal segment that was difficult to tax. To compensate for the narrow tax base, past governments imposed high tax rates that discouraged compliance and suffocated trade and industry. The corporate tax rate was as high as 60 percent, and the sales tax rate often reached 50 percent. Effective tax rates exhibited large discrepancies arising from subjectivity and arbitrariness in tax administration, both de jure and de facto. The wide-ranging exemptions and discretionary powers with respect to tax waivers contributed to a culture of tax evasion and corruption.

To address these structural problems, the government undertook reforms aimed at achieving comprehensiveness, efficiency, equity, and fairness (Uganda Revenue Authority 2004). A critical step was the creation of the semi-autonomous Uganda Revenue Authority (URA) in 1991. A uniform 17 percent value-added tax (VAT) was adopted, replacing the sales tax and the commercial tax levy (CTL). Tax holidays were repealed in 1997, and the finance minister's authority to give waivers of taxes and import duties was repealed in 2001. Various investment incentives were introduced to promote entrepreneurship and technological progress, such as initial allowances for acquisition of plant and machinery, exemptions on imports of industrial inputs, and generous depreciation allowances on specified physical assets. A further noteworthy innovation is that taxpayers can pay their taxes through commercial banks, which creates de facto decentralization of tax collection while saving costs for the government. Finally, the reforms aimed at developing a culture of compliance through taxpayer education, expeditious settlement of complaints, and other public relations efforts to improve customer satisfaction.

Despite improvements in the legal structure of the tax system, a number of problems continue to hinder revenue performance. The first is the culture of tax evasion, a legacy of the old corrupt and predatory system.[5] The system also still suffers from limited human capacity and resources, which often prevents fulfillment of reform plans and promises. For instance, although the law provides for a thirty-day maximum waiting period for tax credit and VAT refunds, customers often wait longer (Chen, Matovu, and Reinikka 2001).

One major accomplishment of the tax reforms was to remove some features of the system that made it highly regressive. These included the export tax on cash crops that transferred the burden of taxation to the farmers. The dismantling of discretionary powers and arbitrariness in the system should help to reduce the patronage advantage of high-income individuals and large corporations, and this too is likely to increase progressivity in the effective tax burden.

In an effort to promote private-sector development, the tax reforms have included strategies that reduce the effective cost of capital through exemptions on capital imports, tax holidays, and generous depreciation allowances. The reforms have made Uganda more competitive for foreign direct investment than its East African Community neighbors. The marginal effective tax rate for machinery in 1997 was –3.9 percent (i.e., a subsidy) in Uganda, compared to 12 percent in Kenya and 31 percent in Tanzania (Chen, Matovu, and Reinikka 2001).

These investment incentives raise an issue with respect to the impact of tax reforms on employment. Like other countries in sub-Saharan Africa (SSA), Uganda faces the challenge of increasing employment to improve the living standards of the population. The country's tax reforms have not targeted job creation, and they have not brought any changes in the direct cost of labor. The effective employment levy has remained at 10 percent, much higher than in neighboring East African countries (0.1 percent in Kenya and 4 percent in Tanzania). The problem is not that tax costs of employment are very high; it is that the current tax system, just as the old one, does not provide any explicit tax incentives for job creation.

To promote job creation and avoid excessive capital intensity of production, the tax authority could adopt measures to provide incentives for firms to hire more workers. Given that wage rates are already low, a wage subsidy— under which firms would collect benefits for existing workers as well as new ones—is not likely to produce the desired effects on employment. In contrast, an employment tax credit could put more people to work by requiring firms to hire new workers in order to collect the tax credit. For this to produce the desired impact on employment, the government would have to establish an effective monitoring system to avoid fraud. The Ugandan government could build on its earlier successes in the area of tax reform to use the tax system to promote job creation and increase living standards.

Performance in Domestic Revenue Mobilization

Following the introduction of tax reforms, revenue increased substantially. In real terms (in 1997–1998 prices), tax revenue almost tripled between 1989–1990 and 1996–1997, and the tax/GDP ratio rose from 5.9 percent to 11.9 percent (Table 2.5). From 1996–1997 to 2003–2004, tax revenue growth slowed, and the tax-GDP ratio grew only to 12.8 percent.

This slowdown raised concerns about the efficacy of the reforms. In its early years, the URA performed well and benefited from strong support from both government and external development partners, especially the UK and

Table 2.5 Tax Performance by Major Category from 1989–1990 to 2003–2004: Real Value and as Percentage of GDP and Total Revenue

Category	Real Revenue (billion shillings, base 1997–1998 = 100)			As % of Total Revenue			As % of GDP		
	1989–1990	1996–1997	2003–2004	1989–1990	1996–1997	2003–2004	1989–1990	1996–1997	2003–2004
Tax revenue	264.2	778.3	1,377.1	90.3	98.7	98.5	5.9	11.9	12.8
Income tax	2.3	111.1	314.9	0.8	14.1	22.5	0.1	1.7	2.9
(= direct taxes)									
PAYE[a]	2.3	41.7	156.6	0.8	5.3	11.2	0.1	0.6	1.5
Other[b]	0.0	69.4	158.3	0.0	8.8	11.3	0.0	1.1	1.5
International trade taxes[c]	181.7	539.1	746.2	62.1	68.4	53.4	4.0	8.2	6.9
Export duties	44.1	2.7	0.0	15.1	0.3	0.0	1.0	0.0	0.0
Customs duties	82.0	287.4	327.3	28.0	36.5	23.4	1.8	4.4	3.0
Excise duty	23.7	110.8	147.5	8.1	14.1	10.6	0.5	1.7	1.4
Import VAT	32.0	138.1	271.3	10.9	17.5	19.4	0.7	2.1	2.5
Indirect domestic taxes[d]	67.0	100.4	242.8	22.9	12.7	17.4	1.5	1.5	2.3
Other tax revenue	13.2	27.7	73.2	4.5	3.5	5.2	0.3	0.4	0.7
Nontax revenue	28.5	2.9	9.2	9.7	0.4	0.7	0.6	0.04	0.08
Total revenue (tax revenue + nontax revenue)	292.7	788.4	1,398.4	100	100	100	6.5	12.0	13.0

Sources: Uganda Revenue Authority's electronic database, and Ministry of Finance, Planning, and Economic Development, *Background to the Budget*, annual editions.

Notes: a. PAYE = pay as you earn. b. Other income taxes include corporate tax, presumptive tax, and withholding tax. c. International trade taxes include export duty, import duty, excise duty, and VAT on imports. Other items usually included in international taxes are withholding taxes, temporary road licenses, commission on imports, reexport levy, and hides and skins levy. d. Indirect domestic taxes = sales tax and VAT, excluding VAT on imports.

the World Bank. Although the extensive autonomy granted to the URA was essential in its initial success, this autonomy became increasingly contested, especially by the Ministry of Finance. Accusations of corruption among the staff and complaints from the public about harassment by the staff undermined the URA's support from the government. At times, the URA reportedly was at odds not only with the minister of finance but also with the president (Therkildsen 2004). Another institutional challenge faced by the URA was the uneasiness among the national staff vis-à-vis the heavy presence of expatriate "experts" on the URA payroll. This undermined staff morale and contributed to alienating the URA from taxpayers.

Performance was also affected by the shift in tax structure. After the 1996–1997 tax reforms, the share of direct taxes increased, whereas that of indirect taxes (including taxes on international trade) decreased (see Table 2.5). The trade tax to GDP ratio declined, as falling import duties were not matched by a proportionate increase in import VAT. This was partly a result of the exemptions on investment inputs and partly a reflection of the substantial share in total imports of government and international agencies, which are exonerated.

Direct taxes rose sharply from 0.1 percent of GDP in 1989–1990 to 3.4 percent in 1996–1997 and 5.9 percent in 2003–2004. This may have had unintended regressive effects, insofar as low- and middle-income households among the salaried population began to shoulder a disproportionate share of the tax burden. The evidence suggests that there are significant unexploited potentials for revenue mobilization, due to constraints in administrative capacity as well as to incomplete dismantling of tax exemptions.[6]

One source of unexploited revenue is taxation of real estate, especially urban housing and private land. Currently taxes are levied only on rental income, at a rate of 20 percent, and these are poorly collected. No property taxes are collected on owner-occupied houses, and we are not aware of any official discussion within the government or with the donor community about the establishment of such a tax. Even with a modest tax rate in the range of 1–2 percent on the market value of the property, the URA could raise considerable revenue. An important advantage of pursuing a real estate tax is that it would be progressive: owners of high-value property in urban areas are high-income households and businesses. In contrast, if the tax on rental income is passed on in the rental price, this tax may be regressive. Implementing a property tax would be a challenge given the poor state of the real estate records. Moreover, such an initiative is likely to encounter some opposition from the urban elite. The government could invest its political capital to support such an initiative, however. The amount of financial resources necessary to establish an inventory of private property would be justified by the expected yield in terms of government revenue.

Although Uganda has outperformed most of its SSA counterparts in economic growth, it is still lagging behind in the area of revenue mobilization (see

Table 2.6). For example, Kenya's average tax/GDP ratio in the years 1990–2001 was 21.6 percent, double that of Uganda at 10.8 percent. This again suggests that there are large unexploited potentials for increasing revenue mobilization.

Restructuring the Uganda Revenue Authority

In response to the unsatisfactory performance in tax collection and accusations of endemic corruption in tax administration, the government initiated a massive restructuring of the Uganda Revenue Authority. The objective is to make the URA leaner and more efficient by getting rid of corrupt staff, reducing centralization, and improving staff morale.[7]

The reforms also emphasize building good relationships between the URA and taxpayers and other stakeholders such as tax consultants, lawyers, and the manufacturing association, so as to educate the public about tax laws and procedures and improve compliance. The Large Tax Payer Office was reformed so

Table 2.6   Tax Performance and Structure: Uganda Compared to Other Sub-Saharan African Countries, Averages for 1990–2001

Country	Tax/GDP Ratio	Real Per Capita GDP (1995$) in 2002	Annual Growth of Per Capita Real GDP
Uganda	10.8	359	3.4
Botswana	22.3	4,102	2.6
Burkina Faso	8.1	281	1.2
Burundi	15.9	143	–3.0
Cameroon	10.3	700	–1.4
Congo, Dem. Rep.	4.0	90	–7.8
Congo, Rep.	10.0	700	–1.5
Cote d'Ivoire	18.0	776	–0.9
Ethiopia	11.9	124	1.4
Ghana	12.1	429	1.7
Guinea	11.0	633	1.4
Kenya	21.6	322	–0.7
Lesotho	38.5	648	2.6
Madagascar	9.0	215	–0.7
Mauritius	19.5	4,538	4.2
Namibia	29.5	2,203	0.8
Senegal	16.4	618	1.0
Seychelles	35.1	8,071	2.8
Sierra Leone	8.6	165	–4.9
South Africa	24.3	4,020	–0.5
Swaziland	28.2	1,553	0.4
Zimbabwe	22.3	521	–0.8

Source: Authors' computations from World Bank (2004g).
Note: Only countries with at least four years of data in the 1990–2001 period were included in the sample. Growth rates of GDP are averages of annual growth rates.

that it handles all three categories of taxes (direct, indirect, and duty/customs), which previously were handled by separate departments. In the past, large taxpayers were subject to frequent audits in fishing expeditions by URA agents, often looking for easy targets for corruption. The new reforms aim to establish a more systematic risk assessment system to target audits on the basis of tax payment and compliance history, among other factors. According to the URA management, the early results of the restructuring are encouraging.

External Assistance and Debt

The development assistance community responded enthusiastically to the Museveni government's adoption of macroeconomic stabilization and reform programs and its dedication to pro-growth policies. The government moved quickly to implement several International Monetary Fund (IMF)/World Bank programs, starting with the 1987 Economic Recovery Program, followed by the structural adjustment program in 1989. In addition, Uganda was one of the few countries on the continent to initiate its own in-house Poverty Eradication Action Plan (PEAP), which eventually became the foundation of the Poverty Reduction Strategy Paper endorsed by donors in 2000 in the context of the enhanced Heavily Indebted Poor Countries (HIPC) initiative.

Official development aid disbursements increased from US$300 million in 1987 to US$834 million in 1995 and US$1.16 billion in 2004. Grants became increasingly important as a source of finance for government expenditures. By 2003–2004, grants routed through the government budget were equivalent to 9.6 percent of the country's GDP (see Table 2.7).

Uganda has also experienced an increase in private external resources. In 2003, foreign direct investment reached US$283 million, compared to US$125 million in 1995 (World Bank 2004d). The increase in private inflows may be attributed to the improvement in political stability and macroeconomic reforms, including liberalization of the capital account and foreign exchange market.[8]

The NRM government inherited high levels of external debt as a result of reckless borrowing by previous regimes. With lending in support of the economic reforms, debt levels continued to accumulate in the early years of the NRM regime. The ratio of debt service to exports grew from 41 percent in 1985 to a staggering 81 percent in 1990. Beginning in 1990, however, debt sustainability indicators started to improve (see Figure 2.6). This change was due to the improvement of economic performance and to debt relief and a shift away from private debt toward concessional multilateral debt.[9]

In April 1997, Uganda became the first country to qualify for debt relief under the HIPC initiative, receiving US$650 million in debt relief, equivalent to a 20 percent reduction in the country's debt stock. The country received further debt relief under the enhanced HIPC initiative, amounting to US$1.3 billion, equivalent to another 40 percent of its external debt. The funds released by this

Table 2.7 Government Budget Financing, 1987–1988 to 2003–2004 (billion shillings)

	1987–1988	1988–1989	1989–1990	1990–1991	1991–1992	1992–1993	1993–1994	1994–1995
Revenue and grants	11.5	32.1	111.0	205.5	278.6	604.8	677.2	785.1
Total revenue	5.0	17.9	90.8	135.3	184.0	291.1	394.7	531.2
Grants	6.5	14.2	20.3	70.2	94.6	313.8	282.5	253.9
Expenditures	28.0	64.9	180.6	278.1	475.0	781.8	893.4	910.1
Recurrent expenditures	24.7	60.9	98.3	128.7	285.1	323.5	416.8	501.3
Development expenditures	19.6	28.8	76.6	134.1	250.0	393.7	431.9	404.0
Domestic debt service	−16.3	−24.8	5.7	15.3	−60.0	64.7	44.8	4.8
Financing	16.5	32.8	69.5	72.6	196.5	177.0	216.3	125.0
External financing (net)	8.7	19.4	91.8	63.2	140.4	200.8	243.2	211.7
Domestic financing	7.8	13.4	−22.3	9.4	56.0	−23.8	−27.0	−86.7
As % of GDP								
Revenue	1.3	2.1	7.0	7.9	7.1	8.0	9.7	10.8
Grants	1.7	1.7	1.6	4.1	3.7	8.7	6.9	5.2
Expenditures	7.5	7.6	13.9	16.3	18.4	21.6	22.0	18.5
Deficit (including grants)	−4.4	−3.8	−5.4	−4.2	−7.6	−4.9	−5.3	−2.5
Deficit (excluding grants)	−6.2	−5.5	−6.9	−8.3	−11.2	−13.5	−12.3	−7.7
As % of expenditures								
Total revenue	17.8	27.7	50.3	48.7	38.7	37.2	44.2	58.4
Grants	23.2	21.8	11.2	25.2	19.9	40.1	31.6	27.9
Deficit financing	59.0	50.5	38.5	26.1	41.4	22.6	24.2	13.7

continues

Table 2.7 Continued

	1995–1996	1996–1997	1997–1998	1998–1999	1999–2000	2000–2001	2001–2002	2002–2003	2003–2004
Revenue and grants	947.8	1,057.7	1,199.2	1,357.7	1,576.9	1,881.0	2,014.6	2,253.8	2,936.6
Total revenue	622.8	747.0	801.5	950.7	1,010.3	1,083.5	1,253.6	1,434.0	1,669.2
Grants	325.0	310.7	397.7	407.0	566.6	797.5	761.0	819.8	1,267.5
Expenditures and net lending	1,097.0	1,183.2	1,246.2	1,454.1	1,847.4	2,240.9	2,590.8	2,770.1	3,103.7
Recurrent expenditures	568.2	658.2	740.7	891.2	977.3	1,131.2	1,428.4	1,586.5	1,864.5
Development expenditures	489.7	442.0	502.5	560.6	771.5	1,005.7	1,042.5	1,142.0	1,186.8
Domestic debt service	39.1	83.0	3.0	2.3	98.6	104.0	119.9	41.6	52.4
Financing	149.2	125.5	47.0	96.4	270.5	359.9	576.2	516.3	167.1
External financing (net)	209.4	173.7	196.0	263.2	212.6	336.8	484.2	535.0	298.9
Domestic financing	–60.3	–48.2	–149.0	–166.8	57.9	23.1	92.0	1.3	–100.3
As a percentage of GDP									
Revenue	11.2	12.4	10.6	11.6	11.3	10.9	12.2	12.2	12.7
Grants	5.8	5.1	5.2	5.0	6.3	8.0	7.4	6.9	9.6
Expenditures and net lending	19.7	19.6	16.4	17.7	20.6	22.5	25.2	23.5	23.6
Deficit (including grants)	–2.7	–2.1	–0.6	–1.2	–3.0	–3.6	–5.6	–4.4	–1.3
Deficit (excluding grants)	–8.5	–7.2	–5.9	–6.1	–9.3	–11.6	–13.0	–11.3	–10.9
As percentage of expenditures									
Total revenue	58.9	67.9	64.5	65.5	57.8	50.7	50.7	52.6	54.7
Grants	30.7	28.2	32.0	28.0	32.4	37.3	30.8	30.0	41.5
Deficit financing	13.6	10.6	3.8	6.6	14.6	16.1	22.2	18.6	5.4

Source: Ministry of Finance, Planning, and Economic Development, *Background to the Budget*, annual editions.

Figure 2.6   Uganda's Debt Indicators

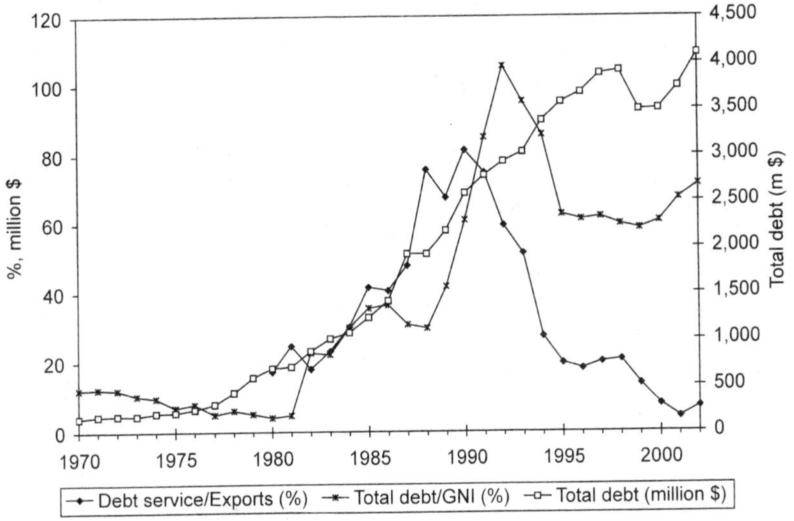

Source: World Bank (2004d).
Note: GNI = gross national income.

debt relief were earmarked for investment in social sectors, including the universal primary education program, but financing gaps in these sectors have persisted (Nannyonjo 2001).

Potential Adverse Effects of External Assistance

Large inflows of external assistance may have adverse effects on the economy through various channels. These include "Dutch disease" effects, pressures on monetary policies, and the crowding out of domestic revenue. There is also concern that aid cutbacks, due to aid fatigue or policy reform reversal, could threaten the sustainability of government programs.

The potential "Dutch disease" effects of aid arise when a large inflow of resources leads to appreciation of the national currency, making the country's exports less competitive and making imports cheaper. This has adverse effects on domestic production of tradable goods in both the manufacturing and agricultural sectors.

Large inflows of aid also increase pressure on the targets for inflation and net domestic credit specified in the government's agreements with the IMF and the World Bank.[10] When the Central Bank issues Ugandan shillings in exchange for the hard currency supplied by aid, this limits exchange-rate appreciation, but it increases the domestic money supply and could lead to inflation. When the

Central Bank attempts to neutralize ("sterilize") this effect on the money supply by selling government bonds, this pushes up interest rates with negative effects on private-sector borrowers. The Central Bank thus faces difficult trade-offs.

Excessive reliance on donor funds also has implications for sustainability of the external debt burden. External loans have accounted for about 40 percent of donor inflows in the postwar era, according to the annual reports of the Bank of Uganda. Low export growth exacerbates the debt-service problem.

Aid may also have negative indirect effects on domestic revenue mobilization. The issue is whether aid crowds in or crowds out domestic revenue. To the extent that the activities funded by aid generate new jobs and incomes and directly or indirectly facilitate private-sector production and trade, this will increase the tax base and cause tax revenue to increase. But high inflows of aid may reduce the incentives for increasing tax revenues via reforms and stronger enforcement mechanisms that are often politically costly. At the same time, the influx of aid creates a foreign public sector that is out of reach of the tax authority. Apart from the forgone revenue, exonerations of aid-related incomes and expenditures have perverse demonstration effects on local taxpayers, particularly since those employed by the foreign public sector have much higher incomes than their domestic counterparts.

In the case of Uganda, the positive effects of the surge in aid inflows over the past decade seem, on balance, to have offset these potential negative effects. In other words, aid may have caused "more gain than pain" (Nkusu 2004).

The Dutch disease effects appear to be limited. Sluggish export performance is primarily due to structural constraints and exogenous shocks, especially the collapse of coffee prices. The effects of aid on the exchange rate were minimized thanks to an institutional arrangement whereby aid funds are held at the Central Bank, rather than intermediated in the private foreign exchange market (Kasekende and Atingi-Ego 1999). This arrangement strengthens the Central Bank's ability to influence short-run movements in the exchange rate. The Central Bank resorted to sales of treasury bills in order to mop up excess liquidity resulting from releasing shillings for aid-funded spending. This put some upward pressure on interest rates, but it helped to keep inflation low.

On the other hand, as discussed earlier, tax revenue growth has slowed since the mid-1990s, following a substantial increase in the early 1990s. There have not been careful empirical analyses of direct and indirect effects of aid on domestic revenue mobilization in Uganda, but insofar as crowding out has indeed occurred, this would be an important caveat to our assessment of the net impact of external assistance.

The Budgetary Process and Expenditure Management

The NRM's initial Economic Recovery program, focused on rehabilitation and stabilization of the economy, took a gradualist approach to reform with strong support from the World Bank (Mitra-Datta 2001). In the mid-1990s the government and the donor community began to focus more on capacity building, civil service reform, decentralization, and private-sector development. An important part of the effort to promote economic growth and poverty reduction was the reallocation of public expenditures from defense toward social sectors, especially education and health.

The Disarmament, Demobilization, and Reintegration Program, 1992–1996

On coming to power, the NRM integrated many soldiers from the former national army into its own forces. This effort to build national cohesion caused the size of the military to swell to more than 90,000 men, a level that was clearly unsustainable given the scarcity of resources and massive reconstruction needs. It became clear to donors and the government alike that reform of the military was indispensable for the success of public finance reform and macroeconomic stabilization. In this context, the government—with the help of the donor community—launched a program to demobilize and reintegrate the ex-combatants into civilian life.

Initially, the NRM was reluctant to downsize the army because it was concerned about insurrection in the north. As rebel activity subsided in the early 1990s, the government undertook efforts to downsize the army. One motivation was to allow ex-combatants to contribute to economic activity by reintegrating them into civilian life. A second was to restructure government expenditure, freeing public resources for more productive uses.

Before the restructuring, military expenditures accounted for more than one-third of the government's recurrent expenditures. Imports of arms, ammunitions, and military accessories amounted to 22 percent of the country's total imports in 1988 (Colletta, Kostner, and Wiederhofer 1996a, 323). The World Bank Public Expenditure Review in 1991 pointed out the heavy burden of defense on the government budget and recommended a shift of expenditures toward social and economically productive sectors. At the same time, the government had concluded that military reform was consistent with its security needs. The government requested technical and financial assistance for demobilization from the World Bank and other donors. Donor involvement in the initial stages of planning the program was instrumental in generating external financial support.

In October 1992, legislation was passed to create the Veteran Assistance Program (VAP), the objective of which was to organize and implement the demobilization of the former combatants and their integration into civilian life. The structure of the VAP was fairly decentralized and participatory, including a board and executive secretariat at the national level, committees and officers at the district level, and veterans' representatives at the local level.

The government encouraged veterans to settle in rural areas to prevent a potential rural-urban exodus. The expectation was that the program could make significant positive contributions to the local economy, through both the multi-plier effects of veterans' spending and the supply effects of new productive ac-tivities undertaken by the demobilized soldiers in their communities. By the end of 1996, more than 36,000 soldiers had been demobilized in the three phases of the program (Table 2.8).

The funding of the Disarmament, Demobilization, and Reintegration (DDR) program was a joint effort of the Ugandan government and donors. The total cost for all three phases was 40.5 billion Ugandan shillings, equivalent to roughly US$37.7 million, of which 79 percent came from bilateral donors

Table 2.8   Cost of the Uganda Disarmament, Demobilization, and Reintegration Program, 1992–1996

	Phase I	Phase II	Phase III	Program Total
Number of soldiers demobilized	22,903	9,308	4,147	36,358
Cause of demobilization				
Voluntary	36%	8%	0%	25%
Downsizing	32%	51%	45%	38%
Medical reasons	22%	28%	44%	26%
Demobilization (US$)	1,213,334	1,073,255	803,180	3,089,769
Per veteran (US$)	53	115	194	85
% of total	7.2	9.2	8.8	8.1
Reinsertion (US$)	14,138,314	8,707,489	5,003,159	27,848,962
Per veteran (US$)	617	935	1,206	766
% of total	83.8	74.5	54.6	74.8
Reintegration (US$)	190,792	301,189	1,826,926	2,318,907
Per veteran (US$)	8	32	441	64
% of total	1.1	2.6	19.9	5.7
Administration (US$)	1,336,548	1,055,435	1,307,453	3,699,435
Per veteran (US$)	58	113	315	102
% of total	7.9	9	14.3	9.6
Contingencies (US$)	0	552,045	221,381	773,426
Per veteran (US$)	0	59,309	53,384	112,692
% of total	0	4.7	2.4	1.9
Total (US$)	16,878,987	11,689,413	9,162,099	37,730,499
Per veteran (US$)	737	1,256	2,209	1,038
% of total	100	100	100	100

Source: Colletta, Kostner, and Wiederhofer (1996a), Tables 2.1, 10.1–10.3.

Notes: The figures are converted from Ugandan shillings into US dollars using the official ex-change rate (obtained from the Bank of Uganda's annual reports) for the years covered by the pro-gram: 1,195.02Ush/$ for phase I (1993 exchange rate), 979.45Ush/$ for phase II (1994 exchange rate), and 968.65Ush/$ for Phase III (1995 exchange rate).

(UK, United States, Denmark, Netherlands, and Sweden), 10 percent from multilateral donors (World Bank, the United Nations Development Programme [UNDP], and the United Nations Children's Fund [UNICEF]), and 11 percent from the government. The cost per veteran rose from US$737 per veteran in the first phase to US$2,209 per veteran by the third phase. The higher costs in phases II and III reflect mainly a series of cost adjustments to the program informed by the experience from phase I.[11]

The DDR generated substantial budgetary savings, improved veterans' welfare, and generated positive externalities for local communities. The defense budget declined from 35 percent of recurrent expenditures in 1989–1990 to 15 percent in 1992–1993. Leakages were minimal, and it was estimated that about 90 percent of the costs of the program went to the beneficiaries. Each veteran received, on average, almost US$1,000 in cash, roughly five times the country's per capita income in 1993. Assuming that the average size of veterans' families was similar to the national average, this means that each veteran's family received an amount equivalent to the yearly income of the average Ugandan household. The veterans' families were less endowed with physical assets than other families, however, and the benefits from the program were insufficient to close this gap. Although the veterans invested a significant portion of the payments into income-generating activities, after their first year of civilian life they were earning less than half as much as the average Ugandan household (Colletta, Kostner, and Wiederhofer 1996a, 325).

At the community level, initial fears of violence and disruption were unfounded. There was very little evidence of veteran-induced crime in the communities. Instead reintegration had favorable impacts, as veterans spent on goods and services and undertook investment activities.

The overall positive experience with DDR in Uganda is attributable to several factors. First, government commitment and ownership of the program ensured political support at the highest level and helped to build credibility of the program. Second, cooperation of the military establishment itself was essential, especially at the disarmament and discharge stage. Third, donor support played a key role both in the conception of the program and in its funding. Fourth, encouraging resettlement in the rural area made reintegration easier, as the veterans were able to engage in activities that were in line with their limited skills. These lessons one day could prove useful in northern Uganda. At present, however, failure to resolve that conflict has contributed to a post-DDR increase of defense expenditures (see Table 2.9).

Sectoral Expenditure: Performance over the Medium Term

In the post-DDR period, the NRM government has faced three challenges in budget management: a meager pool of resources, an unbalanced distribution of resources across sectors, and weak budget execution. The government has

Table 2.9 Expenditures by Sector as Percentage of GDP

	1987–1988	1988–1989	1989–1990	1990–1991	1991–1992	1992–1993	1993–1994	1994–1995
General administration	3.6	1.3	2.5	2.3	2.4	3.6	3.7	4.1
Defense	2.3	2.5	3.2	3.0	2.2	1.7	2.2	2.3
Public order and safety	0.0	0.5	0.6	0.8	0.7	0.5	0.9	1.1
Education	1.3	1.3	1.5	1.4	1.8	1.4	1.4	1.4
Health	0.2	0.4	0.5	0.5	0.6	0.5	0.6	0.5
Community social services	0.0	0.4	0.3	0.3	0.1	0.2	0.3	0.2
Agriculture	0.0	0.0	0.0	0.0	0.0	0.1	0.1	0.2
Roads	0.0	0.0	0.0	0.0	0.0	0.2	0.3	0.2
Water	0.0	0.0	0.0	0.0	0.0	0.0	0.0	0.0
Other economic affairs and services	0.0	1.0	1.3	1.7	1.1	0.4	0.5	0.7
Interest on external public debt	0.0	0.0	0.0	0.0	0.0	0.0	0.0	0.0
Interest on domestic public debt	0.0	0.0	0.0	0.0	0.0	0.0	0.0	0.0
Repayment of domestic public debt	0.0	1.3	1.0	0.7	3.4	0.0	0.0	0.0
Repayment of external public debt	0.0	0.0	0.0	0.0	0.0	3.3	3.3	2.1
Other	0.0	0.0	0.0	0.0	0.0	0.0	0.0	0.1
Total expenditures as % of GDP	9.8	8.8	10.8	10.8	12.4	11.9	13.3	12.9

continues

Table 2.9 Continued

	1995–1996	1996–1997	1997–1998	1998–1999	1999–2000	2000–2001	2001–2002	2002–2003	2003–2004
General administration	2.6	2.2	3.4	2.3	2.9	4.2	4.0	2.8	2.4
Defense	2.3	2.5	2.2	3.2	2.8	2.5	2.6	2.5	2.8
Public order and safety	1.1	1.1	1.1	1.2	1.2	1.3	1.3	1.4	1.3
Education	1.0	1.2	1.2	1.8	2.1	1.8	1.9	1.5	1.4
Health	0.5	0.7	0.5	0.6	0.6	0.7	0.9	1.0	1.1
Community social services	0.2	0.2	0.3	0.2	0.4	0.2	0.2	0.3	0.2
Agriculture	0.1	0.1	0.1	0.2	0.3	0.4	0.5	0.5	0.3
Roads	0.1	0.1	0.1	0.9	1.3	1.5	1.7	1.3	0.5
Water	0.0	0.0	0.0	0.2	0.2	0.2	0.3	0.3	0.2
Other economic affairs and services	1.0	1.2	1.0	0.4	0.3	0.3	0.4	0.5	0.4
Interest on external public debt	0.0	0.0	0.6	1.7	0.4	0.3	0.0	0.0	0.0
Interest on domestic public debt	0.0	0.0	0.3	0.3	0.2	0.3	0.0	0.0	0.0
Repayment of domestic public debt	0.0	0.2	0.0	0.8	0.0	0.0	0.0	0.0	0.0
Repayment of external public debt	1.9	1.3	1.2	1.3	1.5	0.9	1.5	3.0	3.4
Other	0.2	0.2	0.2	0.5	0.3	0.5	1.8	0.6	0.5
Total expenditures as % of GDP	10.9	11.0	12.2	15.4	14.7	14.9	17.0	15.7	14.5

Sources: Uganda Bureau of Statistics electronic database; Bank of Uganda, *Annual Report*, annual editions; Ministry of Finance, Planning, and Economic Development, *Background to the Budget*, annual editions.

Note: "Other" includes civil service pensions, compensation for East African Community employees, transfers to international organizations except the East African Community, other transfers, employment costs, and Entandikwa credit scheme.

had difficulty in reducing defense expenditure below 2 percent of GDP. Although it is necessary to address insecurity in northern Uganda, defense expenditures need to be closely monitored. Overruns and nonprogrammed allocations observed in defense expenditures (and public administration expenditures) undermine budget discipline. Moreover, as discussed below, greater emphasis should be placed on the negotiation process as a solution to the conflict in the north.

According to the government's PEAP, the priority in expenditure should be social sectors, including health and education. As a fraction of GDP, funding to the health sector rose from 0.5 percent in the mid-1990s to 1.1 percent in 2003–2004, and that to education peaked at 2.1 percent in 1999–2000 but then slid back to 1.4 percent (see Table 2.9).

In the health sector, the abolition of user fees in 2001 is said to have enhanced access to health services by the poor, but the quality of services remains low (World Bank 2002c; Deininger and Mpuga 2005).[12] Maternal and child health indicators are still poor, and immunization coverage has stagnated. The gravity of the situation is compounded by new health risks. Malaria has reached endemic levels. Human immunodeficiency virus/acquired immunodeficiency syndrome (HIV/AIDS) remains an important health challenge despite the remarkable success achieved in controlling the epidemic from the late 1980s to the mid-1990s thanks to the approach called Abstinence, Be faithful, and use Condom (ABC).[13] War-affected areas are afflicted by diseases caused by poor hygiene and psychological problems caused by trauma. Ironically, despite these needs at home, Uganda has become an exporter of medical professionals to Western countries and South Africa.

In the education sector, government policy has focused mainly on achieving universal primary education (UPE). This goal was introduced in the Five-Year Plan of 1972–1976 under Idi Amin and reiterated in Obote's Recovery Program but never implemented. A fresh commitment came in Museveni's manifesto for the 1996 presidential election. In January 1997, the government initiated the UPE program with World Bank support.[14] Implementation has yielded some positive results in terms of enrollments and closing the gender gap in education.

The education sector also recorded improvements in efficiency, partly thanks to pioneering tracking studies carried out by independent researchers and public education campaigns that publicized their results. The first tracking study was launched in June 1996, with support from the World Bank and the Swedish International Development Agency, supervised by a task force with representatives from government, donors, the private sector, and nongovernmental organizations (NGOs) (Ablo and Reinikka 1998). One effect of these studies was to spotlight leakages in the flow of funds from the center to the final users. Between 1996 and 2001, the fraction of central government funding that effectively reached schools rose impressively, from 36 percent to 90 percent (World Bank 2002c).

Despite this progress, educational outcomes still fall considerably short of the Millennium Development Goals. For example, the student/teacher ratio has declined from 110 to 85, but this is still much higher than the target of 40. School dropout rates remain high, especially for girls. Low pay contributes to low staff morale. Yet quantitative evidence shows that access to education is one of the most important factors for the transition out of poverty in Uganda (see Appleton 2001; Lawson, McKay, and Okidi 2005).

Toward Efficiency and Transparency?

Uganda's first Medium Term Expenditure Framework (MTEF), laying out objectives, priorities, and budget allocations, was adopted in fiscal year 1998–1999 to provide a three-year rolling public expenditure plan, a step first recommended in the World Bank's 1993 Public Expenditure Review. In principle, the MTEF is guided by the long-term development framework established by the PEAP. Taking into account macroeconomic targets agreed upon with the IMF, the Ministry of Finance establishes sector-wide budgetary *ceilings* that reflect the priorities in the MTEF. Integration of donor project money into the MTEF started in 2004, so as to increase budget predictability and improve the allocation of public expenditures.

The country has also taken steps to enhance democracy and accountability in the budgetary process and expenditure management. Participation in budget preparation has been expanded to include representatives from all major stakeholders: the central government's line ministries and departments, local governments, Parliament, donors, civil society organizations, the Uganda Revenue Authority, and the office of the auditor general, as well as the cabinet. Public expenditure management has been decentralized with the aim of improving efficiency in the delivery of government services. Fiscal decentralization faces a number of challenges, however, including weak capacity at the local level, weak mechanisms for channeling and monitoring resources, and lack of local control over resource allocation due to limited capacity to generate revenue locally.

International development partners provide technical and financial assistance for budget preparation consultations at the national and local level. As noted above, donors also have supported budget tracking studies that provide valuable inputs into the monitoring and planning processes. So far these have been confined to the health and education sectors, but they could be extended to all sectors and publicly funded programs.

Nonstate actors, including NGOs, audit firms, and research institutions, are playing an increasingly important role in the budget process, helping to raise public awareness on issues of allocation and efficiency in budget management, abuse of public office, and corruption. For example, the Uganda Debt Network monitors the use of resources from the Poverty Action Fund (PAF), which was created after Uganda qualified for debt relief under the HIPC initiative to ensure that resources from debt relief were channeled to priority programs that directly benefit the poor.[15]

The government also has sought to improve communication with the public by producing booklets such as *A Citizen's Guide to the Budget Process,* which was translated in seven local languages. Other publications include *The Budget at a Glance* and *The Budget Performance Report,* which give development and recurrent budgets and actual spending by sector, revealing which sectors have spent above or below their respective budgets.

Even though substantial improvements have been made in the budgetary process, several challenges remain. First, the integration of project aid into the MTEF is still weak, and donor disbursements often fall short of commitments. Second, the participation of local governments and civil society is constrained by lack of capacity and the short time given to sector working groups to prepare budget framework papers.[16] Third, the fact that budget framework papers are not output oriented makes monitoring of outcomes difficult.[17] Fourth, a few sectors such as defense and public administration continue to lack budget discipline, as seen through budget overruns, posing a constraint to efficient resource allocation and prioritization of needs. Finally, the MTEF is criticized for not sufficiently taking into consideration the long-term development priorities of the PEAP (see Bategeka 2004).

Social Costs of Budget-deficit Targets and Aid Ceilings

The financing of budget deficits has important implications for interest rates, inflation, and exchange rate stability. In the early years of postwar reconstruction, the Ugandan government ran high deficits owing to low domestic revenue. In subsequent years, aid flows increased, and these played a larger role in funding the government's budget. Since 1999, the ratio of grants to total government expenditures has exceeded 30 percent, and it stood at 41.5 percent in 2004 (see Table 2.7).

In an effort to minimize potential adverse effects of aid inflows on inflation and the exchange rate, the Ministry of Finance imposes sectoral expenditure ceilings on all ministries and government bodies. Given limited domestic revenue, these amount to caps on aid utilization. The ceilings include all forms of aid—grants, loans, in-kind aid, and technical assistance—and they include project aid as well as aid channeled through the government budget.

This policy can be criticized on two grounds. First, there is no evidence of a significant effect of aid on inflation or the exchange rate in Uganda. In fact, even as the aid intensity of the budget has increased in recent years, inflation has gone down and the real exchange rate has not appreciated. One reason for this is that a significant portion of aid covers expenditures abroad on goods and services paid in foreign currency. This is the case for imported equipment and supplies and for technical assistance salaries that are deposited in bank accounts abroad. As these funds never actually enter Uganda, they are not exchanged for shillings and thus have no impact on domestic liquidity. They do not affect the exchange rate, interest rates, or the inflation rate. At a minimum, these kinds of aid should be excluded from calculations of expenditure ceilings.

Second, the imposition of aid ceilings forces ministries to take painful decisions in cutting expenditures. The inclusion of project aid in the ceilings worsens the problem, as the ministries have no or very little control over the volume and timing of project-based aid. When such aid causes total spending to exceed the ceilings, the ministries must compress expenditures in other activities in the sector. The combination of low domestic revenue and ceilings on aid has resulted in low execution rates of development programs. In the health sector, for example, the provision of services is growing at a much slower pace than demand, even as doctors and nurses remain unemployed because the Ministry of Health has to "watch its ceilings." One wonders which targets matter most: the social targets embodied in the country's Millennium Development Goals for the year 2015, or the short-run macroeconomic targets for inflation, the exchange rate, and the budget deficit.

This discussion suggests that new methods of aid management need to be explored to allow the country to finance its development programs and meet the immense social needs of the population. In the end, budget ceilings are not just abstract numbers: they translate into untreated diseases, unemployed health care professionals, unschooled children, poor infrastructure, and suboptimal progress in improving living standards. These development failures, in turn, can translate into political instability. As a first step, the determination of the sectoral budget ceilings ought to be reformed to exclude aid that has no impact on domestic liquidity. More generally, the objective of minimizing the potential adverse effects of aid on the exchange rate and inflation should be weighed against the imperative of financing the government's development agenda.

National Security and Fiscal Policy

The ongoing insecurity in northern Uganda and the wider region, especially in Sudan and Democratic Republic of Congo (DRC), has important implications for Uganda's fiscal policy. On the revenue side, insecurity depresses performance both directly, by preventing the collection of revenue, and indirectly, by undermining production and trade. Conflict and instability in neighboring countries exacerbate revenue losses. For example, the country loses large amounts of revenue on goods that are smuggled across the DRC-Uganda border. On the expenditure side, insecurity compels the government to make difficult choices about the allocation of resources between defense and productive sectors. The best strategy is a multifaceted approach that in addition to fighting the insurrection emphasizes development programs, emergency relief, and peace negotiations.

Development as Peacebuilding

Investing in local development in the north is needed not only to reconstruct the economy but also to achieve peace and political stability. Apart from redressing grievances, development opens new opportunities and expectations, especially for the young people who otherwise serve as a reserve army for rebel organizations. To be sure, much of the recruitment into rebel forces in Uganda is done by force, but it is still the case that the absence of economic opportunities lowers recruitment barriers. Insecurity is to some extent a development problem and must be addressed as such.

In collaboration with its development partners, the Ugandan government has undertaken initiatives aimed at economic empowerment of local communities in the north. Examples include the World Bank–supported Northern Uganda Social Action Fund, European Union (EU)–Karamoja projects, and EU-Acholi projects, which invest in infrastructure development, vocational training for war returnees and orphans, the development of microcredit schemes, strengthening of local capacity to manage and monitor projects, and community counseling. These programs have achieved some success, but they have been hampered by problems including lack of capacity and high costs due to lack of a reliable transportation network. Combined with lack of security, the constant mobility of communities, especially in the case of EU-Karamoja projects, complicates the planning and delivery of services.

Negotiation and Reconciliation Efforts in the North

Economic assistance complements political and diplomatic efforts to resolve conflict. Initiatives to find a peaceful settlement of the conflict in the north have encountered a number of difficulties. One has been the lack of direct face-to-face negotiations between the government of Uganda and the LRA's "single real decision maker," Joseph Kony (International Crisis Group 2005b, 1).[18] Progress also has been hampered by the lack of direct involvement by the United States.[19] So far, the diplomatic process has been spearheaded by the "European Troika" of Norway, the UK, and the Netherlands. The United States has been reluctant to press the government of Uganda to negotiate with the LRA, which it has condemned as a terrorist organization. The United States has invested much more political capital in the Sudanese peace process, an investment that paid off with the signing of a peace agreement between the SPLA and the government in Khartoum. The International Crisis Group (2005b, 8) argued that "Washington should recognize that as distasteful as the LRA is, a settlement would save Uganda from much additional suffering and also help smooth implementation of the Sudanese peace deal."

As the conflict in the north drags on, the government of Uganda runs the risk of losing patience and going for a military solution. History has shown that when pushed into a corner militarily, the LRA reacts by inflicting more brutality on the civilian population. From the standpoint of the civilian population, the military approach thus is a lose-lose solution.

Limited cease-fires offered unilaterally by the government have proven ineffective. The LRA has made it clear that it is more interested in a comprehensive package that addresses its two key concerns: the security of its leaders and fighters and a peace dividend in the form of economic opportunities. A comprehensive program of demobilization, disarmament, and reintegration will be vital to the peace process.[20] The constraints to peace negotiations are not insurmountable, but addressing them will require more political effort from the government and more financial backing from donors.

The Karamoja Disarmament Program

A series of efforts has also been undertaken in Karamoja to resolve the chronic insecurity in the region. With the help of the donor community, the government started a disarmament program in December 2001. The major objectives of the program were to enlist support through sensitization programs, end terrorism by the armed Karamojong, stop illegal trafficking of guns from Sudan and Kenya, work closely with Kenya to ensure concurrent disarmament of the Turkana and Didinga, resettle and rehabilitate those who voluntarily surrender their guns, ensure social and economic transformation in Karamoja, train and deploy security forces (Uganda People's Defense Force [UPDF] and local defense units) to stop armed incursions and gun trafficking, and strengthen police and the judiciary to ensure adequate administration of justice. According to several sources familiar with the program, to date it has collected about 11,000 guns out of an estimated 40,000 guns held by the Karamojong warriors.

Several factors have hampered the success of this disarmament process. The pastoral communities are reluctant to surrender their guns because this would expose them to attacks from neighboring tribes (Action for Development of Local Communities 2000). Lack of gainful economic activities for the youths who voluntarily surrender their guns has led to recurrence of cattle rustling and conflicts. The local defense units deployed in the area are often ill trained, and UPDF forces are not adequately prepared to back them up. Finally, the lack of cooperation and trust among the senior local leadership in the region perpetuates clashes and interclan raids.

Regional Conflicts

The involvement of the Ugandan army in the DRC conflict in the 1997–2001 period was politically and economically costly, depreciating the government's political capital and imposing a heavy burden on the budget. Although revenues were raised from exploitation of resources in DRC, a substantial fraction of the proceeds went into private pockets instead of government coffers (United Nations Security Council 2001).

The conflict in Sudan has complicated the rebellion in northern Uganda, as noted above, owing to the support that the LRA has enjoyed from the Khartoum government. The signing of the January 2005 Comprehensive Peace Agreement between the government of Khartoum and the Sudan People's Liberation Movement (SPLM) was a major breakthrough, but its effective implementation was hampered by the tragic death of SPLM leader John Garang only one month after he was sworn in as first vice president of Sudan. The peace agreement itself has important weaknesses, especially the fact that it tends to marginalize the smaller opposition groups (International Crisis Group 2005a). In addition, disputes between the SPLM and the Khartoum government over oil-revenue sharing and border demarcation remain a challenge to peacebuilding in Sudan. The role of the international community will be critical for the success of Sudan's peace agreement, and this in turn could have a major impact on the prospects for peace in northern Uganda.

Conclusion

The NRM regime has recorded significant success in moving Uganda from chaos back onto the path of development. Since 1995, the country has emerged as one of the strongest economic performers on the continent, recording high and steady GDP growth rates while keeping inflation under control. The government's early commitment to reform and reconstruction attracted funding from donors and contributed to building domestic political support. Another important institutional factor was the establishment of "agencies of restraint" that enhanced government credibility domestically and internationally. Prime examples are the URA, with its semiautonomous structure; the PEAP, which institutionalizes a commitment to poverty alleviation; the MTEF, which provides a framework for the allocation of resources; and the constitutional reforms that aim to democratize the budgetary process.

Nevertheless, the country faces serious challenges. High budget deficits and trade deficits, and the lack of diversification of the export base, in the end could compromise the sustainability of macroeconomic performance. At the microeconomic level, the main weakness is that the benefits of economic growth have not been widely shared. Growth appears to have benefited disproportionately the richer segments of the population. One reason is that growth in agriculture, the main source of livelihood for the majority of the population, has lagged behind, and its terms of trade vis-à-vis other sectors have deteriorated. At the regional level, the north continues to be marginalized economically. Inequitable growth poses serious threats not only to the sustainability of the country's macroeconomic performance but also—most importantly—to political stability.

Uganda's development challenges will require both higher volumes of resources and better management of expenditures. The country faces a paradoxical situation. On the one hand, if it is to have a chance of meeting its Millennium Development Goals, the country needs to spend more to build social infrastructure, increase the workforce, and raise worker morale in the social sectors. On the other hand, the government adheres to stringent short-run macroeconomic targets that force it to compress expenditures, even when this means turning down generous offers of development assistance.

We have argued that the government can raise overall levels of expenditure and increase allocations to social sectors and infrastructure without undermining macroeconomic stability in two ways. First, there is room for raising more domestic revenue. Second, the economy can absorb higher levels of aid. The evidence examined in this study suggests that there is substantial unexploited potential for raising tax revenue. Following the establishment of the Uganda Revenue Authority in 1991, tax revenue expanded, but it tapered off starting in the mid-1990s even as more aggressive reforms were enacted. The weak performance in revenue collection is attributable to inefficiencies in tax administration, especially due to corruption, and to failure to diversify the tax base. The restructuring of the URA is supposed to alleviate the problems of administrative inefficiencies, but more can and should be done to explore avenues for diversifying the sources of tax revenue. Among other avenues, the URA should establish an inventory of urban real estate and initiate mechanisms for collecting property taxes.

There also is room for increasing the use of aid, provided that new mechanisms for managing resource inflows are established. Careful examination of the composition of aid would allow the authorities to determine what portion of aid will be spent on domestic goods and services, with potential impacts on the exchange rate and inflation. The portion of aid that is spent instead on imported goods and services—especially when these do not compete with domestic production—should not be considered in the determination of expenditure ceilings.

The government's efforts to promote private enterprise have generated positive results, as evidenced by rising inflows of foreign investment. It is imperative, however, to keep a healthy balance between incentives for foreign investment and incentives for domestic investment. National entrepreneurs argue that the government currently exhibits a bias in favor of foreign investors, granting them liberal tax holidays and other generous allowances. Moreover, tax policies have encouraged capital accumulation without commensurate gains on the employment front. Given high levels of unemployment, the government should consider establishing tax incentives for job creation in the private sector. In this regard, an employment tax credit would be more appropriate than wage subsidies, since wages are already low and the tax credit could be collected only upon proof of creation of new jobs.

In sum, in attempting to meet the expectations of its external and domestic constituencies, the government has achieved a mixed record. The government has been on good terms with the lending community, thanks to its strong record in macroeconomic stability and commitment to reforms. But the government's score with the general citizenry is less stellar. Excellence on the macroeconomic policy front will not impress the people when their children are not able to attend school and when hospitals are understaffed and undersupplied. Having demonstrated its capacity to engineer strong aggregate economic performance, the Ugandan government now needs to prove its capacity to bring every citizen to the dinner table to share in the fruits of that performance. Efforts to promote greater transparency in the budgetary process and expenditure management can be a positive step in this direction, but they are not enough. Greater economic and political inclusion will be the ultimate test for the contribution of public finance to building a stable state and promoting sustainable economic growth in Uganda.

Notes

1. Yoweri Museveni, *The New Vision* (Kampala: New Vision, 2005), 3.
2. Conservative estimates suggest that cumulative income loss due to war from 1965 to 1994 amounted to about half of 1995 gross domestic product (GDP) (Matovu and Stewart 2001). This estimate is obtained by comparing actual GDP to the level that the country would have achieved if it had performed at the average rate in sub-Saharan Africa (SSA). These estimates are conservative given that SSA's performance has been very poor, whereas, as recent record demonstrates, Uganda is able to perform much better than the SSA average in the absence of conflict.
3. United Nations Office for Coordination of Humanitarian Affairs, 2005b, 8. The figure for internally displaced persons (IDPs) fluctuates according to the security situation. The figure on IDPs is as of March 2005 and reflects IDPs fed by the World Food Program (WFP) and not necessarily the number of IDPs in the whole country.
4. Kasekende and Atingi-Ego (1999) argued that although aid flows accompanied and financed economic reforms, the reforms were indigenously induced rather than "bought by aid."
5. Gauthier and Reinikka (2001) found that tax evasion was more prevalent among small firms, whereas large firms enjoyed more tax waivers, implying that medium-sized firms shouldered a disproportionately large share of the tax burden.
6. An example is the exemption of income tax for employees of the police and prison services (Ayoki, Obwana, and Ogwapus 2005).

7. The restructured URA comprises six echelons instead of eleven, five commissioners instead of eleven, and twenty-four assistant commissioners instead of more than forty. The positions of deputy commissioners have been eliminated, and those of principal and senior revenue officers have been replaced by one position of manager. The reforms of the URA also include complete computerization of the tax collection system, including risk assessment and management mechanisms, which should reduce delays in the processing of consignments while maximizing compliance.

8. See Atingi-Ego and Sebudde (2004) for a discussion of exchange rate regime shifts and capital account liberalization.

9. For further discussion of Uganda's external debt, see Chapter 9 by Patricia Alvarez-Plata and Tilman Brück.

10. The "financial planning" model, which constitutes the framework for macroeconomic policy in Uganda and other countries under IMF and World Bank programs, initially was conceived to ensure external solvency, but the current version of the model includes inflation control. For a critique of this model, see Easterly (2002).

11. For example, education support for veterans' children in phase I was judged inadequate and was raised. Starting with phase II, predischarge orientation, health care support, and training funds were provided. Phase III introduced information and counseling for veterans and substantially greater support for training.

12. The first attempt in 1990 to introduce user fees in health care as a way of improving performance of the public health system was met with opposition on the grounds that imposition of fees would discriminate against the poor in access to health. The fees were eventually established in 1993. Despite provisions for exemption for the poor, the fees in practice were applied uniformly across districts (Kapiriri, Norheim, and Heggenhougen 2003). Complaints against adverse effects on access to health care for the poor motivated the abolition of the fees in 2001.

13. Uganda's ABC approach to HIV/AIDS prevention was instrumental in curbing the spread of the epidemic from the late 1980s to the mid-1990s (see Cohen 2003).

14. Initially, the government committed to providing free education for four children per family. In 2002, the policy was revised to cover all children of school-going age. See Bategeka, Ayoki, and Mukungu (2004) for a discussion of funding for universal primary education.

15. The PAF is part of the funds budgeted under the MTEF. Although other programs within the MTEF may be subject to cuts owing to lack of resources during budget implementation, the government guarantees that the funds budgeted for PAF programs will be 100 percent available over the financial year. The resources available for programs funded by PAF increased from about 8.5 percent of the total budget in 1998–1999 to 24 percent in 2003–2004. In the latter year, the funds in the PAF came from the government's own resources (60 percent), debt relief savings (20 percent), and donor support (20 percent) (Ministry of Finance [Uganda], *Background to the Budget,* annual editions).

16. The sector working groups (SWGs), institutionalized in Uganda's planning and budgeting process since 1996, are the forums where central (finance, public service, local government) and line ministries (health, education) and external stakeholders, including donors and civil society, coordinate sectoral planning and budgeting.

17. The National Integrated Monitoring and Evaluation System, located in the office of the prime minister, takes this issue into consideration.

18. So far, negotiations have been conducted through contacts between the government's chief negotiator, former State Minister Betty Bigombe, and Kony's second-in-command, Vincent Otii. Bigombe's work has been constrained by limited logistical, political, and diplomatic support.

19. The United States has, however, played a major role in funding of humanitarian operations (United Nations Office for Coordination of Humanitarian Affairs 2005c).

20. Under the 2000 Amnesty Act, more than 15,000 rebels have surrendered, but so far, according to several sources, only about 4,000 have received their reintegration packages. Obstacles have included delays in formulating a national framework for coordination and implementation, inadequate funding, inadequate flows of information to LRA fighters due to lack of safe zones, and ongoing investigations by the International Criminal Court that discourage rebels from surrendering.

3

Aid, Public Finance, and Accountability: Cambodian Dilemmas

Paul Smoke and Robert R. Taliercio Jr.

When the Cambodian peace accords were signed in 1991, setting up a United Nations transitional administration, the country's public finance system was poorly developed. In 1993, after UN-brokered elections formally initiated a political process to recover from decades of conflict, the Royal Government of Cambodia (RGC) began to take steps to modernize the public sector and transform its focus from the military to developmental objectives. Although progress has been made on a number of fronts, the present system has deep flaws rooted in the country's complex political dynamics and relations with external actors. More than fifteen years after the peace accords, Cambodia still faces enormous political and technical challenges in transforming the public sector into a well-functioning entity able to meet the basic needs of its population.

This chapter reviews the recent evolution of the public finance system in Cambodia and its role in national development in a postwar environment. Our broad perspective is that public finance reform is not just a technical matter: it must take account of the local context and the larger role of the public sector in promoting economic and social development, including democratic governance. Political considerations dominate the public-sector landscape and influence the shape of all key fiscal reform efforts.

In Cambodia today, a "peace and security" mentality permeates the thinking of many actors, both in the coalition government and among the international aid donors. In the area of public finance, policy is subjected to the litmus test of how it will affect political stability. The latter is assumed to depend on safeguarding and expanding the existing patronage system: priming the patronage pump is accepted as the "price of peace." This dynamic is used to justify the adoption of a reform framework with formal principles that in practice are often subjugated to the perceived need to use resources to maintain fragile alliances that benefit the various elements of the ruling coalition, including the military.[1]

The peace and security mentality leads to a series of systemic dysfunctions. Revenue is affected in a number of ways, ranging from the siphoning of revenue collections away from the Treasury for political uses to the discretionary use of tax law. Selective tax enforcement and the private pocketing of public revenue result in low compliance and low revenue yields. The civil service is used for patronage to keep government coalition partners together. Expansionary political pressure on the size of the civil service, in the context of low revenue collections, contributes to a reluctance to raise low wages for civil servants, and this creates disincentives for them to report for work and deliver services. Public expenditures often do not reach their officially intended beneficiaries—instead they are used to secure political support. Spending is concentrated in Phnom Penh and provincial capitals and is heavily devoted to administrative and indirect costs. When expenditures do reach the public, they tend to favor the middle-income and wealthy strata. The new decentralization initiative thus far has been somewhat more transparent, and perhaps more pro-poor, than other public resource allocation mechanisms, but it accounts for a small share of expenditures, and its integrity could be threatened as it grows.

When there is peace, the system is seen to be working, and peace and security proponents claim success. When the threat of instability flares, as it did during power-sharing negotiations after the 2003 national elections, the mentality justifies expanded patronage designed to stabilize the situation, such as the dramatic increase in senior ministerial positions created to build a cross-party coalition government a year after the elections. Whatever their political logic, such patronage-oriented measures promote an atmosphere that invites corruption and deepen the problems of the system. Although something of a caricature, this picture captures the basic consequences of the prevailing peace and security mentality.

In stark contrast to the peace and security mentality is a nascent "developmental" mentality in which the Cambodian state is seen primarily as a facilitator of economic growth and poverty reduction. This view—which is the dominant one in the official, public discourse—is largely consistent with the current worldview of the international financial institutions (IFIs), the "Washington Consensus" updated to incorporate the important institutions and governance. Although Cambodia's ruling elite to some extent may have adopted this approach as a facade for international consumption, the developmental mentality is gaining credibility in some segments of the state, and it has resulted in a degree of reform momentum. Some senior civil servants who push for a more developmental perspective, including an influential group of technocrats in the Supreme National Economic Council (SNEC), now wield considerable influence over economic and social policy.

The true position of the international donors with respect to these competing paradigms is not always obvious. Officially, the IFIs tend to support the developmental mentality, whereas some bilateral donors sympathize more with the peace and security mentality. In the post-9/11 world, the peace and security mentality is seen by some bilateral donors as a way to avoid a "failed state" that could serve as a terrorist haven. Others may simply accept the political logic of patronage more than the IFIs. This balance changes over time. In the wake of a power struggle in 1997 that left one of the country's two prime ministers in firm control, many donors, including the International Monetary Fund (IMF) and several bilateral agencies, froze aid to register disapproval of what they perceived as an overt violation of political process. A number of donors, however, fairly quickly adopted a more accommodating view, grounded in the peace and security logic, and restarted support, particularly once new elections were announced. Japan and Germany resumed aid, for example, whereas the United States took longer to reengage. These varying and shifting positions underscore the lack of consistency in the donor community's approach to supporting the RGC.

The tension, negotiations, and compromises between the developmental mentality and the peace and security mentality help to explain the trajectory of Cambodia's public finance system. The coexistence of these two currents of thought within the state itself, at times in alliance with nonstate actors including private sector groups, donors, and non-governmental organizations (NGOs), underlies both the progress made in some reform areas and the lack of progress in others.

The next section provides a brief historical overview of Cambodia's social, political, and economic context. Other topics are a summary of the evolution of the public finance system in the past decade; a discussion of the four major reform areas of public financial management, civil service reform, decentralization, and natural resource management; and an analysis of challenges that cut across these major areas. We conclude with some thoughts on what might lie in the future.

Historical Context

Cambodia's total population is about 11 million, with an estimated annual growth rate of 2.5 to 3 percent. It is one of the poorest countries in the world, with an annual gross domestic product (GDP) per capita of US$350. Three-quarters of the workforce is employed in subsistence farming. Literacy levels are low, with only 35 percent of the over-fifteen population able to read and write. Ethnically the country is fairly homogenous, consisting of 90 percent Khmer, 5 percent Vietnamese, 1 percent Chinese, and 4 percent others. The public sector is small, with the RGC budget accounting for only about 11 percent of GDP in 2001.[2]

Political and Social Landscape

Cambodia has a fractious modern political history. In 1863, King Norodom accepted a French offer of protection from Vietnam in exchange for access to the country's natural resources. After Cambodian independence in 1953, King Sihanouk dominated Cambodian politics until he was overthrown by Lon Nol in 1970. The Khmer Rouge, a resistance movement led by the notorious Pol Pot, took power in 1975. As many as 1.7 million people are estimated to have been executed or to have died from hardship during the four years of Khmer Rouge rule. Vietnam intervened to drive out Pol Pot in 1979 and created the single-party People's Republic of Kampuchea, led by the forerunner of today's Cambodia People's Party (CPP). Civil war with the ousted Khmer Rouge raged throughout the 1980s, and a movement to restore the monarchy also emerged.[3]

The United Nations brokered a three-way peace agreement among the CPP, the Khmer Rouge, and the royalists that was signed in Paris in 1991. The agreement established a constitutional monarchy and called for internationally supervised elections, which were held in 1993. In the interim, Cambodia was administered by the United Nations Transitional Authority in Cambodia (UNTAC), at the time the largest such operation in UN history. Although UNTAC endeavored to build up domestic governance capacity, the results were mixed, perhaps not surprisingly given the difficult starting point. Some efforts focused on strengthening the capacity of the Ministry of Economy and Finance (MEF) to manage public finances, but the de facto approach was to use expatriate "advisers" as line managers. This enabled the core functions of MEF to be carried out reasonably well, but it sidelined the building of local capacity.

The main contestants in the 1993 elections were the CPP under Hun Sen, who had served as prime minister under the Vietnamese-backed regime since 1985, and the royalist United National Front for an Independent, Neutral, Peaceful, and Cooperative Cambodia (FUNCINPEC) Party under Prince Norodom Ranariddh, son of King Sihanouk.[4] Ranariddh won the election, but Hun Sen, who effectively controlled the military, sought a cogovernance arrangement. A coalition government was formed in which Ranariddh and Hun Sen respectively became first and second prime ministers. This power-sharing arrangement, which was replicated in ministries and throughout government institutions, was highly controversial, and it has often been blamed for a multiyear paralysis of much government activity. Many observers criticized the UN for allowing the CPP to maintain its power in this way, against the "rule of law" (or developmental) outcome of the 1993 elections, but the peace and security mentality prevailed, most likely out of a deep fear of reigniting civil war.

This fragile power-sharing arrangement collapsed in July 1997 amid factional fighting. Prince Ranariddh went into exile (although FUNCINPEC was not fully driven from the bureaucracy), and Hun Sen assumed power as the sole prime minister. The immediate international reaction was outrage, but some donors saw opportunities for greater stability and progress in a situation where one party had control. Hun Sen quickly organized an election in 1998, in which the CPP won a narrow victory and FUNCINPEC secured a junior role in a new coalition. The 1998 election also saw the electoral debut of the opposition Sam Rainsy party, named after its leader, a reform-minded former minister of finance.

The most recent elections, held in July 2003, again resulted in a CPP victory, but afterwards it took a full year to negotiate a coalition government. Again, perhaps fearing a return to hostilities, the international community essentially sat on the sidelines while this process played out. Patronage concerns appear to have dominated the extended negotiations. Critics argue that the CPP in effect bought off FUNCINPEC and marginalized the Sam Rainsy party, exacerbating the basic public finance problems explored below.

In addition to the peace and security mentality, there are other obstacles to establishing effective public management and democratic governance.[5] First, traditional perceptions of power and authority are very hierarchical, so concepts of broad-based accountability are not well understood in many circles. Second, Khmer culture has an aversion to conflict and losing face, and this often constrains vigorous debate on public decisions. Third, the country was in a state of turmoil for so long that social cohesion has been seriously undermined. Finally, the legacy of the centralized socialist system during the 1980s reinforced hierarchical behavior.

There now appear to be some openings for public sector reform. Frequent power shifts in recent decades have created a degree of opportunism in Khmer society. As the political landscape changes, people rush to position themselves favorably relative to each new power configuration. It is not unusual to meet people who have been in the Khmer Rouge, FUNCINPEC, and CPP at various times. This could mean that some people will attempt to capitalize on the introduction of public-sector reform and decentralization, although of course this could be done in ways that undermine the goals of these efforts, rather than supporting them. The vibrant NGOs that have emerged in some parts of the country provide some foundation for the development of greater community cohesion and more democratic decisionmaking. The central government has been so ineffective, for so long, that the service delivery aspect of its relationship with Cambodian citizens is tenuous at best. Some of the reforms that are planned or now underway in service delivery and decentralization may be able to build government credibility and engage citizens, creating a dynamic that will take on a life of its own and perhaps undermine the patronage mentality.

Economic Situation

Cambodia's economic performance has generally improved in the postconflict period, with one period of serious disruption in 1997 following the controversial change of government and the East Asian financial crisis.[6] Since the restoration of political stability in late 1998, the country has achieved fairly high economic growth under what the IMF and the World Bank consider to be a relatively positive macroeconomic environment. Inflation has been stable in recent years, as has the exchange rate, and the international reserve position has strengthened. There has also been some progress on structural reform: an important commercial bank relicensing program has been completed, general fiscal administration is improving (including tax and customs), and there has been progress with key commercial laws needed to meet the requirements for World Trade Organization (WTO) accession.

Economic growth has raised living standards and reduced poverty head counts. Between 1993–1994 and 2004, per capita household consumption rose 32 percent in real terms. The percentage of the population living under the poverty line was estimated at 35 percent for 2004. Growth has been narrowly based, however (World Bank 2003a). It has relied heavily on the garment sector, which employs only a small fraction of Cambodia's population, and on tourism-related activities concentrated in Phnom Penh and Siem Reap (site of the Angkor Wat complex). As discussed below, some potentially productive natural resource sectors remain substantially "underground," not only damaging economic development but also undermining a productive revenue source for the cash-starved RGC. Inequality has risen over the past decade, owing in part to the widening gap between rural and urban areas and in part to widening inequality *within* rural areas.

There are potential risks to sustained growth for Cambodia. First, tourism and foreign exchange earnings would likely be damaged from a slowdown in the world economy. Second, much remains to be done to create a stable business environment and attract foreign investment, including continued development of the legal framework and provision of better infrastructure services that serve as production inputs. Third, given the lack of competitiveness of Cambodia's garment sector, the expiry of the Multi Fiber Arrangement in 2005 put pressure on Cambodia's main foreign exchange earner. The enactment of protectionist measures by the United States against Chinese garment exports (and China's voluntary restraint in the European market) provides some breathing space, but Cambodia's need to diversify its export base has come into stark relief. Fourth, higher external debt-service obligations will increase fiscal pressure. Finally, uneven growth and rising inequality could lead to social unrest. Too narrow a focus on peace and security in the short term, to the detriment of a more developmental stance—given the assumption that a significant share of peace and security investments are nonproductive—could undermine long-term prospects for growth, poverty reduction, and social stability.

The Evolution of Public Finance

There is little readily available data on the public finances of Cambodia prior to the post–peace accord government.[7] The picture painted in the early postaccord data is rather grim. The World Bank's first Public Expenditure Review (PER) for Cambodia (World Bank 1999b) reported the following:

- Between the 1993 elections and 1997, the RGC financed only 30–40 percent of total public expenditures from its own resources, relying heavily on international assistance.
- Government expenditures in the early and mid-1990s were dominated by defense and security, with modest attention given to basic developmental public service needs.
- RGC revenues started from an extremely low base—roughly 4 percent of GDP in 1991—and remained very low by developing country standards and relative to neighbors.
- There was a huge underground economy, particularly in forestry and gem mining, which undermined public revenues.
- There were numerous tax and duty exemptions, including some, such as ad hoc customs "exemptions," that were irregular and others, such as investment incentives, that were legal.
- There was little formal cost recovery for public services, yet in some sectors, such as health and education, consumers were paying substantial informal fees.
- Basic public accounting and financial management systems were highly limited and did not provide adequate safeguards, resulting in high fiduciary risk to public funds.

Since the first PER, some progress has been made.

Revenues

On the revenue side, Cambodia still has one of the smallest public sectors in the world. Some steps were taken to improve tax administration in the 1990s and into the present decade, and these efforts received greater prominence with the adoption of the Public Financial Management Reform Program (PFMRP) in 2004. Total revenue reached 10.8 percent of GDP in 2002 (tax revenue accounted for 7.7 percent).[8] The RGC expects to increase the level of public resources to 12 percent of GDP by 2010 through further improvements in tax administration and tax policies, though the recent discovery of oil could generate a very significant increase in Cambodia's share of revenue to GDP. Efforts are also planned in nontax revenue administration, including improving transparency in state asset management.

Expenditures

On the expenditure side, the RGC has made some major changes that are consistent with the evolution of a system recovering from conflict to one that focuses on development (see Table 3.1). From 1998 to 2001, government spending on priority developmental sectors, particularly health and education, dramatically increased from 1.4 to 3.2 percent of GDP. Expenditure growth has also been occurring in other key sectors, including agriculture, infrastructure, and rural development, and future increases are budgeted in many of these sectors.

This reallocation to priority developmental sectors was financed through both increases in revenues and reductions in expenditures in defense and security. Defense and security expenditures declined from a peak of 47.3 percent of Treasury-executed expenditures (4.8 percent of GDP) in 1997 to 25 percent (3.2 percent of GDP) in 2001. These savings were largely realized from reductions in the size of the armed forces and cuts in operational expenditures. Defense and security, however, are reportedly subject to off-budget financing, including from natural resource rents.[9]

Turning to distributional impacts of expenditures, the poorest 40 percent received 39 percent of education spending and 50 percent at the primary level (Table 3.2a). This is a significant increase from their share five years earlier. The operational efficiency of this expenditure at the facility level has not been assessed, however. In health, the bottom 40 percent of the population received only about 30 percent of public spending (Table 3.2b). Inequality was most ev-

Table 3.1   Treasury-Executed Spending by Function, 1996–2001 (US$ million)

Function	1996	1997	1998	1999	2000	2001
Core government	214.1	200.1	196.5	190.8	233.7	221.8
General administration	58.2	49.7	73.7	66.2	115.2	111.6
Defense	111.2	103.4	83.4	88.1	80.1	71.7
Security	43.8	46.1	38.8	35.3	36.9	36.9
Judiciary	1.0	0.9	0.6	1.2	1.5	1.6
Economic services	37.0	44.6	26.3	49.5	49.8	73.4
Agriculture	7.1	8.2	4.9	6.5	9.2	17.1
Transport	10.5	12.9	5.0	9.0	20.4	27.9
Public works	8.9	8.2	3.5	7.7	18.8	23.4
Other transport	1.6	4.7	1.5	1.4	1.5	4.5
Other economic services	18.7	23.0	16.0	33.3	19.2	26.3
Environmental protection	0.8	0.5	0.4	0.6	1.0	2.0
Rural development	1.9	1.3	1.6	4.1	3.2	7.8
Social services	66.5	67.2	53.3	92.1	98.6	122.4
Health	16.5	18.6	11.8	33.0	26.5	34.2
Recreation, culture, and religion	2.0	2.4	1.8	2.6	7.2	8.4
Education	31.0	28.7	26.7	39.9	42.3	56.3
Social protection	17.1	17.5	12.9	16.6	22.5	23.5
Other	22.3	3.2	5.3	12.3	11.4	9.7
Debt service	22.3	3.2	5.3	8.6	8.0	7.7
Other not classified	—	—	—	3.7	3.4	2.0
Total	341.9	316.4	283.0	348.8	396.7	435.1

Source: Modified from World Bank (2003a).

ident for national facilities, whereas district hospitals provided the most important benefits to the poorest group. There have been recent efforts to provide health services through alternative nonprofit channels, bypassing the government agencies (Dugger 2006). In the short run, this may improve service delivery and poverty targeting, but in the long run, it risks undermining the development of a well-functioning public sector.

There are multiple reasons for the lack of a sufficiently strong poverty focus in public spending. Technical and administrative factors include inadequate sectoral plans and strategies and weak linkages between plans and budgets. Political factors, however, are the key. Relatively better-off and politically connected groups who benefit from public expenditures can undermine reorientation to the poor, and poor budget management allows diversions of resources intended for public expenditures.

Although increases in social service spending are generally considered positive, there are also concerns that inadequate attention is being given by the RGC and international donors to other key sectors, notably agriculture, rural

Table 3.2a   Share of Education Subsidy Received by Income Quintile (RGC Spending)

Quintile	I	II	III	IV	V	
	Percentage of Government Subsidy Received, 2002 estimate					
Total	19	20	19	19	23	100
Primary	25	25	21	17	12	100
Lower Secondary	11	14	19	22	34	100
Upper Secondary	7	7	13	26	46	100
Post-Secondary	1	0	12	22	65	100

Source: World Bank (2003a).

Table 3.2b   Share of Health Benefits Received by Income Quintile (RGC Spending)

Quintile	I	II	III	IV	V	
	Percentage of Benefits Received, 1999 estimate					
Total	13	17	26	24	20	100
National hospital	4	7	11	15	63	100
District/province hospitals	21	15	29	29	6	100
Health centers	13	26	33	26	2	100

Source: Calculated from World Bank (2003a).

development, and economic services (Beresford et al. 2004). Despite some increases in expenditures in these areas, they account for a smaller percentage of GDP than social services. They can, however, be seen as critical for sustainable economic development, on which the public sector ultimately must rely for its resources.

External Assistance

Over the 1996–2001 period, external assistance flows (US$2.672 million) were significantly higher than government expenditures (US$2.122 million). Of the total aid, only US$190 million was provided as budgetary and balance-of-payments support. The remainder—US$2.264 million for projects and programs and US$220 million in humanitarian assistance—bypassed the state. Reasonable people can debate the desirability of heavy dependence on foreign aid, but to some extent it seems inevitable in a poor country like Cambodia. More worrying than the sheer volume of external assistance is the fact that the bulk of it is not reflected in the RGC budget or disbursed through the National Treasury. Such off-budget arrangements undermine the integrity of the national budgetary system and raise concerns about resource use excessively reflecting donor priorities or being allocated in uncoordinated ways that exacerbate interministerial competition. We return to these issues below.

Major Reform Areas

In this section we consider four aspects of public-sector reform in Cambodia that are intimately linked to the public finance system. The first two, public financial management and the civil service, relate to the foundations for transparent and accountable public resource use. The third, decentralization, is a cornerstone of RGC attempts to build legitimacy and improve resource allocation. The fourth, natural resource management, is included because it could provide a highly productive source of public revenue. This section describes the achievements and failures in these areas, and the subsequent section highlights some of the underlying constraints on performance.

Public financial accountability is at the heart of an effective development and poverty reduction strategy. In theory, Cambodia's legal framework provides for a system in which policymakers and managers are accountable to citizens. The constitution provides that the National Assembly and Senate have the power to "approve the national budget," that "tax collection shall be in accordance with the law," and that "the National Budget shall be determined by law."[10] The government "determines the national priorities" to be addressed by the budget, and the Council of Ministers (CoM) then adopts expenditure directives for the MEF to use in budget preparation.[11] Guided by central oversight ministries, the line ministries deliver the goods and services provided for in the budget. Thus, the budget should be the principal instrument for resource mobilization and expenditure policy and management.

There is considerable evidence, however, that the budget does not fulfill this key role and that resources do not reach intended beneficiaries. Breakdowns in the chain of accountability, which persist often because of the peace and security mentality, create various "governance failures." The National Assembly does not provide adequate oversight of public financial management, and citizens do not have effective mechanisms to demand that oversight. Policymakers deliver limited resources, including wages, to service providers through the budget, in part because revenues are low. Revenues are low, in part, because taxpayers will not pay for poor services, and they face few, if any, consequences for nonpayment. The lack of resources underlies a civil service with both weak capacity to deliver service and strong incentives to divert funds. Weak internal and external controls reinforce possibilities for undetected abuse.

Public Financial Management

Cambodia's existing public financial management (PFM) system is in a very weak state. Budget execution suffers from delays and unpredictable releases of funds, even for salary payments, undermining operational planning and resulting in a buildup of arrears. Deficient accounting and reporting systems increase opportunities for corruption. Indeed, in some ways, Cambodia's current system performs worse than those of countries suffering more recent conflict, implying that progress has been slow in relative terms. For example, in Rwanda civil servants are paid through the banking system, and Afghanistan is moving in this direction, whereas in Cambodia they still are paid cash, with obvious implications for "leakages." In 2005, a new PFM Reform Program began to address this by planning for greater use of the banking system for taxes, civil service wages, and payments to suppliers.

Frustration with poor budget performance has led MEF and the Ministries of Health and Education to find ways of channeling funds that bypass the rigidities, delays, and uncertainties created by the centralized budget execution process. These pilot initiatives, the Accelerated District Development program (ADD) and the Priority Action Program (PAP), have forced some modifications in spending priorities. By targeting a narrow set of outcomes without making major changes in the overall budget system, these efforts illustrate how the developmental mentality has been able to gain limited ground when it is seen as relatively nonthreatening to the interests that benefit from the status quo. The impact of these pilot initiatives, however, has been muted by liquidity constraints and inadequate control. Execution rates for priority sectors have trailed those for the civil administration as a whole, despite streamlined disbursement mechanisms.

The policy challenge is how to consolidate and deepen recent initiatives while gradually addressing the structural constraints imposed by weak institutions and limited capacity. The RGC officially recognizes the need to improve budget execution, cash management, and the control environment in the PFM Reform Program. But in spite of a comprehensive legal framework and a multiplicity of controls, reform does not address weak financial management practices that undermine transparency and accountability. Widespread anecdotal evidence suggests, for example, that "facilitation" of Treasury transactions—in which a small percentage of the transaction amount must be "kicked back" to secure the release of budgeted funds—is a common practice.

Despite some progress in improving audit functions, public oversight of financial management remains weak. Legislation establishing the National Audit Authority (NAA), passed in March 2000, provides for an institutional framework consistent with international standards. The NAA is independent of the executive, reports to the National Assembly, enjoys financial and administrative autonomy, and is authorized to determine the scope and methods of audits. As its first assignment, the NAA conducted an audit of the 2001 budget implementation. This was completed in September 2002 and submitted to the National Assembly, but it has yet to be made public. The MEF's General Inspection Department undertakes compliance audits at the agency level, but its effectiveness is limited, in part because there does not appear to be a strategic or risk-based audit. Most line ministries do not have formal internal audit units.

The other critical link in the expenditure management chain is public procurement. Competitive bidding was introduced in stages, beginning in 1995, but the fiduciary risk is still rated. Reasons include weaknesses in the regulatory framework; the absence of a sovereign procurement law with a single focal point for monitoring and enforcement; inadequate capacity at the line ministry level; the ability of civil servants to negotiate contracts directly with contractors and suppliers, encouraging unofficial "deals," and a loophole in the 1998 Build-Operate-Transfer (BOT) subdecree, which encourages concession awards through direct negotiation. Suppliers and contractors, as well as government procuring entities, often admit to being confused about the rules.

Legislative oversight of public spending, including procurement, is provided by the National Assembly and its Finance and Banking Committee (FBC), though the link between legislative oversight and accountability is weak. The FBC reviews the RGC's budget proposal and financial statements before submitting them to the plenary session. Although there is active debate, FBC deliberations are neither public nor published. Parliamentarians and senators have the authority to propose budget reallocations, but rarely do so. Debates on the draft budget are reported in the press, though coverage has tended to focus on investigations of corruption rather than on expenditure policy. Recently questions have emerged about the Assembly itself. There have been press allegations about inappropriate procurement on the contract for the new National Assembly building and reports that wood for the new building is from an endangered, protected species. Improving accountability is hampered more generally by weak transparency. The budget, for example, is not very accessible, nor is it disseminated widely. Budget execution data are not made public, and basic civil service information is closely guarded. Civil society is not consulted by the assembly on budgetary issues, and audit reports are not made public.

Although capacity is a factor in this overall weak performance, the poor governance environment is surely at its core. The dominance of the patronage system has long hindered a more aggressive approach to genuine reform. The recently adopted PFM Reform Program focuses on making the budget credible in terms of delivering resources in a timely and predictable manner to budget managers, strengthening financial accountability of budget managers, and carrying out extensive MEF departmental and procedural reforms. These reforms are intended to address many of the problems noted above, but it is too early to tell how effective they will be.

Civil Service Reform

Another key factor underlying poor public-sector performance is the absence of an effective system of incentives and accountability mechanisms in the Cambodian civil service. The current civil service is based on the one established in 1979 by the State of Cambodia, which was fully controlled by the CPP. The State of Cambodia civil service was inherited by the coalition government in 1993, very little change having taken place under UNTAC, which did not see transformation of the civil service as part of its mandate (Doyle 1998). The RGC faced the challenge of absorbing FUNCINPEC officials alongside the existing CPP-dominated apparatus. From the beginning, there has been a sense that the civil service existed to serve the needs of the dominant political parties—the civil service as patronage rather than service provider. Merit is not the normal basis for recruitment and promotion. Nor are there adequate systems to control the establishment. Civil servants are not assigned to posts (there are few specified posts in ministries), so that changes in establishment size are subjective and not amenable to reasoned argumentation. This reduces transparency and exposes the system to allegations of and opportunities for patronage. Evidence also suggests problems in the geographic and sectoral deployment of civil servants (redeployment from the center to provinces is needed, for example, in agriculture and health).

The overall size of the civil service has grown since the mid-1990s, as political pressures to hire overwhelm any sense of need to deal with weak hiring, promotion, and establishment control practices. According to the numbers in the budget laws, public-sector employment has grown from 148,353 in 1994 to 167,778 in 2003. But one indicator of the problematic nature of civil service management is the fact that the RGC does not use one set of official numbers when counting its civil servants. The budget law uses one set, and the Council for Administrative Reform (CAR), a cabinet-level policy office based in the Council of Ministers, uses another that is drawn from the Human Resource Management Information System (HRMIS). With the completion of a recent civil service census, the budget law should be based on CAR data. CAR, however, has not made these data public or allowed their use outside of CAR. MEF must rely on information directly from ministries for budget preparation. Though there are claims that the recent census and the payroll automation led to the removal of more than 9,000 ghost workers, this is not apparent in the MEF budget law or the CAR figures, nor in the difference between these sets of figures. Without producing a consistent establishment register, the system cannot properly control posts and staff within ministries and provinces.

Although the most critical issues facing the civil service are the lack of a merit-based system and effective control, the most pressing problem facing civil servants themselves is the low level of pay, relative not only to wage levels outside the service but also to the cost of living (Table 3.3). Cambodia's ratio of average civil service wage to per capita GDP is very low (roughly 1.3 in 2003). With the exception of a very limited number of high level staff (approximately 700), most civil servants earn very little in either absolute or relative terms. Moreover, the compression ratio (average pay of the highest category to the lowest category) is very low by international standards.

One way of beginning to improve the civil service would be to increase wages for high-priority posts. But the peace and security mentality–justified need to feed the patronage system has resulted in a preference for raising all salaries across the board, with only limited decompression for a small set of selected civil servants. Some argue that civil service salaries cannot be increased because the resulting disequilibrium vis-à-vis the military and police would cause discontent. Thus, extremely low wage levels have been maintained.

The current pay structure, coupled with the lack of merit-based practices, is sufficient neither to motivate civil servants nor to attract the necessary quan-

Table 3.3   Median Monthly Remuneration of Cambodia's Civil Service, 2002 (US$)

Category	Level of Education	US$/month	Compression Ratio
A	Secondary school + 4 years	40	1.9
B	Secondary school + 2 years	32	1.5
C	Secondary school	26	1.2
D	Other	21	—

Source: World Bank (2003a).
Note: Compression ratio = average pay of the highest category to the lowest category.

tity of qualified candidates to the civil service. Indeed, the extremely low pay levels encourage corrupt practices by blurring the lines between the public and the private. Anecdotal evidence indicates that civil servants survive, and in some cases prosper, thanks to patronage networks in which they pass resources up to their patrons and down to their clients. Reports of job buying abound.

There seems to be no good technical alternative to the eventual adoption of a transparent, merit-based system, reinforced by higher pay through sequenced and targeted salary increases and increased access to the CAR HRMIS database as the unified source of civil service information. But all this is a tall order. It would be neither feasible nor sensible, for example, to enact an across-the-board pay increase for the Cambodian civil service, especially without improved management, given the problems noted above and the fiscal constraints. But progress could be made through the introduction of a parallel, phased merit-based management and higher, decompressed pay for selected high-priority sectors, functions, and skills. This is being piloted in MEF in the context of the PFM Reform Program, and it may be rolled out to additional high-priority ministries. There is now some space for well-designed pilots, which represents a breakthrough in the developmental over the peace and security mentality. As with the PAP, this experience suggests that when reforms are perceived to be nonthreatening (i.e., nondestabilizing and controllable), progressive experimentation can occur.

UNTAC is sometimes blamed for the lack of development of bureaucratic capacity. Doyle (1998, 4) for example, argued that "if UNTAC had combined control and training, it might then have handed over a more stable, responsive, and effective bureaucracy." Yet it is hard to imagine that UNTAC could have implemented radical bureaucratic modernization in its short mandate, given the panoply of other problems it was addressing.

More important has been the post-UNTAC behavior of the donor community in hampering development of state capacity. A focus on "delivering results," with its emphasis on the short term, has led donors to bypass when possible—and "capture" when not—the civil service. The donor practice of hiring the "best and brightest" from the civil service to work on donor projects has undermined capacity development and fueled resentment against perceived donor shortsightedness. Just as civil servants "sold" their allegiance to political parties in return for a low but steady wage, along with access to rents, they were also willing to sell their services to donors, often the highest bidders. In this sense, short-term-oriented donor approaches have perpetuated patronage practices initiated by the dominant political parties.

Decentralization

A few years ago it would have seemed improbable to suggest that the highly centralized RGC would even consider strengthening subnational governments.

Yet today the country is undertaking a seemingly ambitious program of deconcentration and decentralization as an element of the public-sector reform.[12] Deconcentration refers to the strengthening of the provinces and municipalities (PM), which are simply arms of the center that provide capacity building, technical assistance, and monitoring functions. Decentralization refers to the creation of local governments at the commune and sangkat (municipal commune) or CS level; these receive resource allocations from the center. In principle, the communes have a modest degree of autonomy, and unlike the provinces they are governed by elected councils.

The PM and CS have existed since the French colonial era. At times, the provinces were heavily managed by the center, but there have also been periods when provincial governors were fairly autonomous because the center was weak. The CS served only as a vehicle for central/PM communications with rural villages and urban neighborhoods. This entire system deteriorated during the protracted conflict. After the 1993 elections, the center reexerted control over the provinces, and as the stability and capacity of the RGC increased and its focus shifted toward development, awareness of the potentially important role of subnational governments began to emerge.[13]

Much of the impetus for decentralization grew out of donor efforts in the immediate postconflict period. A key feature of UN support in the 1990s was the Cambodia Resettlement and Reintegration (CARERE) Project, which assisted returned refugees who had been displaced during the Khmer Rouge and Vietnamese years by building basic infrastructure.[14] CARERE developed from an emergency relief project to a subnational institutional development and capacity-building project (CARERE 2). In 1996 the UN Capital Development Fund financed the Local Development Fund (LDF), which piloted participatory service planning and delivery systems in two communes in each of two provinces. This evolved into CARERE 2's Seila (Khmer for *foundation stone*), which introduced local governance mechanisms in additional provinces. The RGC was barely involved in early stages of these experiments, which were undertaken through UN engagement with provincial-level officials. Over time the RGC took notice, and when CARERE 2 ended in 2000, the RGC Seila Task Force assumed responsibility for Seila with UN assistance under the Participatory Local Governance project.[15]

Seila developed a process for the planning, financing, and delivery of demand-responsive public services through local development committees. It also created a provincial system of capacity building, technical assistance, and monitoring of the CS processes managed by Provincial Rural Development Committees (PRDCs), which were chaired by governors and included representatives of subnational offices of RGC ministries. A system of formula-based intergovernmental transfers was developed to support the PM (Provincial Investment Fund; PIF) and CS (the LDF). The PRDCs allocated PIF funds to PM departments, and Commune Development Committees (CDCs) allocated LDF resources to proposed projects.

Seila's influence led to greater emphasis on development of the CS (decentralization) than on the PM (deconcentration). Its systems and procedures provided the basis for developing the CS as a level of local government, the PM as support agents of CS councils, and key central agencies as regulators and facilitators of the CS system. Many basic features of Seila were adapted for the 2001 decentralization laws and subsequent regulations that defined the CS system. For example, CDCs became elected Commune Councils, and the LDF (channeled from the UN through commercial bank accounts) became the Commune Sangkat Fund (channeled from MEF through the Treasury system).

A number of factors help to explain how a donor project came to provide the basis for CS decentralization in Cambodia. First, the RGC remained weak and in disarray well into the 1990s. The UN's success in brokering elections (and perhaps its decision not to challenge Hun Sen's bid to stay in power despite the 1993 election results) gave it credibility to effectively bypass the RGC in developing experimental subnational institutions and processes under CARERE and Seila. Second, some key ministries and the provincial governors must have seen opportunities in Seila for improving their influence, access to resources, and capacity, so they were happy to cooperate. Third, the LDF started in northwest provinces that benefited from the return of Cambodians who were educated in the ways of international donors during years spent in refugee camps at the Thai border. These areas also experienced a proliferation of NGOs generously funded by post-1993 international contributions and skilled in community organization and local service delivery. Initially, many of these NGOs viewed Seila as unwelcome competition, but they learned over time to benefit from and integrate themselves into the Seila system.

These realities explain why Seila was able to establish itself and operate effectively, but not why the RGC eventually decided to create a system of elected CS councils. Again, a number of factors appear to be important. The first is simply that CARERE and Seila were successful in delivering services. The system was responsible for thousands of rural infrastructure projects that could not have been delivered by central ministries and PM departments. In the process it created considerable capacity and awareness at provincial, district, commune, and village levels. This created internal pressures on the RGC to institutionalize the experiment and expand it into other areas. Second, major donors vigorously support democratic participation. RGC leaders were undoubtedly aware that substantial funds would be forthcoming to develop local governments if they accepted such practices, even if they did not really understand them or support them in the way the donors did. Third, the CPP, comfortable after the 1998 electoral victory, must have seen opportunities to create well-financed structures to extend the patronage system of governance and consolidate power at the grassroots level. The CPP also must have been fairly certain that it would dominate local elections, as its base of support is rural, whereas FUNCINPEC had been stronger in urban areas.

Decentralization and deconcentration have faced some challenges.[16] The problematic RGC institutional structures, systems, and procedures—including poor revenue generation, high dependence on aid and technical assistance, a weak civil service, and primitive budgeting and financial management—could undermine the performance of the subnational system over time.

The PM remain primarily arms of the center, and efforts to restructure their roles and functions are at an early stage. A number of issues are of particular concern:

- First, there is no final clarity on what *deconcentration* means. At one extreme, it could involve improving capacity of PM administration to serve national ministries more effectively. At the other, the PM could be given discretion in allocating resource envelopes among and within sectoral departments and playing a greater role in provincial personnel management. The RGC's 2005 decentralization strategy points to the latter approach, but this was rushed through with substantial donor input and has not yet been formalized into law; how it will play out remains to be seen.
- Second, accountability is a major question. PM governors are appointed by and accountable to the Ministry of Interior. In addition, the PM do not have elected representative bodies. These were proposed by the 2005 decentralization strategy, but the shape they will take, and when, is unknown.
- Third, although the 1997 Provincial Budget Law provides an initial basis for limited fiscal deconcentration, it does not provide clarity on PM functions and competencies, gives the PM little discretionary power, and allows the PM only modest "own revenues" with centrally fixed bases and rates. The Provincial Development Plan (PDP) was conceived as a broad resource allocation guide but is presently used only to program off-budget resources, primarily the Seila PIF, and only a small percentage of PDP projects are ever implemented. Linking the PDP to regular RGC operations could be an important part of developing a deconcentrated system.
- Finally, the experimental approaches to deconcentration thus far taken by a few ministries are limited, diverse, and not entirely consistent. Some, such as the ADD and the PAP discussed above, are not really deconcentration—they bypass the PM to get money to subprovincial service delivery agents. The off-budget Seila approach is more developed and consistent, but there are also important concerns, including how PIF resources are allocated by the PRDC Executive Committees, bypassing the Provincial Treasury.

At the CS level, although limited empowerment may be an appropriate first step in building credibility and capacity, and the CS elections were generally considered acceptable,[17] what is happening cannot be considered true devolution. The CS have few roles, functions, resources, and capacities, and the system faces great challenges:

- First, the legal framework is weak, with the lack of attention to CS own-source revenues of particular concern.[18]
- Second, the CS fund is limited. After the 2002 elections, the need to finance many additional CS greatly diluted the volume of resources flowing to individual communes that had participated in Seila. It is not clear that the resources provide enough incentive and opportunity for citizen engagement and local capacity building.
- Third, the institutional support structure is in flux, with profound implications for accountability. PRDCs continue to function in Seila provinces, and similar structures have been created in non-Seila provinces, but their long-term role is not defined relative to other structures.[19]
- Fourth, many individual communes will not be viable planning and budgeting entities in the foreseeable future. The case for consolidation is strong, but it cannot be done before the next local elections in 2007, and seems unlikely later. Deconcentration may involve use of districts (subdivisions of provinces) as service delivery agents that could in effect "compete" with larger CS councils. If communes prove politically difficult to dissolve, they could serve as a lower consultative tier, with planning and budgeting authority vested in a higher tier. On the other hand, they could simply be consumed by districts, which would be easier for the center to use in institutionalizing the patronage system at the local level.
- Finally, the present decentralization law treats urban sangkats the same as rural communes. Rural areas were the focus of Seila, and as a result some rural communes have greater capacity than urban areas. Service roles differ between sangkats and communes. Area-wide planning is particularly critical in urban areas owing to scale economies and externalities, but although small elected sangkat councils within municipalities receive unconditional transfers, the municipalities themselves do not. Despite compelling logic to fund municipalities, it seems unlikely that the CPP will provide substantial independent resources to jurisdictions that have tended to support the opposition.

In sum, the political motivations for rapidly transforming Seila into an official local government system have produced positive reforms. At the same time, the lack of attention to details in framing the system have left some major gaps, inconsistencies, and questions as to what comes next. Decentralization could provide a window for governance reforms that work their way up to influence the central level. Or the CS system could be overtaken by the patronage practices that plague the RGC. Efforts began in 2006 to draft an Organic Law on Decentralization that would do much to determine the fate of subnational governments and their eventual effects on Cambodia's governance and resource allocation.

Natural Resource Management

Cambodia enjoys one of the highest natural capital endowments in East Asia, with 1.5 hectares (3.7 acres) per capita of total land. Some 60 percent of Cambodia's land area is classified as forested, including 24 percent in protected areas or forests. Cambodia has the most productive freshwater fishery in east Asia, with production estimated at 300,000 to 400,000 tons per year. Freshwater resources, estimated at more than 40,000 cubic meters per capita, rank second in the region behind Laos, and the percentage of annual withdrawals of available freshwater is the lowest in the region.[20]

High levels of natural resource endowments are a mixed blessing. Developing countries with few natural resources grew two to three times faster than natural resource–abundant countries over the past fifty years (Ascher 2002). This is the result, in large part, of the availability of revenues—official and unofficial—from the exploitation of natural resources. These provide an "easier" mechanism for supporting the state apparatus than developing institutions that are accountable to the populace at large and hence support more broadly based, private-sector-led, economic development.

As in many postconflict states, physical, human, and social capital were severely damaged in Cambodia. The country's forests, agricultural land, fisheries, and mineral resources were the only high-value assets available for distribution to appease warring factions and consolidate control over territory and populations. Lingering physical insecurity and weak property rights enforcement led to rapid resource exploitation, as formal property rights had been destroyed by the Khmer Rouge, and large-scale displacement of populations undermined traditional claims that had facilitated natural resource management in communities with no formal property rights system. At the same time, as noted above, there is high demand for unofficial revenues to support the poorly paid, patronage-based civil service and military and to finance political campaigns, generating additional incentives for trading away sustainable use of resources for short-term financial gains. Harvest rights were sold to international and domestic investors through highly nontransparent processes, on terms that initially placed few controls on nonsustainable practices and did not consider impacts on local populations.

Although still relatively abundant, Cambodia's natural resources are under increasing pressure. Reorienting governance of natural resources could improve rural livelihoods, reduce the potential for conflict, contribute more substantially to economic growth and exports, provide improved environmental services, and increase public revenues. This could also reinforce reforms in other areas, such as private-sector development. Steps have been taken to improve natural resource management, but a strong coalition of vested interests both within and outside the government will continue to resist further reforms. The big challenge is to reduce their influence.

The RGC's main mechanism for natural resource management has been to contract large areas to Cambodian and foreign investors. Some fifty-seven official land concessions for agriculture (primarily for tree crops), covering 940,000 hectares, have been granted since the early 1990s, ranging in size from 500 hectares to more than 300,000 hectares. Over the same period, thirty forest concessions covering more than 6 million hectares have been granted. Fisheries concessions were introduced in the late 1980s, and by 1999 there were 270 lots covering more than 950,000 hectares. In addition to these "official" concessions, a number of others have been granted by the military on lands ceded to it in 1994, generally without coordination with the Ministry of Agriculture, Forestry, and Fisheries or the Council of Ministers. The borders of these concessions, when defined, often overlap official concessions, forests, or protected areas.

The concession system has not been an effective mechanism for providing public goods. Concessions were usually granted through ad hoc and nontransparent processes. Designation of resources to be granted were not based on feasibility assessments, prior and conflicting claims on resources were neither identified nor resolved, investors were not adequately screened to ensure technical and financial capacity to fulfill contract obligations, and government institutions were unable to enforce the contracts. The result has been poorly implemented concession plans with little generation of "expected" public goods. Direct revenues from concessions accruing to the National Treasury, if any, have been limited. No revenues from economic land concessions have been paid, reflecting the low rate of land utilization by concessionaires (estimated at less than 2 percent).[21] Official forest revenue, originally forecast at US$50 to $100 million per year, has averaged less than US$10 million owing to pervasive evasion of royalty payments. Some argue that timber exports have been used to finance a "parallel military budget" and have served as a lucrative source of rents for high-level officials, which would help to explain the opacity and low revenue productivity of concession management (Le Billon 2000). Whether off-budget military financing is conducive to long-term "peace and stability" is an open question. Again, there may be a trade-off between short-term and long-term considerations in building peace in Cambodia.

Under increasing pressure to recognize the poor performance, as of 2000–2003 the RGC cancelled about 40 percent of existing concessions and commercial fishing lots. Concerns regarding the inability to control the rate of logging in forest concessions have led to requirements for submission and review of strategic forest management plans. In addition, a suspension on logging in concessions and a moratorium on log transport are currently in effect, though it is not clear to what extent these measures are effectively enforced. Reports of illegal logging abound. Illegal land swaps—in which public entities "exchange" government buildings and lands for other properties, assets, and sometimes cash—were frequently reported in the press in 2005.

In sum, RGC management of natural resources has provided limited public benefits to most Cambodians. Instead, small but powerful elements of the population have dominated the sector. The RGC has signaled, at the highest levels, its acknowledgment of the past shortcomings in natural resources management, and it has recently taken several actions to suspend or reduce inefficient activities. The RGC has also indicated its intention to reorient natural resources policy to be consistent with larger reform strategies. To what extent this will happen remains to be seen.

Cross-Cutting Issues

Reforms in all the areas discussed here—financial management, civil service, decentralization, and natural resource management—involve improving transparency and accountability. When these take root, reform-minded managers and citizens have the information and power needed to improve resource use, and government legitimacy can be enhanced. Unfortunately, the current state of the public sector in Cambodia works against such dynamics. Information is nonexistent, inaccurate, or unavailable. Lines of accountability are often blurred but usually hierarchical. Capacity and performance incentives are typically weak.

Throughout this chapter we have referred to the key role of the peace and security mentality with its attendant political patronage—and its thus-far meek challenge from a more developmental mentality—in defining opportunities for reform in Cambodia. Within this larger set of political dynamics is a set of cross-cutting factors that we see as critical in influencing the form, degree, and pace of public-sector financial reforms: reform process management, reform strategy, capacity enhancement, and the role of international donors. We believe that modest inroads can be made in establishing a more developmental approach to public-sector reform if each of these is handled appropriately.

Reform Process Management

Perhaps the greatest challenge in bringing about public finance reform in the complex Cambodian environment is how the process is managed. Lines of accountability in the Cambodian system are hierarchical (particularly within ministries) and often ambiguous (particularly across but also within ministries)—a situation that is conducive to conflict and patronage. The MEF, for example, is the clear leader on public financial management reform issues and should be able to introduce reforms and issue regulations that other ministries must follow. Yet even this seemingly basic expectation can be undermined when officials in other ministries have the right connections to key politicians, or when the military is powerful enough to act independently in generating resources irrespective of MEF regulations, or when international donor projects require specific forms of record keeping and reporting that undermine a consistent approach.

In other matters, reform can be immensely more complex. Civil service reform, for example, involves among others the Council on Administrative Reform, which reports to the CoM; the Ministry of Interior (MOI), which has responsibility for general public administration; and the MEF, which provides the resources for salaries. A key constraint to civil service reform has been the maneuvering of various ministries to protect their institutional interests or those of their powerful internal leaders. Similar situations exist with other types of reform, such as decentralization, where the MOI, which is in the main position of legal authority on this matter, often clashes with MEF on fiscal and financial issues, the Ministry of Rural Development on matters related to rural institutional structures, the Ministry of Planning on planning issues, and so on. These ministries have direct connections to political parties and leaders that affect their influence and behavior.

Even single ministries are not monolithic entities, and there are powerful pockets of resistance to reforms within particular ministries. For example, MEF has had trouble with its own Tax and Customs Departments regarding the implementation of reforms in these critical public finance areas. The situation within ministries has become even more complex because, as noted above, many new ministerial and subministerial positions were created as part of the patronage-driven, coalition-building response to the last national elections. Now there are many more senior officials in position to push poorly conceived reforms or undermine good ones.

In this context, there are two dominant concerns with the management of the reform process. One is the (probably intentional) lack of clarity regarding reform responsibilities and the weak coordination across and within agencies. Attempts to coordinate reform have been numerous but not very successful. Interministerial committees abound, but often they represent primarily the interests of the ministries that chair them, or they are captured by senior politicians. Better interagency coordination might be realized under more neutral leadership, although some political will or protection to enforce reforms is also needed.

A second concern is the excessive ability of high-level officials to push or retard reforms. An intervention from the prime minister, for example, can quickly alter reform progress, whether contrary to or consistent with official

RGC policy—and whether or not intentions behind the action are consistent with the normative purpose of the reform. Thus, personalized and often arbitrary intervention in the management of public-sector reforms complicates the process. There are signs that inroads can be made against the hierarchical, patronage-dominated mentality that pervades the system, but this is neither easy nor rapid.

Reform Strategy

There are two basic ways to push public-sector reforms in Cambodia, where the de facto role of government is fairly distant from the role that is generally seen as desired in an effective developmental state. One approach is authoritarian: a senior official, in alliance with other powerful actors, forcefully promotes an important reform. Even in such a case, and even where the intentions are consistent with the normative goals that underlie the reform in development thinking (by no means a given), the rapid adoption of reforms does not mean that they will be successful—for example, that transparency will be built quickly, the public will understand how to use information, civil servants will have capacity to respond to public needs, and so on. And it seems unlikely that such an approach can succeed in Cambodia without some coincidence of interest between reformers and political elites, or some pressure on the latter from external or internal sources. There are a few examples where this "powerful champion" approach has assisted reform in Cambodia, but it seems unreliable as a primary strategy.

The other possibility is to take a more gradual, step-by-step approach. This appears to hold more promise, and it may be supported by the "powerful champion" approach as part of an overall strategy. An interesting example in Cambodia is the limited decentralization to the CS, which was the product of a complex and lengthy interaction among international donors, the RGC, and citizens who became engaged in the semipublic process surrounding development of the reform legislation and framework. At first glance, the new system may appear to be, at best, inconsequential. Communes have few responsibilities and few sources of revenue, whereas decentralization specialists often highlight the importance of clearly defined roles for each level of government to ensure accountability. At this early stage, however, the decision not to assign major functions to the CS may be beneficial. CS councils face many service needs, and in the foreseeable future most will not have the capacity to meet more than a few of them. Requiring the CS to provide more services early on could raise unattainable expectations and result in failure. Providing elected CS councils with modest resources to address a few local priorities of their own choosing serves the dual purpose of beginning to build their political credibility and enhancing their capacity to deliver services. When such a dynamic begins to take hold, limited inroads against the tide of patronage politics seem more likely.

The pursuit of alternative public resource management and service delivery mechanisms may be viewed as opportunities, but they may also have problematic consequences that must be balanced against their gains. We saw, for example, that attempts to contract out natural resource management have not fared well, but perhaps this could have been avoided if appropriate mechanisms could have been put in place to regulate contractors and enforce contracts. Sequencing of activities may be critical. On a more positive note, we saw that bypassing the state to involve nongovernmental contractors in health service delivery has been productive. Will such arrangements undermine the development of a responsible and capable state? Or can these experiences be institutionalized such that both the state and nonstate actors play important but different roles in managing and delivering public services?

Most key public-sector reforms are not one-time actions. They are complex processes in which a number of elements have to work together. In the Cambodian environment, it is important to do what can be done by relatively sweeping reforms, such as making better information available to the public to improve transparency. But the process by which the various actors learn how to use and respond to new information is another matter. This requires a careful strategy, with reform-minded civil servants, international agencies, and civil society groups always looking for openings to push reform forward. Modest steps are more likely to see the light of day than massive changes, and if successful, they can lay the groundwork for broader reforms. Once in place, reforms can take on a life of their own. For example, CS residents who have gotten used to having a say in how public resources are used under decentralization may not easily allow this role to be constrained if the government tries to backtrack. In a similar fashion, if taxpayers start to become accustomed to rule-based revenue generation with one tax, they may resist attempts at corruption and demand a similar approach to other forms of revenue generation. The real key to taking even modest steps is the entry point—how to get key RGC actors to agree to do things differently, which requires making a reform attractive or at least nonthreatening to them, or else imposing a degree of pressure that the international community has rarely brought to bear to date.

Capacity Limitations

A critical issue in public finance reform, noted repeatedly above, is whether the capacity to make the system work properly can be developed. Adopting appropriate systems and incentives is critical, but people have to be able to use those systems and respond to those incentives. It is probably not an exaggeration to state that few senior RGC officials understand the substance and intent of many aspects of official reform policies and that few civil servants have the skills to perform required functions in a reformed system.

Some observers do not feel that this is a major problem for certain aspects of reform, such as decentralization. This is because many systems and training mechanisms being promulgated are based on well-tested Seila experiences. But these emerged slowly with enormous levels of external technical assistance. They are now being extended rapidly into areas with little or no previous exposure to them. Decentralization is no longer an experiment. It is being integrated into an RGC system that will have to change rapidly to accommodate new ways of operating but in fact is resisting many changes.

Public-sector reforms will not function well simply because people have attended a few seminars. Training needs to be focused on specific things people will use. Ideally, it should be integrated with the adoption of new procedures that are part of the reform agenda. Follow-up training and periodic, hands-on technical support are also needed, along with vigilance to ensure that reforms are not corrupted by status quo politics. It is also important to emphasize that capacity development is not just technical—governance aspects of transition are the most challenging aspect of reform.

Capacity building is a process, and inherently one that takes time. It needs to be guided by a strategy that builds capacity incrementally, within a system in which incentives for appropriate behavior are beginning to emerge. There is a need for an ongoing search for entry points that can begin to make a difference, and capacity building has to be directly linked to these as much as possible.

The Role of International Development Agencies

The critical role of international development agencies in public finance reform was emphasized above, as were some of the problems associated with their behavior, such as their preference for off-budget funding. Some observers have criticized the donors for focusing too much on supporting social services at the expense of agriculture, rural development, and economic services. This may mean that the donors are failing to contribute as much as they could to economic development, the ultimate basis for a strong fiscal system and poverty reduction.

Donor fragmentation has been a critical problem in Cambodia. Public-sector reform support activities have been untidily shared between the United Nations Development Programme and the World Bank, among others. On occasion the Ministry of Economy and Finance has been caught between conflicting advice on fiscal and financial reform from the International Monetary Fund, the World Bank, the Asian Development Bank, and some of the bilateral donors. Similarly, the Ministry of Interior has been provided with uncoordinated technical advisers on decentralization from the UNDP, German Technical Assistance (GTZ), and the Asian Development Bank. The donors often have divergent views on reform, and their bickering about the "best" structures allows the RGC to maintain its patronage approach and ignore the resulting damage to revenue generation and public expenditure management.

Development partners also share some of the blame for weak capacity in Cambodia's public sector. Spending on technical assistance (TA), comprising personnel, training, and associated operational expenditures, accounts for about 45 percent of the external assistance portfolio, excluding humanitarian assistance (World Bank 2003a). This means that TA spending is two to three times greater than total RGC spending on civil service wages. Although TA inputs make an important contribution, over time there must be a shift toward capacity development of Cambodians and public institutions. The donors' project-driven "short-termism" has given short shrift to institutional capacity building, despite much rhetoric to the contrary. There is a need for creative thinking about how to rechannel some TA funds, including salary supplements paid to civil servants, toward wage expenditures in the context of a capacity development drive.

There are some positive examples, and more possibilities are on the horizon. Donors recently have been developing with RGC a pilot initiative to pay merit- and performance-based allowances to officials and staff working on priority reform programs. Under the Merit-Based Pay Initiative (MBPI), which commenced in 2005, a small number of MEF staff (about 6 percent in the first stage), after careful evaluation of qualifications and merit, are being "bumped up" to a higher pay scale. The MBPI is financed mainly by donors, but the RGC is initially financing 12 percent of the cost, with a commitment to increase its share over time. Initial reports indicate that MBPI is keeping officials in the office more and focusing them on their responsibilities and performance. Two other ministries—Commerce and Land Management—are considering the same initiative, and others are interested as well.

On the donor coordination front, the Public Finance Management Reform Program is a good example, with ten donors working together in a sector-wide approach and agreeing to abide by a set of "partnership principles" to guide interactions with the RGC and each other. There has also been good cooperation from multiple donors on Seila for several years. Donor coordination is difficult because the RGC rarely has coherent policies that they are willing to use to guide donor support. And if donors have different takes on the peace and security versus developmental approaches to public-sector reform, the situation is even more difficult. Clearly, stability concerns have contributed to donor failure to demand deeper reform, despite pro-reform rhetoric to the contrary. Some changes might be realized through pressure from the public, but it seems likely that external pressure will be needed to back reforms that begin to supplant the clientelistic and secretive mode of doing business in Cambodia.

Conclusion

The RGC has made some progress—significant in some areas, less so in others—with public finance reform since the late 1990s. Perhaps most striking are the steps toward decentralization. For all of its limitations, this is a dramatic change in the Cambodian public sector. Beyond that, the most notable progress has been in areas in which central oversight agencies and line ministries have partnered to implement reform. An example is the PAP in education and health, which has moved line agencies toward improved pro-poor targeting and may have had a positive impact on outcomes. Forestry remains more problematic—policy reform proceeded well but implementation floundered, perhaps owing to the role of the military in this area. Reforms in civil service and tax policy and administration fall between the two extremes. The RGC has adopted some civil service reform, but in the context of the struggle for control over the vast patronage potential in this area, key flaws have been ignored and overall progress has been slow. On the tax front, there was progress in revising the Law on Investment and strengthening tax administration, but these measures fall short of resolving core problems related to the ability to reward favorite partners and control access to public resources.

One factor which may explain the differential success is the degree of consensus (or at least, lack of controversy) about the nature and priority of the reform. Decentralization, perhaps because it was not well understood or was seen to have a different purpose than reformers intended, has been relatively well accepted, at least at its current modest scale, although currents of resistance have emerged. On PAP there was broad agreement between the RGC and the donors that getting resources to the front line of service delivery was crucial. In the case of civil service reform, there is not yet agreement either among competing central agencies or between the RGC and donors on the nature of needed reform. Nor has there been agreement between the RGC and donors, or among the donors, on tax policy. There have been differences of opinion about the benefits of tax incentives, with bilaterals generally favoring greater incentives to attract investors, and multilaterals typically opposing incentives in light of the need for higher revenues. Experience to date suggests the critical importance of building consensus as a foundation for reform and of keeping reform simple.

A second factor behind uneven results is that the RGC tends to rely on ad hoc approaches for systemic problems. A prominent example is the PAP, which in effect is a parallel budget system operating in a small set of ministries, without a plan for how to expand or institutionalize it into regular budget operations. Limited capacity and political resistance make such approaches inevitable, and as noted above they can create productive inroads into reform. They do have potential costs, however. Paradoxically, the more successful such measures are in solving specific critical problems, the less urgent systemic reform becomes, and the more easily the political elite can pursue business as usual. Another potential cost is that these limited reforms occupy existing capacity, diverting attention from more comprehensive reform. Of course, the key question is whether success with the limited experiences will alarm those who lose from reform and undermine further change or empower those who benefit and create a momentum for further progress.

In the near future, there appear to be few prospects for a dramatic change in Cambodia's political landscape. The CPP consolidated its position through power-sharing arrangements negotiated after the last election, and to some extent the political patronage price of that deal will have to be paid. The military, although less prominent than before, remains a key player. This relative stability may be good news for keeping conflict at bay, at least for the time being. But the consolidation of a durable peace founded on broad-based economic development will require bold systemic reforms that deal decisively with the problems discussed above. There appears to be some recognition by senior politicians of the costs of the semi-dysfunctional system, and there are nontrivial external and internal pressures for reform. An incremental approach that focuses on more limited, less controversial reforms—strategically selected to build a base for more systemic reform and generate sustainable pressure from donors and/or Cambodian voters—seems to be within reach.

The future of public finance reform in the medium term will depend on the extent to which consensus is reached among the RGC and its various key donors. Generating and maintaining consensus is laborious, and it requires consistency and steadfastness that does not always seem possible on the donor side. More important, it also requires an opening on the government side, which often must be nurtured by reformers. When both of these "preconditions" are present, reform will be more likely. When they are not, the status quo is more likely to prevail. Even when initial reforms occur, progress can be sustained only if attention is given to limiting their capture by the system of political patronage that continues to prevail in Cambodia.

Notes

1. A clear example of how this perspective has affected Cambodia is the way the country's vast forest resources have been manipulated to create mutually beneficial power-sharing relationships among key political actors (see Le Billon 2000).

2. These basic country statistics are taken from World Bank and *New York Times* websites.

3. For more information on Cambodia's political history, see Chandler (1996); Brown and Timberman (1998); Curtis (1998); Hughes (2003); and Cambodian Institute for Cooperation and Peace (2004).

4. The Khmer Rouge defected from the peace agreement and opted to return to war but without the international support it had received in the 1980s.

5. For further discussion, see French (1994); Ovesen, Trankell, and Ojendal (1995); Biddulph and Vanna (1997); and Curtis (1998).

6. The information in this section is drawn primarily from World Bank (2003a, 2006a) and from discussions with government and donor officials.

7. The information in this section is drawn primarily from World Bank (1999b, 2003a) and from discussions with government and donor officials.

8. By way of comparison, the revenue/GDP ratios in Sri Lanka and Vietnam in the 1999–2001 period were 17.0 and 20.6 percent, respectively (World Bank 2003a).

9. This has been a difficult area for donor engagement. A World Bank project on military demobilization failed after misprocurement was declared on a major contract.

10. An analysis of this power is available in "Cambodian Law of Public Finance," Thematic Publication of Legal Reform Unit, no. 3, Office of the Council of Ministers, June 2000.

11. "Organic Budget Law" (Kram no. 93-1, December 28, 1993), Article 26.

12. The reform program is based on the National Strategic Development Plan (2006), the Public Financial Management Reform Program (2004), and the Decentralization and Deconcentration Strategy (2005).

13. The Cambodia decentralization is very recent, and there is little formal literature on the process, so most of the analysis here is based on interviews and observations. Useful sources include Turner (2002); Smoke (2003); and Blunt and Turner (2005).

14. For more information, see UNICEF, "Cambodia's Recent History: CARERE 1." Available at www.uncdf.org.

15. For more information see UNICEF, "The Seila Initiative." Available at www .uncdf.org. See also Romeo (2000).

16. The issues discussed here are given a fuller treatment in Smoke (2003).

17. Human Rights Watch (2002); Neutral and Impartial Committee for Free and Fair Elections in Cambodia (2002); Sam Rainsy Party (2002), and Ye and Ngep (2002).

18. References on various aspects of fiscal decentralization in Cambodia include Prud'homme and Smoke (2000); Royal Government of Cambodia (2001b; 2004); and Eng and Rusten (2004).

19. Provincial Offices of Local Administration are the main legal interface between CS councils and PM, Provincial Treasuries play a role in CS finances, and Provincial Departments of Rural Development played a technical support role under Seila. There is no clarity on how to coordinate these activities, and the institutional choices will influence the degree of control the center has over CS activities.

20. This section is based on World Bank (2004a).

21. Some concessions have paid deposits to the Ministry of Agriculture, Forestry, and Fisheries.

4

Building Fiscal Provisions into Peace Agreements: Cautionary Tales from Guatemala

Pablo Rodas-Martini

In the mid-1990s, a series of peace accords brought an end to more than three decades of violent conflict in Guatemala. Although the Guatemalan state emerged intact from the conflict, the accords advanced an ambitious state-building agenda as part of the effort to secure a lasting peace. A distinctive feature of the accords is that they include an explicit commitment to raise the ratio of government revenue to gross domestic product (GDP), so as to provide funding for increased social expenditure and for new democratic institutions. Implementation of the fiscal provisions of the accords has proven difficult, however, since the political obstacles to these reforms did not disappear with the signing of the peace accords.

Background: The Armed Conflict in Guatemala

Guatemala's guerrilla insurgency started in 1960. The leftist government of Jacobo Arbenz had been deposed in 1954 by anticommunist groups who invaded the country from Honduras with the support of the United States. Some national sectors believed that the democratic route had been closed and that changes could only be promoted by the force of arms.

Although the guerrilla movement started as a national effort, it soon became involved in the Cold War that prevailed at the world level. The military governments were aligned with the United States, whereas the guerrillas, known as the Guatemala National Revolutionary Unity (URNG), adopted a Marxist ideology. The triumph of the Cuban revolution that had taken place in 1959 also influenced the Central American guerrilla movements.

The armed conflict in Guatemala acquired dimensions similar to those of El Salvador and Nicaragua, but it transpired less visibly and probably with greater cruelty. The Commission for Historic Clarification estimated that about 200,000 persons died. The conflict went beyond deaths in combat, disappearances, and torture. It reached extremes of genocide: whole villages were razed to the ground as part of a military policy to deny the guerrillas social support. The greater fault was the army's, but neither were the guerrillas blameless of crimes.

With the crumbling of socialism in the USSR and in Eastern Europe, the Central American guerrilla movements lost much of their international support. The Sandinistas were defeated in Nicaragua in 1990 in democratic elections, thus ending the counterrevolution that was supported by the United States. In El Salvador, a peace accord was signed in 1992, ending a civil war that had reached the very streets of the capital.

In Guatemala, the democratic government of Vinicio Cerezo took office in early 1986. His government held the first talks with the guerrillas. The attempts to reach an accord were not successful, however, owing to the unease of the military. After the fall of the Berlin wall in 1989, prospects improved. The government of Jorge Serrano, who took power in 1991, formalized talks with the guerrillas, a process that continued under his successor Ramiro de Leon.

During the presidency of Alvaro Arzú, who took office in January 1996, the peace process accelerated. It culminated in the symbolic signing of an agreement between the government and the URNG on December 29, 1996, ending thirty-seven years of internal conflict. The Guatemalan peace process produced a series of accords, the first of which had been signed in 1994 (see Table 4.1). The accords recognized that the country suffered from social and economic backwardness, in some cases going back to the colonial period, and that the state was weak in all terms. Even today, Guatemala has the lowest tax ratio (taxation/GDP) in Latin America, with the consequent weakness in public expenditure. The accords also recognized the presence of an exclusionary state under which the indigenous population suffered de facto discrimination.

Four key sectors were involved in negotiating the Peace Accords: the government; the army, which was part of the government but had its own profile and represented a state within the state; the business sector, which was not represented officially but always had a negotiator present; and the URNG guerrilla movement. Despite the fact that the opposition parties and civil society were not consulted, the national reaction to conclusion of the peace agreements was very favorable.

The Peace Accords received great attention from the international community. They became the principal framework for allocating assistance to the country. The United Nations had mediated the negotiations, and in 1997 the Security Council created the United Nations Verification Mission in Guatemala (MINUGUA) to supervise compliance with the accords. The mission operated until 2004.

Table 4.1   Overview of the Guatemalan Peace Accords

Specific Accords	Date Signed
Timetable accord for negotiations for a firm and lasting peace in Guatemala	March 29, 1994
Global accord on human rights	March 29, 1994
Accord for the resettlement of communities uprooted by the armed conflict	June 17, 1994
Accord for the establishment of a commission for historic clarification of human rights violations and acts of violence that have caused suffering to the Guatemalan people	June 23, 1994
Accord on the identity and rights of the indigenous population	March 31, 1995
Accord on socioeconomic aspects and the agrarian situation	May 6, 1996
Accord on strengthening of civilian power and the role of the Army in a democratic society	September 19, 1996
Accord on definitive cease-fire	December 4, 1996
Accord on constitutional reforms and the electoral regime	December 7, 1996
Accord on the basis for incorporation of the Guatemalan National Revolutionary Unit into legality	December 12, 1996
Accord on the timetable for the implementation, compliance, and verification of the Peace Accords	December 29, 1996
Accord on a firm and lasting peace	December 29, 1996

Fiscal Policy in the Peace Accords

Unlike the Nicaraguan case, in which peace came through elections and not ne-gotiations, or the case of El Salvador, in which the accords were relatively nar-rowly focused,[1] the Guatemalan Peace Accords were very comprehensive, not only in number but also in the scope of commitments in them. Many of these commitments involved public expenditure and therefore had fiscal repercussions.

Although some estimates were made of the financial commitment implicit in the Peace Accords, this was difficult to quantify precisely since much de-pended on how the letter of the accords was interpreted. For example, one of the many commitments of the "Accord on the Identity and Rights of the In-digenous Peoples" provides that "a Maya University or indigenous higher study institutions will be promoted." What financial sum does such a commit-ment represent? The accords did not specify the size of the faculty or student body, nor whether the university would be financed wholly or in part with pub-lic funds.

The government estimated the total cost of the accords at US$2.6 billion. Table 4.2 shows the principal items as well as a breakdown between internal and external resources necessary to support them. It was believed that interna-tional cooperating bodies would contribute 70 percent of total implementation costs.

Table 4.2 Peace Programs: Costs and Financial Requirements of the Projects

Programs	Total Cost (US$ million)	Internal Resources (%)	External Resources (%)
Area of action 1: Reinsertion of displaced persons and demobilized combatants	330.5	21.8	78.2
Reinsertion of displaced populations	175.4	29.9	70.1
Demobilization of former combatants	42.5	14.4	85.6
Support for victims of the armed conflict	38.2	12.2	87.8
Clarification of historic facts	500	10.0	90.0
Community development for peace	74.0	12.2	87.8
Area of action 2: Integrated human development	1,245.7	38.5	61.5
Emergency assistance for populations in extreme poverty	121.8	14.2	85.8
Cultural preservation of indigenous peoples	23.7	11.1	84.6
Education	197.6	38.9	61.1
Health	202.0	20.0	80.0
Social security	11.0	27.6	72.4
Housing	166.0	64.8	35.2
Infrastructure	446.4	44.3	60.2
Participation of women	58.1	58.6	41.4
Area of action 3: Sustainable productive development	351.8	32.4	67.6
Labor reform and training program	21.6	5.6	94.4
Agriculture and livestock, forestry, fishing, and environmental development program	257.3	38.8	61.2
Land financing program	70.0	17.7	82.4
Investment support program, employment, and export promotion	2.9	18.0	82.0
Area of action 4: Strengthening and modernization of the democratic state	692.8	16.4	83.6
Legal and constitutional reforms	3.2	10.0	90.0
Strengthening of human rights organizations	14.6	17.1	82.9
Modernization of the executive branch	260.6	13.4	86.6
Modernization of the legislative branch	6.1	16.8	83.2
Modernization of the judicial branch	35.2	10.0	90.0
Public security	149.9	23.8	76.2
Strengthening of tax collection	21.0	9.5	90.5
Support for local development councils	16.0	10.0	90.0
Municipal government strengthening	19.4	9.9	90.1
Land register and cadastre	50.0	20.0	80.0
Development and execution of peace program	40.0	24.3	75.8
Modernization of the army	76.9	13.3	86.7
Grand total	2,620.8	29.7	70.3

Source: Gobierno de Guatemala (1997).

The Socioeconomic Accord, signed in May 1996, is distinctive in that it contains explicit commitments on government revenue and expenditure. These included a clear mandate to increase the tax ratio by 2000 to 50 percent over the 1995 level, which would have brought it to 12 percent of GDP. No mention was made, however, of specific tax measures that would have to be adopted, such as a value-added tax or income tax. The commitment to the 12 percent goal, a crucial innovation of the Guatemalan peace process, derived not only from the recognition of the country's low tax burden in comparison to the rest of the region but also from observation of the challenges of financing implementation of the Salvadoran peace process owing to the absence of such a commitment. In fact, during the negotiations the URNG asked for a higher figure but finally compromised with 12 percent.

Fiscal Provisions in the Guatemalan Peace Accords (1996)

"Fiscal policy (revenue and expenditure) is the key tool enabling the State to comply with its constitutional commitments, particularly those relating to social development, which is essential to the quest for the common good. Fiscal policy is also essential to Guatemalan sustainable development, which has been impaired by low levels of education, health care and public security, a lack of infrastructure and other factors which militate against increasing the productivity of labor and the competitiveness of the Guatemalan economy.

"Budgetary policy should respond to the need for socio-economic development in a stable context, which requires a public spending policy consistent with the following basic principles:

a) Giving priority to social spending, the provision of public services and the basic infrastructure needed to support production and marketing;
b) Giving priority to social investment in health care, education and housing; rural development; job creation; and compliance with the commitments entered into under the peace agreements . . . ;
c) Efficient budget performance, with an emphasis on decentralization, redistribution and auditing of budgetary resources.

"Tax policy should be designed to enable the collection of the resources needed for the performance of the State's functions, including the funds required for the consolidation of peace, within the framework of a tax system consistent with the following basic principles:

a) The system is fair, equitable and, on the whole, progressive . . . ;
b) The system is universal and compulsory;
c) The system stimulates saving and investment.

continues

Continued

"The State should also ensure efficiency and transparency in tax collection and fiscal management so as to promote taxpayer confidence in government policy and eliminate tax evasion and fraud.

"Bearing in mind the need to increase State revenues in order to cope with the urgent tasks of economic growth, social development and building peace, the Government undertakes to ensure that by the year 2000, the tax burden, measured as a ratio of gross domestic product, increases by at least 50 percent as compared with the 1995 tax burden.

"The failure to fulfill tax obligations deprives the country of the resources needed in order to address the backlog of social needs affecting Guatemalan society. The Government undertakes to impose exemplary penalties on those who engage in various types of tax fraud, to modernize and strengthen tax administration and to give priority to spending on social needs."

Source: Accord on Socioeconomic Aspects and the Agrarian Situation, signed in Mexico, May 6, 1996.

The accord also contained commitments to increase public expenditure in education, health, and housing by 50 percent (again, as a share of GDP) over the same period. Additional resources were also necessary to strengthen the institutions created under the 1985 constitution and to finance the new democratic processes arising out of the accords. The parties concluded that the Guatemalan state had to expand its role and that this required additional resources. Greater expenses and greater income: that was the fiscal mandate of the Peace Accords.

Proposal of a Fiscal Pact

By the end of 1998, it was evident that the goal of increasing the tax ratio to 12 percent by the year 2000 would not be reached. The newly created Superintendence of Tax Administration (SAT), which assumed tax collection functions with a degree of autonomy from the Ministry of Finance, could not be asked to perform miracles. Attempts to reform tax policies had not succeeded. For example, a proposed reform of the property tax was rejected, paradoxically in the face of opposition by indigenous small holders in the highlands, despite the fact that the tax would have fallen on the large landed estates.

Rather than consigning fiscal matters to a narrow set of experts, it became clear that these questions needed to be debated broadly by the key national sectors. At the end of 1998, a few months before the end of its period in office, the government of President Alvaro Arzú decided to create a Fiscal Pact Preparatory Commission made up of expert economists from different ideological tendencies and a constitutional lawyer. Its mandate was to present a proposal of "principles and commitments" that would be discussed with representative sectors of Guatemalan society until a Fiscal Pact could be concluded.

The commission did not propose specific tax reforms but defined a general framework or guidelines toward a fiscal policy. The 12 percent goal was also rescheduled to 2002, as it was impossible to reach in 2000. The commission presented its proposal at the end of 1999, a few days before the new government of Alfonso Portillo took office. Once the document was available, the Commission of Accompaniment to the Peace Accords invited society representatives to react to the proposal of the experts.[2] Numerous entities sent comments in writing. The Commission of Accompaniment proceeded to meet with the business sector and civil society groups separately, in what was to be called a pendulum strategy. As soon as it was possible to approximate the positions of the key sectors, formal negotiations were started, but by this time a consensus had already been reached on a good part of the document. More than 140 organizations signed the document on May 25, 2000. Although the principles and commitments remained fairly general and did not include specific tax measures (always more controversial), they did make fiscal policy more precise than the Peace Accords had done.

The private sector and civil society continued to negotiate on concrete tax reforms. In the interim, however, the Portillo government was in dire need of resources, and it jumped the gun by taking a package of reforms to Congress. Given this urgency, the business sector and civil society finally agreed to a Fiscal Pact that included increasing the value-added tax (VAT) from 10 to 12 percent and increasing the maximum income tax rate from 25 to 31 percent.

The Congress, however, approved the government proposal instead of the reforms agreed upon in the Fiscal Pact. Months later, in 2001, the government finally approved another set of measures that took into account much of what the Fiscal Pact had suggested, including the controversial increase of VAT to 12 percent. By then, however, there were many charges of corruption against the government, and the measures had the support only of the ruling party.

In 2004, with the new government of Oscar Berger in place, an attempt was made to rescue the Fiscal Pact, as once again the government was in need of funds. The Constitutional Court (CC) had recently declared the Tax on Mercantile and Farm Enterprises (IEMA) unconstitutional,[3] and as a result the tax ratio threatened to fall to pre–Peace Accord levels. In other words, the government sought to use the Fiscal Pact, not to reach the 12 percent target of the Peace Accords but simply to stem plummeting tax collection and explosion of the fiscal deficit. A new commission, called the Technical Commission, proposed tax changes that were finally approved with amendments by the Congress, after a hard negotiating process, but the impact of these reforms has been very modest.

On the positive side, the Fiscal Pact brought traditionally opposing sectors into dialogue with each other to seek agreement on a subject as sensitive as taxes. Thanks to the Fiscal Pact, there is a better understanding of fiscal matters among the general population, not only because of the studies prepared for the Commission but also because of the ample coverage that the subject received in the press.

On the negative side, the Fiscal Pact's ambition of generating a national consensus has limited the government's ability to take initiatives on fiscal matters. Business sectors and civil society now want all measures to have their prior approval, which bogs down fiscal policy. Moreover, the Fiscal Pact has served as a pretext for political parties not to pronounce on fiscal matters during electoral campaigns, instead merely promising that, if elected, they will promote reforms arising out of the pact.

Tax Collection Performance

Guatemala's tax collection stood at 8 percent of GDP in 1995 and had reached 8.8 percent in 1996, the year in which the Peace Accords were signed (see Table 4.3). Collection continued to increase, albeit modestly, until it reached a maximum of 11 percent in 2002. The goal of 12 percent was never reached—neither by the original target date of 2000 nor by the subsequent rescheduled target of 2002. After this date, tax collection deteriorated further still, in clear violation of the Peace Accords.[4]

Tax collection figures must be taken with a certain amount of caution, as Guatemala still keeps its national accounts using the base year of 1958.[5] Only now is the Bank of Guatemala making new estimates, and preliminary results

Table 4.3   Gross and Net Tax Burden, as a Percentage of GDP

Year	Gross Tax Burden	Net Tax Burden
1995	8.0	N.A.
1996	8.8	N.A.
1997	9.4	8.8
1998	9.3	8.7
1999	9.9	9.4
2000	10.0	9.5
2001	10.3	9.7
2002	11.0	10.5
2003	10.7	10.3
2004	10.8	10.3

Source: Superintendence of Tax Administration (SAT) (2005).
Note: N.A. = not available.

(still unofficial) indicate that the GDP should be adjusted downward between 15 and 20 percent. If confirmed, tax collection as a percentage of GDP would edge up above 12 percent while doing nothing to address the fiscal concerns that originally motivated the target: mainly, the precarious provision of public services by the Guatemalan state.[6]

The structure of taxes is presented in Table 4.4. It is evident that indirect collection predominates over direct collection, with the former fluctuating between 75 and 80 percent. Among indirect taxes, VAT occupies first place, accounting for more than 40 percent of total taxation since 1996.

Customs duties gradually declined; they fell from close to 25 percent in the mid-1990s to approximately 10 percent in 2004 as a result of continued efforts to open the economy through trade liberalization.[7] High tariffs no longer exist in the country; instead there are four main bands: 15 percent for consumer goods, 10 percent and 5 percent for intermediate inputs, and 0 percent for capital goods. The signing of free trade agreements, notably the Dominican Republic and Central American Free Trade Agreement (DR-CAFTA) with the United States is expected to reduce tariff collection even more.[8]

Unlike tariffs, selective taxes (in particular on fuel), which have fluctuated at around 10 percent of the total, will continue to occupy an important place in total revenue collection. These taxes have the advantage that they are relatively easy to collect and that they tend to be inelastic, as consumers react slowly to changes in prices.

Direct taxes come from three main sources: income tax, the IEMA, and the "extraordinary and temporary" taxes in support of the Peace Accords. The latter two can be considered variants of an income tax because they are creditable to income tax, making it possible to collect a minimum amount under this rubric. As in many developing countries, direct taxation has fallen principally on companies, owing to the administrative difficulties in taxing individuals.

In brief, the Peace Accords have not brought an appreciable change either in tax collection levels or structures. Rather, tax collection has followed a trend similar to that of other developing countries unaffected by violent conflict. Namely, the VAT, at the suggestion of the international agencies, has become the most important tax, whereas tariffs have decreased in response to trade opening, and income tax has been stagnant owing to the difficulty in collecting it.

After the signing of the peace agreements, there was considerable optimism that the tax ratio would be increased to 12 percent by 2000. Today, no one dares set a date: we are in 2007, and the goal remains unmet. Did Guatemalan society really believe that the ratio would reach 12 percent but then realize that it was a harder task than it had imagined? Was it a false promise to bring about the end of the conflict that was then deliberately not complied with? Was it trickery to lure donor organizations to throw millions of dollars into the country, when there was no real will to reach the goal? It is difficult to discern the truth, and national players surely disagree in their answers.

Table 4.4 Tax Structure (%)

Year	1995	1996	1997	1998	1999	2000	2001	2002	2003	2004[a]
Total	100.0	100.0	100.0	100.0	100.0	100.0	100.0	100.0	100.0	100.0
Direct taxes	20.7	23.9	22.4	20.6	21.8	22.1	24.3	26.4	25.9	24.5
Income tax	20.1	17.7	12.5	13.9	13.6	13.3	14.8	13.2	13.3	15.0
Property and similar taxes	0.5	0.3	0.2	0.1	0.1	0.1	0.1	0.0	0.0	0.0
Extraordinary and temporary solidarity tax	0.0	5.9	9.7	0.3	0.0	0.0	0.0	0.0	0.0	0.0
Tax on mercantile and farm enterprises	0.0	0.0	0.0	6.2	8.1	8.6	9.4	13.1	12.6	3.9
Extraordinary and temporary tax in support of peace	0.0	0.0	0.0	0.0	0.0	0.0	0.0	0.0	0.0	5.6
Indirect taxes	79.3	76.1	77.6	79.4	78.2	77.9	75.7	73.6	74.1	75.5
Value-added tax[b]	36.0	42.5	44.8	45.8	46.7	47.3	43.8	44.7	45.8	42.3
VAT imports	20.1	21.9	24.1	26.9	26.6	27.9	26.7	27.2	28.5	29.3
VAT domestic	16.0	20.6	20.6	18.9	20.1	19.4	17.1	17.5	17.3	18.4
Customs duties on imports	23.6	17.5	15.0	14.5	13.6	12.0	12.4	11.7	11.8	11.0
Distribution of petroleum and derivatives	8.9	7.2	9.2	10.9	10.5	9.3	10.2	8.3	7.4	8.0
Licenses/fees	2.8	2.3	1.7	2.0	1.9	1.2	1.0	1.0	0.9	1.3
Circulation of motor vehicles	1.9	1.3	1.4	1.2	1.1	1.2	1.4	1.3	1.3	1.2
Oil and hydrocarbon royalties	0.1	0.1	1.4	0.2	0.0	2.6	1.8	2.0	2.5	2.2
Exit tax	0.1	0.1	0.1	0.7	0.7	0.9	1.0	0.8	0.8	0.9
Distribution of beverages	2.1	1.7	1.5	1.9	1.9	1.3	1.6	1.6	1.4	1.0
Tobacco	2.1	1.9	1.8	1.7	1.3	1.4	1.5	1.4	1.4	1.2
Distribution of cement	0.0	0.0	0.0	0.0	0.0	0.0	0.4	0.4	0.4	0.4
Others	1.6	1.4	0.8	0.5	0.5	0.7	0.6	0.5	0.5	0.4

Source: Available at http://www.minfin.gob.gt/.

Notes: a. The figures for 2004 are preliminary. b. The VAT credit refunds to the exporting sector are not deducted from 1995 to 2000, but they are deducted as of 2001.

Vertical Distribution of Taxes

It is possible to evaluate the incidence of taxation in Guatemala in its vertical distribution by deciles but not horizontally across ethnic groups or regions. To date, three studies have been made on the former, but none on the latter. The first study was prepared by Galper and Ramos (1992), the second by Larios (2000), and the third by Arthur Mann (2002b). Given the fact that the first two have been questioned in respect to methodology, we will concentrate on the third and most recent.

Table 4.5 shows that the overall incidence of taxation in Guatemala is approximately neutral: the contribution of each decile fluctuates around 20 percent. This would mean that the "global progressivity" mandated for tax collection by the Peace Accords has not been accomplished.[9]

Each tax shows somewhat different results. Direct taxation is regressive or neutral in the first deciles and progressive in the last deciles. Indirect taxation is essentially neutral except in the last decile, where it turns regressive, a finding that is not surprising when one considers that the propensity to consume (as opposed to save) declines with greater wealth.

Personal income tax appears to be paid exclusively by the top deciles. As indicated earlier, however, in Guatemala income tax is collected principally from businesses. Insofar as companies transfer the tax to the consumer, as if it were VAT, direct income taxes are really indirect, and their incidence is not accurately captured in these figures. This is important to mention because sectors of the Left in Guatemala have strongly proposed an increase of income tax on companies, believing it to be highly progressive, whereas they do not propose such an increase in income tax on persons because they believe this would affect the middle class. The rationale for this position is questionable.

VAT is neutral in the middle eight deciles, but regressive in the first (10.2 percent) and the last (7.8 percent). The results are quite similar for VAT on imports and domestic goods and services. The most strongly progressive tax is that on the circulation of vehicles, but it remains a minor source of revenue.

In a postconflict country such as Guatemala, a question that arises is what should be prioritized: the collection level or tax distribution? In general, it may be easier to achieve distributional objectives through expenditure, in which case the priority on the revenue side is to raise the collection level.

Luxury taxes are sometimes mentioned as a way to further both objectives. As discussed below, the Guatemalan constitution (or at least, the interpretation of it by the Constitutional Court) prohibits luxury taxes by proscribing "double taxation" (since luxury products and services are already subject to VAT). Despite this, however, it is possible to tax certain products—as is done with vehicles (the burden is built into the road tax) or liquors and fuel (distribution is taxed)—or to impose a higher VAT rate for certain products. Goods that could be subject to luxury surcharges include transportation vehicles such as automobiles, private aircraft, and yachts.

Table 4.5 Effective Tax Rates by Deciles of Household Income, 2001 (%)

Tax	1	2	3	4	5	6	7	8	9	10	Total
Total direct	4.5	4.0	4.0	3.8	3.8	3.8	3.6	3.6	4.2	5.8	4.7
Personal income	—	—	—	—	—	—	—	—	0.5	1.6	0.7
Income and IEMA taxes on companies	4.4	3.9	3.9	3.6	3.6	3.7	3.5	3.5	3.6	3.9	3.7
Exit tax	0.1	0.1	0.1	0.2	0.1	0.1	0.1	0.1	0.2	0.3	0.2
Equity	—	0.0	—	—	0.0	—	—	0.0	—	0.0	0.0
Total indirect	16.5	14.8	15.6	15.2	16.4	16.7	16.5	15.6	16.4	13.5	15.1
VAT imports	7.4	6.4	6.4	6.0	6.1	6.4	6.0	6.7	5.9	4.8	5.5
VAT domestic	2.8	3.0	3.5	3.8	4.2	4.2	4.3	4.1	3.9	2.9	3.5
Customs duties	2.7	2.3	2.4	2.3	2.4	2.8	2.5	2.4	2.8	2.5	2.6
Beverages	0.2	0.2	0.4	0.3	0.4	0.4	0.5	0.5	0.4	0.2	0.3
Tobacco	0.4	0.1	0.3	0.3	0.7	0.3	0.5	0.3	0.3	0.2	0.3
Petroleum	2.5	2.2	2.1	2.0	2.0	2.0	2.1	2.1	2.3	2.0	2.1
Stamps	0.3	0.3	0.3	0.2	0.2	0.2	0.2	0.2	0.2	0.2	0.2
Circulation of vehicles	0.1	0.1	0.1	0.1	0.1	0.2	0.2	0.2	0.4	0.4	0.3
Cement	0.2	0.1	0.1	0.1	0.1	0.1	0.1	0.1	0.1	0.1	0.1
Fares	0.1	0.1	0.1	0.1	0.1	0.1	0.1	0.1	0.1	0.2	0.1
Others	—	—	—	—	—	—	—	—	—	—	—
Total	21.0	18.8	19.5	19.0	20.2	20.5	20.1	19.3	20.6	19.3	19.7

Source: Mann (2002b).

The property tax also could increase both revenue and progressivity. This is an extremely controversial tax in Guatemala, as seen in the failure of the attempt to reform it after the signature of the Peace Accords, and it is also made difficult by the lack of a national cadastre. There are some experiences in and around the capital, however, which show that municipalities may succeed in increasing property tax collection if they are able to provide neighborhoods with proper streets and other community services.[10]

Support of the International Community

With the Peace Accords, Guatemala captured the attention of international aid donors. They applauded the end of the armed conflict and showed a willingness to finance different components of the program that the government presented to them (see Table 4.2). Implicitly or explicitly, the donors obviously conditioned their support on advances in the implementation of the accords.

Table 4.6 shows the flows of international aid to Guatemala in the period from 1997 to 2003. Although the total is substantial, the average annual disbursement of about US$200 million is less than 1 percent of the Guatemalan GDP. The largest share of this aid has come from multilateral agencies. The Inter-American Development Bank has been the single largest donor. Given the fact Guatemala will have to repay these loans with interest (albeit at a more favorable rate than on the international market), the net impact on the country is reduced further. Among bilateral donors, the United States occupies first place, providing roughly half of all bilateral aid.[11]

Table 4.7 shows that the flow of official development assistance to Guatemala has been relatively modest and compares it to aid received by Nicaragua in the same period. Family remittances to Guatemala have been considerably larger than aid (see Table 4.8), with a correspondingly greater macroeconomic impact, in particular on the exchange rate, which has appreciated in recent years. According to the 2000 US population census, the number of Guatemalans living in that country was 480,665, roughly half of whom entered the United States between 1990 and 2000.[12] Remittances certainly are taxed when they enter the country, but they become liable to VAT when spent on consumption in the formal sector and eventually even to income tax on the companies who make these sales, so that the public purse benefits from this entry of resources.

Impediments to Increasing Revenues

This section reviews some of the major obstacles that have been encountered in efforts to increase tax revenues in Guatemala in recent years.

Table 4.6   Financing by Aid Donors (US$ million)

Country/Agency	Amount Subscribed as of December 2003	Accumulated Disbursements 1997–2002	Disbursements 2003[a]	Amount Available
Bilateral cooperation				
Germany	91.8	8.6	20.4	62.8
(loans)	19.0	N.A.	4.0	15.1
(grants)	72.8	8.6	16.4	47.8
Canada	66.7	35.3	11.9	19.4
Denmark	1.1	N.A.	1.1	0.2
Spain	10.7	N.A.	N.A.	10.7
United States	433.5	329.1	54.6	49.8
Finland	4.3	N.A.	1.7	2.6
France	0.3	N.A.	0.1	0.2
Italy	16.6	5.4	4.2	7.0
Japan (loan)	49.0	20.2	3.4	25.4
Norway	54.4	14.6	12.6	27.2
Netherlands	66.5	42.9	13.2	10.3
Sweden	46.2	23.5	10.5	11.5
Switzerland	8.4	N.A.	3.1	5.4
Total Bilateral	849.5	479.6	136.9	232.6
Multilateral cooperation				
CABEI[b] (loans)	384.2	N.A.	45.9	338.3
IADB[c]	1,013.9	485.7	58.0	521.8
(loans)	988.8	481.4	52.5	506.4
(grants)	25.1	4.3	5.5	15.4
World Bank	558.6	193.8	31.5	292.1
(loans)	555.2	192.3	31.4	290.6
(grants)	3.4	1.6	0.1	1.5
United Nations	29.9	N.A.	17.2	9.9
OAS[d]	22.5	N.A.	7.9	14.6
European Union	230.0	N.A.	29.4	200.6
Total Multilateral	2,239.0	679.5	189.8	1,377.2
Grand Total	3,088.6	1,159.0	326.7	1,609.8

Source: Inter-American Development Bank (2004).

Notes: a. Disbursements made by sources of financing to government and nongovernmental organizations. b. CABEI = Central American Bank for Economic Integration. c. IADB = Inter-American Development Bank. d. OAS = Organization of American States. N.A. = information not supplied by agencies or embassies.

Tax Administration

Several aspects of the performance of Guatemala's SAT are shown in Table 4.9 in comparison with international parameters and Central American countries. It is evident that Guatemala still has ample room for improvement.

Although international consultants have offered a relatively favorable assessment of the SAT (DevTech 2001), the agency would seem to replicate

Table 4.7 Indicators of Assistance to Guatemala and Nicaragua

	1995	1996	1997	1998	1999	2000	2001	2002	2003
Guatemala									
Aid (% of central government expenditures)	18.9	15.3	18.0	12.8	15.2	12.5	9.2	9.4	7.9
Aid (% of GNI[a])	1.4	1.2	1.5	1.2	1.6	1.4	1.1	1.1	1.0
Aid (% of gross capital formation)	9.5	9.7	10.9	6.9	9.2	7.7	6.1	5.7	6.0
Aid per capita (current US$)	21.0	18.9	25.1	21.6	26.5	23.2	19.4	20.7	20.1
ODA[b] and official aid (US$ millions)	209.8	193.6	264.4	233.4	293.3	263.6	226.6	248.7	247.0
Nicaragua									
Aid (% of central government expenditures)	125.5	171.7	71.5	97.0	93.8	74.2	103.3	64.4	95.8
Aid (% of GNI)	23.1	31.2	13.2	17.8	19.0	15.0	24.4	13.3	21.0
Aid (% of gross capital formation)	93.0	109.1	39.0	54.4	45.4	38.4	67.2	35.6	54.3
Aid per capita (current US$)	147.5	205.1	87.9	125.3	136.2	110.7	178.8	96.9	152.0
ODA and official aid (US$ millions)	652.9	933.8	411.5	602.6	673.2	561.5	930.5	517.5	833.2

Source: World Bank (2005f).
Notes: a. GNI = gross national income. b. ODA = Overseas Development Administration.

Table 4.8   Entry of Foreign Exchange from Family Remittances (US$ millions)

Year	Total
1995	416.5
1996	375.4
1997	408.0
1998	456.4
1999	465.6
2000	563.4
2001	592.3
2002	1,579.4
2003	2,106.5
2004	2,550.6

Source: BANGUAT.

Table 4.9   Benchmarks of Tax Administration

Indicators	Benchmark International	Benchmark Central America	Guatemala Actual
Magnitude evasion VAT	10%	25%	33%
Number of internal tax administrators for every 1,000 persons in the national population	1–2	0.27	0.17
Ratio between number of active taxpayers and tax administrators	150–250:1	81:1	51:1
Administrative cost as % of total internal collection	1%	1.5%	3%

Source: DevTech (2001).

faults that are common to other institutions in the country. In less than eight years, for example, SAT has had six superintendents, an excessive rate of turnover, especially if we take into account that the superintendent is designated, in theory, for an indefinite time. The institution has also not been immune to the phenomenon of corruption: the second to last superintendent is at present in prison for corruption.

Tax Incentives and Exemptions

Fiscal incentives have long been common practice in developing countries for the purpose of promoting objectives such as economic growth and industrial development. Guatemala is no exception. Exemptions and incentives have reduced the taxable base of VAT, income tax, and tariffs, among others.

The past decade has seen the abolition of numerous incentives and exemptions that existed for diverse sectors, such as tourism or poultry production. Despite these advances, there is still discussion in the country on the level of incentives and exemptions that remain in effect. In a study of "tax expenditure," in the form of deductions, credits, exclusions, and exonerations, Mann and Burke (2002) concluded, on the basis of the method of "sacrificed revenue," that the tax expenditure was equivalent to 7.3 percent of GDP in the year 2000. The most important components were exemptions from VAT on exports (1.4 percent of GDP), the deduction of 36,000 quetzals granted to persons under income tax (1.3 percent of GDP), exemption of customs duties on temporary imports for the *maquilas* (1.1 percent of GDP), and exemption of VAT for temporary import of inputs for *maquilas* (0.8 percent).

Mann and Burke explained, however, that it would be a mistake to conclude that tax collection would rise by this amount if these exemptions were eliminated. Using the method of "net increase in fiscal revenue," which allows for behavioral changes in response to the elimination of incentives, they calculated that the net gain would be closer to 3.2 percent of GDP. In sum, despite some progress in curtailing the incentives and exemptions that have eroded tax collection in the past, appreciable scope remains for further reforms to increase collections.

Constitutional Restrictions

Most constitutions contain principles that limit the power of the state to create taxes, in order to protect individuals against abuse by the authorities. Guatemala is no exception to this rule. The Political Constitution of 1985 develops these tax principles more than previous constitutions, however, and more than the constitutions of other Latin American countries. Some commentators have called the results "taxation padlocks," as they make legislative reform of taxes and the work of the customs administration very difficult.

The principle of "taxpaying capacity," established in Article 243, says that the taxation system must be just and fair and that tax laws must be structured according to the capacity to pay. It prohibits confiscatory taxes and double or multiple internal taxation and states that there is double or multiple taxation when one generating event attributable to the same taxpayer is taxed two or more times.

This article has been open to capricious interpretation by different Constitutional Courts, some of which have nullified tax reforms under the subjective argument that charges are not fair or just. Of course, there is no obvious parameter for delimiting what is considered just and fair. For example, fines imposed for noncompliance with tax obligations have been deemed confiscatory. Also, the prohibition on double taxation has prevented the imposition of taxes on luxury goods and has even created difficulties for selective taxes on fuel, cigarettes, or liquors (taxes that are common in most countries) under the argument that these products are already burdened by VAT. Successive governments have had to have recourse to complicated justifications to avoid suppression of these taxes.

The appeals continuously filed against tax reforms by pressure groups are not limited, however, to these arguments. Tax reforms have often been appealed by recourse to other articles of the constitution that appear to have no relation to taxation. For example, recourse has been had to Article 2, which speaks of the duties of the state; to Article 4 on liberty and equality; to Article 24 on the inviolability of correspondence, documents, and books; to Article 39 on private property; to Article 41 on the protection of the right to property; and to Article 43 on liberty of industry, commerce, and work.

At the end of 2003, the Constitutional Court declared the IEMA unconstitutional on the grounds that it violated the constitutional obligation of the state to promote the economic development of the nation, grant incentives to industrial enterprises, and protect the formation of capital, savings, and investment as well as Article 243 relative to payment capacity. Overnight, more than 10 percent of the country's total tax intake was endangered. As noted above, the IEMA tax was simply a way to collect income tax in advance, as it was creditable to it. In another case, the VAT itself narrowly escaped being declared unconstitutional, surviving a court challenge on a 3–2 vote.

In brief, although the Peace Accords clamor for an increase in public expenditure, which should obviously go hand in hand with increased tax revenues, the constitutional framework built in 1985 erects a series of checks and limitations to progress on this front. To a great extent, the failure to achieve the 12 percent goal is due to the continuous interventions of the Constitutional Court, which have sapped tax reform efforts.

Corruption and Cynicism

Given the fact that corruption has been a recurrent phenomenon on the Guatemalan political scene, the population has become impregnated with a culture of tax evasion that leads it to rationalize lack of payment: why pay tax if they are going to steal it? This logic erodes taxation, and it is applied equally by large, medium, and small businesses as well as the individual taxpayer.

In periods when the perception of corruption has diminished, for example during the Arzú (January 1996–2000) and Berger (January 2004–present) governments, the argument is heard less often, but it is always present. People have, to a certain extent, become cynical. Even when the press is not reporting corruption scandals, they assume that the authorities are involved in shady business. These doubts cast shadows on any political party that comes to power, as many citizens believe that politics are "dirty" and that the rulers, whoever they may be, are taking advantage of the national coffers.

The Informal Economy

A fifth impediment to increasing revenues is the large size of the country's informal economy. The World Bank estimated that 51.5 percent of GDP was informal in 2003. The informal sector does pay a percentage of its income in taxes—for example, in the form of VAT when buying in the formal economy, but by definition their informality means that the sector is not supervised by the tax administration. The informal sector does not issue invoices or pay income tax. Over time, it could be expected that formality will increase, which would lead to greater taxation. This medium- and long-term process will not generate important increases in taxation in the short term, however.

Evolution of Public Expenditure

Public expenditure has increased modestly since the signature of the Peace Accords (see Table 4.10), rising from 9.4 percent of GDP in 1996 to 13.8 percent in 1999 and then slipping to 12 percent in 2004. Despite the rhetoric of peace, the advance in the implementation of the commitments established for the state has been slow.

Expenditure has not increased more owing to difficulties in increasing tax revenue; otherwise it would have repercussions on the fiscal deficit. The deficit has been kept under control since the signing of the Peace Accords: it reached a maximum value of 2.8 percent in 1999 and fell to 1 percent in 2004.

The modest increase in public expenditure has not allowed for full compliance with the commitments of the Peace Accords. In the same way as tax revenue, the commitments on the expenditure side have been diluted as the years have gone by.

Moreover, the country has fallen into the euphemistic practice of identifying almost every expense on human development, infrastructure, and governance as part of compliance with the Peace Accords. Consequently, the presidential reports presented each year to Congress, and the government reports presented to the consultative groups of the aid donors, have painted a relatively optimistic picture of supposed advances in the Peace Accords. This points to the problem in postconflict countries of how to differentiate peace implementation from those expenditures that form an inherent part of the development of countries. When and how should peace commitments be supplanted by the latter?

Table 4.10 Public Expenditure of the Central Administration (% GDP)

Description	1995	1996	1997	1998	1999	2000	2001	2002	2003	2004
Total	9.4	9.4	10.7	12.5	13.8	12.8	12.9	12.4	13.4	12.0
Government administration	1.6	1.7	1.9	2.1	2.2	2.1	1.7	1.7	1.8	1.6
Judicial branch	0.2	0.3	0.4	0.4	0.5	0.5	0.6	0.5	0.6	0.6
Government direction	0.5	0.2	0.2	0.1	0.1	0	0	0	0	0
Tax administration	0.3	0.6	0.8	1.0	1.0	0.9	0.5	0.5	0.5	0.4
General services	0.4	0.3	0.1	0.3	0.4	0.3	0.4	0.4	0.4	0.3
Other administration activities[a]	0.2	0.3	0.3	0.2	0.2	0.3	0.3	0.3	0.3	0.3
Defense and internal security	1.3	1.1	1.1	1.2	1.3	1.5	1.6	1.3	1.4	1.0
Defense	0.9	0.8	0.6	0.6	0.6	0.7	0.9	0.6	0.6	0.4
Internal security	0.4	0.4	0.5	0.6	0.7	0.7	0.8	0.7	0.8	0.7
Social services	4.0	4.0	4.6	5.8	6.1	5.8	6.3	6.3	6.7	6.3
Health and social assistance	0.8	0.7	0.8	0.9	1.2	1.0	1.1	1.0	1.0	0.9
Labor and social welfare	0.7	0.7	0.7	0.8	0.9	1.0	1.1	0.9	1.4	1.2
Education	1.5	1.5	1.7	2.0	2.3	2.2	2.5	2.3	2.4	2.3
Culture and sports	0.1	0.1	0.1	0.1	0.1	0.2	0.2	0.2	0.2	0.2
Urban and rural development	0.7	0.8	1.0	1.0	1.0	0.8	1.1	1.4	1.3	1.3
Other social service activities[b]	0.1	0.2	0.4	0.8	0.1	0.5	0.4	0.5	0.3	0.4
Economic services	1.4	1.6	2.2	2.4	2.9	2.2	1.9	1.9	2.3	1.9
Transportation	0.9	1.1	1.6	1.7	1.8	1.3	1.2	1.2	1.1	1.1
Farm	0.3	0.2	0.2	0.3	0.4	0.3	0.5	0.5	0.5	0.4
Other economic service activities[c]	0.2	0.1	0.4	0.5	0.5	0.5	0.1	0.2	0.7	0.3
Public debt	1.0	1.1	0.8	1.1	1.3	1.2	1.4	1.2	1.2	1.2
Interest, commissions, and other expenses	1.0	1.1	0.8	1.1	1.3	1.2	1.4	1.2	1.2	1.2

Source: Available at http://www.minfin.gob.gt/ (2004).

Notes: a. Includes the legislative branch and foreign affairs. b. Includes science and technology, housing, and environment. c. Includes energy, tourism, industry, and commerce.

Distributional Incidence of Public Expenditure

Vertical Distribution

To date, the one study of the vertical distribution of public expenditure in Guatemala was carried out by the World Bank (2003b) on the basis of information provided by the First National Survey of Living Conditions (EN-COVI), conducted in the year 2000. The lack of previous studies is due to the paucity of household surveys in the country.[13]

Table 4.11 presents the results for education and health.[14] Expenditure in pre-primary education is progressive, being more oriented toward the poor; expenditure in primary education is roughly neutral; and expenditure on secondary education and tertiary education is regressive. Specific interventions, such as the school breakfast program, scholarships, and other subsidies, are not well taken advantage of by the poor. Overall, public education expenditure is neutral, contrary to the progressive incidence that would be expected for a country like Guatemala.

Expenditure on health is no better. The most regressive item is hospitals, which benefit the poorest quintile least. The health posts and community centers are more focused on the poorest. Given the resources that the hospitals absorb, health expenditure benefits the third and fourth quintiles most.

In comparison with other countries with similar income levels, the principal allocations to human development are badly distributed. Moreover, intuition would suggest that many items of public expense, whose incidence cannot be evaluated, such as public security and foreign affairs, are regressive, as these expenses tend to be made principally in the capital or mainly benefit the middle and upper layers of society.

Although in the case of taxation it is argued that an increase in revenues is more important than the incidence, in the case of expenditure, especially for a country with as many needs as Guatemala, it is undeniable that increases in the level of expenditure should go hand in hand with improvement in progressivity. Clearly, much more needs to be done on this front.[15]

Horizontal Distribution of Expenditure

The data presented in Table 4.11 suggest that vertical inequalities are overlaid with horizontal inequalities between Guatemala's indigenous and nonindigenous populations. According to the official statistics, indigenous people comprised 43 percent of the population but received only 37 percent of public expenditures on education and 40 percent of public expenditures on health in 2000. Given that public expenditures should help to redress disparities in private expenditures, these numbers reflect substantial cleavages in Guatemalan society.

Table 4.11 Distributional Incidence of Public Spending on Education and Health, 2000 (% of total benefits or net public subsidies received by each group)

	Total	By Quintile					By Ethnicity		By Area	
		Q1	Q2	Q3	Q4	Q5	Indigenous	Non-Indian	Rural	Urban
Education—Total	100	17	21	21	21	21	37	63	59	41
Pre-primary	100	39	18	24	14	4	64	36	76	24
Primary	100	21	25	23	21	10	42	58	69	31
Secondary	100	3	12	23	31	32	22	78	36	64
University	100	3	12	23	31	32	22	78	36	64
Demand-side programs										
School feeding	100	16	25	27	20	11	43	57	79	21
Scholarships	100	9	4	23	16	48	47	53	28	72
School materials	100	18	24	24	20	13	35	65	69	31
School transport	100	0	2	15	56	27	8	92	3	97
Health—Total	100	17	18	23	25	17	40	60	64	36
Hospital	100	13	16	21	29	22	33	67	58	42
Health center	100	20	23	28	20	9	51	49	67	33
Health post	100	40	22	27	6	5	53	47	98	2
Community center	100	39	20	23	8	10	71	29	87	13
Memo for comparison										
Share of total population	100	20	20	20	20	20	43	58	61	39
Share of poor population	100	36	36	29	0	0	58	42	81	19
Share of total consumption	100	5	9	13	24	54	24	76	37	63

Source: World Bank (2003b).

Regional data on per capita public education expenditure are presented in Table 4.12. It is interesting to note that, with the exception of Petén (which is very sparsely populated), the highest per capita expenditure occurs in the metropolitan region, despite the fact that it has the lowest levels of poverty. Once again, this would suggest poor targeting of the public expenditure in essential areas such as education.

Although the geographical allocation of the public expenditure in Guatemala remains far from optimal, prior to 1985 it was even more concentrated in the metropolitan region. The 1985 constitution required that an important percentage of the ordinary resources of the state be channeled to municipalities in the interior (data not shown in the earlier tables, which are limited to addressing the expenditure of central government). In addition, social funds (government entities that target expenditures to poorer regions) have become important since the 1990s.

Expenditure Priorities of International Aid Donors

The government of Guatemala classifies international assistance into four broad categories: (1) growth, stability, and competitiveness; (2) equity, social protection, and human development; (3) natural resources and the environment; and (4) modernization of the state. Details on aid in the pipeline in 2004 are shown in Table 4.13.

If we compare Tables 4.2 and 4.13, we find that both the first postwar government and the aid donors assigned priority to economic development and human development, followed closely by governance and improvement of

Table 4.12 Expenditure on Education Per Capita, by Region

Region	% Relative Poverty	Indigenous Prevalence	Public Expenditure (dollars PPP[a])			
			1999	2000	2001	2002
Metropolitan	11.7	14.5	141.6	142.9	142.0	110.9
Southeast	65.5	5.0	93.8	102.7	113.9	98.2
Southwest	72.1	64.9	92.1	101.5	112.3	98.0
Central	43.1	45.5	91.6	96.0	106.4	91.8
Northwest	79.2	77.1	84.8	89.7	101.1	89.8
Northeast	49.9	13.1	81.0	86.1	117.5	86.6
North	75.3	93.5	84.8	87.5	97.6	79.6
Petén	59.3	28.7	179.2	205.1	213.4	188.3
National average			102.9	108.7	119.0	99.3

Source: Cely, Mostajo, and Gregory (2003).
Note: a. PPP = purchasing power parity.

Table 4.13 Matrix of Aid Agencies and Sectors, 2003 (US$ million)

Sectors	Germany	Canada	Denmark	Spain	US	Finland	France	Italy	Japan	Norway	Netherlands	Sweden	Switzerland	OAS[a]	CABEI[b]	IDB[c]	WB[d]	UN	EU	Totals
Growth, stability, and competitiveness																				
Productive infrastructure				0.3	0.6									0.1	85			0.1		85.7
Local development		7.4		0.4			0.1	4.1						0.1		49	16	0	4.2	80.7
Energy/roads	10								25					0.2		112	19	0.1		166
Small and medium enterprises	1.5										0					46		0	7.4	55.5
Training/labor market				1.7				0.1		0.4				0.2		9.9				12.3
Technology						0								1		14				14.6
Commercial integration		0.5						0.9						0.9						2.3
Competitiveness	1.5			0.1								0.1		0.1		8.2	25	0		34.8
Financial sector	0.7															79	128	0.3		208
Subtotal I	14	7.9	0	2.5	0.6	0	0.1	5.1	25	0.4	0	0.1	0	2.6	85	318	187	0.4	12	661
Equity, social protection, and human development																				
Pre-investment																3.2	0.1			3.3
Social investment	8.7				8.5		0			1.7		0.1		0.1	85	14				109
Health	0.8	2.1						0.8		0.7		1.5				51		2.3	9.2	76.9

continues

Table 4.13 Continued

Sectors	Germany	Canada	Denmark	Spain	US	Finland	France	Italy	Japan	Norway	Netherlands	Sweden	Switzerland	OAS[a]	CABEI[b]	IDB[c]	WB[d]	UN	EU	Totals
Education	5.3	4.6			8.4					3.4	0			1.3		0.1	54	0.4	26	104
Urban development and housing												1.6								1.6
Resettlement and lands												0.2					19	0		19.3
Indigenous sector, gender, and culture	0.6			0.6			0	0.1		2.4	0.1	2.1		0.1		0.2		0.8	0.5	7.7
Human rights	0.4	4.8	0		2		0			3.3	0.2	0.9	0.4	0.4				0.5	10	23.1
Emergencies										0.1										0.1
Peace process										0.3	0.8	0.1	0.4	0.8				1.5	18	25.4
Human development	2.7					2.6	0	0.9		0.6		0.6		0.9		3.1		0.1	2.5	10.4
Subtotal II	19	12	0	0.6	19	2.6	0	1.8	0	13	1.1	7.1	0.8	3.5	85	72	73	5.7	67	381
Natural resources and environment																				
Agriculture				0.6	13			0.2		1.4			0.2	0.3		23		1.6		40
Water/sanitation/ irrigation	21			2.4											85	50		0	11	169
Natural resource conservation	0.1				3.9					0.6	6.2		0.5			4.2		0.6	2.8	19.2
Subtotal III	21	0	0	3.7	17	0	0	0.2	0	2	6.2	0	0.7	0.3	85	77	0	2.3	14	228

continues

Table 4.13 Continued

Sectors	Germany	Canada	Denmark	Spain	U.S.A.	Finland	France	Italy	Japan	Norway	Netherlands	Sweden	Switzerland	OAS[a]	CABEI[b]	IDB[c]	WB[d]	UN	EU	Totals
Modernization of the state																				
Dialogue and democracy	2.3									0.4				6		0.1		0	12	23.7
Justice/security			0.1	0.2	2		0			1.2		1.6	0.4	0.1		7.4	14	1	25	53.2
Economic sector							0					0.4					16	0		0.4
Fiscal and tax sector					0.7					0.7						0.3	16			17.1
Support to executive/governance				1.3			0				3.1			0.7		4		0		9.8
Customs and land cadastre										1.6			3.5					0.2	1.9	7.1
Municipal and regional development	6.2														85	19			25	134
Others	1			2.4	11					8.4				1.3		25	1.3	0.2	44	94.9
Subtotal IV	9.5	0	0.1	3.9	13	0	0.1	0	0	12	3.1	4.4	3.9	8.1	85	56	32	1.4	108	340
Totals	63	19	0.2	11	50	2.6	0.2	7.1	25	27	10	12	5.4	15	338	522	292	9.9	201	1,609

Source: Inter-American Development Bank (2004).

Notes: a. OAS = Organization of American States. b. CABEI = Central American Bank for Economic Integration. c. IDB = Inter-American Development Bank. d. WB = World Bank.

the democratic state. The first sector—which includes productive infrastructure; the financial sector; support for micro-, small, and medium businesses; labor and public training; competitiveness and commercial integration—absorbs roughly 40 percent of total aid. The second—covering social investment, health, housing, gender, culture, the indigenous sector, human rights, and lands—represents close to 25 percent. The third—which includes agriculture, potable water, sanitation, irrigation, and the environment—receives approximately 15 percent. Finally, the remaining 20 percent is channeled to the fourth sector, which includes activities related to the process of modernization of legislative, judicial, and executive institutions and the municipalities and development councils.

The macroeconomic effects of international assistance have not been a topic of much concern in Guatemala, given its relatively low levels. Problems related to appreciation in the exchange rate are attributed to remittances from Guatemalans working abroad, the amount of which far exceeds aid from the international agencies.

Efforts to Reform the Budget Process

Congress tends to make only minor changes to the draft budget sent to it by the executive branch (see Table 4.14), in part because the ruling party held the majority in the legislature in the 1996–2000 period and again from 2000 to 2004. A larger difference tends to arise between the budget as approved by Congress and the ultimate execution of the budget. In some years, execution has been almost 20 percent below what was budgeted. Major disparities occur at the ministerial level, as there are ministries and secretariats that underexe-

Table 4.14   Expenditure Budget (millions of quetzals)

Year	Presented by Executive	Approved by Congress	Executed	Executed/ Approved (%)
1995	9,559.7	9,812.7	8,263.3	84.2
1996	11,345.6	11,345.5	9,418.1	83.0
1997	13,840.9	13,840.9	11,843.1	85.6
1998	15,982.1	16,402.8	15,929.9	97.1
1999	19,289.7	19,402.5	19,282.0	99.4
2000	22,310.3	22,310.4	19,802.2	88.8
2001	24,933.1	22,780.7	22,179.3	97.4
2002	26,049.1	23,938.7	23,512.3	98.2
2003	27,229.7	29,688.6	27,542.1	92.8
2004	33,020.9	33,020.9	27,069.4	82.0

Source: Available at http://www.minfin.gob.gt (2005).

cute while others overexecute. Unfortunately, the ministries and secretariats that have underexecuted include priority institutions such as the Ministries of Education and Health.

Nevertheless, Guatemala has made great efforts in recent years to improve the financial management and control of public resources through the Integrated Financial Administration and Control System (SIAF) supported by the World Bank.[16] SIAF now serves as the basis for executing and tracking internal operations, budget formulation discussions with the Ministry of Finance, and issuance of financial statements to the Comptroller General's Office (OCG) for ex-post audit.

Financial management units have been created and are responsible for agency budgets, accounting, and cash management operations. Accounting data entered into the system become instantly available through fiber optic cable to all appropriate users in real time, forming the basis of an audit trail and preventing the payment of nonbudgeted commitments.

Arrears to suppliers have been virtually eliminated, with payments now made on average within seventy-two hours after entry of data into SIAF. This compares to an average of three months in the mid-1990s, resulting in overcommitments, loose controls, and a supplier/agency practice of entering the long payment queue before services or goods were actually delivered. This required a reengineering and simplification of procedures in the Ministry of Finance: some 130 steps to effect payment have been reduced to twelve. The sharp reduction in payment periods, along with complementary reforms in procurement procedures described below, has contributed to sharply reduced prices for many goods sold to the government.

Transparency has been enhanced, as more than 1,000 users in the public administration have access to SIAF accounts for their respective responsibilities. Full access in real time to budget performance is provided to the Offices of the President and Vice President, the Finance Commission of the Congress, and the OCG. In addition, an Internet website (http://sicoin.minfin.gob.gt) in operation since mid-1998 is updated monthly.

Public investment is being reformed in collaboration with the Secretariat of Planning (SEGEPLAN) through the design of new procedures and manuals covering the formulation, evaluation, and monitoring of projects; the creation of a virtual database for investment projects; and linkage with a supporting software system that will include a georeferenced national investment map.

Training has been a top priority of the project. Since 1996 thousands of public employees have attended courses on SIAF at the national university and a major private university. These courses disseminate the system to potential entrants into the government as well as to private-sector accountants and auditors.

Despite these important gains, a substantial reform agenda remains. First, timely reporting and oversight of budget execution need to be strengthened. SIAF already provides early warning signals on budget, cash management, and public credit operations. The mere existence of such tools and information does not, however, ensure their full or proper use.

Assessing budget performance and redirecting expenditure toward important social goals is a second priority. An ultimate goal of financial management reforms is to create the framework for a results-oriented budgeting process. This means moving from a detailed focus on incremental annual changes to a more comprehensive understanding and multiannual review. This also involves moving from the large amount of physical indicators already in the system (which have no explicit links to unit costs) to a more selective and cost-based assessment of budget performance.

Budget oversight not only by Congress but also by the media and the public in general, is undermined by (1) knowledge gaps about SIAF programs and their use; (2) unduly complicated reporting of budget execution by the executive branch; and (3) institutional capacity constraints among legislators in budget preparation, oversight, and evaluation.

Finally, the strengthening of the audit function has been hampered by the lack of modern legislation that would permit the OCG to proactively concentrate on problem areas and selective auditing, rather than requiring a review of all government financial transactions, and would allow for systems reviews, outsourcing selected audits to private firms, and reducing requirements that all financial transactions be recorded on paper.

Transparency and Corruption

The System of Information on Contracts and Acquisitions of the State, known as Guatecompras, is another recent expenditure-management initiative, backed by the World Bank and the United Nations Development Programme. This is an Internet-based electronic market that the government uses to buy and contract goods and services.

Guatecompras increases transparency in the procurement process. Businesspeople become aware of opportunities, public agencies that buy know all the bids available, and citizens can oversee the processes and know the prices paid for each acquisition. The goals are greater competition, less corruption, and greater efficiency.

Guatecompras also allows for government acquisitions to be used as an instrument to promote an expanded and diversified private sector, because it facilitates protection against monopolies, encourages gradual growth of productivity, and makes possible the expansion of local economies and small and medium enterprises.

On the revenue side, the Ministry of Finance (MINFIN) and SAT provide information on their websites, including not only statistics but also studies on fiscal matters that have been commissioned from international consultants. In other words, the Internet has become, as in many countries, the most important tool for accentuating transparency, for it facilitates the early divulgence of information and unlimited access. These recent advances in the tools of transparency are not due to the Peace Accords but rather are part of the process of technological evolution that computers and the Internet permit.

Despite these initiatives, corruption is still a serious problem. The previous government (the Portillo administration, which governed from 2000 to 2004) has a reputation as one of the most corrupt. The president fled to Mexico and is still at large, his vice president spent several months in prison, and other officials of that government have been prosecuted—all this in spite of the reforms described above. In this sense, the nominal public expenditure executed is fiction. As a result of corruption, effective public expenditure that reaches the citizens is lower than what is recorded in the accounting data.

Two principal types of corruption have affected Guatemala. The first is the appropriation of public resources by government officials, either by diverting funds to phantom companies or by taking bribes for the granting of public contracts and so on. The other type consists of granting public works contracts to companies belonging to relatives or close friends. This second type is "more sophisticated," because instead of overt appropriation of public resources there may only be a restriction on competition. In theory, SIAF and Guatecompras should lead to a reduction of both of these scourges.

It is not surprising that Guatemala has a low score in the Transparency International (TI) rankings of countries according to perceived corruption. In 1998, when the country was first included in the TI list, it ranked 60 out of 85 countries (a lower ranking denotes more corruption). In 2004, Guatemala ranked 123 out of 146 countries (Transparency International 2004).

The post of the transparency and anticorruption commissioner was created with a mandate to guide and advise the president and the ministers of state in respect to the adoption of mechanisms to prevent, detect, and eradicate corruption and to promote transparency. This post replaced a commission that was created for these purposes in 2003, an effort that did not prosper, ironically owing to problems arising from lack of transparency. Given the fact that it is an incipient institution, it is too early to evaluate its results.

Conclusion

Guatemala's experience regarding compliance with the Peace Accords surely has similarities to and differences from other international experiences. This concluding section looks at the Guatemalan peace process in context and examines some key contrasts.

First of all, the end of the conflict did not come because of international pressure. The international community certainly cooperated in the reaching of peace. Spain contributed to holding the first meeting between the government and the guerrillas in October 1987. During the negotiation process, Sweden and especially Mexico and Norway also contributed actively, offering their territories as venues for numerous encounters.[17] The UN also played an important role during and after the negotiations. The United States was interested in ending the conflict as well: with the end of the Cold War, the polarization existing in Guatemala came to be seen as an anomaly that atrophied normal development.

Although the international community helped to press both sides to make their positions more flexible, the conflict came to an end primarily by decision of those involved: the government, the army, and the guerrillas. This differs from many peace processes in which the international community practically forced an end to the conflict.

Second, the Peace Accords in Guatemala were exceptional in their breadth and depth. As already mentioned, in Nicaragua there were no peace accords, and in El Salvador the accords were very limited in their scope. In Guatemala, twelve agreements were signed, and an international and national framework was created to oversee their implementation.

In 1985, a National Constituent Assembly had approved a new political constitution for Guatemala. In the Assembly, parties of a wide range of ideologies were represented, and only the guerrilla Left was absent. The constitution represented the first great national accord on the guidelines that would govern the performance of the Guatemalan state. The Peace Accords were an important complement to this new constitution. The Peace Accords, for example, addressed matters that had been dealt with quickly in the constitution, such as agrarian issues and the rights of the indigenous peoples.

Third, Guatemala has failed to increase tax collection, so that it has not been able to comply effectively with the agreements in the Peace Accords. The goal of 12 percent of GDP has not been reached, and therefore many of the commitments established in the accords have not been met. The adoption of more aggressive policies to address social needs, for example, has been undermined by lack of funding and serious problems of inefficiency. Little has been done to promote rural development or to resolve the core problem of access to land. And with some exceptions, most national institutions remain weak and subject to patronage-driven personnel changes after each change of government.

Since the signing of the Peace Accords there have been three governments in Guatemala. Although the different governments have mentioned the relevance of the Peace Accords and say that they are contemplated in public policy, it is undeniable that interest in the accords has decreased. Almost a decade after the signing of the final peace accord, there is a doubt as to whether it would not have been more realistic to approve more modest Peace Accords that could have been complied with more effectively (like those of El Salvador). Did the Guatemalans agree to unrealistic Peace Accords with which it would be impossible to comply? This is a question that will always persist.

Fourth, Guatemalans have defined the pace of implementation in the peace process, not international donors. Just as national players essentially determined the end of the conflict, compliance (or noncompliance) with the accords has been principally a national responsibility.

Guatemala has had several Consultative Group meetings, at which its peace program has been evaluated and criticized by the international donors and by representatives of Guatemalan civil society. In one form or another, the governments have passed the test of the donors, and the impression has been left that although there is no effective compliance with the many commitments in the Peace Accords, it is not the case that the governments do not respect them or do not take them into account in their public policies. The present administration has refused to call a new Consultative Group, with the argument that the needs for external resources are minimal.

Finally, the Peace Accords have mixed and competed with other economic agendas. One of these is macroeconomic stability and in particular control of the fiscal deficit. This budgetary restriction means that there are discrepancies between the greater public expenditure that the Peace Accords require and the containment of expenditure that macroeconomic stability demands in the absence of higher revenues.[18]

The Peace Accords also complement and compete with what might be called a strategy of poverty reduction along the lines suggested by international agencies.[19] The reduction of poverty would be in consonance with the accords, but the strategy does not necessarily build on the instruments agreed upon when the Peace Accords were signed.

Another agenda, a more competitive one, is structural reform. The country has privatized and deregulated, again along the lines suggested by the international agencies. For sectors on the Left, this type of reform enters into contradiction with what was agreed upon in the Peace Accords, although the accords mentioned nothing in this regard. The critics hold that these pro-market processes contradict agreements that were of a more social and political nature.

A related agenda is the economy's growing openness. Guatemala has signed a series of free trade agreements (FTAs), of which the most recent and the one with the greatest potential impact is the one negotiated with the United States, which entered into effect in 2006. This insertion into the world economy could be considered an unavoidable phase of globalization. The Peace Accords, however, were essentially national accords and hardly pronounced on these subjects of international economy. And once again, sectors on the Left point to contradictions between what was agreed upon and the impacts that could result from this greater economic opening.

These features of the national and international context help to explain the limited success so far in implementing the statebuilding agenda set forth in the Guatemalan Peace Accords. Public finance is a central part of this agenda, as the accords call for increasing revenue and expenditure to extend government services so as to redress the exclusion and inequities that underpinned the conflict. The country's economic elite did not embrace this agenda unequivocally, and the leverage of the international community and former guerrillas to press for compliance was modest at best. Moreover, although the accords were popular domestically, no systematic effort was made to mobilize popular support for their implementation. Even though public opinion strongly favors larger public expenditures, there is no corresponding awareness of the need to increase revenues. Under these circumstances, it is not surprising that the Peace Accords failed to trigger a great transformation in Guatemalan society. Instead, historians are likely to view the accords as just one step in a lengthy process of political and socioeconomic development.

Notes

1. Essentially, the Salvadoran accords were limited to purging the army, strengthening democratic institutions, and supporting reinsertion of the guerrillas.

2. The commission was made up of members of government and the ex-guerrillas, whose objective was to monitor compliance with the accords.

3. IEMA, a tax on net assets or gross sales, was a way of guaranteeing minimum collection of income tax, as it was creditable to it. The private sector consistently opposed it.

4. The shortfall is even greater, in that the gross tax ratio includes collection that is refunded to exporting companies (exports are subject to 0 percent VAT). The more relevant tax burden is the net rate, which as shown in Table 4.3 tends to be 0.5 percent less than the gross rate. The Peace Accords did not specify whether the tax-ratio target should be gross or net.

5. Guatemala has the oldest base in the world, according to the IMF's International Financial Statistics (IFS).

6. Another slight underestimate of the tax ratio in Table 4.3 is that the recent figures do not include the property tax, whereas they were included when the Peace Accords were signed. It is no longer recorded, as the municipalities now collect most of this tax. In 2003 it represented 0.14 percent of GDP.

7. The fall in relation to GDP has been close to 1.9 to 1.1 percent. This reduction has been partially affected by the increase of VAT on imports, as shown in Table 4.4.

8. According to the Economic Commission for Latin America and the Caribbean (2004), taxation in Guatemala would be reduced by close to 4 percent of total taxation with the implementation of DR-CAFTA, although the positive impact on growth could compensate part of this fiscal loss through a greater intake of other taxes, particularly income tax and the value added tax.

9. The overall tax burden based on household survey data is 19.7 percent, much higher than that obtained by the division of the tax collected into the GDP (which, as already seen, does not reach 12 percent). This discrepancy is attributed primarily to the fact that the household survey does not capture the totality of the national income (total income represented by the survey is only 62.3 percent of the income reported in the national accounts). The assumption that the underestimate of income is proportional across all deciles is obviously a strong one. If the degree of underestimation varies

across deciles, the finding of overall neutrality would be affected. If survey income is more severely underestimated for poorer households (e.g., owing to failure to capture nonmarket incomes), then the true tax incidence is more progressive than shown in Table 4.5. If, on the contrary, it is more severely underestimated for richer households (e.g., owing to stronger incentives for concealment), then the true tax incidence is more regressive.

10. Figures for 2003 indicate that 271.8 million quetzals (the equivalent of 0.14 percent of the GDP) in property taxes were collected, 99.7 percent directly by the municipalities.

11. The data do not include aid from US and European nongovernmental organizations (NGOs). There is no record of these figures, but they are believed to be substantially less than official development assistance.

12. The International Organization of Migration estimates that the migrant population could well be more than a million. The enormous gap between these estimates could be due to the fact that many migrants, given their illegal status, "escape" from the census, fearing deportation.

13. Before ENCOVI, only a Survey of Family Income and Expenditure (ENIGFAM) had been made in 1998–1999 and a much older one in the 1979–1981 period.

14. It is possible to carry out this exercise only for public services that are consumed directly by households, for example, education and health. Expenditure on public goods to which specific consumption in each household cannot be assigned, such as roads and security, cannot be subjected to this type of evaluation.

15. To monitor this, it is crucial to periodically hold new ENCOVIs to allow for replication of the World Bank exercise.

16. SIAF has been an integral process that envisions a new legal framework, reengineering of processes, permanent training, application of state-of-the-art technology, public-sector telecommunications network, telecommunications and hardware equipment, liaison with the banking system, a government electronic gateway, and software that is the tool to support all this government modernization process. For details, see World Bank (2002a).

17. The number of meetings held by each country was as follows: Mexico, 9; Norway, 4; Spain, 2; and Sweden, 1.

18. The International Monetary Fund (IMF) has played a minor role in Guatemala. Since the Peace Agreements the country has had just two agreements: one in 2002 and the other in 2003. In both cases the IMF has not disbursed any credit.

19. Guatemala does not have a formal poverty reduction strategy, as do some other countries, including Nicaragua and Bolivia.

5

National Ownership and International Trusteeship: The Case of Timor-Leste

Emilia Pires and Michael Francino

This chapter analyzes the public finance dimensions of building a new state "from scratch" in Timor-Leste (East Timor), beginning with the establishment of the United Nations Transitional Administration in East Timor (UNTAET) in 1999 after two centuries of Portuguese colonial rule and a quarter century of Indonesian occupation. There were no guidelines for designing a new state, nor any comparable experiences, with the partial exception of the UN administration in Kosovo that had begun the previous year. The statebuilding enterprise was marked by numerous misunderstandings between the Timorese leadership, which had almost no prior exposure to public administration, and the international community, which had no experience of inheriting what appeared to them to be a tabula rasa. In recounting this experience, we draw on our perspectives as participants in this process from the national and international sides.

We sketch the historical background of Timor-Leste, with particular focus on public finance; provide a brief chronology of key events during the UNTAET period; and recount the formation of the Ministry of Planning and Finance (MPF). We also discuss the issues and debates around resource mobilization and cover the budget and expenditure execution. We analyze some economic failures and efforts to address issues related to capacity development, then conclude with some lessons and tentative recommendations for future missions and some reflections on the role of public finance in statebuilding.

Historical Background

To understand the challenges faced by the Timorese in the statebuilding and economic reconstruction process, it is worth examining briefly the country's history under Portuguese and then Indonesian rule.

Timor-Leste is the eastern half of the island of Timor.[1] The western half is the Indonesian province of West Timor, the island having been partitioned between the Portuguese and the Dutch colonial rulers of what is now Indonesia in a series of diplomatic agreements beginning in 1851. Across the Timor Sea to the south is Australia, just 500 kilometers (300 miles) away. Also part of the national territory are the smaller islands of Ataúro and Jaco and the enclave of Oecussi situated in the eastern part of West Timor.

The Portuguese Colonial Period

Timor became known to the Portuguese in the sixteenth century, although they did not formally establish colonial rule in Timor-Leste until 1769. Timor-Leste became an "autonomous district" of Portugal in 1896, with its status changing between district and province several times until 1951, when it was again made a province (Vaz 1964).

The Portuguese hold on the territory remained tenuous until early in the twentieth century in the face of resistance from the liurais (kings) of the many small kingdoms of Timor-Leste and several indigenous rebellions, some lasting as long as thirty years (Jolliffe 1978; Dunn 1983). From 1912 onward, these small kingdoms gradually were incorporated into an administrative system of districts, each with a Portuguese administrator. The Portuguese governed by indirect rule through the liurais, playing on the ethnic diversity of the population to keep the Timorese divided and easier to control (Thatcher 1993).

Portugal was neutral during World War II, but neither Australia nor Japan respected that neutrality. The Australians invaded Timor in 1941, and the Japanese invaded two months later to fight the Australians. An estimated 40,000 Timorese died during the war, which left the island desolate and economically ruined.[2] At the end of World War II, Portugal quickly reestablished control.

In the first five-year plan of Portuguese Timor, in the 1950s, almost half the money available was earmarked for the reconstruction of Dili, the capital city. The remainder was divided evenly between development of agriculture and livestock resources and the construction of infrastructure in the hinterland. A primary school system was set up, and by 1974 there were 456 schools with some 60,000 students.[3] Illiteracy rates nevertheless remained high, at more than 90 percent, with a school attendance rate of only 40 percent by that date (Ranck 1977).

It was not until 1963 that some of Dili's streets were paved and electricity introduced. The main link with the outside world was the airport at Baucau, also completed in 1963. Until new port facilities were constructed in Dili harbor in the mid-1960s, the unloading of vessels was carried out by using landing barges. Fuel was unloaded by rolling drums into the harbor and letting the current slowly carry them to the beach—a method still in use as recently as 1990. By the late 1960s there was an embryonic tourist industry, and coffee, rubber, and copra were being exported in modest quantities. Grain production had increased, as had sweet potato and manioc crops, and by 1974 the province was close to being self-supporting in food production (Thatcher 1993).

Despite this progress, Timor-Leste was a drain on the Portuguese exchequer, with domestic revenues covering only about half of the cost of administration.[4] Sources of domestic revenue included taxes on exports and imports and a personal tax imposed on every male household head, irrespective of whether or not he had a job.[5] There were also electricity fees in Dili (for those who had a meter), and water and land taxes, again mainly applicable to those living in the capital.

Under the Missionary Agreement between the government and the Catholic Church, the church was considered a partner in human development activities in Timor-Leste. The government provided teachers and school materials to the church, which in turn provided educational services. The church also enjoyed tax exemption privileges. Each church mission also had a small health clinic for which the government provided some medicine and nurse training for one catechist, ensuring a basic minimal medical service.

The colonial administration was both paternalistic and repressive. Any attempt by Timorese to become politically active led to exile in Africa or Portugal. The Portuguese secret police (International and State Defense Police; PIDE) were active, and there was tight censorship of the press, radio, and other media coming into the province. It was not until 1967 that outside journalists were allowed into the colony. These factors resulted in the lack of an independence movement.

In 1974, after the overthrow of the Marcelo Caetano regime in Portugal, there was a call from the new Portuguese authorities for the establishment of political parties in Timor-Leste.[6] The first to form was the Timorese Democratic Union (UDT), representing Timorese and Mestizo elites and other conservative interests. This was followed by the Timorese Association of Social Democrats (ASDT), a nationalist party with social democratic ideals that soon changed to become the Revolutionary Front for the Liberation of Timor-Leste (FRETILIN). A third party, the Timorese Popular Democratic Association (APODETI), advocated integration with Indonesia as an autonomous province.[7] Its rhetoric was anticolonial and antiwhite (Ranck 1977).

In 1974–1975 the Portuguese administration attempted to lead the Timorese through an accelerated decolonization process, with these three political parties competing for power. This was a period of chaos, confusion, and turmoil, but it was also characterized by feelings of pride, exhilaration, and hope (Thatcher 1993). There were three issues on which the general population seemed to agree: (1) a need for improved education; (2) a desire for Western-style employment; and (3) nonintegration with Indonesia (Jolliffe 1978; Nicol 1978).

The clumsiness of Portuguese attempts at decolonization, combined with naïveté on the part of Timorese political leaders and destabilizing tactics emanating from Jakarta, culminated in a three-week civil war between FRETILIN and UDT in August–September 1975—an event that continues to haunt Timorese society. FRETILIN won the war and took over the administration of the territory. On November 28, 1975, FRETILIN declared Timor-Leste independent, a unilateral act not recognized by the international community. Indonesia responded by invading Timor on December 7, 1975. In June 1976 Timor-Leste was formally incorporated into Indonesia. The Indonesian occupation would last for twenty-four years, in the face of determined Timorese resistance, both active and passive.

Indonesian Occupation

During the Indonesian occupation, money flowed into Timor-Leste, most going into unsuccessful campaigns to "win the minds and hearts" of the Timorese. According to Indonesian government sources, Timor-Leste received the largest central government allocation on a per capita basis of any Indonesian province, but this allocation included the budget for the occupation army. More roads and bridges were constructed, mainly to facilitate military movement from one end of the island to the other to control what were termed terrorists and rebels. They were not in the main built to serve the Timorese population, who for most of the Indonesian period were not allowed to travel more than five kilometers from their homes without special permits.

The gross domestic product (GDP) per capita in Timor-Leste in 1996 amounted to about a third of the Indonesian level. The Indonesian government subsidized civil servants' wages with rice rations or goods to compensate for low wages.[8] Officially, transfers from the Indonesian government covered some 85 percent of current and investment expenditures. Taking into consideration the (underreported) exports from Timor-Leste, high levels of corruption, and other administrative inefficiencies, the actual net flow of resources into Timor-Leste was probably considerably lower (Joint Assessment Mission 1999).

As Indonesia's control strengthened, it imposed a personal tax that, unlike the Portuguese system, was applied to all with an income. Land and water taxes were charged where possible, and import and export taxes existed on most goods and commodities, as did license fees of all types.

The Catholic Church, as the largest institution in Timor-Leste after the state apparatus, continued to enjoy a number of privileges. The Indonesian government again considered the church as a development partner and provided more assistance than it had received from the Portuguese administration, or for that matter from the current one. In the field of education the Indonesian government not only provided teachers and materials but also constructed school buildings.[9] The church also expanded its health care activities during this time. Wherever the government had a health clinic, so did the church. The church clinics were generally preferred to the state clinics by the people, because of their distrust of anything Indonesian.

Independence Struggle

After the Indonesian invasion, many Timorese sought refuge in the mountains, where they supported the resistance led by FRETILIN. Constant bombings forced them to come down from the mountains in 1979, at which point they were relocated in "resettlement villages," distant from both their homes and the zones of fighting, where they were subjected to a rigorous system of internal control.

The occupation and continuous military campaigns had a devastating effect. Many Timorese died of hunger. Others were imprisoned or disappeared. People were not allowed to grow their own food. Meanwhile, land outside the villages was devoted to the cultivation of cash crops for export in agricultural projects set up by the military. Land was transferred to migrants from areas outside Timor-Leste as part of the government's "Indonesianization" strategy. Timor-Leste's lingua franca, Tetun, was banned, and Bahasa Indonesian was taught in schools. Informers, directed by appointed elders (*katuas*), became responsible for the surveillance of groups of ten to fifteen families (Taylor 1994).

By 1979 FRETILIN was almost destroyed as an organization. All of its original leaders had been captured or killed, leaving behind a small group led by Xanana Gusmão that managed during 1980 to reorganize the movement. One of the first steps was the creation of the National Council of Maubere Resistance (CNRM), set up in 1987 in an effort to restructure the resistance movement along more inclusive, nonpartisan lines. Xanana Gusmão resigned from FRETILIN, helping to constitute the Armed Forces for the National Liberation of Timor-Leste (FALINTIL), until then the armed wing of FRETILIN, as a nonpartisan, national force. FRETILIN, in turn, rescinded its claim to be sole legitimate representative of the Timorese people. The changes also involved recognition of the role of all nationalists—such as students and political parties such as UDT—in the struggle for self-determination.

The massacre of independence supporters, mainly youth, at Dili's Santa Cruz cemetery on November 12, 1991, sparked a resurgence in opposition to Indonesian rule and refocused the world's attention on the Timor-Leste cause. Xanana Gusmão's capture and jailing in November 1992 was followed by the jointly awarded Nobel Peace Prize in 1996 to Timor-Leste Bishop Carlos Belo and leading Timor-Leste international spokesperson José Ramos-Horta, events that also helped to keep Timor-Leste alive on the world's agenda.

Indonesian President Suharto's fall from power in 1998, following a collapsing economy and widespread street protests, raised hopes that Jakarta would finally reconsider its position on Timor-Leste. In June 1998 the new president,

B. J. Habibie, announced that he was willing to consider giving Timor-Leste a "special status" within Indonesia. This was not considered sufficient by Timorese independence supporters. Following a series of United Nations–backed talks, Indonesia and Portugal signed an agreement on May 5, 1999, to allow the Timorese to determine their future in a United Nations–supervised referendum.

These developments sparked a further restructuring of the Timorese resistance. At an April 1998 convention in Portugal, the National Council of Timorese Resistance (CNRT) was established as the umbrella body for all Timorese resistance organizations. The CNRT name and flag were used by the United Nations Mission in Timor-Leste (UNAMET) on the August 30, 1999, ballot paper to represent the independence option. A resounding majority—78.5 percent of the voters—supported independence.

From Referendum to Independence

On September 4, following the announcement of this result, a local militia organized by the Indonesian military went on a rampage. "Black September," as the Timorese describe the systemic campaign of violence, looting, and arson, sent the CNRT into survival mode, scrambling to escape from the violence and to save as many lives as possible. The violence stopped only after President Habibie announced on September 12, 1999, that Indonesia would accept a UN peacekeeping force for Timor-Leste and with the arrival in Dili of the first troops of the international intervention forces, led by Australia, on September 20.

Dealing with the resulting humanitarian crisis required the resources of both the UN and the CNRT. Common sense dictated that the CNRT leadership should be involved because they knew the terrain and had the trust of the people, yet UN officials pointedly refused to involve them on the spurious grounds that they were members of a political party. Most UN officials in fact saw Timor-Leste as a "failed state" rather than a country that had successfully fought a twenty-four-year war of independence. This faulty perception colored their attitudes toward Timorese on a variety of levels.

At the time, the lead author of this chapter was in Jakarta, the Indonesian capital, coordinating a small Timorese think tank at the request of CNRT president Xanana Gusmão, who had been asked by the UN to prepare a development plan for postreferendum Timor-Leste. Xanana described the kind of administration he foresaw for Timor-Leste, a small and lean bureaucracy. A major focus of discussions centered on what to do with the FALINTIL, which had begun as the armed wing of the political party FRETILIN and was transformed during the period of resistance by Xanana as its commander into the Timorese national armed forces. This was one group within Timorese society that could not be neglected, given that without them we would not even have been discussing a development plan.

This was not the first time the Timorese had met to devise a plan for the country. In two previous forums, Timorese from all over the world, including from inside Timor-Leste, had come together to discuss future plans. The first forum took place in Algarve, Portugal, in October 1998, where approximately forty Timorese of different professional and political backgrounds met at the invitation of José Ramos-Horta (who later became foreign minister and in 2006 would become interim prime minister) to start brainstorming about a development plan for Timor-Leste. A follow-up conference took place in Melbourne, Australia, in April 1999, where more than 300 people met, half of them Timorese and half international friends, to produce the first Timorese Strategic Development Plan.

By the time many of us met again in Jakarta, our self-confidence was rather high. We felt confident in our ability to organize a conference with the aim of enlisting international aid to support us at the beginning of our self-governing process, until such time as we could produce enough revenues of our own to support the kind of expenditure we envisaged. During this time the World Bank approached us, and we began to establish a close informal relationship with them. Perhaps realizing our ignorance, the Bank took five of our economists to Washington as part of a training package. Initially we welcomed the Bank's help in our discussions on future plans for our country. Partly due to the crisis resulting from the events of Black September, however, which was accompanied by movement restrictions that affected the regularity of our meetings with Xanana, who was under house arrest, the planning discussions became more and more exclusive, often taking place between the World Bank and our leader only. The perception grew that the Bank had adopted the driver's seat of our planning processes, and this was accompanied by a loss in confidence in our own ability to drive the car again.

Nevertheless, we managed to organize ourselves sufficiently to enable us to take part in the World Bank–led Timor-Leste Joint Assessment Mission (JAM) in October 1999. At this point, the Timorese counterparts for the World Bank and the international community were mainly drawn from the Timorese diaspora. Inside Timor, most of the suitable people were just trying to survive the events of Black September. With financial assistance from the World Bank, we were able to put together a team of Timorese, including some crucial people from inside Timor. That intense month of working together in the JAM with international counterparts was a steep learning curve for the Timorese. Again we had another opportunity to discuss the kinds of governmental structures we wanted to create in Timor-Leste, including the number of ministries and the type of economy. We were exposed, for the first time, to how to put together a costing exercise for reconstructing a country from scratch.

UNTAET arrived in Dili on October 25, 1999, in the person of the Special Representative of the Secretary-General (SRSG), Sergio Vieira de Mello. World

Bank officers felt that UNTAET would be the most appropriate organization to employ capable Timorese to continue the work that they had already started with the JAM. There was no contingency plan to ensure Timorese participation in case UNTAET failed to do this, which is what in fact happened. It took UNTAET at least six months to establish its operations on the ground. Meanwhile, due to the urgency of mobilizing funds for the reconstruction process, the World Bank pushed on, working with a small nucleus of Timorese who at that time were part of the CNRT team supporting Xanana. Here again the Bank had an advantage over UNTAET, as the latter did not recognize CNRT as its counterpart, leading to much confusion in trying to identify appropriate counterparts.

The first donor pledging conference took place in Tokyo on December 17, 1999. Under the World Bank's leadership, the conference was very successful in raising the required funds: a total of US$523 million, of which $157 million was humanitarian aid and $366 million was in support of administrative capacity building and reconstruction.

The Timorese were focused on ensuring that we still played a key role in decisionmaking, specifically regarding how these funds were to be allocated and the approval process for programs and projects. At the time, we felt that the funds given to us by the international community were indeed ours, and hence we needed to make sure the money was used in the most appropriate way. In almost everything the World Bank consulted with us very closely. We never received an answer, however, to our question of where we Timorese would be in the structure that was going to be set up to manage the funds, the Trust Fund for East Timor (TFET). We were not looking to manage the funds ourselves, as we knew we had no capacity to do so. What we wanted to know was where the body was that was going to decide where to spend the money. We felt very strongly that our technical people needed to be part of that body, to ensure that funds were directed toward activities that we Timorese considered a high priority. Even the setting up of TFET was not a topic discussed in detail with the Timorese. We did not realize that we had two trust funds until very much later in the process. Nor did we understand that the second one, the Consolidated Trust Fund for East Timor (CFET) created by UNTAET, was meant to be our embryonic Treasury Single Account.

Some may say that it was naive of us to think that we should be managing the process. But when the Bank wanted a decision that was being opposed by some other international agency, we would be brought in immediately to become the arbitrator. We tended to decide in favor of the World Bank, because in spite of everything it was the only organization at the time that took pains to explain to us most of the things that were happening around us.

UNTAET had been given responsibilities by the 1999 United Nations Security Council Resolution 1272 that far exceeded those of any previous UN mission, with the exception of the Kosovo mission. It was responsible for security, law, and order; establishment of an effective administration; assurance of the provision of basic services; coordination of humanitarian, rehabilitation, and development assistance; and assistance in the establishment of conditions for sustainable development. An ambitious mandate indeed.

Immediately upon his arrival in the country, Sergio Vieira de Mello established a National Consultative Council (NCC), consisting of eleven Timorese representatives from the CNRT and four international staff. The council advised de Mello, who had full legislative and executive powers, on issues ranging from which laws to adopt to the rebuilding of shattered infrastructure and the provision of basic government services.

Six months later, after registering dissatisfaction from both the Timorese and international community, Sergio Vieira de Mello saw the need to broaden the NCC to make it more inclusive. At the same time, he felt it was time to bring the Timorese into the executive side of the government as part of the learning process. At the May 2000 Tibar Conference near Dili, an attempt by the CNRT to regain control of the reconstruction process that brought together Timorese and internationals to discuss ways of moving forward, de Mello launched the idea of a joint cabinet, which later became known as the first East Timor Transitional Administration (ETTA). He delegated as much of his executive powers as he was allowed to the ETTA. The NCC became the National Council (NC), a fully Timorese body with twenty-six appointed members, which was more representative of Timorese society. The new joint cabinet consisted of eight ministries, four led by Timorese and the others by internationals. A few weeks later José Ramos-Horta was added as minister of foreign affairs, bringing the Timorese total to five.[10]

On August 30, 2001, elections took place for the Constituent Assembly (CA), an eighty-eight-member body to write the first Timor-Leste constitution. This body replaced the NC, and the cabinet also changed to reflect the elected parties and become fully Timorese, led by a chief minister who was accountable to the SRSG. This was part of the capacity building of the leaders who would take the reins as UNTAET withdrew.

It was during this term that the Planning Commission was created to formulate the first Timor-Leste National Plan as part of UNTAET's strategy to set some directions for the future. At the same time donors were asked to prepare for another round of pledges for the next three years, the Budget Office having indicated there was a fiscal gap of approximately US$90 million for that three-year period.

Timor-Leste's first presidential election took place on April 14, 2002, between two candidates. There was no doubt in anyone's mind who was going to win, but democracy demands more than one contender! Francisco Xavier de Amaral, previous president of FRETILIN, did the honors of trying to compete with Xanana Gusmão, who won a landslide victory.

In hindsight, perhaps it would have been better to have invested the money spent on this election in the parliamentary election that had been promised by the UN but never took place.[11] We were told this election could not take place owing to the fact that there were not enough resources. So the Constituency Assembly made use of one tiny clause of their mandate that gave them the right to turn themselves into the first National Parliament of Timor-Leste without having to go back to the people. It appears that UNTAET did not feel that the clause was important enough to alert the people in their civic education program as part of the preparation for election. This continues to be a source of friction among many groups in Timorese society, and it undermines the current government's legitimacy in the eyes of the people.

On May 14, 2002, a second donor pledging conference took place in Dili. The donors were presented with the *East Timor Vision*, a booklet prepared by the Planning Commission containing Timor-Leste's first National Development Plan, the document that became the focus of all donor aid funds. The conference again was very successful in mobilizing external resources.

Three days later, on May 17, a new UN body, the United Nations Mission of Support for East Timor (UNMISET), was set up for a twelve-month period. Unlike UNTAET, UNMISET was no longer the administration. Instead, it was mandated to provide assistance to core administrative structures critical to the viability and political stability of Timor-Leste. It did so through the provision of 100 professional advisers.

May 20, 2002, witnessed the swearing in of the first president of an independent Timor-Leste, and the new Timorese government took office. By this time, the huge stock of goodwill that had existed between Timor-Leste and the international community had been largely dissipated, with profound consequences for future development efforts. In retrospect, there were faults on both sides. The civilian UN presence in Timor-Leste was too large and often unproductive. It pushed up prices, distorted economic relations, and, arguably, did little to develop the capacity and institutions that the new country desperately needed. The Timorese, for their part, were very anxious to seize control of the government apparatus without commensurate understanding of what was involved. On the international side, a smaller program with better qualified people, sustained over a longer period of time, could have been to everyone's advantage.

The Ministry of Planning and Finance

The nucleus of the MPF was formed with the establishment of the Central Fiscal Authority in January 2000. The report "Timor-Leste: A Strategy for Rebuilding Fiscal Management," prepared shortly thereafter by the Fiscal Affairs Department (FAD) of the International Monetary Fund (IMF), became the charter document for Timor-Leste's Central Fiscal Authority (CFA).[12] The scope of the report is succinctly stated in its preface:

> Mr. Sergio Vieira De Mello, the Special Representative of the Secretary-General (SRSG) in charge of the United Nations Transitional Administration in East Timor (UNTAET) requested technical assistance from the International Monetary Fund (IMF) in designing a wide range of fiscal institutions. . . . The work included the design of a Central Fiscal Authority and its particular areas of responsibilities: tax policy, tax administration, customs administration, and public expenditure management, including budget preparation and the development of a government treasury.

By and large, the report's recommendations were followed, although not always in detail or in the sequence recommended.

The Treasury was established on June 30, 2000. The MPF Budget Department was made responsible for developing the state general budget. The Treasury contributes to the budget preparation cycle by providing analysis and reports on budget implementation to the Council of Ministers (CoM) and to multinational agencies such as the World Bank, the Asian Development Bank, and the IMF (Kumar et al. 2004).

The basic accounting framework for Timor-Leste is the CFET, which operates as a Treasury Single Account.[13] The annual budget sets out the expected government revenues and the proposed appropriations for the fiscal year. An Appropriations Law provides for the appropriations from the CFET to the line agencies for the fiscal year. In preparing financial accounts, the Treasury follows the guidelines laid down by the International Accounting Standards Committee and the Institute of Internal Auditors (Kumar et al. 2004).

A Revenue Service for Timor-Leste was established under Regulation 1999–2001, and from 2000 to 2002 taxation laws were refined, new taxes introduced, and various taxation guides produced (Calcott 2004). A Large Taxpayer Unit was created for taxpayers with a turnover greater than US$1 million. Audit and Appeals Units were also set up. Administration and collection of taxes from the Timor Sea were based in a separate division, because applicable taxation laws were distinctly different from those applied to domestic taxes.[14]

The Customs Service, another MPF department, was given responsibilities to (1) regulate the import and export of goods or classes of goods, (2) establish and administer appropriate schedules of tariffs for the purposes of revenue collection, (3) collect trade taxes and duties, and (4) fight fiscal evasion and customs fraud. A Customs Code approved by the Council of Ministers in 2003 governs customs administration, principles, and activities (Lopes 2004).

A National Planning and Development Agency (NPDA) was set up within ETTA in 2000. This organization was responsible for providing a post-UNTAET national planning development framework and for coordinating resource mobilization efforts with bilateral donors, the World Bank, the Asian Development Bank, UN agencies, and nongovernmental organizations (NGOs). It was charged with coordinating five existing units: (1) the Economic Planning and Projects Assessment Unit, (2) the Donor Coordination Unit, (3) the Gender Affairs Unit, (4) the Environmental Protection Unit, and (5) the Census and Statistics Unit. These units were staffed mainly by international personnel, with an average of six staff members per unit, but local staff were also recruited during the UNTAET period and given initial training on the respective units' functions (Pires 2004).

With the establishment of the second Transitional Government in 2001 following elections for the Constituent Assembly, the NPDA was abolished, and a Planning Commission composed of five government members and five civil society members took its place. The Planning Commission was mandated to prepare the first National Development Plan (NDP) for Timor-Leste, which became the central instrument for mobilization and coordination of external funds for the first Timorese government.

Within twelve months of independence, the Planning Commission was abolished. The Donor Coordination Unit and the Economic Planning and Projects Assessment Unit merged to become the National Directorate for Planning and External Assistance Coordination (NDPEAC) under the new MPF. The NDPEAC has two divisions: the Planning and Monitoring Division and the External Assistance Mobilization and Coordination Division.

Revenue Development

The first mission from the IMF's Fiscal Affairs Department in February 2000 considered both the medium-term need "to regenerate tax and customs systems to provide sufficient revenue to finance a significant portion of current public expenditures" and the short-term need "to raise revenue to cover the most urgent public services, and to ensure that finances are properly controlled and managed." To these ends, the mission made a number of recommendations:

- The draft regulation on temporary customs duties (5 percent), various excise taxes, and sales taxes (5 percent) to be collected at the border should be reviewed by UNTAET and brought to the NCC as soon as possible.
- As soon as possible, appropriate regulations should be drafted to implement the proposed package of service taxes on hotel receipts, restaurant receipts, private accommodations rentals, government rentals, and vehicle rentals.
- A review should be conducted immediately to determine the best means of establishing a minimum threshold for the application of a

final withholding tax on wages, and the tax should be introduced as of July 1, 2000.

- A 5 percent presumptive tax on coffee sales was recommended, to be effective as soon as possible.
- A tax regime should be considered for small businesses, to be effective as soon as practicable. A similar tax should also apply to larger unincorporated businesses and the professions; the longer-term objective should be to reintroduce, when administrative constraints allow, a more developed personal income tax for this purpose.
- A corporate profits tax should be considered for January 2001. It should be made as simple as possible and information about this and other taxes should be published in advance.
- An airport departure fee of ten dollars should be collected on exit; a new car registration fee of twenty dollars should be imposed; airport and port user charges should be determined and implemented as soon as practicable; electricity charges for businesses should be reimposed as soon as possible.

There were also proposals for excise duties on beer, wine, spirits, and tobacco as well as for a levy on soft drinks. Efforts to mobilize domestic revenue by implementing these recommendations took place within the context of large-scale external resource inflows.

External Resource Mobilization

External funds came into Timor-Leste through multiple channels. In October 1999, the World Bank–coordinated JAM recommended external assistance of US$300 million over three years for reconstruction and rehabilitation activities. In a parallel planning and budgeting exercise, UNTAET asked for US$700 million to cover the expenditures associated with the presence of the peacekeeping forces (PKF) and the 1,500 civilians on the UN staff, from the assessed contributions of UN member states. In addition, in September 1999 the UN's Consolidated Inter-Agency Appeal (CAP) requested approximately US$200 million in voluntary contributions to address humanitarian and emergency relief to be coordinated by the Office of Co-ordination of Humanitarian Assistance (OCHA).

All of these involved budgeting of external resources on behalf of Timor-Leste. Meanwhile, the IMF calculated a figure of US$30 million in recurrent budget needs for fiscal year 1999–2000, estimating that half of this would be covered by domestic revenues. Thus there were many cooks in the kitchen, all baking different kinds of cakes.[15] Nonetheless, these efforts succeeded in securing substantial international assistance for Timor-Leste.

Table 5.1 summarizes the international financial support to Timor-Leste from 1999–2000 to 2004–2005. Total aid disbursements peaked at $236 million in fiscal year (FY) 2000/01 ($519 million including United Nations Police [UNPOL] and PKF operations).

Timor-Leste witnessed the establishment of at least five distinct aid delivery mechanisms: (1) the CFET, which focused on mobilizing funds for the government's recurrent expenses, rehabilitation of administrative buildings, civil service capacity building, and the justice sector; (2) the TFET, administered by the World Bank in collaboration with the Asian Development Bank, which mobilized funds for reconstruction work in health, education, agriculture, community development, private-sector development, transport, power, water, and sanitation; (3) projects funded and implemented by NGOs; (4) projects funded and implemented by UN agencies; and (5) projects funded by bilateral aid donors and implemented through NGOs and contractors.

Domestic Resource Mobilization

Table 5.2 outlines the government's revenue performance from FY 1999–2000 to FY 2003–2004. Although revenues from domestic sources increased through-

Table 5.1   Trends in International Assistance for Timor-Leste from FY 1999–2000 through FY 2004–2005 (US$ million)

Type of Assistance	1999–2000	2000–2001	2001–2002	2002–2003	2003–2004	2004–2005
Development and technical assistance on-budget	63.0	120.6	145.7	119.1	107.9	108.2
Development and technical assistance off-budget	26.6	33.6	33.4	36.7	25.8	16.3
UN Security Council posts				13.8	8.0	7.0
Humanitarian assistance	84.1	29.7	11.8	3.4	1.8	0.9
Budget and commodity support	27.1	44.6	31.8	31.1	32.6	21.8
Donor administrative expenses	1.1	7.3	5.5	4.6	4.5	3.9
Total assistance	201.9	235.8	228.2	208.7	180.6	158.1
Memo items						
UN Police (UNPOL)	33.1	51.9	45.4	26.7	15.7	5.1
UN PKF	65.6	231.1	145.0	104.4	74.7	12.9
Grand Total	300.6	518.8	418.6	339.8	271.0	185.1

Source: Government of Timor-Leste, Ministry of Planning and Finance, "Registry of External Assistance Database" (unpublished).

Note: Bilateral military assistance program not included in these data.

Table 5.2   Revenue Performance from FY 2000–2001 to FY 2003–2004 (US$ million)

	2000–2001	2001–2002	2002–2003	2003–2004
Total revenues	25.39	26.99	45.68	67.25
Tax revenues	15.46	18.08	17.00	24.76
Nontax revenues		2.44	2.30	4.48
Timor Gap oil and gas revenues	9.93	6.47	26.38	38.01
Other revenues[a]		4.4	4.92	5.65
Power sector		2.0	2.87	3.53
Aviation		1.1	1.00	1.08
Port		1.3	1.05	1.04
Donor budgetary contributions	31.56	22.74	32.53	34.76
Grand total	56.95	84.13	83.15	107.76

Source: Annual Financial Report and Accounts for Timor-Leste (2001–2004).

Note: a. Owing to the nature of the agencies involved, revenues here are not included as part of the state revenues. These are retained by the respective agencies to cover their own operating costs.

out this period, they were insufficient to meet the full expenditure requirements of all agencies. The gap was financed by donor budgetary contributions, which covered 55 percent of the budget in FY 2000–2001 and diminished to 32 percent in 2003–2004.

The first taxes introduced under UNTAET were custom duties on imports. These were in place by March 2000. Income tax was introduced in February 2001. The first US$100 per month of income was completely exempt, and the tax was largely paid by government employees. Other employers were notified of their responsibility to withhold income taxes from employees and remit these to the government, but there were few large-scale employers other than government itself, and even fewer who paid more than US$100 a month to local staff. The poor, who made up the vast majority of the Timorese population, contributed very little to state revenues.[16]

Table 5.3 presents a breakdown of the tax revenues for the fiscal years 2000–2001 to 2003–2004. Taxes on commodities consistently accounted for approximately 60 percent of the total. Income taxes accounted for approximately 30 percent, with the remainder coming from taxes on services.

The Timorese leadership initially was reluctant to introduce taxation. CNRT president Xanana had appealed to diaspora businesspeople to return to Timor-Leste in 1999, specifically asking them to prioritize importing basic products. CNRT also encouraged local businesses to join with Indonesian businesspeople to increase their capacity. CNRT was reluctant at this juncture to tax basic products that were sorely lacking in the country. The MPF international staff, however, insisted that the state's expenditures be covered by raising revenues and that taxing imports was one effective way of doing this.

Table 5.3   Breakdown of Tax Revenues from FY 2001–2002 to FY 2003–2004 (US$ million)

	2001–2002	2002–2003	2003–2004
Taxes on commodities	10.66	9.83	15.48
Sales tax	3.25	3.37	4.34
Excise taxes	4.29	3.44	7.23
Import duties	3.10	3.01	3.92
Export duties	0.11	0	0
Taxes on income	5.38	5.26	6.65
Individual income tax (ETTA)	0.53	0.52	0.58
Individual income tax (other)	1.94	2.16	2.31
Special withholding tax	1.26	0.87	1.92
Business/corporate taxes	1.66	1.70	1.84
Taxes on services	2.03	1.89	2.63
Total tax revenue	18.08	16.98	24.76

Source: Annual Financial Report and Accounts for Timor-Leste (2001–2004).

The Timorese were not against taxing luxury items such as cars, beer, and tobacco, items that mostly came to serve the international staff. But ironically, these became tax free, even when the import duties were imposed on all goods, because the majority of these items were imported on behalf of some agency claiming to be tax exempt. For example, there was a little shop within UN-TAET grounds that sold alcohol and other goods very cheaply to the international staff. These same goods were often bought and then sold outside at a profit, thus creating black market activities.[17]

The Timorese leadership particularly objected to the introduction of income taxes at a time when the economy was stagnant, many Timorese remained homeless, and not all humanitarian aid coming into the country was reaching the population that required it. To ensure the good will of the people, the leadership argued that the first priority should be to create opportunities for people to work and rebuild their lives.

Quick Impact Projects (Quips) introduced by the UN created short-term employment in public works in an effort to disburse money to poor people, but these projects were not seen by the Timorese leadership as sustainable in the long term. Initially the only Timorese receiving substantial cash incomes were local UNTAET staff and others fortunate enough to work for NGOs. Given the small numbers of Timorese with such jobs, there was little income to tax.

The international staff was the one component of society that was contributing something substantial to the cash economy at the time. Shops brought in goods to sell to the internationals, who were the only people who could afford to buy even relatively simple items such as vegetables.

Yet there was strong international pressure on the Timorese leaders and officials to see the budget process from the point of view of revenues and expenditure. From the outset, the Timorese were told repeatedly that state expenditures had to be paid for by revenues collected by the state and that they should not depend on the international community for this. The government needed to prove to the donors that it was serious about raising its own revenues through its own sources. Hence it was critical, according to the international staff, that a tax system be set up immediately and that citizens should get the message that they had tax responsibilities.

The Timorese leadership was aware of the importance of domestic revenues. Independence was more to them than just raising the flag and singing the new national anthem. They understood that everyone had to contribute to rebuilding. After all, the twenty-four years of resistance had been supported financially mainly by the ordinary people. But they were also aware of social realities. When people did not have enough to feed their families, they felt that introducing taxes would send the wrong political message. The leadership vigorously disputed the speed and sequence with which the tax system was being implemented. They felt that premature decisions could not only lead to failure but also discredit the government in the eyes of the public.

Under great pressure from the donors, the Tax Department of the Ministry of Finance began the process of collecting taxes so as to show at the next donors' conference that Timor was on its way to financial sustainability. Given the lack of administrative capacity and enforcement regulations at the time, it was very difficult to collect tax. Invoices were issued to potential taxpayers who often did not understand how the figures were calculated. This not only created antagonism, but in many cases resulted in a refusal to pay, particularly by NGOs.

The Timorese assumed that the initial US$15 million revenue target proposed by the IMF was supposed to come from Timorese taxpayers and argued strongly that this was unrealistic. In reality, the IMF was intending that the bulk of the taxes would come from the bigger entrepreneurs, such as the boat-hotel in Dili harbor that provided accommodation to UN staff. When the time came to collect these taxes, however, the embryonic administration was not in a position to do so, because UN contractors were declared by UN lawyers to be exempt from tax payments.

There was much debate even over the question of whether the local Timorese employees of the international financial institutions (IFIs), UN, bilateral aid agencies, and international NGOs should be required to pay income tax. Only after prolonged negotiations was it accepted in principle that the local staff should be liable to pay income tax.

Should International Staff Pay Any Tax?

There were numerous heated discussions around the topic of whether or not internationals should pay tax. The Ministry of Finance and the Timorese leadership agreed that tax should be paid by all internationals working in Timor-

Leste unless there was a specific legal basis for their exemption. (For example, UN employees other than Timorese nationals were exempt from tax under the Vienna convention.) They also agreed that import taxes should be levied on all goods imported into the country unless a specific legal basis existed for excluding them.

With some honorable exemptions, such as Sergio Vieira de Mello and the head of the World Bank mission in Timor-Leste, both the UN and the donors fought hard for the broadest possible interpretation of the privileges thought to flow from the status of both national and international donors. As a consequence there were bitter fights between international officials at the Ministry of Finance and international officials of donor organizations over this issue, with the latter winning.

The failure to be able to effectively tax the international staff who were liable for tax was a bitter blow to the Ministry of Finance. The donors and the UN, who disagreed about many things, were as one on their inviolable right to a complete exemption from taxes, not only for themselves as individuals and for goods imported for their direct use but also for their contractors and goods imported for reconstruction. Only the World Bank took a more constructive attitude.

UNTAET was obliged to refer everything to New York, where UN headquarters monitored and resisted any threat to UN tax privileges. The position of local employees of international organizations and NGOs was not clear in law, but they ferociously defended every inch of ground. Even when UNTAET offered to pay the taxes of international staff working with NGOs, provided that they were prepared to declare the income they were receiving, the answer was still No. The donor organizations made three basic arguments against paying taxes. First, they argued that if international staff was to pay tax, or to be charged import taxes on goods bought out of the aid funds, this was the same as contributing toward budgetary support. Second, they were dead set against taxes being levied on any income paid out of aid money because, they argued, expatriates were already paying tax in their countries of origin and should not be required to pay tax again. Third, they argued that no other country where they had worked ever applied such levies, so why should Timor-Leste be different?

The debates over taxing international staff were conducted mainly among the internationals themselves, between those working for the Ministry of Finance and the donor institutions. But the Timorese leadership also felt that it would be fairer to tax the highly paid international staff, particularly those with very high salaries ranging from US$5,000 to US$10,000 a month, rather than trying to raise revenue from local people who were struggling to rebuild their lives. They understood that this would be a temporary measure because eventually the internationals would leave, but it would have given the right message to the people. The system that emerged instead was perceived by many Timorese to be unfair, in that extremely high earners were favored with exemptions. At the same time, the purchasing power of the internationals was seen to be distorting the local economy, as the price of goods increased exorbitantly (for discussion, see Carnahan, Durch, and Gilmore 2006).

In hindsight, there should have been more discussion between UNTAET and the CNRT to seek a consensus on the best way to approach domestic resource mobilization. A division of labor in which the CNRT would sensitize the Timorese people to the need to introduce taxes and engage their collaboration, and in which UNTAET would sensitize donors to be more open to the priorities advocated by the CNRT, could have ensured a much smoother process. Had UNTAET and other donors viewed Timor-Leste as the winner of an independence struggle and not as a failed state, and had they engaged the CNRT as an equal partner, more attention would have been paid to local concerns.[18]

The Power Sector

The electric power sector could have been a good revenue source if well managed. Instead it was a disaster. Immediately after the 1999 destruction, intensive efforts began to restore electricity to Dili and the surrounding villages. With assistance from the UK Department for International Development (DfID), UNTAET managed to operate a number of power stations and a distribution system, but this lasted only as long as DfID funds were available. By the end of 2000, Dili and surrounding villages were subject to frequent power cuts and sometimes consecutive days of darkness.

From the outset, the power sector was not able to implement a billing system to ensure cost recovery. The new government of Timor-Leste inherited this problem from UNTAET. Ironically, the inability to implement charges for electricity use conferred disproportionate benefits on internationals with their air conditioners and numerous household appliances. In effect, this was a donor-financed benefit that did the average Timorese little good. High fuel costs exacerbated the problem. Indonesia had provided heavily subsidized fuel to Timor-Leste. Independence meant a loss of these subsidies, and at the same time world fuel prices were rising.

Donors objected, and rightfully so, to their budgetary support funds going to subsidize electricity consumption by clients such as restaurant owners and international staff. The boat-hotel that housed UN staff alone drew upon one generator's entire supply of energy to keep its operation going. The power sector was eating a good portion of the government budget, as shown in Table 5.4.

This problem led to an acrimonious confrontation between donors and the government. The donors, represented by the World Bank, wanted to see the management of the power sector contracted out immediately. The government argued that the public first had to be satisfied by the delivery of a reliable source of energy, before being asked to pay for it. The public by this time had completely lost confidence in the government's ability to deliver electricity, and the public servants responsible for reading the electric meters refused to

Table 5.4   Power Sector Revenue and Expenditure Performance (US$ million)

	Revenue	Expenditure	Government Subsidy
Fiscal year 2000–2001		>7.18	
Fiscal year 2001–2002	2.0	8.85	6.75
Fiscal year 2002–2003	2.87	9.3	6.5
Fiscal year 2003–2004	3.53	9.7	6.56

Source: Annual Financial Report and Accounts for Timor-Leste (2001–2004).

do so because they were being assaulted by home owners. On several occasions, the minister responsible for the sector had his house stoned when the city plunged, yet again, into darkness. Contracting out, in the government's view, would simply transfer the problem to the private sector in a situation where the rule of law and security were not yet guaranteed.

A compromise was reached a few months before Christmas 2003, when a donor provided new generators that would guarantee a twenty-four-hour electricity supply until Christmas. The government developed a public relations program to prepare the public for the introduction of prepaid meters and then allowed management of the sector to be privatized, with the cost of power to consumers to be set by the government. The cost of electricity remained high, and most people could not afford it, a warning sign that the situation would not be sustainable in the long term. As of October 2005, Dili still had power cuts of six to eight hours per day.

Timor Sea Revenue

There are great uncertainties about the amount of revenues that Timor-Leste will receive from its offshore petroleum resources. This is one reason the government of Timor-Leste is making considerable efforts to expand nonpetroleum revenues.

At the same time, there is also an understanding that the Timor Sea resources belong to future Timorese generations as well as to the current generation. In light of this, the Timor-Leste government has adopted a policy to save all First Tranche Petroleum (FTP) revenues, representing the royalty component of Timor Sea revenue. This policy has two aims: first, to secure savings for income and development when the oil revenues cease; and second, to force the current generation into economic diversification, rather than relying on income from oil production. Indeed, the Timorese leadership initially wished to sequester all Timor Sea revenue and not just royalties, and there were heated debates about this in the run-up to the preparation of the 2001–2002 budget.

Table 5.5 shows the amount of Timor Sea revenue that has been made available for allocations to line agencies through the CFET and the amount held in the separate FTP account as national savings by the Banking Payments Authority.

Estimates for the Timor Sea revenue are based on projections of production, world oil prices, and the exchange rate. These estimates rely heavily on factors outside the control of both the government and the project operators. World market oil prices have an enormous impact on the actual amount of Timor Sea revenues received. Prices have ranged from about ten dollars per barrel in the late 1990s to about sixty dollars in 2005. This volatility leads to disproportionate changes in Timor-Leste revenue, much of which is based on profits rather than sales. When high capital costs are netted out, a 10 percent change in world oil prices can lead to a 20 or 30 percent change in revenue.

Another source of uncertainty is the fact that oil revenues only come from one petroleum project, the Bayu Undan field.[19] Although this may change with successful resolution of maritime boundary disputes with Australia, or if new petroleum projects proceed, currently any technical or production problems at Bayu Undan have a direct impact on Timor-Leste revenues. In late 2003, for example, drilling problems at Bayu Undan led to a dramatic fall in expected revenues. The operating companies were able to recover from some of these problems, and rising world oil prices more than restored revenues, but similar problems could occur in the future. The Bayu Undan project will not be completed until a pipeline and liquified natural gas plant are built and become fully operational. Until then, risks to revenue remain particularly high.

For these reasons the government takes a cautious approach toward the use of periodic windfall gains from temporarily high petroleum prices. The planning process is based on the assumption that the current high levels of petroleum prices will not be sustainable and that prices will trend downward in coming years.[20]

Table 5.5   Timor Sea Revenues (US$ million)

	2000–2001	2001–2002	2002–2003	2003–2004
CFET–Timor Gap revenue estimates		6.00	23.80	17.10
CFET–Timor Gap revenue actual	6.79	6.47	26.38	38.01
First Tranche Petroleum (FTA)				
Timor Gap royalty	3.14	4.22	3.1	3.3
Timor Gap royalty interest		0.07	0.07	0.06
Cumulative FTP savings	3.14	7.43	10.6	13.96

Source: Annual Financial Report and Accounts for Timor-Leste (2001–2004).

The Budget

The combined sources budget (CSB) of Timor-Leste covered funds drawn from five separate sources: (1) the CFET, controlled by the government; (2) the TFET, managed by the World Bank; (3) bilateral and multilateral funds managed by the individual donor organizations; (4) UNTAET funds from the assessed contributions to the United Nations; and (5) the Capacity Development Posts Fund managed by the United Nations Development Programme.

In total, the CSB averaged around US$200 million per annum in the fiscal years from 2000–2001 to 2003–2004. The CFET, the only portion directly managed and administered by the government, averaged around US$75 million per annum. It included three categories of expenditure: salaries and wages, goods and services, and capital investments for development projects.

The first (minuscule) national budget was prepared by the Timorese under the auspices of the CNRT, but subsequent budgets were prepared by international staff in close consultation with the respective ministries and the IFIs. It was not until after independence that Timorese officials again actively participated in the budget preparation process.

The formal budget process for the government-managed CFET begins when the Minister of Planning and Finance proposes to the CoM both the timelines and the process for the development of the annual budget. Once approved, the MPF Budget Office sends a memo to that effect to all the other state agencies. Each ministry then forwards expenditure costs to the Budget Office. If for some reason the Budget Office does not accept these figures, it seeks a solution that is mutually acceptable to both parties. The resulting figures are incorporated into a budget proposal that is submitted to the CoM for executive approval. The Budget Office then prepares the Budget Law to be submitted to the National Parliament for final approval.

Planning is meant to augment the budget process, but owing to the degree of complexity and the weak capacity skills of staff involved, best use has as yet to be made of the systems in place. The country did not have a comprehensive development plan until after independence, and even then it took a further two years to develop a bureaucratic culture to link planning to the budgetary process. In the meantime, planned activities often were not reflected in the budget, and vice versa.

To cite one example, in an effort to eradicate illiteracy, the decision was made to prioritize education in the budget. That translated into allocating more money to the sector, but no discussions took place on how that money should be spent. There was no analysis of how many people were actually illiterate, or what their age ranges were, or how many children were attending school, or whether those outside school were not attending. Some programs commenced that did not work. For example, in some areas classes were set up to provide education for illiterate adults, but they only lasted a few weeks because after attending some classes, people complained they did not have time owing to their need to earn a living. Concentration on the young would have been more pragmatic.

Impact of External Resources on Sector Allocations

The CFET budget preparation process was more participatory than that of the larger TFET. Like the CFET, the TFET budget initially went to NCC sessions for approval. At these sessions, a one-page TFET budget was presented by the World Bank, showing the amounts already allocated. Not realizing that this presentation constituted a "consultation" process, the NCC automatically approved these allocations. From the first budget prepared by CNRT technical groups, there was pressure from both the World Bank and the IMF for a "pro-poor" budget. This concept was welcomed by the Timorese, who believed that this meant the priority would be agriculture, on which most of the poor depended for their livelihoods.

The international concept of a pro-poor budget was different, however. "Pro-poor" meant that most funds had to be allocated to education and health. The advisers helping the Timorese prepare the budget constantly emphasized that the more pro-poor the budget looked, the better in terms of finding favor with donors.

Education and health received about 34 percent of the total available funds from FY 1999–2000 to FY 2003–2004 (see Table 5.6). For the most part, CFET allocations mirrored the CSB allocations, mainly owing to the pressure from the international community for the CFET budget to be seen as pro-poor. Clearly, external resources had an impact on the national budget allocation. At the time, one could have been forgiven for viewing the government as one large NGO trying to do all the right things to compete for donors' funding.

With hindsight, agriculture should have received higher priority. The imperative should have been to increase the capacity of farmers to produce. How could hungry and ill children go to school? How can one talk about poverty reduction and not create opportunities to enable the poor people to earn a living in the first place?

In addition to agriculture, small to medium enterprises are critical to poverty reduction in Timor-Leste. Here, too, there were missed opportunities both to invest in capacity building and to stimulate the local economy. For example, there were numerous requests from TFET projects administered by the World Bank for school chairs and desks. In the rush to produce results and be seen to produce them, most of these were ordered from outside the country, when perhaps the funds could have been better used to increase the capacity of the small to medium local entrepreneurs. They were hungry for work, and the competition among them would have kept prices to a minimum while increasing their skills.[21] The international donors need to be cognizant that capacity

Table 5.6   Sectoral Allocation of Combined Sources Budget, FY 1999–2000 to FY 2003–2004 (US$ million)

Sector	
Basic services	301.9 (34.0%)
Education and training	195.2
Health care	106.7
Production-related sectors	91.2 (10.3%)
Agriculture, forests, fisheries	70.6
Natural resources and environment	10.4
Private-sector development	10.2
Basic infrastructure and housing	207.4 (23.4%)
Communications	7.1
Housing and urban development	5.2
Power	67.2
Transport	81.7
Water supply and sanitation	46.3
Governance	287.2 (32.3%)
Public-sector management	113.9
Local government and civil society	10.7
Rights, equality, and justice	30.4
Security and peacebuilding	64.5
External relations	37.8
Total	887.6 (100%)
Funding sources	
Total CFET appropriations	302.5 (34.1%)
UN-funded critical posts	21.8 (2.5%)
Bilateral military assistance	7.3 (0.8%)
Donor programs	561.4 (63.2%)

Source: Democratic Republic of Timor-Leste Ministry of Planning and Finance (2005a).

building takes time and that investments in long-term results are more beneficial and sustainable than the "quick and dirty" approaches that were so often used in Timor.

The international organizations came to Timor-Leste with their own rules and standards, and they were not willing to acknowledge that the country had its own standards and values. In the eyes of the Timorese, the stance of the internationals was "we know best, we bring the ideas, and we bring the rules . . . so you just have to comply with them." When it came to the security sector, these attitudes almost led to disaster.

The Security Sector

Anyone familiar with Timor-Leste's history would understand why FALINTIL, the armed wing of the resistance movement, was highly regarded by the people. As far as most Timorese were concerned, without FALINTIL there would have been no independence. Yet when members of the international community landed in Timor-Leste, they behaved as though they viewed the guerilla forces as bandits. One assumes this was due to ignorance of Timorese history and perhaps to lessons learned in other situations where there were many militaristic elements competing for power—Somalia and the Balkans come to mind. Whatever the reasons, the international community made a crucial and potentially dangerous mistake when it was reluctant to recognize or help FALINTIL, which had voluntarily disarmed and gone into cantonment in Aileu, about 50 kilometers south of Dili.

There was international consensus that Timor-Leste was going through an emergency phase and that food needed to be distributed to one and all. The FALINTIL soldiers in cantonment were excluded, however, which was inexplicable to the Timorese. There seemed to be no plan for the treatment of this group, and the development agencies had rules against assistance to military forces. Extraordinary maneuvering had to take place to enable food to reach them. This became an explosive issue for the Timorese, who perceived this as showing disrespect for the resistance struggle and for the strong Timorese cultural imperative that food must be shared with those without. Luckily for the stability of the country, the Portuguese government understood the problem and supported the FALINTIL soldiers.

The remainder of the international community appeared to be oblivious to how close to disaster the situation had come. They were unaware of the enormous pressure they put on the Timorese leadership, particularly on CNRT president and FALINTIL commander Xanana, who had to mediate between the sentiments of the local people and those of the internationals. Many UN PKF impositions were obeyed only because of a direct appeal from Xanana. He explained that there would be incidents and international rules that in Timorese eyes were unfair, but that until we were independent these rules should be respected. He emphasized that international administration would only be for two years and that the people should see it as an exchange for the peace and freedom for which they had fought for two and a half decades.

At the Lisbon conference in June 2000, Xanana made an appeal to the international community that something had to be done about the FALINTIL fighters. They could not be abandoned in Aileu simply because the international community was unable to help a military force. Originally, the Timorese planned for Timor-Leste not to have a military force. Instead there would only be a police force. In the absence of an acceptable plan for the FALINTIL fighters, however, the Timorese leadership decided to create a defense force. After intensive lobbying, the international community agreed to commission King's College in London to undertake a study on the future of FALINTIL.

The King's College study (Centre for Defence Studies 2000) recommended that FALINTIL be set up as an apolitical volunteer force accountable to civil authority. A regulation establishing the national defense force, known as Falintil–Timor-Leste Defense Force (F-FDTL), was passed on January 31, 2001, and the F-FDTL came into being the next day. The study also recommended that recurrent costs of the defense force should be borne by the government and that all initial training, infrastructure, and equipment for the new force be provided via in-kind assistance from donor countries.

At a current strength of around 1,500, the F-FDTL has two light infantry battalions, a naval component with two patrol boats, a training center, force logistics and communications units, and a military police unit. In 2002 a Secretariat of State for Defence was established to provide civilian oversight as well as financial and management guidance. There is still a considerable gray area in relation to potentially overlapping responsibilities with the Timor-Leste National Police Force (PNTL), a situation that creates confusion for budgetary processes.

Table 5.7a summarizes the available information on defense spending in Timor-Leste in the five years from 1999–2000 to 2003–2004. The United Nations reported the cost of the PKF operations at US$620 million. CFET appropriations amounted to about US$18 million during the period. Bilateral military assistance amounts generally were not available, but these were well in excess of the funds provided by the government in the CFET budget. Clearly this is not a sustainable level of defense spending for Timor-Leste. The national budget allocation to the PNTL does not reflect much PNTL-incurred expenditure, because until independence the police force was UNTAET's responsibility. Table 5.7b shows what was spent on PNTL in this period.

UNPOL has funded repairs to buildings, vehicle maintenance and running costs, communications, and large amounts of equipment. Handovers have been completed, but the PNTL budget makes no provision for maintenance of equipment and buildings. There are clear indications that a funding gap will emerge when UNPOL support to the PNTL ceases.

In May 2006 fighting broke out between the armed forces (F-FDTL) and the police (PNTL). In light of the history sketched above, this should not have come as a surprise. F-FDTL had been created only reluctantly after appeals from Xanana Gusmão, whereas the international donors clearly felt that PNTL was the institution responsible for border and internal security. The attention given to both institutions, including their budget allocations, reflected this.

Table 5.7a   Expenditures for Defense, FY 1999–2000 to FY 2003–2004 (US$ million)

	1999–2000	2000–2001	2001–2002	2002–2003	2003–2004	Total
UN PKF	65.6	231.1	145	104.4	74.6	620.7
Donor programs						
CFET appropriations	—	2.5	4.2	4.9	6.1	17.7
Total	65.6	233.5	149.2	109.3	80.7	638.5
Expenditure as % GDP	19.8	58.0	37.4	28.3	20.5	33.4

Source: Democratic Republic of Timor-Leste Ministry of Planning and Finance (2005a).

Table 5.7b   UNPOL, CFET, and Donor Expenditures on Police Programs for FY 1999–2000 to FY 2003–2004 (US$ million)

	1999–2000	2000–2001	2001–2002	2002–2003	2003–2004	Total
UNPOL	33.1	51.9	45.4	26.7	15.6	172.8
Donor programs	0.2	0.5	0.6	0.6	0.6	2.5
CFET appropriations	4.6	4.7	6.7	8.1	8.5	32.7
Total	37.9	57.1	52.7	35.5	24.7	208.1
Expenditure as % GDP	11.4	14.2	13.2	9.2	6.3	10.9

Source: Democratic Republic of Timor-Leste Ministry of Planning and Finance (2005a).

Yet most Timorese regarded the personnel of F-FDTL as heroes. Many officers of the PNTL, in contrast, had lower status because they were recruited disproportionately from the western part of the country where they had earlier served in the Indonesian police force and therefore had the required police experience. Their behavior toward the citizens with regard to human rights was poor and became an increasing source of concern.[22] The situation was further exacerbated by the rivalries within the new Timorese government. The F-FDTL was perceived as a body loyal to President Xanana. His rivals proceeded to strengthen the PNTL by creating two new units, the Rapid Intervention Unit and the Border Patrol Police, who were equipped with automatic weapons. Meanwhile the F-FDTL troops were poorly armed, sidelined, and confined to barracks.

Budget Execution

Budget execution starts after the appropriations are approved by the National Parliament. The Treasury releases quarterly Expenditure Authorization Notices, based on the requests by the line ministries and agencies, subject to availability of funds.

There are three ways of making payments:

1. Direct payments are processed by Treasury for amounts less than US$500. Treasury can also process amounts greater than US$500 if an existing contract is already in place—for example, for the payment of electricity and telephone bills or temporary staff.
2. Procurement procedures are applicable for purchases in excess of US$500. The Procurement Division tenders and enters into negotiations with the supplier, and in the final phase a purchase order or contract for the goods and services is signed. Following completion of the procurement process, the payment requests are submitted to the Accounts and Payment Unit of Treasury.

3. Under the supply modality, the government allocates approximately US$1 million annually for the purchase of stationery and office supplies for all bureaucracies. This allocation is managed and controlled by the MPF Directorate of Supply.

The payment procedures are complex and time-consuming. Although they are intended to ensure transparency and accountability, there are loopholes and lapses due to inefficiency, lack of understanding of the procedures, or corruption. Budget execution has been chronically low: in fiscal years 2003 and 2004, for example, only 75 percent of the amount appropriated was actually spent, despite the country's urgent needs.

In teaching the Timorese good practice in public finances, the international staff involved in the budget process instilled a fear of spending. As a result, low budget execution is attributable not only to lack of capacity in implementing the work but also to the centralized control over nearly all expenses. When dealing with the Ministry of Finance, one hears the constant refrain, "Careful, careful . . . Let's not make mistakes. Otherwise the donors won't give us any more aid."

To cite one example involving the president's office, the current garage that has the contract for repairs to government cars belongs to a group of veterans. Unfortunately, this garage lacks the equipment and technical human resources to handle many repairs, and a car from the president's office that was repaired there came back in worse condition. The office decided to take the car to a more professional garage, which not only repaired the car properly but guaranteed its work for at least six months. The Finance Ministry refused to reimburse the president's office on the grounds that the expenditure was done outside budget regulations.

The tension between the desire of the central Treasury to maintain tight control over process and spending and the desire of government agencies to enjoy greater flexibility in resource use is as old as government itself and probably will last as long as government. In Timor-Leste the Treasury was strong from the beginning, whereas the line ministries were generally weak. There is now talk of instilling a "service" mentality in the Treasury, but this is easier said than done.

When corruption is spoken about in Timor-Leste, it is referred to as KKN (corruption, collusion, and nepotism). The allusions are not just to money but to money coupled with politics. There are complaints that only those who have high-level contacts or are members of the winning political party are able to enter the public service.

Petty corruption is common in the form of bribes for service delivery, such as a few extra dollars accompanying a passport application or a couple hundred dollars to avoid paying tax at the border when bringing in goods. Preferences in provision of services go to people whose family members are in the public service or who are friends of parliamentarians or ministers. The whole situation is further facilitated by the fact that many parliamentarians have businesses of their own.

To date most of the corruption cases that have come before the courts do not involve public funds, although there have been at least half a dozen that did. Due to the discretion given to public servants in terms of procedures and the lack of an effective mechanism to inform the public of their rights in relation to the services provided by government departments, there is ample room for rent-seeking. More and more people have become accustomed to paying the bribes to facilitate continuation of their businesses.

Capacity Development

The international community provided generous assistance for capacity development and capacity-building programs (see Table 5.8).[23] Sadly, the results on the ground do not reflect the huge amounts invested.

Almost all donors who invested in capacity-building projects used expatriate advisers as the main modality for delivering assistance. The concentration on this modality resulted in some neglect for formal training programs for national staff. Indeed, in some respects the large influx of expatriate personnel, thought to be essential to avoid a total collapse of public services in the early phase of the postconflict transition, quickly turned into a nightmare.

Timor-Leste's fiscal management system, designed largely by the Bretton Woods institutions, is "world class" in its extensive monitoring and control mechanisms. This system requires a pool of highly skilled personnel to operate it, however. Timor-Leste lacked the necessary skills. Faced with the need for the Timorese to acquire sufficient skills quickly, the MPF decided to rely heavily on expatriate advisers giving one-on-one training, at a cost to the donors of approximately $25 million over five years. Shortly before the end of UN-TAET's mandate, MPF with a total staff of 564 had the largest number of expatriate advisers: seventy-nine out of the total of 225 advisers employed for all government sectors. In comparison, in spite of the fact that 80 percent of Timorese depended on agriculture for their livelihoods, the Ministry of Agriculture (with 253 staff) had only five advisers. This graphically reflects the emphasis

Table 5.8   Capacity-Building Programs (US$ million)

	1999–2000	2000–2001	2001–2002	2002–2003	2003–2004	Total
Donor programs	3.2	15.3	19.2	23.7	17.6	79.1
UN assessments	—	—	—	13.8	8.0	21.8
CFET appropriations	1.4	1.9	2.3	3.9	3.2	12.9
Total	4.6	17.2	21.5	41.5	28.9	113.9

Source: Democratic Republic of Timor-Leste Ministry of Planning and Finance (2005a).

on fiscal discipline rather than on increasing rural production and improving the welfare of the majority of the people.

With the passage of time, the cost effectiveness of the capacity-building program has emerged as an issue. The one-on-one approach to staff development implicit in the use of expatriate advisers led to limited numbers' receiving training. A related issue is the extent to which there has been effective skills transfer.

To exacerbate matters, the Timor-Leste government, like many other post-conflict governments, has used public service employment as a peace dividend for members of the ruling party, often marginalizing or rejecting capable people who are not of the same political persuasion.

Finally, capacity development has been further impeded by the fact that donor organizations, UN agencies, IFIs, NGOs, and UNTAET divisions were offering much higher salaries than the Timorese public service, and this competition resulted in the best skilled workers opting for the higher salaries. This is a common problem in the developing world, but it was particularly acute in Timor-Leste, a tiny country with a limited pool of educated human resources that was swamped by a huge international presence.

Conclusion

The UN's statebuilding effort in Timor-Leste between 1999 and 2002 was rushed, chaotic, paternalistic, and only partly successful. It was done in an environment of crisis, psychosocial trauma, and competition for power. In other words, it had much in common with other statebuilding initiatives.

As much as the Timorese needed UN intervention in 1999, the UN also needed Timor-Leste to shore up its own flagging reputation. At the time, the UN was under pressure from sections of the international community to prove its competence following high profile "failures" in the Balkans, Somalia, and Rwanda. UNTAET had to succeed, or at least appear to succeed, because Timor-Leste was the UN's last chance, according to its critics, to demonstrate its continuing relevance in the post–Cold War era.

The challenge faced by the UN staff and the Timorese was to transform a land left in ashes and a people traumatized by a long history of repression. Starting from the legacy of colonial rule and occupation, they sought to create something resembling a modern state that was built upon local knowledge, traditions, cultural practices, and resources.

Many senior UN personnel saw their primary objective as establishing the "shell" of a state upon which the Timorese could further develop their own system of government. Their primary aim was to build institutions—not schools or roads or public utilities. They sought to build a political framework conducive to social stability, future investment, and development by introducing democracy, developing institutional capacity, and establishing the rule of law.

The UN adopted a "top-down" approach that sought to ensure political stability through a power-sharing formula that gave Timorese leaders power within the administration and then later in government. An alternative "bottom-up" approach was advocated by many NGO groups, and the UN experimented with that when Sergio Vieira de Mello appointed the National Council, whose twenty-six members were selected from all different groups and organizations within Timor-Leste. For the most part, however, the top-down model prevailed, and the UN field staff relied on a handful of influential local political leaders. This distorted legitimate local governance and may have sown the seeds for some of the occasionally violent opposition to government that has occurred since.

The UN did set up the shell of a state, upon which the Timorese are continuing to build administrative and governance systems. Yet it also must be recognized that the UN's need to succeed, and appear to succeed, often took priority over the long-term objective of setting in place a political framework that would lead to future stability through inclusive democratic participation in Timor-Leste.

Among the lessons that can be drawn from the state-building efforts in Timor-Leste are the following:

• *Keep institutional rivalries to a minimum.* There must be high coordination among donors, UN agencies, and IFIs, even if that means setting up one office to make sure this happens. Rivalries among the international agencies caused the Timorese a great deal of confusion as they were putting their own government structures in place.

• *Keep the number of aid delivery mechanisms to a minimum.* The World Bank–managed TFET was successful in rehabilitating essential infrastructure and delivering services in a situation where no government institutions existed and it was urgent to meet people's basic needs. But the transition to self-government would have been smoother if from the beginning these sectors were funded from a single trust fund. Instead UNTAET set up CFET to fund recurrent costs of the government. As government structures were established, the TFET Project Management Units became parallel structures that often were in direct conflict with the government structures rather than complementing them.

• *No country is a "blank slate."* Internationals should not assume that there are nó skills available in the country. In many instances inexperienced UN staff who were learning on the job were instructing Timorese with better skills and many years of experience. This led to poor decisions, of which the treatment of FALINTIL was an example.

• *Transfer skills.* Time is needed for locals and returning diaspora to acquire skills to be able to operate the systems that have been set up. In the beginning, internationals were doing line function jobs. When the pressure came from donors to bring Timorese into the bureaucracies, the internationals abruptly became "advisers" and no longer took responsibility for the results produced. The tasks of expatriates must be framed so that time can be allocated properly to developing the necessary skills locally.

• *Set a good example.* Values that Timorese leaders developed during the period of resistance were eroded when they came into contact with the globalized world. When the international community makes a decision to rebuild a country and set up new governance institutions using the rhetoric of the world's "best practices," this must be done very carefully. It is human nature to copy the example being set by the powerful and worldly "outsiders." What were some of the behaviors that the Timorese learned from the foreigners? The internationals fought tooth and nail to avoid paying tax on either salaries or goods brought in for their benefit.[24] Many were more interested in building their résumés than in rebuilding Timor-Leste. On top of being very well paid, they demanded fringe benefits such as cars for both business and personal use. At the beginning of the UN administration, the Timorese generally were happy to do voluntary work, but as they observed the behavior of internationals and became aware of their salaries and perks, the idea of doing any voluntary work quickly ceased. In other words, it was the selfish "me" attributes that were copied rather than the altruistic attitudes.

• *Communicate and explain actions to the local people.* In Timor-Leste, the UN was very good at communicating with the international community but did a very poor job of communicating with the Timorese. This may have reflected the greater need to be seen to be succeeding outside of Timor-Leste rather than within it. Better communication would improve understanding about the whole process and help the people to be more accepting of decisions that may appear harsh but are necessary for future sustainability.

Both parties to postconflict reconstruction need to accept that nation building is a very long-term exercise. What internationals can help to do is to install or renovate the basic structures of governance. What happens after that is largely up to the local population. Given the scale of the intervention in Timor-Leste, UNTAET itself became a major source of disruption, both social and economic. A tiny country, still largely dependent on subsistence agriculture, was hurled almost overnight into the twenty-first century. The international community was willing to devote enormous resources to Timor-Leste, but it had much more difficulty adapting to local norms and recognizing the need and potential for local solutions.

Notes

The authors are grateful to Patsy Thatcher for both research and editing assistance.

1. The official name of East Timor is now the Portuguese Timor-Leste; although the names can be used interchangeably, in this book we use Timor-Leste.

2. The death toll calculated from statistics for Timor from 1920 to 1970 in Agencia Geral do Ultramar (1974).

3. These figures include a few church schools, twenty Chinese primary schools, and one Chinese secondary school (Thatcher 1993).

4. Interview with Jose Barbosa, former senior civil servant of the Portuguese government in Timor-Leste, October 10, 2005, Melbourne, Australia; see also Dunn (1983).

5. The personal tax was collected throughout the territory via the local district and subdistrict authorities. The Portuguese government used to conduct a yearly census whereby everyone and everything they possessed would be registered. It was through this means that they would identify who was eligible to pay personal tax, based on the male household head's being within a certain age group considered to be employable, irrespective of whether he was holding a job. In cases in which the male head of household had neither a job nor land to work from, he could either join others in the same position and work collectively on state-owned land to produce goods that would then be exchanged for his share of personal tax, or he was cashiered into corvée labor on government projects such as roads until his debt was considered paid. Overall the amount of individual tax levied was small, however, and it was considered by many as mostly symbolic (interview with Jose Barbosa, October 10, 2005).

6. The overthrow of the right-wing Caetano regime by young military officers was sparked by wars of independence being fought in Portuguese Africa. The new regime moved quickly to decolonize.

7. APODETI's principal source of strength and political inspiration was the Indonesian Consulate in Dili.

8. The failure of the UN and the Timorese government to replicate this practice during the transition to independence was resented, particularly by former civil servants who felt they were entitled.

9. After independence, this caused friction between the church and the newly formed Timor-Leste government, which wanted to take back these schools for the government system but was unable to do so because the buildings were built on church land. Another cause of tension between the church and the government was the issue of payment of teachers. After independence, the government wanted to stop paying the salaries of teachers in the Catholic schools, but it was pressured into continuing the practice. During the transition period, UNTAET made an agreement with the church to take on more students than its normal capacity on the basis that UNTAET would assist with teachers' salaries. This strategy was based on the fact that the church still had an educational infrastructure in place, whereas the state's educational infrastructure had been completely destroyed. UNTAET wanted to see children in school rather than on the streets while waiting for the state to rebuild all the necessary schools.

10. The other Timorese-led ministries were Economic Affairs, Infrastructure, Social Affairs (education and health), and Internal Administration. The ministries of Political Affairs, Judiciary, Security and Defense, and Public Finance were led by internationals.

11. The mandate of the eighty-eight-member Constituent Assembly was to draft the country's first constitution. Once this task was completed and the constitution ratified, people expected another election to elect those to govern. According to the new constitution, the Parliament would have sixty-five members.

12. The mission that prepared the report was composed of Steven Symansky (head) and François Corfmat, both of the FAD, and William Crandall and David Webber, both consultants.

13. Treasury Single Account in the Timor-Leste context means that all public revenues are credited into the Consolidated Fund of Timor-Leste account, and all payments are debited from that account.

14. The taxation law for the Timor Sea was a legacy of agreements reached prior to UNTAET.

15. This of course resulted in coordination problems. For example, it was not until late 2005 that Timor-Leste managed to build up a system that could track all capital investment projects financed outside the national budget that had recurrent cost implications.

16. The poor were affected by rapid inflation, however. The Indonesians had heavily subsidized such basic commodities as rice and fuel, and the loss of these contributed to a popular perception that the government was taxing the poor.

17. Despite evidence that these products leaked into the local markets, the UN was very resistant to any curtailment of privileges in this regard. It was also hard to argue that the military serving in Timor-Leste under conditions of considerable discomfort should have been taxed for the temporary benefit of the country they had come to protect. The average peacekeeper was a poorly paid soldier, often from a poor country.

18. We are referring here to the early years of the UNTAET period. After the CNRT was wound up in 2001, there was no longer a single channel for interactions with the Timorese leadership.

19. In the next two or three years, exploration of the Phoenix field may commence.

20. The MPF Budget Office works on two future scenarios. In the "high case" scenario it estimates that Timor Sea revenues will be US$279.9 million over the next four years; in the "low case" scenario it estimates Timor Sea revenues to be only US$49.8 million (Democratic Republic of Timor-Leste Ministry of Planning and Finance 2005a).

21. It was galling for the Timorese to learn that many contracts for items their people could have produced were given instead to firms in Indonesia.

22. Apart from the recruitment policies, part of the blame for this lies in the poorly coordinated training provided to PNTL officers by the UN personnel who came from more than forty disparate international police forces. In contrast, the training given to the F-FDTL was carried out by only two international groups.

23. Not included in Table 5.8 is another US$32 million declared by donors during Sector Investment Program (SIP) exercises. Total spending on capacity-building advisory services and staff training in Timor-Leste over the five-year period was almost US$145 million.

24. It is understood and accepted that internationals should be well paid. Perhaps the employer should be prepared to pay the taxes, so that the internationals are seen as contributing rather than just being rapacious.

6

The Budget as the Linchpin of the State: Lessons from Afghanistan

Ashraf Ghani, Clare Lockhart,
Nargis Nehan, and Baqer Massoud

Maintaining a monopoly on the use of force is often cited as the fundamental attribute of states. More than a thousand years ago, however, the philosopher Ibn Qutayba wrote of the equal importance of two additional attributes of a state: fiscal sustainability and justice. Summarizing what has come to be known in Islamic thought as the "circle of justice," he wrote, "There can be no government without an army, no army without money, no money without prosperity, and no prosperity without justice and good administration."[1] This notion neatly captures the ideas that no force can be created without a fiscal basis and that an endurable and enduring fiscal basis in turn requires justice and fair play. In postconflict settings, where establishing the monopoly on the means of force often remains a challenge, the budget can be a critical instrument of statebuilding. This chapter examines the role of the public finance system in Afghanistan in the 2001–2004 period.

The Budget Cycle as the Linchpin of the State

To become an instrument of legitimacy, a public expenditure system must be predictable. This in turn has a number of prerequisites. First, resources necessary for making payments must be available on time and in full. When a postconflict country is dependent on donor flows for much of its revenue, before domestic revenue sources have been consolidated, it is incumbent on donors to provide that predictability. Second, the rules for allocation and transfer of funds must be agreed upon. Third, criteria of accountability and reporting must be agreed upon in order to establish trust in the capacity of the recipients across levels and functions of the government. Fourth, decision rights at various levels of government must be made clear. Fifth, when new systems are being created, the balance between short-term centralization to create accountability and medium-term delegation of authority that is necessary for sustainability must be kept clearly in view.

A revenue system is the other side of the coin. To satisfy the minimum condition of being a state, a country must generate sufficient revenue to meet its recurrent expenditures. Collection of revenue on a transparent, effective, and accountable basis is an even stronger challenge than constructing the payments system. The payments system is redistributive, whereas the revenue system is extractive. Opportunities for corruption and collusion are even greater. Authority here can be fragmented if various levels of government turn into autonomous centers of revenue extraction, thereby undermining the unity of the state and imposing unpredictability on economic actors. A clear strategy for establishing a sustainable fiscal basis from domestic revenue, therefore, must be a critical part of statebuilding.

The willingness of the citizens to contribute to the public exchequer depends on their appreciation of the state's effectiveness in delivery of services and public investment to improve their well-being. Social justice—across various provinces or districts or across social groups, be it among men and women or young and old—can be measured through budgetary allocations and expenditures. Only if these are reflected completely and transparently in a budget can citizens hope to begin to hold their governments accountable. Thus the circle of policy and practices again closes on the centrality of the budget as the instrument of policy.

The exercise of preparing and agreeing upon a budget can be an important tool in capacity building for governance, particularly in situations where resource allocation among ethnic or social groups is hotly contested in an atmosphere of distrust and where a coalition government is in place. The agreement on a budget by the cabinet is an important mechanism in shifting conflicts over resource allocation into the arena of a transparent political process.

Developmental expenditures can take the shape of either budget support to state expenditure or donor-managed projects. The central criterion for evaluation of public expenditure must be the extent to which it becomes the vehicle for creation of wealth and bonds of solidarity and trust among the citizens. Given that leadership and management are critical constraints in most postconflict conditions, the aid system should be harnessed to maximize the impact of the existing leadership and management. Today, however, the bewildering variety of requirements that the current unharmonized aid system imposes on postconflict countries necessitates that the bulk of the energies of people put in positions of leadership of the economy is devoted to translating the aid pledges into commitments and disbursements, rather than to the creation of wealth and generation of revenues that would provide the true basis of sustainability.

For resource flows to reinforce and sustain the legitimacy of governance, the locus of decisionmaking must reside in the government. If, instead, the government is merely one of multiple centers of autonomous decision rights in the allocation of resources, then stakeholders pursuing their immediate interests rather than long-term goals will seek patronage from these alternative centers. This will further fragment the authority of the new government and jeopardize its quest for legitimacy.

Public Finance Reform in Afghanistan: The Context

On December 22, 2001, power was transferred to Hamid Karzai as chairman of the interim administration, an institutional arrangement agreed to in a conference convened in Bonn in late November 2001 by Lakhdar Brahimi, the Special Representative of the United Nations, and backed by the United States and major powers.

The Bonn Agreement, signed by an unrepresentative group of Afghans, envisaged a series of institutional transitions. The goal was a process that would culminate in direct election of the head of state by the people of Afghanistan, a first in the history of the country. The benchmarks of the Bonn process were (1) creation of the interim administration, to be followed within six months by convening of an Emergency Loya Jirga (Grand Assembly), whose representatives were to be elected with supervision by the United Nations; (2) election of a head of state by the Emergency Loya Jirga for a period of two years; (3) drafting of a constitution; (4) convening of a Constitutional Loya Jirga to modify and improve the constitution; and (5) the holding of elections. This ambitious schedule was to be underwritten by deployment of the International Security Assistance Force (ISAF), the first deployment of which took place in December 2001 in Kabul, and supported by a flow of resources pledged in a conference held in Tokyo in January 2002. ISAF's presence was intended to preempt the possibility of recourse to force by armed groups to change the rules of the game agreed to in the Bonn process.

Between the Communist coup of April 1978 and the collapse of the Taliban in December 2001, Afghanistan had been the scene of a brutal Soviet invasion, ten-year occupation, civil war, and proxy regional war. The cost to the country in destroyed infrastructure and lost opportunities during this period was estimated by the World Bank to have been US$240 billion.[2]

As is common during prolonged conflicts, norms of legality were seriously compromised in Afghanistan, as most of the combatants operated through networks on the margins of established legal norms. Currency was printed outside the country and included multiple printings with the same serial numbers. Its value eroded severely. At times it took a basket of currency notes to buy a basket of goods. Deficit financing through orders at times literally written on the back of envelopes destroyed any notion of fiscal accountability. Two distinct currencies functioned in the north and the south, the northern one trading for roughly half the value of that in the south.

Neither the Soviet-backed regime, nor the mujahadeen, nor the Taliban had been able to gain control over the entire territory of the country. Large swaths were under the control of individual big men or loose and shifting alliances of commanders. Formal revenue mobilization was among the lowest in the world, but individual power holders were able to tax trade, farmers, mining, and other extractive industries. Years of drought further exhausted the coping strategies of the ordinary people, and Afghans acquired the distinction of being the largest refugee population in the world.

Resistance to the Taliban was carried out by a significant but small force around the leadership of Ahmed Shah Massoud, who was assassinated on September 9, 2001. In the wake of the September 11 bombings, the US-led coalition made an alliance with these opposition commanders and supplied them with both cash and matériel to spearhead the drive for ousting the Taliban. As a result, Afghanistan witnessed the reemergence of individual strong men in positions of authority in a number of key provinces.

Despite the years of conflict, a body of administrative rules survived as well as a number of people with a strong identification to a functioning unitary system of government. National sentiment was quite strong, and there were no separatist movements. The Afghan population defined the crisis as one of the absence of a legitimate state that would satisfy their aspirations for security, order, and prosperity. It took time to persuade other actors, ranging from Group of 8 nations and the development and humanitarian agencies to the international security presence, to embrace the goal of statebuilding.

Despite this difficult context, the benchmarks established in Bonn were completed on time, and Hamid Karzai was elected president in a contested election in October 2004. The remainder of this chapter outlines the policies and reforms that were implemented in the public finance system in Afghanistan from October 2001 to the end of 2004.

The Aid System: An Asset and a Constraint

The aid system currently exists as a parallel series of bureaucracies, each with its own revenue, expenditure, and reporting systems. These multiple and fragmented systems are not linked through a budget process that would ensure accountability either to the citizens of donor countries or to the citizens of beneficiary countries. Only the policy process embodied in national budgets can provide this coherence and accountability. When aid is channeled through the budget process, it can be a great asset in the statebuilding process. When channeled outside the budget process, however, it can instead become a constraint. This section sketches the multipronged strategy adopted by the Afghan government in raising international resources.

External Debt Arrears

An initial priority was to clear Afghanistan's arrears to the international financial institutions (IFIs) to make the government eligible to receive grants and highly concessional loans from these organizations. The government met this objective by persuading bilateral donors to contribute US$47.3 million in grants to clear these arrears. These payments were made directly by donors to the lenders, with no financial involvement by the Afghan government.[3] The government also sought forgiveness of past debts owed to bilateral donors.[4]

Multilateral Trust Funds

The bulk of the aid pledged at the January 2002 Tokyo conference was spent on humanitarian assistance, with UN agencies, nongovernmental organizations (NGOs), and private contractors in the position of direct implementers and decisionmakers. The result can be described as a "dual public sector"— one controlled and managed by external actors, the other by the Afghan government (see Figure 6.1 and Table 6.1).

The strategy of the Afghan government was to secure a greater share of external funds and decision rights for the government. To this end, the Ministry of Finance strongly advocated the creation and use of multilateral trust funds: the Afghanistan Reconstruction Trust Fund (ARTF), administered by

Figure 6.1 Afghanistan's Dual Public Sector: Expenditure Budget 2002–2004

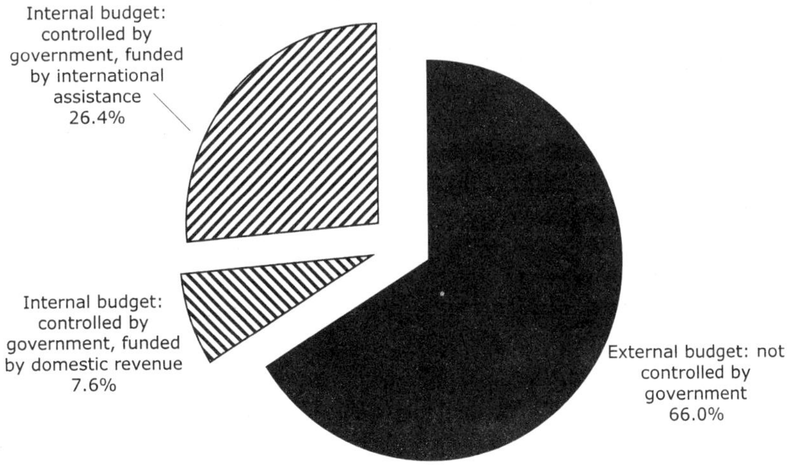

Internal budget: controlled by government, funded by international assistance 26.4%

Internal budget: controlled by government, funded by domestic revenue 7.6%

External budget: not controlled by government 66.0%

Source: Government of Afghanistan, Ministry of Finance, "Financial Report 16/7/1381 (October 2004)," Kabul, 5.

Table 6.1   Expenditure in Afghanistan, 2002–2004

	US$ million	Percent
Internal budget	1,581.1	34.0
Funded by international assistance	354.8	7.6
Funded by domestic revenue	1,226.3	26.4
External budget	3,075.0	66.0
Through United Nations	1,957.0	42.0
Through nongovernmental organizations	413.0	8.9
Through private companies	705.0	15.1
Total expenditure budget	4,656.1	100.0

Source: Government of Afghanistan, Ministry of Finance, "Financial Report 16/7/1381 (October 2004)," Kabul, 4, 6, 32.
Note: Data refer to January 2002 through March 2004.

the World Bank for civilian expenditures, and the Law and Order Trust Fund (LOTFA), administered by the United Nations Development Programme for payments to the police and expansion of the security infrastructure. Ensuring that these multilateral trust funds were supported was critical to the government's goal of bringing predictability, transparency, and accountability to its recurrent expenditure. A number of bilaterals, led by the Netherlands, the Scandinavian countries, Canada, and the UK, channeled a substantial part of their contributions through these trust funds. India, Oman, and Pakistan also provided budget support to the government at an early stage.

When the Minister of Finance assumed the post in July 2002, there were no funds in the Treasury to meet either recurrent or development expenditures, and more than half of his time had to be spent on advocacy with donors to provide resources to ARTF or the budget to meet basic salary payments. This diverted time and energy from internal management issues. Drawing on the reports of the ARTF monitoring agent hired by the World Bank, however, the government was able to analyze leaks in the expenditure system, and the Ministry of Finance aggressively pushed for accountability and transparency. The success of this approach was shown when the European Union and Canada agreed to enhance their contributions to the ARTF and Japan broke precedent by making its first payment into the Trust Fund, followed by Saudi Arabia and several other Arab countries.

A distinctive feature of the ARTF is a clear commitment to design and enforcement of rules that promote transparency and accountability at all levels of government, helping to set the parameters of law-bound behavior in the future. This strategy entailed bringing all recurrent government expenditure, regardless of whether it was from domestic revenue or international sources, within the purview of monitoring arrangements of ARTF. Expenditures were classified by the external monitoring agent as eligible for reimbursement or as ineligible and nonreimbursable. The allocation of ARTF expenditures through the budget helped to entrench the budget as the central instrument of policy. The system required a government float to undertake the initial payments; reimbursement by ARTF funds was quick but conditional upon satisfactory implementation of the rules. Breach of rules not only risked freezing the flow of resources to the government collectively but also could result in a deduction in allotment for the particular department. After a three-year period of operation, the percentage of ineligible expenditures had fallen substantially, and the regularity, detail, and accuracy of reporting had increased dramatically. Resource allocation became completely transparent, as the Ministry of Finance had no discretionary power: its role was simply to enforce the rules. All major policy decisions were taken through the budget process at the cabinet level and in the ministries once the budget was set.

Program Loans

The Ministry of Finance also reached agreements with the Asian Development Bank (ADB) and the World Bank to give program loans to Afghanistan. This proposal was initially received with a high degree of skepticism, as even well-functioning governments in developing countries have difficulty in meeting the conditions of program loans. Afghanistan, however, quickly established a stellar reputation not only for meeting the conditions of program loans but also for meeting ambitious targets on revenue generation and reform agreed upon with the International Monetary Fund. The program loans were made available to the government in cash, enabling the cabinet to exercise decision rights over the disbursement of the funds. The first program loan from the ADB provided an insurance mechanism for meeting expenditure commitments, as the World Bank–administered Trust Fund would only reimburse expenditures after they had been certified as eligible by the monitoring agent. As the process of reimbursement usually entailed a minimum of ninety days, access to program loans enabled the government to avert being shut down a number of times.[5]

National Programs

The Ministry of Finance formulated the notion of national programs to ensure that the flows of donor resources would meet the priorities announced in President Karzai's speech in Tokyo. The National Transport Program, National Emergency Employment Program, National Solidarity Program, National Health Program, National Education Program, National Irrigation and Energy Program, and National Stabilization Program were among the first to be translated into realities on the ground. At the heart of these programs was the approach of empowering the poor directly through investing in social solidarity and institutional development at the village level. In each of these programs, a small group of core donors had to be initially persuaded to fund the program, agree on the strategy, and translate the overarching strategy into procedures, processes, and organizations on the ground.

From the perspective of the heightened expectations of the Afghan population, the programs were slow to develop. The challenge is that the people expect delivery of services by a fully functioning state that both represents them and is accountable to them. The government, however, is not only burdened by the institutional legacy of the past but also faced with the task of coordinating an international aid system that cannot coordinate itself.

A Compact for Development

The government sought donor funds for a medium-term compact for development, presenting the document *Securing Afghanistan's Future* to the Berlin conference on March 31–April 1, 2004. The conference resulted in a pledge of US$8.2 billion for the next three years and an acknowledgment by the international community that Afghanistan needed US$27.5 billion in public investment between 2004 and 2011 to launch it on a path of sustained growth of 9 percent per annum.[6] This stood in sharp contrast to the donor-driven "needs assessment" that had provided the basis for the US$4.5 billion pledged in Tokyo in January 2002. Based on a visit to the country of less than one week, the needs assessment had not only proved unrealistic in its cost estimates—erring in some infrastructure projects by a factor of ten—but also failed to grasp the centrality of the task of statebuilding. A team of more than 100 people worked on *Securing Afghanistan's Future*, with Clare Lockhart, Michael Carnahan, and Ashraf Ghani providing day-to-day coordination and producing the final synthesis. The cabinet debated the document, and after the incorporation of President Karzai's final directions, it was subjected to a month of intense scrutiny by donors prior to its final release at the Berlin conference.

The most significant achievement of President Karzai and his team was to produce a consensus with the donors that the goal in Afghanistan was to build a state geared to the delivery of value to a citizenry that would hold it accountable. At the beginning of 2002, the international partners had other goals, such as providing humanitarian assistance or supporting pet programs. By December 2004, the visions of the international community and the Afghan government were aligned around the centrality of statebuilding. One result was that actions to coordinate security and revenue generation, hitherto considered impossible, became the subject of serious attention and the focus of collaboration.

Coordination of Aid Flows

Knowing that it could not persuade the donors to channel all their resources through the government, the Ministry of Finance confronted the challenge of coordination of the flows. A number of mechanisms were devised to achieve this. A rule on selectivity was put in place, whereby donors were asked to focus on three critical sectors each. If a donor wanted to engage in more than three sectors, it had to contribute US$30 million to each of the sectors and make a minimal contribution of an additional US$30 million to enter another sector. A number of consultative groups, chaired by cabinet ministers, were formed around each of the national programs with the participation of the relevant donor agencies, to provide strategic direction and coordinate implementation. In addition, a monthly coordination meeting chaired by the minister of finance provided the donors and the government with a forum to review challenges and celebrate accomplishments. The annual Afghanistan Development Forum, convened and chaired by the government in Kabul, became the mechanism for providing the government and the donors with a setting in which to engage in a productive dialogue on the strategy of statebuilding pursued by the government. The budget process provided the government with the vehicle to make its preferences explicit to the donor community and to channel donor resources to the priorities of its citizens.

Problems with US Aid

The Ministry of Finance made a concerted effort to persuade the US government that the time for investment in Afghanistan was the current moment, arguing that US$1 million at that point could save US$10 million in the future. This lobbying effort proved successful in 2004 when, at the recommendation of a US Treasury team that worked closely with the Afghan Ministry of Finance, President George W. Bush recommended and obtained from Congress an exceptional mid-term allocation of US$1 billion for Afghanistan and then sought other supplemental funds. This success proved to be a mixed blessing.

Implementation of the enlarged US commitment was entrusted to the US Agency for International Development (USAID). After having been reduced in size and importance over several decades, USAID suddenly faced the task of administering exceptionally large programs simultaneously in Iraq and Afghanistan. Severely limited in the number of people it could place in Afghanistan and essentially becoming a contracting agency, USAID's reach exceeded its grasp. It desired to enter into program after program, promising large sums of money and asking other donors to shift their priorities elsewhere. Yet USAID could neither mobilize the funds in time nor establish control over its layers of contractors. To take one example, a significant number of school buildings that were supposed to be constructed by September 2004 were not actually completed. Although Afghan firms that were the ultimate subcontractors would be paid around US$50,000 for a school, the cost to USAID could be as high as US$250,000.[7]

Continuity was another problem, as USAID went through at least four managers of its country office in a three-year period. It should be mentioned, however, that the US embassy also assembled in the Afghanistan Reconstruction Group (ARG) an exceptional team of talented individuals from the private and public sectors that has worked closely with the Afghan government to put forward a planning framework for devising and implementing strategies. There is a need to draw lessons from the past to enhance the effectiveness of aid provided by the United States and to ensure that it becomes a magnet for trade and investment and not the mechanism for producing a syndrome of dependency.[8]

Domestic Revenue Generation

True sovereignty is inconceivable without a sustainable, internally generated fiscal base. This can be provided only through a strategy for generation of wealth coupled with a social contract on rights and obligations of citizenship. The Staff Monitored Program with the International Monetary Fund (IMF) linked the generation of specific revenues to well-defined institutional reforms in the Central Bank and Ministry of Finance. The government continuously defined a "stretch revenue target" that exceeded the agreed target with the IMF, and meeting these stretch targets became an important vehicle for moving toward self-sustainability. The Afghan team has been clear that the donors must see the light at the end of the tunnel, a period within which the security costs, civilian salaries, and operational and maintenance costs of the development programs can be met fully from domestic revenue. Projections made in preparation for Berlin indicated that the recurrent budget in seven years would be around US$1.5 billion. Only by relentless rationalization of existing revenues and creation of new sources of revenue can such a stretch target be realized. Internal and external stakeholders must realize that the target can be met, but that this will require careful attention to political economy and the types of resistance that will be mobilized by narrow groups bent on advancing their own interests at the expense of national sustainability.

Currency and Banking

In early 2002, the afghani, Afghanistan's currency, far from being the dominant means of exchange, had conceded ground to other currencies from the dollar to the Pakistani rupee and the Iranian rial. Having declined nearly 1,000-fold in value, a basket of afghanis was needed to acquire a basket of goods. Deficit finance had reigned supreme for over a decade, with notes being printed in the Soviet Union and then in Russia. Finding sets of notes with the same numbers was not uncommon. Furthermore, in the northern provinces, notes printed in Europe—called the Jumbesh currency—were trading for half the value of the notes circulating in Kabul. In some valleys in central Afghanistan, a third form of currency was also in circulation. The Central Bank had no deposits of currency, and the Interim Government was put in the ironic situation of buying afghanis for dollars in the open market and using the currency thus acquired for payment of salaries.

International experts presented the government with three options on the currency front: full dollarization, meaning that the dollar would become the sole currency of the realm; partial dollarization, meaning that the dollar would be legal tender until a new afghani was issued; or issuing a new currency. They recommended partial dollarization, arguing that a new currency could not be issued in a period of less than two years and that there were major logistical and social risks entailed in issuing a new afghani. President Karzai chaired daily meetings of the coordination committee of the cabinet for a week on this issue. He posed the key problem of how the government would explain partial dollarization to the Afghan population. His relentless focus on the symbolic importance of the currency for statebuilding forced a reexamination of the assumptions upon which the recommendation of the international experts was based. The committee recommended that a new Afghan currency be introduced, with the reduction of three zeros from the old currency.

The finance minister was assigned the role of chairing a task force to delineate the time line and recommend mechanisms for implementation. The task force met every day for a month until it reached consensus. On the legal front, a key issue was the amount of old currency that could be exchanged by a single individual. The task force decided against an imposition of limits, arguing that this would simply result in long lines, as those with money could simply hire their dependents to satisfy the limit.

The search for mechanisms focused on finding existing resources that could be harnessed without creation of a major new infrastructure. The solution was found in the networks of the *hawala,* dealers who were specialists in currency exchange and transfer. Consultations with representatives of these networks quickly revealed that they had a sophisticated infrastructure spanning the length and breadth of the country and that they could be quickly persuaded that a new currency would simplify their transactions immensely. In addition, pride in putting their networks at the service of a national cause was an important enabling factor. A small commission to enable them to bear some of the additional expenses was also agreed upon. An international donor agreed to provide the resources to hire the planes and helicopters needed for the logistics. On this basis, an initial period of three months was delineated as the time of exchange.

The other critical decision involved printing. As the adoption of the euro had created surplus capacity in the printing presses of European countries, the Central Bank carried on intensive discussion with a number of printers, choosing several who could guarantee a security level to the new afghani matching that of the euro.

Once the task force had achieved consensus, the results were presented to the cabinet, which endorsed the approach and passed the enabling decree. The governor of the Central Bank then took over the task of implementation.

Several challenges were successfully faced during implementation. First, as the logistics support from the donors did not materialize in time, the timetable had to be set back by one month, and the resources of the Afghan security forces had to be mobilized.[9] Second, the rate of exchange of currency was so rapid that organizing the burning of old notes in a timely manner posed a challenge. A dedicated incendiary had to be constructed by artisans in Kabul and manual processes of burning had to be organized in the provinces—not a small task, as the equivalent of sixteen tons of notes was collected. To ensure transparency, teams of ministers and members of the international community were sent to the nodal points across the country to supervise the burning of old notes. Third, to ensure that no further notes were being printed, the old facilities in Russia had to be destroyed. Fourth, there were fears that people in remote areas would not be able to participate in the process of exchange, but the public relations campaign, coupled with the ability of the *hawala* dealers to mobilize their networks, proved more than equal to the task. The currency exchange was completed one month after its initial target date.

Success in the currency exchange served as a symbolic means of unification of the country. It also established the credentials of the transitional government with its international partners and with the population, who greeted the reform with spontaneous celebrations. Children flashed the new notes as a sign of national pride and a harbinger of a stable currency.

Banking sector reform proved more difficult. Four major issues needed to be addressed: a legislative basis for defining the functions of the Central Bank and for the entry of the private sector into banking needed to be established; the state-owned banks needed to be reorganized; the Central Bank needed to be strengthened, both to perform as the banker of the government and to regulate the banking sector effectively; and financial institutions, ranging from microfinance to venture capital funds, were needed to support the legal economy in general and small and medium enterprises in particular. A clear vision on building the banking system as a credible payments system and a mechanism of providing access to credit is essential to stability and unity of the country.

The IMF was the major interlocutor in formulation of the necessary legislation. Two constraints emerged that would be repeated across other arenas. First, international partners insisted upon a legislative model that was largely derived from theoretical precepts, rather than a clear analysis of institutional constraints and mechanisms that would satisfy the requirements of theory. Second, when the legislative department of the Ministry of Justice was confronted with a complex piece of legislation taken off the shelf from another legal tradition, it had serious difficulties rendering it into the traditions and language of the country. Granting of licenses to a number of international banks was carried out rapidly after the decision by the cabinet to accept the English text of the legislation as binding, thereby considerably easing transfer of money to and from Afghanistan.

Reform of the state-owned banks moved very slowly, and this task still needs to be confronted. The government faced severe constraints in adopting an effective system of payments across the country. Difficulty in paying security forces and civil servants across the country was later identified as a key constraint to stability. Two of the state-owned banks had cash assets of more than US$100,000,000, but the government was unable to utilize these assets to ease the severe shortage of credit for entrepreneurs or to reshape these banks to provide an effective payments system. Many branches of the Central Bank remained effectively under the control of local commanders and provincial governors.[10] The Ministry of Finance and the governor of the Central Bank repeatedly raised the issue of security of branches in the provinces and requested support from the international community, but the request was not met.

A clear vision on a financial architecture has been slow to emerge. Although some schemes were initiated on microfinance, and the government sponsored the creation of a venture capital scheme and sought risk-guarantee mechanisms,[11] a comprehensive credit system did not emerge. As a result, latent assets cannot be tapped. The use of mortgages to unleash the capital inherent in housing assets was not tackled credibly, impairing efforts to develop livelihoods as a linchpin of the counternarcotics strategy. The inability of the Central Bank during its first two years to open letters of credit for developmental projects caused significant delays in implementation of key infrastructure projects.

Treasury Reform

Treasury was a domain where informal rules had subverted the formal rules of the game, creating an organized culture of corruption. The formal rules required submission of payment forms to the Ministry of Finance. After approval by the Budget and Treasury departments, these were to be sent to the Central Bank for payment to the government ministries, and from the ministries' departments of finance to the secondary budget units in the central government or the provinces. The informal rules of the game required that at each of the critical nodes, queues were developed, and facilitation arrangements were required to move the process forward. When a government employee received her or his pay in cash from a bonded trustee at the end of the process, the amount usually would be as much as 25 percent less than the entitlement. An analysis of payment of customs duties in July 2002 revealed that an Afghan citizen who needed to pay two dollars in duties usually ended up paying eight dollars in bribes and spent as much as seven days running between different government departments to obtain the necessary signatures.

Transformation of the Treasury into a predictable and transparent organization required a number of major changes. A financial management firm was brought in to computerize the process within the Ministry of Finance, and similar computerization was undertaken in the Central Bank. The technical process was achieved rapidly, enabling the Ministry of Finance to issue printed checks to the Central Bank. The introduction of new technology resulted in an organized Luddite movement to incite employees against the computers, blaming them for the breakdown in the well-honed networks of corruption. The real tasks then became mapping and remapping of the existing processes and recruiting new personnel with the necessary commitment to a culture of accountability and transparency. As a result of the reengineering of processes, the previous organization in which a number of individuals were continuously assigned to the accounts of specific ministries was disrupted, and Treasury personnel were separated from the facilitators and bonded trustees who would require illegal commissions to carry out their work.

The assumption of the Treasury post by Nargis Nehan launched the department on a rapid process of systematic transformation. She brought a number of elements into a coherent strategy. First, she streamlined the payments process by setting a deadline of four days for processing any request from a ministry and by assigning dates for issuing checks to the ministries on a predictable schedule, thereby eliminating the queues and processes of facilitation to move a request to the top of the queue.

Second, reporting from the ministries and provinces to the Ministry of Finance and from the Ministry of Finance to the cabinet was organized in a systematic manner. The Treasury required and obtained information from all the line ministries on the payments of salaries to all government employees, enabling the cabinet to track the degree of success and failure in the predictability of payments across the country. By linking processing of future allotments to submission of timely reports, the Treasury was able to create a system of rule-bound behavior. A marker of the degree of success of this process is that by December 2004, fully 65 percent of the provinces were reporting their incomes and expenditures within the first ten days of every month to the Ministry of Finance. Key requirements were the organization of data into categories that reflected citizens' concerns, collecting these by geographic unit to ensure evenhandedness in distribution of resources, and regular reporting.

Third, the system of allotment to the provinces was made predictable. A turning point in the transition to formal rules came in a meeting with the directors of the departments of health, education, and finance from the provinces, where in response to queries and criticism, Nehan provided charts that showed the amount of funds in each of the provincial accounts and the method of allocation based on a computerized program. The meeting ended with a full endorsement of her leadership.

The restoration of the payments system was a key element in reassertion of the authority of the state. Given the complex logistics and the terrain of the country, the goal of paying all employees of the government on the same day across the country remained unfulfilled and will take significant investments in the banking system and information technology to be achieved. This goal was formulated in July 2002, and technical assistance was mobilized to study its feasibility. The report by an international consulting firm argued that it would take at least five years. Internal brainstorming in the Ministry of Finance, however, produced a series of recommendations for changing the existing manual systems and reorganizing the staff of the Central Bank and two state-owned banks to deliver direct payments to employees. By December 2004, ten ministries and other central government organizations were being paid through this new method. For the first time, an employee received her or his salary in an envelope containing the exact amount of the payment. The process not only enhanced the effective pay of the employee but also resulted in a significant reduction of the number of ghost workers in whose names bonded trustees were previously collecting salaries. As part of its reform initiative, the Ministry of Finance also formulated a strategy to enhance the capacity of the post offices across the country, as a mechanism for both payments and savings.

To enable the flow of finances from donors through the government account, international firms had been contracted through the World Bank's first postconflict grant to exercise key functions in financial management, audit, and procurement. The challenge became to build capacity to ensure that these responsibilities were transferred to Afghan leaders, managers, and officials. Nargis Nehan led a "localization" initiative to update skills of existing staff and to recruit new staff through a transparent and merit-based process. She also led an initiative to reexamine the use of information technology and systems, investigating the borrowing of information management systems from Iran that were already in Persian, rather than continuing with systems imported via Western firms that were unsuitable in terms of complexity and language.

Although reform of the Treasury entailed centralization within the Ministry of Finance, the medium-term strategy required the creation of systems in both the provinces and the line ministries, where decision rights would be delegated, and integrated information management systems would allow monitoring to check adherence to the rules. In the spring of 2005, the process was inaugurated in the provinces. Creation of the capacity in the ministries has been much slower, as a fiscal management project for the whole government is dependent on clarification of functions of each ministry and removal of overlapping functions. As different donors are working as lead nations with different ministries, there is a risk that information management systems and organizational models are being created that will require considerable expense and effort to integrate subsequently into a unified system.

In contrast to the fragmented picture on information management systems, the creation of the Single Treasury Account is one of the enduring accomplishments of the transitional government. Creation of this account and adherence to it has been enshrined in the constitution. All government flows now are organized into subaccounts in the Central Bank, and the Ministry of Finance is able to keep track of the revenue and expenditures on a timely basis. Prior to the creation of the Single Treasury Account, there were hundreds of separate government accounts in the Central Bank and state-owned banks. A single department of the Ministry of Finance, for instance, had more than forty accounts. As different individuals had decision rights over the withdrawal from these accounts, the budgetary rules could constantly be subverted in practice. The existence of these multiple accounts also enabled various organizations to collect money in the name of the government without reporting it as part of the revenue of the state. The resulting degree of opaqueness is captured by the fact that in Afghan year 1382 (2003–2004), more than US$40 million was brought to the revenue of the government through closure of these accounts. The entire revenue of the government in that year was US$207 million. Creation of the Single Treasury Account also limits potential abuse of rent from natural resources, as any agreement to divert royalties from natural resources would be a violation of the constitution.

Reform of Revenue

Consideration of domestic revenue mobilization brings the economy of state-building into sharp relief. In Afghanistan, the period under review was characterized by widespread violations of the constitution and other laws and by informal systems subverting the formal rules of the game. Customs illustrates the first, and taxation illustrates the second.

Customs and Tariffs

The collection of tolls or customs has always been an important part of the revenue of governments ruling over the current territory of Afghanistan. Between 1929 and 1978, customs revenue provided the most important component of the domestic revenue. Depending on the trading partners, a few provinces have loomed particularly large in collection of customs revenue. The Afghan government found itself in a situation in which provincial governors or militia commanders, sitting astride border points, collected the revenue, determined policy, gave preferential treatment to their favorite merchants, and spent the money as they wished. By contrast, provinces that were not on transit routes had practically no resources. From 2002 to 2004, Iran was the key conduit of the transit trade—the overland shipment of goods from the Gulf to south

Asia—making Herat the most important gateway for collection of revenues. At the same time, the large number of military units who had gathered under Commander Massoud and were stationed in and around Kabul could not be paid, as the international community refused to provide the resources to pay these men.

President Karzai addressed this problem in May 2003, convening first the National Security Council and then the cabinet to produce a consensus on the need for centralization of revenue. He then addressed the nation and a gathering of the *ulema* (religious scholars), making it clear that he made his own continuation in service dependent on progress on this issue. After this public declaration, he ordered all the governors and commanders with major customs revenue to come to Kabul. Having kept them waiting for four days, he then drafted a decree on centralization of revenue, obtained the signatures of all of the commanders and provincial governors, and promulgated it as public policy. The Ministry of Finance was tasked with implementing the presidential decision. Teams from the ministry were sent to all the provinces in June and July, and the minister of finance undertook an intensive tour of the revenue-producing provinces. By July 2003, more than US$20 million in cash had been brought from the provincial deposits to the Central Bank, and formal restoration of a unitary system of government in the fiscal area was established on the ground.

The success of the process is rooted in history. As studies of provincial-level administration by the World Bank reveal, Afghans across various walks of life, including those serving in provincial administrations, considered restoration of the unitary system to be highly desirable.[12] Despite the disappearance of manuals of administration, the memory of rules was extremely strong. In addition, the Afghan public associated local control over customs with unaccountable if not outright despotic or predatory individuals and groups. There was a consensus in the country that centralization of the revenue was a marker of the reemergence of the Afghan state. The issue as framed by the Ministry of Finance was one of restoration and implementation of rules rather than imposition of arbitrary centralization. The Islamic theory of governance in Afghanistan has been unitary, and the election of President Karzai by the Emergency Loya Jirga in June 2002 was a key enabling factor in centralization of revenue. In mosque after mosque, the Ministry of Finance asserted that the edict of a legitimate ruler, from whose legitimacy the governors and commanders derived their authority, was being implemented. Therefore the issue was not a one-time handover of "tribute" from the provincial treasuries of some local big men but rather the implementation of the constitution and laws of the land.

The reassertion of formal rules had its limits, however. Even though all formally registered customs revenue was submitted to the government, three significant areas of departure from the formal rules persisted in practice. First, in some of the key border points, a double bookkeeping system emerged, with one set of books submitted to the capital but another kept on the ground. Second, at least ten border crossings became points of entry for very large quantities of goods without having been recognized as customs posts. Revenue collected in these locations went to militia commanders and various networks of big men. Third, discriminatory local-level policies favoring groups of merchants aligned with militia commanders or local big men persisted, allowing cronies of these power brokers to compete on terms very unfavorable to honest merchants. The net effect of these three practices was that significant amounts of potential revenue did not find their way to the coffers of the government. Discussions with the international security forces persistently focused on a strategy whereby deployment of coalition forces and their Provincial Reconstruction Teams (PRTs) would be aligned with the goal of government control of customs and border crossings. These problems have yet to be fully resolved. The amount at stake is not small: preliminary assessments indicate that an additional US$300–600 million per year can be garnered from removing these three constraints. This compares to an estimated domestic revenue in 1384 (2005–2006) of about US$320 million (International Monetary Fund 2005a).

In parallel to centralization of customs revenue, the Ministry of Finance embarked on an ambitious program of tariff reform. The major issues were simplification of the complex system of classification into a transparent system, promulgating an exchange rate based on the market rather than administrative fiat, simplification of customs procedures and practices, creation of modern infrastructure for customs, crafting a customs law aligned with best international practice, and building information management systems and human resources. After a fair amount of groundwork had been done to formulate the elements of the strategy, Jelani Popal assumed the post of the director general of customs and deputy minister of finance for revenue and customs and galvanized the process that moved it forward.

Prior to the reform, the rules of the game were extremely opaque. The Customs House in Kabul, for instance, in 2002 was producing three different tariffs in response to inquiries. Up to twenty-four signatures were required, every step of the process entailing the payment of a "gift." There was a high degree of unnecessary centralization, requiring, for instance, signatures from the office of the director general of customs on various items of imports. The biggest problem was the artificial exchange rate, for although the dollar was trading in the open market for fifty afghanis, the rate of exchange at the customs house was six afghanis, leading to dramatic undervaluation of imports. The reform process had to face the challenge that simplification of tariff categories, which should have been welcomed by importers, could also involve an effective increase in rates of payment. Therefore, the work had to be done with considerable care and analysis. In the policy proposal to the cabinet, the tariff structure was reduced from more than 120 categories to 4, with rates of 5, 8, 10, and 14 percent. The president ordered the introduction of a new category of 4 percent on all imports of machinery for private investment projects, to signal the special attention of the government to this group of potential investors. After a one-week trial period resulted in a protest movement, discussions between the government and merchants prompted the introduction of a further category of 2.5 percent covering most food imports and construction materials such as cement.

The process of reaching agreement on the new tariff structure reveals the complexity of the dynamics of interaction among importers, and the toll that the absence of credible representative organizations in the private sector exacts from bargaining over such issues with the government. Prior to submission of the new tariff to the cabinet, the Ministry of Finance engaged in extensive consultations with various categories of merchants. Some merchants, however, insisted that they had not been consulted, construing the willingness of the government to openly and transparently consider all their inputs as tantamount to the right of veto over the decision of the government. It is interesting that those individuals who voiced the loudest concerns over not being consulted did not show any records of having imported anything during the previous year or having paid any substantial amounts in customs. There was also the issue that some of the merchants considered 200 or 400 percent margins of profit to be their natural rights. Others wanted the tariff to be geared exclusively to their short-term interest in reexporting goods illegally to the neighboring countries, a practice that led the government of Pakistan to impose a unilateral ban on a list of imports from Afghanistan, in violation of international conventions and the Afghanistan Transit Trade Agreement between the two countries.

On the other hand, some of the merchants voiced legitimate grievances when the tariff was implemented on a trial basis. One week of discussions between government and merchant representatives produced an agreement: the new exchange rate and the simple tariff categories would be retained, but the government would agree to the introduction of a category of 2.5 percent, shift certain items within the tariff categories, and put the new system into effect on March 21, 2004, the beginning of the Afghan calendar and fiscal year. The new system went into effect on the agreed date, and except for a minor protest in Khost, where the erstwhile Communist government had granted special concessions that were now removed, there was no hitch in implementation. Afghanistan now has the simplest tariff system in the region and is in a position to use the tariff as an instrument of developmental policy and revenue collection. The rise in revenue has been substantial (International Monetary Fund 2005a), but realizing the full customs revenue potential awaits the removal of three constraints identified above.

Preparation of a new customs law internalized the lessons learned from the preparation of the banking laws. Instead of presenting the legislative department of the Ministry of Justice with an off-the-shelf product, the team from the Ministry of Finance, assisted by international advisers, worked closely with colleagues from the Ministry of Justice to reach agreement. By December 2004, when Popal, who had contributed his services as a volunteer without pay, resigned from his post, a coherent strategy for the next five years was in place. At the heart of this strategy was creation of information management systems that went beyond enabling Afghanistan to adhere to the best international practice. Investing in people was a very significant part of this strategy, and the customs department obtained approval from the Civil Service Commission to recruit staff on a transparent basis and to pay them on an enhanced scale of salaries. The draft law also provided special incentives for customs officials to seize illegally imported goods and to combat corruption in the export of narcotics.

In sum, customs and tariff reform followed a holistic strategy that combined attention to a complex range of policy issues, relentless management of details, and patience to deal with stakeholders who would shift their positions or claim that those who had provided inputs and dialogue were unrepresentative. Over the decades, the official Chamber of Commerce has become an organization whose leadership is appointed by the Ministry of Commerce. Some new organizations have come into existence, but these are led by Afghans who have lived many years abroad and are fluent in foreign languages, and it is not clear that they actually represent the consensus of the merchant community in general. The challenge for the merchant community is to acquire an organizational infrastructure, with transparent systems of selection and representation; to agree on mechanisms of consultation with the government; and to understand both the potential and limits of a consultative process, as the government in the end must make policy decisions based on the interests of the entire nation rather than one segment.

The Telecommunications and Fuel Sectors

The government has been clear that although centralization, simplification, and consolidation of revenue from customs are necessary to fiscal sustainability, they are by no means sufficient. The goal is to increase total revenue on the basis of a wealth-creation strategy and to reduce the proportion contributed from customs and foreign assistance. The first manifestation of this approach for diversification of revenue sources was carried out in the area of telecommunications. The transitional government decided to issue licenses for a mobile telecommunications operator, on the basis of careful work by a team of international experts who were led by the ministers of communications and finance. After approval of the policy by the cabinet, the process of awarding the license was entrusted to a group of international experts, who were provided complete autonomy in their evaluation of bids. Two bids nearly matched each other on technical grounds, but the Roshan group offered nearly US$3 million more than its rival and consequently was awarded the license.

An important issue of discussion was whether the government would give customs concessions or exemptions for the import of telecommunications machinery. The government team insisted that Roshan's projection of potential demand was vastly underestimated and was not willing to provide exemptions. Negotiations were tough, nearly resulting in award of the license to the next bidder. As it transpired, Roshan had indeed underestimated substantially the demand of the Afghan population for mobile phones. The agreement with Roshan provided the precedent on the basis of which the government renegotiated the licenses granted to the Afghan Wireless Communication Company by the Taliban and confirmed by outgoing president Burhanuddin Rabbani prior to the transfer of power to Karzai. Taxes from the telecommunications sector can provide an important source of revenue in the future, provided that the government acquires the capacity to maintain a level playing field and hold the players to international standards of accounting and auditing.

In contrast to the successful strategy adopted in the telecommunications sector, efforts to introduce a transparent regulatory system for the import of fuels, which would have had substantial health, safety, and revenue benefits, did not materialize, as powerful interest groups successfully mobilized against it. Instead, there were attempts to secure concessions, eighteenth-century-like privileges that would have violated the constitution and the laws of the land. Substantial progress was achieved in 2004 on new minerals and oil and gas laws, as the Ministries of Mines and Industry and Finance reached agreement with the World Bank and other international partners on these important policy domains.

Taxation

The most important arena for realization of the goal of fiscal sustainability is taxation. This is a complicated domain, because of the complexity of inherited rules and regulations, the lack of clarity of functions within the government, and the substantial human resources required for simplification as well as conflicting ideas regarding fairness, incentives for development, and creation of a culture in which rights of citizenship go hand in hand with the obligations of citizenship.

An analysis carried out in the Ministry of Finance revealed that there were about 113 laws on the books in the area of taxation, some entailing expenditure of US$1,000 to collect one dollar in revenue to the government. Of course, this did not mean that the revenue collected by the government was the amount paid by the people, as those acting in the name of the government often acted in their own interest or that of local power holders. Simplification of the laws and enforcement of new procedures required a substantial one-time mobilization. Changing the antiquated rent law, for instance, required mobilization of more than 200 individuals to collect more than US$100 million in revenue and taxes from several districts of the city of Kabul. Change of the vehicle registration tax in Kabul would require a three- to six-month mobilization of around 400 individuals and would bring a net benefit of US$20 million to the government.

With the large international presence in Afghanistan, an issue in implementing various taxes, including rental taxes and vehicle registration fees, was whether international agencies and their employees should be tax exempt. In principle, the payment of taxes by the international community not only could help increase domestic revenue capacity but also would provide a demonstration effect that wealthy and powerful people must pay their fair share of taxes. Moreover, the existence of a separate set of rules goes against the principle of equality of all before the law and provides loopholes through which goods could enter under one category and be resold under another, undermining fair competition in the market. Yet the international community's declarations on the importance of enhancing domestic revenue mobilization have not been matched by willingness to consider new initiatives to tap the revenue possibilities generated by their own presence. For example, the introduction of the rental tax in Kabul, which captures some of the windfall profits generated by the foreign presence, although supported by the IMF, was resisted by some in the international community.

A challenge that remains to be settled in taxation policy in Afghanistan is clarification as to whether the Ministry of Finance, alone or in conjunction with one or more other authorities, is the locus of policy and implementation in the area of taxation. Practically every ministry now performs a role not only in collecting revenue but also in setting policy. Such a structure not only suffers from undue complexity but also contains the risks of double or triple taxation as well as unpredictability. The risk is particularly high in the case of municipalities, whose decision rights need to be clarified as part of a holistic strategy on taxes and revenue mobilization.

The Ministry of Finance was able to eliminate export taxes, reduce corporate and individual taxes from 25 to 20 percent, create a large taxpayers' unit, and introduce tax identity numbers for all importers and corporate taxpayers. The number of taxpayers at the end of 2004, however, was fewer than 14,000. Despite this, a group of vocal individuals in the private sector, some of whom have received heavy subsidies for their initiatives from donors, insist that the taxes in the country are too high. Examination of both tariffs and taxes of the neighboring countries reveals that Afghanistan's are the lowest in the region, and among the lowest in the world. But given the shrill nature of the debate, there is need for a mechanism to review the developmental aspirations of the country and to forge a consensus around taxation policy. A key task for the future is substantially reducing, if not eliminating, the gap between the informal and the formal rules. The Afghan people today are taxed for both legal and illegal activities. It is clear that both production and trafficking of drugs are subject to various informal mechanisms of taxation. Further, merchants are subject to informal tolls across the roads. A truck, for instance, was subject in early 2004 to illegal collection as many as twenty-four times from the border town of Hairatan in the north to the city of Jalalabad in the east. Unless the cost of protection is centralized and the flow of legal transactions is subject to an honest system of taxation, creation of a culture of formal and transparent taxation will remain a distant goal. Equally significant, of course, is a transparent system of expenditure where citizens are able to see the value derived from their taxes at work.

The Budget

The Ministry of Finance put forth the concept of the budget as the central instrument of policy. The essence of this strategy was to initially bring all the stakeholders in the government, and then all the stakeholders in the country and the international system, into the same arena and to make the cabinet the center of decisionmaking. This conception is deeply rooted in Afghan history, where government officials desired a predictable system and one locus of decisionmaking, linked directly to flows of resources. Having obtained the president's endorsement of this national objective, the Ministry of Finance devised a number of mechanisms to achieve it.

No-Deficit Financing

First, the ministry enforced the policy of no-deficit financing. This meant a complete break with the practices of the past, as it required strict adherence to rules of budget, procurement, and reporting for release of funds. The magnitude of the task can be appreciated by noting that in the first quarter of 1383, beginning on March 21, 2004, fully 40 percent of applications for cash advances were rejected by the Treasury for lack of compliance with existing rules. A corollary of the policy of no-deficit financing was that the government should be able to project its cash requirements to the Central Bank with advance notice of at least one month. The Central Bank was completely right in requiring this type of notification. Despite considerable progress, however, the Ministry of Finance has been unable to meet this objective.

Centralization of Allocation and Reporting

The underlying reason for the failure to meet the first objective has to do with a second objective of the Ministry of Finance: to make the budget not only its business but also that of all levels of government at first, and ultimately of the citizens at large. Progress in this area was painfully slow. Although coordination between the Ministry of Finance and line ministries improved substantially, the internal reorganization of the budgeting and administrative systems within most ministries progressed only marginally. Neither the information management systems nor the human resources required to ensure that allocations and expenditures were based on priorities and accurately reflected the cost of activities were in place by the end of 2004.

At the heart of this problem was the neglect of the budget as a central instrument of policy in the aid system. It was now common practice for different donors and groups of technical experts to take the lead in recommending changes in parts of complex systems, a practice that contributed to fragmentation and waste of resources. What was required was a coherent program for building the internal budgeting systems across levels and functions of government. Only on this basis could the right balance be achieved between the centralization of allocation and reporting and the delegation of authority to instill ownership and responsibility to the lower levels.

Identification of Personnel

A third focus was the need to tackle the problem of differences between the number of authorized positions and the actual number of staff in a particular ministry or organization. The Ministry of Finance created a database with the help of the British Department for International Development (DfID), entering all the details of government staff who had received salary in a particular month. On this basis, Salam Rahimy, the deputy minister of finance, was able to transform consideration of the recurrent budget from shrill arguments to discussion of figures, numbers, and priorities. It is a credit to his leadership and management skills that the 1383 (March 2004 to March 2005) recurrent budget was a consensus document with the exception of one ministry, which unsuccessfully pressed its case for a much enhanced appropriation in the cabinet.

The staff size issue reflected the so-called 20–80 rule, meaning that 20 percent of the organizations usually account for 80 percent of the expenditures and thereby 80 percent of the problems. In the case of the recurrent expenditure, the organizations that were on the top of the list were Defence, Education, Health, Interior, and the Secret Service. The discussions between Ministries of Defence and Finance for preparation of the 1382 (March 2003 to March 2004) budget were particularly intense, with the Ministry of Defence insisting that the various militia forces within their structure amounted to 250,000 officers and soldiers, and the Ministry of Finance, relying on publicly available intelligence systems, maintaining that the number was closer to 50,000. The process of verification entailed in Disarmament, Demobilization, and Reintegration (DDR) has revealed that the intelligence estimates were quite close to the mark. In the end it was decided that the Ministry of Finance would accept a figure of 100,000 for the Ministry of Defence, provided that the Ministry of Defence agreed on a systematic downscaling during 1382 and 1383 (2003 and 2004). By November 2004, the Ministry of Defence was requested to provide in the 1384 (March 2005 to March 2006) budget for a maximum of 10,000 officers and soldiers from its former ranks.

Discussion with the other major interlocutors in the 20–80 category was equally intense. By the end of 2004, the health ministry had substantially reduced the number of its employees by contracting with the private sector; the secret service was undergoing a systematic reform of procedures and verification of its employees; and the education ministry was receiving substantial help from donors to create databases and systems to verify teachers and personnel on the ground. Nonetheless, it is worth repeating here that the absence of a national biometric database of employees was still severely constraining the ability of the government to know the number of its actual employees and thereby to implement increases in their salaries.

Although the number of authorized positions gradually is being brought under control, and the number of actual positions is being verified manually, it is still impossible to ascertain the number of people who draw multiple salaries simultaneously under different names from different ministries and departments. The Ministry of Finance saw a great opportunity in the presidential and parliamentary elections of 2004 and 2005 to harness modern technology to address this problem and pushed to create a biometric national database or to persuade the UN agencies and donors at least to fund such a database for the civilian and military employees of the government. Its efforts were unsuccessful, however, as the election experts were strongly committed to a manual procedure based on the use of paper cards and verification by ink.

Database on Donor Assistance

A fourth focus was building a database on all donor assistance. Aidan Cox, a United Nations Development Programme (UNDP) staff member seconded to the government at the request of Ministry of Finance, recruited an Afghan team and invested his considerable energies in building its skills and confidence. When Seema Ghani Massoumi accepted the post of the director of the budget in the Ministry of Finance, she not only strengthened this remarkable team but also enlisted it for preparation of the mid-year budget review, the annual budget preparation process, and information sharing and dissemination with the donors and the Afghan public. The workshops that she and Nargis Nehan organized with various groups of Afghan stakeholders were a very important mechanism for ensuring transparency and accountability. These workshops were the pilot for undertaking the preparation of a poverty-reduction strategy paper in 2005, with the goal of using the process to build a national consensus around achievable goals with the available means.

Development Expenditure

Fifth, in budgeting for development expenditure, the 20–80 problem applied to ministries charged with provision of infrastructure. Here a key constraint was the absence of feasibility studies and a lack of understanding of what a fundable project required. As development is the legitimate business of all citizens, everyone in the country has a proposal on the best location of dams for irrigation or generation of power, construction of roads, building of hospitals or transmission lines. Regardless of financial costs or environmental and social impacts, when most ministries proposed projects, they were at best dusting off the proposals of the 1970s, ignoring the changed technologies and design practices or putting forward a one-page proposal for expenditure of tens of millions of dollars. There was also difficulty in grasping the fact that donors were unwilling to fund the expansion of the government sector to implement developmental projects. Older officials, fondly recalling their collaborations in the 1970s with international financial institutions in the creation of state-owned enterprises, were often shocked to learn that these institutions now advocated the dismantling rather than expansion of these enterprises. This tension regarding functions to be performed by the government remains unresolved.

Procurement

A sixth area of work related to the budget was procurement, which has been a severe constraint in both project implementation and timely attention to operations and maintenance. The government hired an international firm to handle procurement for development projects, which made a substantial contribution to ensuring that international procurement was carried out effectively. At the very beginning, however, the firm ignored the advertisement rules of the existing procurement laws, compliance with which would have required a minimal expenditure of less than US$1,000 for the advertisements. This seemingly small incident cast a public shadow—inflamed by a number of newspapers and interest groups within the government—on the government's commitment to transparency.

The most significant challenge, however, was to find a champion for preparation and passage of a new procurement law through the cabinet. The Ministry of Reconstruction took charge of management of the procurement firm and responsibility for preparation of a new procurement law, but passage of the law was delayed until 2006. In the absence of a procurement law that met international best practice, the government's desire to channel more money through the budget remained unfulfilled. Adoption of a new procurement law also was needed to change the relation between Ministry of Finance and line ministries, from one of opposition and constant scrutiny to one of trust based on adherence to accepted rules. Given the ninety-day period of reimbursement from the ARTF and the fact that the weather and logistics put severe limits on the number of days when construction work can be carried out in different parts of the country, adoption of a new law to streamline procurement should have been an urgent task.

Budget Law

Afghanistan had inherited a budget law that received a very favorable review from international experts. Therefore, the task was seen initially as improvement of the existing procedures and introduction of information management systems, rather than preparation of a new law. Subsequently, however, different experts from the same international institutions recommended adoption of a new budget law. Seema Ghani Massoumi prepared a draft budget law that was ready for discussion by the cabinet by the end of December 2004. The shift in the advice of international experts should serve as a reminder that few people in international agencies or bilateral donors have a clear view of the building blocks of a sustainable fiscal system. In each of the reforms carried out by the Afghan government, Afghans had to invest substantial amounts of time to tailor the recommendations of international experts to the context and to build on existing traditions rather than beginning with an off-the-shelf law that had been recently applied in some other context. Major policy decisions were required, in particular, in the area of accounting and auditing. These are highly technical fields where the existing system completely fails to meet international standards, but decisions on which parts of the international system to adopt need considerable attention and thought.

Equity and Equality of Opportunity

An eighth concern was the impact of the budget on equity and equality of opportunity. This issue could not be faced with the existing rules and organizational capabilities. Obtaining the figures on provincial expenditures from line ministries required months of intense discussion and analysis of manual systems of recordings. When the figures were first presented to the cabinet, it came as a shock that the ten poorest provinces of the country were receiving the smallest amounts of allocation. The explanation lies in the investment pattern of the 1960s through the 1980s: provinces that had received investments in those periods required the largest budgets for operation and maintenance and for salaries of staff assigned to provide social services. It is only through collection of relevant data and detailed analysis that the principle of geographic equity, which was unanimously adopted by the cabinet in the 1382 (2003–2004) budget, can be given concrete substance in the procedures and practices of all departments of government.

Reporting

A final area is reporting, both as an instrument of discipline within the government and as a means of binding the citizens and the state as a community. The Ministry of Finance submitted a weekly report on the fiscal condition of the country to the cabinet from July 2002 to December 2004. Using data on expenditures ineligible for ARTF reimbursement that were gathered by the World Bank–appointed monitoring agent, the Ministry of Finance was able to keep the attention of the president focused on this issue and to provide inputs on fiscal matters to cabinet members. The ministry also devised the mid-year budget review as a mechanism to provide monitoring and to establish adjustments between different ministries.

The Finance Ministry relied on three key mechanisms for reporting to the citizens at large. First, in a series of regular press conferences, the ministry team reported on all the categories of income and expenditure. Second, a website was created where all the information was posted and the information on the Donor Assistance Database was disclosed. Third, in response to the questions of the delegates of the Loya Jirga, the minister of finance provided an hour-and-a-half-long report that was broadcast on national television. As the right to information is enshrined in the Afghan constitution, it is hoped that the practice of disclosure and reporting begun during the transitional government will become a routine input into public discussion of how public money creates value.

Security and Public Finance

Transparency of expenditure on the security sector is going to be a particularly important aspect of building trust between the citizens and the government and between the government and the international community. A unified budget cannot be established without full incorporation of the cost of security; and a monopoly on the means of violence cannot be established without the predictability and order created through the accountabilities of a public financial system. Because there was no establishment control in the spring of 2002, the security sector rapidly expanded from a force of fewer than 20,000 in 2001 to a claimed force of more than 400,000 by the summer of 2002, based on patron-client relationships. The international community decided not to support these forces—which they called Afghan militia forces (AMF)—instead choosing to support the newly formed Afghan National Army. Accordingly, domestic revenue had to be mobilized to pay for the militia forces as well as the police. To establish accountability to the Afghan population, it had to be demonstrated that these people existed, leading to the negotiations between the Ministry of Finance and Ministries of Defence and Interior on validation of numbers and people. Although agreement was eventually reached on a target number of 100,000 soldiers and officers to which to reduce the AMF, it became evident as the DDR started that the numbers were not in fact there and that various commanders were diverting the resources. Hence by December 2004, budget discussions concluded that the maximum number of people from AMF that could be retained on payroll in the 1385 (March 2005 to March 2006) budget would be between 8,000 and 18,000. A similar verification process was followed with the Ministry of Interior, but because formal DDR for the police had not begun by the end of 2004, reductions were much slower.

An iris-based identification system would have enabled verification of identity to ensure that one person had only one government job. Anecdotal evidence and data gathered through a pilot program indicated that some individuals were drawing multiple salaries under different names, thereby inflating the number of actual employees of the government and creating distrust regarding transparency of hiring and payments. The database required for such a purpose would have cost around US$100 million. Despite the Ministry of Finance's effort to convince the election team to create a national voter registration database, the UN resorted to a one-time manual database for elections and a separate one for DDR. Currently, there is a proliferation of separate databases in different ministries without compatibility or integration into an overall database. Both accountability and security require investment in information capital. It is imperative that the costs and benefits of such investment are analyzed within a clear framework of statebuilding rather than being dictated by the preferences of individual agencies.

Although President Karzai's policy of no-deficit financing was strictly followed by the Ministry of Finance, deficit financing remained widespread in the northern provinces until June 2003, when revenue was centralized. During this period, a number of profitable state-owned enterprises were being subsidized by the government, yet their workers were not receiving wages and benefits. In implementing the law on state-owned enterprises, the Ministry of Finance cut off subsidies to profit-making enterprises nationwide. Some of the northern commanders threatened to take funds from the banks and allocate them to the enterprises under their control. The Ministry of Finance informed them that if they did so, all payments for salaries would be stopped and that the cause of the nonpayment would be disclosed to teachers and government employees. As a result, subsidies to profitable enterprises and deficit financing were stopped, and the special status of some commanders in overriding the authority of provincial directors of finance was ended.

Revenue from customs and other domestic sources could have been significantly raised had there been international support for protection of customs posts and the branches of the Central Bank and the state-owned banks in the provinces. Requests for such support initially were not acceded to, but thanks to strong backing from the US Department of the Treasury, the US Department of Defense reached agreement toward the end of 2004 on mechanisms to support the efforts of the Afghan government in this regard.

Current plans for a 70,000-strong army, based on discussions with the US military, would require a recurrent expenditure of around US$500 million per year by 2009. When plans for the national police and secret service are taken into account, the recurrent expenditure for security forces could exceed US$1 billion per year. From a fiscal perspective, the question of sustainability of such expenditure is paramount. Even under very optimistic projections for domestic revenue, such an expenditure on security would imply a totally inadequate allocation of resources for human capital, infrastructure, and other vital functions of government. Noting that US expenditure on the coalition and NATO expenditure on ISAF were estimated at US$12–15 billion per year, the Ministry of Finance took the position that since any reduction in the presence of external forces would entail a substantial saving for the international community, there must be a medium- to long-term commitment of security assistance for the Afghan institutions. This would both create the enabling security environment for investment and growth and allow the government to use domestic revenues for enhancing its legitimacy by fulfilling its vital functions. In the absence of such a commitment, current assumptions about the size of the army, police, and secret service will have to be reexamined and more affordable security strategy agreed upon.

Conclusion

The public finance accomplishments in Afghanistan are due to the remarkable teamwork and shared goals pursued by individuals with a high dedication to public value and empowerment of the citizens. It was often remarked that the Ministry of Finance during the transitional government contained a very large number of unpaid volunteers.[13] In the words of Deputy Minister Jelani Popal, they viewed this as service undertaken in return for the investment that the nation had made in their education.

Afghanistan's strategy of dealing with public finances as a critical dimension of statebuilding demonstrates that reforms can take place under difficult circumstances. At the same time, it shows the need for fundamental changes in the international aid system to create sustainable development. In an environment of persistent tensions and great mistrust, the goal of movement toward a state that delivers citizenship rights is best served through processes that are not only technically sound but also politically transparent.

Notes

1. For a discussion of the "circle of justice," with a focus on its historical role in south Asian governance, see Darling (2002).

2. World Bank press release ("Two Decades of Conflict Cost US$240 Billion; Now Afghanistan Will Need $27.5 Billion to Recover") issued on March 30, 2004, for Berlin conference "Securing Afghanistan's Future" held on March 31 and April 1, 2004.

3. Donors included the United Kingdom (US$520 million), Norway (US$10.7 million), Japan (US$8.4 million), Sweden (US$5 million), and Italy (US$3.2 million). Loans from the Asian Development Bank, the World Bank, and the International Monetary Fund were paid off in this manner. Government of Afghanistan, Ministry of Finance, "Financial Report 16/7/1381 (October 2004)," Kabul, 28.

4. The government obtained debt forgiveness from China (9.6 million pound sterling), Denmark (5 million Danish kroner), and Germany (34.5 million pound sterling) (Ibid.). A number of other claims remain to be resolved.

5. As the Central Bank had not yet been reformed, and the funds of the government were not drawing any interest in accounts at the Central Bank, the Asian Development Bank agreed to deposit the proceeds of the first program loan in a special interest-bearing account opened in the name of the government. Withdrawals from this account required the simultaneous signatures of the president and the minister of finance. ADB and international consultants chose the bank where the account was opened. Funds were then transferred to the Central Bank as the need arose for payment.

6. It is worth remarking that the demands voiced by about 225 members of the constitutional Loya Jirga in December 2003 that were costed by the Ministry of Finance amounted to at least US$80 billion. This figure is not high, in comparison to the World Bank's estimate of at least US$240 billion in war-related losses between April 1978 and December 2001 (see World Bank press release, "Two Decades of Conflict Cost US$240 Billion; Now Afghanistan Will Need $27.5 Billion to Recover," March 30, 2004).

7. For an account of this situation, see Rohde and Gall (2005).

8. For an account of US assistance in Afghanistan in the 2001–2004 period, see Ghani, Lockhart, and Carnahan (2005b).

9. The problem arose because the insurance required by the donor's internal procedures could not be secured in time, as it required fulfillment of too many complex conditions. This highlights the need for rapid procedures if donor organizations are to provide timely responses to governments in the immediate wake of conflict.

10. The situation was particularly problematic in northern provinces, where bank branches participated in a series of transactions that in any other context would have constituted crimes.

11. A risk-guarantee facility was secured from the Overseas Private Investment Corporation (OPIC) in early 2002 by the Ministry of Finance; other facilities were sought from the Multilateral Investment Guarantee Agency (MIGA), which took a couple of years to activate, and from other countries, which were not forthcoming.

12. See Afghanistan Research and Evaluation Unit and World Bank (2004).

13. These included Temor Anwaryah in revenue, Wafi Amin in state-owned enterprises, Tareq Formoli as deputy minister of administration, Jelani Popal as deputy minister of revenue, and Ashraf Ghani as minister, among others. None of them drew salary or benefits for their public service.

7

Managing Public Resources: The Experience of the Palestinian "Proto-State"

Rex Brynen

Although the story of public finance in postconflict countries is never simple, it is a particularly complex tale in the Palestinian case. Like Timor-Leste, but unlike Cambodia, Guatemala, Afghanistan, and Uganda, the Palestinian territories have no prior history of statehood. The Palestinian Authority (PA)—established in the West Bank and Gaza (WBG) in 1994, following the Oslo Accords—is certainly a quasi-statelike entity and indeed was intended to represent the foundations of a Palestinian state-to-be. Its powers are sharply limited, however: it controls neither all (or even most) of the territory of the WBG nor any of its international borders. The Palestinian case is also far from being a postconflict one. Although many of the cases studied in this book have been afflicted by transitional or posttransitional violence, in the Palestinian case a final peace agreement has yet to be agreed upon, with permanent status negotiations in 2000–2001 being swept away by the violence of the intifada, Israeli reoccupation of large areas of the West Bank, and the 2006 election of a new Palestinian government headed by the Islamist party Hamas.

Prior to the intifada, the Palestinians were socioeconomically better off than most of the other cases studied in this book. By global standards, they had a relatively high gross domestic product (GDP)/capita (US$1,493 in 2002); high levels of life expectancy (72.3 years), adult literacy (90.2 percent), and school enrollment; and a relatively low level of income inequality (a Gini index of 0.38) (United Nations Development Programme 2004). The Palestinian economy, however, is also highly dependent. More than three-quarters of all Palestinian imports and exports are to Israel. Historically, large numbers of Palestinians also worked in Israel, although this number has diminished sharply since the early 1990s as a result of Israeli security measures. The Israeli shekel is the predominant currency used in the WBG, and prices for most goods are close to those in Israel, where gross national income is more than ten times higher at nearly US$17,000 (World Bank 2007, 288). This pattern of dependence has made the Palestinian economy, and Palestinian revenue collection, acutely vulnerable to Israeli policy and practices.

The occupied Palestinian territories have also been recipients of unparalleled levels of development assistance: some US$8 billion or so between 1994 and 2004, averaging approximately between US$250 and $400 per capita over this period and equivalent to 10–30 percent of GDP per year. Of the cases in this book, only Timor-Leste has received comparable levels of (relative) assistance and for a shorter period of time. In July 2005, the Group of 8 declared its support for even larger amounts of aid—"up to [US]$3 billion per year over the coming three years"—in the context of Israel's impending disengagement from Gaza (UK Foreign and Commonwealth Office 2005). In practice, the election of Hamas in January 2006 saw the suspension of much Western aid.

This chapter will examine the relationship between the Palestinian public finance system and the peace process through the Oslo period (1993–2001) as well as after the intifada that began in September 2000, looking at the political and economic context, revenue generation by the PAPA expenditures, and problems of fiscal sustainability. By way of conclusion, the chapter will look at future challenges to Palestinian reform as well as draw some larger conclusions about fiscal politics in postconflict settings.

A postscript to the chapter will examine the intensified fiscal crisis faced by the PA following the election of a Hamas government in January 2006. The impact, effects, and consequences of this remain in flux, making definitive analysis difficult. Nevertheless, it is possible to draw some conclusions about the relationship between the 2006 crisis and earlier dynamics as well as the use of budgetary pressures by the international community to influence domestic politics in conflict-afflicted countries.

Overview

Although formal Palestinian-Israeli peace talks began in Madrid in October 1991, it was not until September 1993 that a breakthrough occurred in Norwegian-sponsored backchannel negotiations. Under the terms of the Palestinian-Israeli "Declaration of Principles" (better known as the Oslo Accords), the two sides committed themselves to a peaceful resolution of their dispute. It was agreed that an interim self-governing Palestinian Authority would be established in most of the Gaza Strip together with the West Bank town of Jericho. Thereafter, the functional and geographic authority of the PA would be enlarged as Israel withdrew its military forces from additional areas. After a period of presumed mutual confidence building, the two sides would then begin negotiations dealing with the major "permanent status" issues (borders, security arrangements, settlements, Jerusalem, refugees) with the aim of agreeing to a final resolution of their long conflict.

Over the next few years, additional interim agreements were negotiated.[1] These gradually expanded the powers of the Palestinian Authority as well as the territory under its control. Geographically, the WBG became a patchwork quilt of noncontiguous zones of varying Palestinian authority, with the PA exercising both civil and security control in some 17 percent of the West Bank (Area A) and about three-quarters of the Gaza Strip by March 2000. It also exerted responsibility for civil affairs in 24 percent of the West Bank (Area B) but had no authority over the remaining areas or any of its international borders.

The economic powers of the PA, including the architecture of its fiscal regime, were largely specified in the April 1994 (Paris) Protocol on Economic Relations. This called for what amounted to a customs union between the two sides, with Israel collecting customs duties and value-added taxes (VAT) on imported goods destined for the WBG and then transferring these revenues to the PA. Given that no border had yet been agreed upon between Israel and the Palestinian proto-state, there seemed few other alternatives to such an arrangement. This also allowed the PA to make use of Israel's already well-developed capacities to administer trade taxation.

Under the Paris Protocol, the PA was allowed little flexibility in setting customs and excise rates, with some goods subject to import quotas, whereas for others the PA was prohibited from setting rates lower than those used by Israel. The internal VAT rate was fixed by the Paris Protocol at 15–16 percent, just below the Israeli rate of 17 percent. The PA was also given the right to "regulate independently its own tax policy in matters of direct taxation, including income tax on individuals and corporations, property taxes, municipal taxes and fees" (Article V.1). The Israeli shekel was confirmed, de facto, as the primary currency of the Palestinian territories, and the PA was not authorized to introduce its own currency ("Protocol on Economic Relations between the Government of Israel and the PLO," 1994).

Throughout most of the Oslo period, Palestinian sources and international financial institutions alike estimated that economic growth in the occupied territories was slow and even negative. The primary reason for this was Israeli security measures (often taken in response to sporadic acts of violence by Palestinian rejectionist groups) or "closure" that hampered or blocked internal mobility within the West Bank, sharply reduced the number of Palestinian workers in Israel, and severely constrained external trade between the WBG and the outside world.[2] Subsequent reevaluation of this period has painted a slightly better picture, suggesting a real average GDP growth rate of 8.3 percent per year in the 1994–1999 period, or a per capita increase of around 4.3 percent per capita annually (International Monetary Fund 2003c, 22).[3]

Oft-delayed permanent status negotiations between Israel and Palestinian officials finally began in 2000 and extended to early 2001.[4] These failed to produce agreement, however. They were also rapidly overtaken by other events, including the eruption of the Palestinian uprising in September 2000, the end of the Clinton administration in the United States, and the political collapse of Israeli prime minister Ehud Barak and his Labour Party–led coalition. In February 2001 Barak suffered electoral defeat at the hands of his right-wing Likud rival, Ariel Sharon.

With this, and amid the violence of the intifada, the Oslo era of the peace process came to an end. Faced with attacks against its civilian population, Israel further restricted Palestinian labor access, imposed curfews and stringent mobility restrictions, and halted the transfer of customs duties and VAT clearances to the PA. From the spring of 2002 onward, the Israeli Defence Forces also reoccupied most areas of the West Bank that had been under PA control.

As a consequence of such measures, the WBG suffered what the World Bank characterized as "one of the deepest recessions in modern history" (World Bank 2004b, 1). Between 1999 and 2002, GDP per capita dropped from US$1,493 to US$879, unemployment grew from 12 to 31 percent, and the poverty rate (under two dollars a day) rose from 20 to 51 percent (World Bank 2004e, 32). Because of both the suspension of Israeli tax transfers and the sharp contraction of the economy, PA revenues fell precipitously, from US$939 million in 2000 to a mere US$273 million in 2001 (see Figure 7.1).

Figure 7.1   PA Revenues and Current Expenditures, 1996–2005

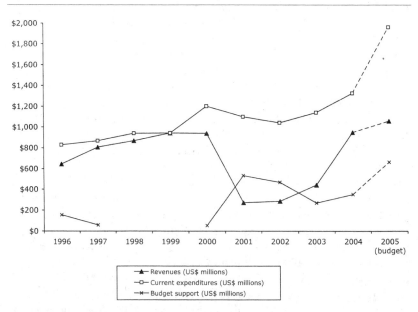

Sources: International Monetary Fund (2003c); Palestinian Authority Ministry of Finance, *2004 Budget* and *2005 Budget.*
Note: There was no budget support in 1998–1999.

Thereafter, the economy stabilized (with GDP of US$934 per capita in 2004), owing to a slight lessening of Israeli security measures, a reduction in violence, and the resumption of Israeli tax clearances in 2003. It in no way recovered to its earlier levels. On the contrary, the World Bank predicted that without a substantial lessening of Israeli restrictions, GDP per capita would gradually continue to erode, dropping to US$807 by 2008 (World Bank 2004e, 3).

Politically, the post-Oslo era was characterized by a number of important new developments. In April 2003 the diplomatic Quartet of the United States, European Union (EU), United Nations, and Russia unveiled a three-stage "Performance-Based Roadmap to a Permanent Two-State Solution to the Israeli-Palestinian Conflict." This called for an end to violence, a return to more normal conditions, a halt to all Israeli settlement activity in the Palestinian territories, and reform of the institutions of Palestinian governance. This would be followed by transition to "an independent Palestinian state with provisional borders and attributes of sovereignty, based on the new constitution, as a way station to a permanent status settlement." Finally, permanent status negotiations would begin leading to full Palestinian statehood (State Department 2003). Both sides reluctantly accepted the plan. The Palestinians were concerned that, as in Oslo, they would once more become stuck in an interim period falling short of full statehood. Conversely, Prime Minister Sharon was reluctant to move quickly to Palestinian statehood, and in any case seemed committed to retaining permanent control over large areas of occupied Palestinian territory.

In the territories themselves, the Sharon government embarked on construction of a separation barrier in the occupied West Bank to separate Palestinian population centers from Israel and the major Jewish settlement blocs. The government indicated its intention to eventually end all Palestinian labor access to Israel. It also announced its intention to "disengage" from Gaza by withdrawing all settlers and military forces from the Gaza Strip in 2005 and to also evacuate four small settlements in the northern West Bank. For an indeterminate period, however, Gaza's borders, airspace, and sea space would continue to be under Israeli control. Despite an advisory opinion from the International Court of Justice confirming the illegality under international law of both Jewish settlements and the separation barrier in the West Bank, construction of both continued.[5]

In November 2004, Palestinian leader Yasser Arafat—by now, isolated by both Israel and the United States—died. Mahmud Abbas ("Abu Mazen") was chosen to succeed him in January 2005 elections. Abbas, like Arafat, was a long-time leading member of the main Palestinian nationalist party, Fateh. Unlike Arafat, however, he was a proponent of political reform and had been critical of the armed intifada.

As a first step, Abbas secured agreement from militant groups for a "period of calm" during which attacks against Israelis would be suspended (and

Israel would, implicitly, show similar restraint). Abbas faced a number of serious challenges, however, in this apparently new, postintifada era: the legacies of Arafat's neopatrimonial style of governance; lawlessness and a proliferation of armed Palestinian splinter groups; the growing popularity of Hamas, the main Islamist militant group; and a Sharon government that resisted implementation of the "Roadmap" and held a vision of a peace agreement very much at odds with Palestinian aspirations. The public finance implications of all this were enormous, with the new Palestinian president facing the simultaneous and often contradictory demands of institutional and fiscal reform on the one hand and political stabilization on the other—all in a context of economic uncertainty and crisis.

Revenues: Dependency, Diversion, and Reform

The sharp political and economic disjunctures experienced in the WBG have meant that there is not so much one story of Palestinian revenue collection as there are several. These include the initial fiscal imbalances in the early years of the PA, problems of revenue diversion and reform, the impact of the intifada, and the fiscal position of the PA under the Abbas administration (see Figure 7.1). Each of these will be explored below.

The Early Years

Prior to the establishment of the Palestinian Authority, tax and nontax revenues in the WBG had been collected by the Israeli Civil Administration, which also provided health, education, and other limited governmental services. The Civil Administration was an extension of the Israeli military occupation authorities, directed by Israel but staffed by more than 20,000 Palestinian teachers, health care workers, and administrative (including tax) personnel. Through the 1990s it collected some US$200 million to $300 million per year, typically consisting of about two-thirds tax revenues and one-third nontax revenues (such as licensing fees and profits from public enterprises) (Khadr 1999, 111).

The first few years of the PA were characterized by the incremental expansion of both its geographic area and its functional authority. With this, of course, came new revenue sources, including clearances of Israeli-collected duties, excise, and VAT on Palestinian imports. Initially, these were inadequate to meet the recurrent costs of the PA's growing responsibilities, as well as the additional start-up costs associated with establishing new administrative and governmental structures. Moreover, Palestinian economic dependence on Israel meant that periods of intensified Israeli mobility restrictions (notably in 1995–1996) could curtail economic activity, and hence revenue mobilization.[6] As a result, donors also provided some US$500 million in start-up, transitional, and budget support through the 1995–1998 period, of which $212.8 million was budget support disbursed through the World Bank–administered, multidonor Johan Jürgen Holst Peace Fund (Brynen 2000b, 180). This represented almost one-fifth of the $2.3 billion in total aid disbursed to the WBG during this period (Brynen 2000b, 114).

By 1999 the PA had achieved a balanced budget of sorts,[7] with some $942 million in revenues and a similar level of recurrent expenditures. Of these revenues, 26 percent accrued from domestic taxation, 12 percent from domestic nontax sources, and 62 percent from Israeli revenue clearances. At 20.8 percent of GDP, this represented a very healthy level of revenue mobilization by the standards of the developing world.

According to one World Bank assessment of PA fiscal performance in this period, there was significant but not substantial scope for improving the rate of domestic tax collection through more effective collection and enforcement, especially given the greater legitimacy of the PA compared to the previous Israeli civil administration (Khadr 1999, 115). The International Monetary Fund highlighted particular weaknesses in income and corporate taxation, which together yielded only 1.8 percent of GDP in 1999 (compared to an average of 5.6 percent for middle-income countries). Some of the reasons for this related to the absence of large corporate structures in the WBG—a legacy, in part, of the Israeli occupation. It was also due to an outmoded and fragmented set of tax laws that varied between Gaza and the West Bank, the lack of an integrated tax administration, and limited administrative and enforcement capacity (IMF 2003c, 87).[8] A number of practices (such as that of estimating revenues and "negotiating" tax bills) also facilitated tax evasion or underreporting. Over time, PA capacities were enhanced and reform of the tax code undertaken, and in March 1999 the highest marginal rates were reduced somewhat in an effort to improve compliance.[9]

Interestingly, (re)distributional issues in the tax system received very little attention in the WBG at this or any other point, from either the PA, the Palestinian Legislative Council, civil society, international financial institutions, or the broader international community. There are several reasons for this: heavy reliance on indirect taxation (the distributional effects were not obvious to most), relatively lower levels of income inequality within the WBG (particularly compared to the income inequality between Israel and Palestine, or compared to a country such as Guatemala, where distributional issues have been highly politicized), an absence of analytical capacity on tax issues in the legislature or civil society, and the overarching issue of continued Israeli occupation and the struggle for Palestinian statehood. Overall, Palestine's heavy reliance on VAT, customs, and excise revenues was probably neither substantially regressive nor progressive in its socioeconomic effects.

To the extent that there was attention to distributional issues, it tended to focus on the PA's decision to issue customs exemptions to returnees, tax breaks to foreign and expatriate investors, business income taxes, and tax breaks in the agricultural sector (including income tax exemptions on agricultural incomes in the West Bank only, a frequent complaint of Gaza farmers). Of these, the question of business taxation received the most attention, with small and medium firms sometimes grumbling that well-connected larger companies were better able to manipulate the tax system (Fjeldstad and Zagha 2004, 204). Adding to this perception were the activities of PA-sanctioned monopolies[10] (such as in the telecommunications sector), the sometimes shadowy activities of semipublic firms partly owned by the PA, and the PA's Investment Promotion Law. The latter offered customs and income tax exemptions of up to five years, and guarantees of low rates for up to twenty years, with the greatest benefits flowing to large foreign and expatriate investors ("Law No. [1] of 1998").

One major problem with regard to revenue generation arose from weaknesses in the design of Israeli-Palestinian economic arrangements under the Paris Protocol. According to the customs union model embodied in the agreement, Israel collected duties on all goods specifically destined for the WBG, whether these entered through Israeli ports or through the Israeli-controlled borders of the West Bank (with Jordan) and Gaza (with Egypt). These revenues were then transmitted to the PA. Many Palestinians do not import directly, however, but rather from or through Israeli middlemen. In this case, the goods seemed to have an Israeli destination at the time of importation, and hence the customs duties and other taxes accrued to the Israeli treasury rather than to the PA. There was also no mechanism for recouping VAT paid by Palestinians on their purchases of local Israeli goods. Some studies estimated that this leakage might be as much as 4–6 percent of Palestinian GDP, or around one-quarter of PA revenues (Khadr 1999, 116). In June 2000 Israel agreed to compensate the PA for some of this leakage and transferred some 200 million shekels ($49 million) for this purpose. The agreement was soon overtaken by the intifada and the suspension of Israeli clearances, however (IMF 2003c, 87).

Another weakness of the Paris Protocol is that it did not permit the PA to issue its own currency supply. On the positive side, reliance on the Israeli shekel (and, to a lesser extent, the Jordanian dinar) had benefits with regard to currency stability in the WBG and eliminated any possibility that the PA might finance its deficits by printing more money (with all the inflationary consequences this would entail). On the negative side, it also prevented the PA from accruing any seignorage revenues from the growth of the local money supply.[11] Here, World Bank analysts reported that were Israel to equitably share its seignorage revenue with the PA, this might amount to an increase in PA revenues of around 0.2 to 0.5 percent of GDP (Khadr 1999, 116).

From Diversion to Reform

As the fiscal situation of the PA began to stabilize through the 1990s, the question of accountability and transparency in public finance increasingly emerged as a central issue. On the revenue side, there were three major components of this: the diversion of revenues to accounts outside of Ministry of Finance control; the growth of a murky array of semipublic, semiprivate PA investments; and the unauthorized revenue collection and monopoly enforcement by elements of the PA, notably the security services.

With regard to the first of these, a detailed IMF study in 2003 found that between 1995 and April 2000, some $709.6 million in PA revenues—or 15 percent of all revenues during this period—were diverted to accounts outside Ministry of Finance control. These comprised $486 million in petroleum excise taxes that were collected by Israel and deposited to an Israeli bank account under the direct control of Arafat and his financial adviser, Muhammad Rashid (also known as Khalid Salam), together with $223.6 million in tobacco and alcohol taxes that were collected by the PA but not transferred to the Ministry of Finance (IMF 2003c, 91). This, of course, generated periodic government liquidity crises, with available PA resources unable to meet budgetary obligations. In response to this, some of these funds (approximately $119 million) were transferred back to the Ministry of Finance or to other government departments. Most, however, were used to finance the investments of the Palestinian Commercial Services Company (PCSC).

By 1999, the shadowy PCSC—run by Rashid—was involved in some sixty-nine commercial activities inside and outside the WBG, ranging from cement to hotels to telecommunications. These had an approximate market value of $700 million in 2003 and perhaps as much as $900 million in 1999. Profits from these investments—estimated at $307 million during the 1995–2000 period—also remained outside Ministry of Finance control (IMF 2003c, 91). Many of these funds were apparently handled through offshore accounts, far from the prying eyes of donors, Israel, or others in the PA (European Anti-Fraud Office 2005).[12]

In addition to the systematic diversion of PA revenues into the PCSC and related investments, the PA also suffered from weak control over the fees and charges levied for certain government services. These tended to be collected (and then spent again) by individual PA ministries, thus inhibiting the ability of the Ministry of Finance to exert oversight and control.

More serious still were the unofficial fees charged—or extorted—by some of the security services. In Gaza, for example, the PA's Preventive Security Force controlled the Palestinian side of the Karni crossing into Israel and charged its own transit fees, which appear to have disappeared either into Preventive Security Force coffers or private pockets. Various security forces also enforced de facto monopolies over certain goods, in exchange for apparent kickbacks. Outright extortion was reported, too. Arafat appears to have tolerated or even encouraged a degree of "self-financing" by (and corruption within) the security services, both to finance them beyond the bounds of the PA budget and as a political reward to loyal supporters.

As these various problems of revenue management became clear, donors began to press for reform. An early instrument of this was the PA/Israeli/donor "Tripartite Action Plan on Revenues, Expenditures, and Donor Funding," first agreed to in 1995 and subsequently revised on several occasions up until 1999. This laid down commitments to specific economic and fiscal actions by each of the parties, to be monitored by the IMF in periodic reports. Many of these commitments were repeatedly violated. Few of the donors had any leverage with Israel, and the United States—the one actor *with* leverage—preferred not to use it. At the same time, collectively the donor community showed neither the will nor the cohesion to apply any sort of strong conditionality to the PA (in part for fear of destabilizing Arafat amid an unstable transitional period in the peace process).

Nonetheless, donor pressure and support for capacity-building and policy reform did gradually bear some fruit. By 2000 the PA had agreed to centralize revenues within a consolidated Ministry of Finance account. It also agreed to an audit of the PCSC.

A second wave of reform resulted from the intifada, the subsequent fiscal compression of the PA, and intensified donor pressure for reform. The growing reliance of the PA on a lifeline of external budget support increased its susceptibility to external pressure for reform. Reform also became a centerpiece of donor efforts, most notably evident in the June 2002 Rose Garden speech by US president George W. Bush on Palestinian statehood (White House 2002)[13] and in the subsequent formation by donors of a high-level Task Force on Palestinian Reform and a series of local Reform Support Groups.

It would be a mistake, however, to see reform solely as a function of external pressures. By this time, local demands for reform had become powerful, amid widespread disillusionment at perceived corruption, cronyism, and inefficiency within the PA. A key turning point came in June 2002 when the former IMF representative in the West Bank and Gaza, Salam Fayyad, was named as the new PA minister of finance. Fayyad proved to be an ardent and effective reformer (Bennet 2003). Widespread improvements were implemented throughout the Palestinian public finance system, including centralization of accounts, improved reporting, and the establishment of a fully transparent and accountable Palestine Investment Fund.[14] The passing of Yasser Arafat and the subsequent election of Mahmud Abbas to the PA presidency in January 2005 provided further impetus for change.

The Intifada and the PA's Fiscal Crisis

Although the intifada may have hastened the processes of public finance reform in Palestine, it also set the stage for a major Palestinian fiscal crisis. As previously noted, PA resources shrank sharply in this period, owing to reduced economic activity, a consequent reduction in tax compliance, and especially the suspension of Israeli customs and VAT clearances.[15] Revenues declined from $939 million in 2000 (21.1 percent of GDP) to $273 million in 2001 and $287 million in 2002 (7.2 percent of GDP). Thereafter, they recovered somewhat as Israel resumed tax transfers, rising to $442 million in 2003 and $948 million in 2004 (28.4 percent of GDP) (International Monetary Fund 2003c and later date supplied by the IMD and the PA Ministry of Finance).[16]

These revenues were clearly inadequate to finance the recurrent costs of the PA (Figure 7.1). The resultant financing gap grew to some $826 million—or a staggering 22 percent of GDP—by 2001 (IMF 2003c, 91).

In view of the strategic importance and ramifications of the Palestinian-Israeli conflict, donors could not allow the fiscal collapse of the PA. Consequently, they provided large amounts of budget support, totaling almost $1.7 billion in the 2000–2004 period. Arab countries were the largest donors, in the form of loans from the Islamic Development Bank, pledges made through the Arab League, and other contributions.[17] The European Union also provided some 225 million euros in direct budget support in 2000–2002. The provision of budget support to the PA was often hampered by a lack of transparency and accountability, reports of corruption, and weak expenditure controls (and hence the inability to determine how fungible budget funds were being used). EU budget support, for example, was slowed at times by allegations that some of the funds might be diverted to support terrorism.[18] In the case of the United States, Washington had little interest in supporting the PA budget while Arafat was still in power. Congressional suspicion of the PA, encouraged by some US domestic lobby groups, made it politically difficult, however, for the administration to provide any funds directly to the PA even when it wanted to. Instead virtually all of the $945 million in aid provided by the United States between 1996 and 2004 flowed through local or US nongovernmental organizations (NGOs) or via US contractors. The exception to this was $20 million in budget support provided when Abbas briefly served as PA prime minister in 2003, and $50 million promised to President Abbas during his visit to Washington in May 2005 (US Agency for International Development 2005).[19]

Because of these political constraints, donors shifted away from providing "raw" budget support to more targeted forms of financial assistance. In the case of the EU, this took the form of a new Reform Support Initiative in 2003. Rather than support recurrent expenditures in general, this provided 90 million euros to support social service provision, the payment of PA arrears to small- and medium-sized enterprises, and technical assistance for reform measures (European Commission Technical Assistance Office for the West Bank and Gaza; European Union 2003).

In the case of the World Bank, a new Public Financial Management Reform Trust Fund was established in April 2004. Even though the World Bank's earlier Holst Fund had been widely considered a success—and, indeed, was praised as a "pioneering example" for other postconflict cases where transitional budget support was urgently required (UN Department of Peacekeeping Operations 2003)[20]—it was not designed to promote transparency or leverage policy reforms. Rather, the PA had simply been reimbursed against demonstrable expenditures. Such an approach was no longer tenable given the publicity surrounding PA diversion of public funds, the real need for reform, and the greater willingness of donors to press for such reforms. Consequently, the new Reform Trust Fund linked the payment of support branches to PA fulfillment of specified benchmarks for reform and fiscal sustainability such as wage containment measures, pension reform, and administrative and legal reforms. By February 2005 the EU and eight other donors had contributed more than $150 million to the Fund (World Bank 2005c).[21]

Despite substantial budget assistance, external financial assistance was not enough to fully plug the PA's post-2000 fiscal gaps. Consequently, it also turned to other sources: commercial bank borrowing, nonpayment of suppliers, and the withholding of VAT refunds and pension contributions. Commercial bank debt reportedly reached $193 million (or 5.4 percent of GDP) at the end of 2003. PA arrears to local suppliers grew from zero in 1996 to around $415 million by 2002 (and a roughly similar level by 2004) (World Bank 2004f, 26). By 2005 the budget appeared as if it had reached the limits of what it could squeeze from this kind of domestic financing.

Overall, the story of PA revenue management is one of the constraints caused by occupation and dependence, the shocks of closure and the intifada, and the diversion of resources for neopatrimonial political purposes by the Arafat regime. All of this laid the groundwork for impending fiscal disaster. At the same time, the very substantial degree of fiscal reform in the late and post-Arafat period is also striking, a consequence of both domestic and donor pressure.

Expenditures: Dynamics and Legacies of Neopatrimonialism

During the Oslo era, PA current expenditures grew in absolute terms from $829 million in 1996 to $942 million in 1999, representing some 19–23 percent of GDP during this period. Thereafter, expenditures sharply increased to $1.2 million (27 percent of GDP) in 2000, in part because of increased social service demands caused by the economic disruption associated with the intifada (IMF 2003c). Thereafter, while stabilizing or declining slowly in absolute terms under the pressure of fiscal crisis, they continued to grow relative to the shrinking economy (Figure 7.1). The PA estimated 2003 expenditures at $1.14 million or 41 percent of GDP. The 2005 budget projected expenditures of up to $1.962 million, or well more than half of likely GDP (Palestinian Ministry of Finance 2005).

Sectoral Composition

The typical composition of a recent budget (2002) is shown in Figure 7.2. In examining this, however, several caveats are in order. First, the budget shows current expenditures, rather than capital spending. Although the PA budget does show a capital component, this generally reflects project-specific donor development assistance channeled through PA coffers (which, in turn, is only a portion of donor-financed capital investment in the WBG). Palestinian-financed public capital investment is essentially nil.

Second, the data for social service expenditures do not include either NGO social service provision (often donor financed) or the health, education, and social welfare services provided to Palestinian refugees in the occupied territories by the United Nations Relief and Works Agency (UNRWA). In 2002 UNRWA's programs in the WBG amounted to a sizable $154 million, a very significant amount given PA social service expenditures of $340 million that same year.[22]

Third, the post-2000 budgets of the PA have also been distorted by the need to provide emergency financing to cash-strapped municipalities, which in

Figure 7.2   PA Current Expenditures by Sector, 2002

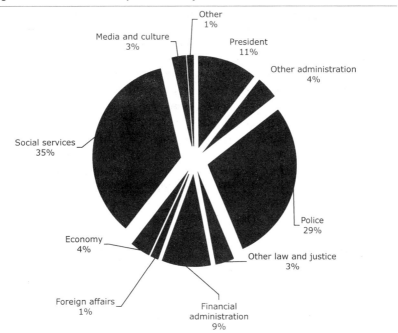

Source: Palestinian Authority Ministry of Finance, *Current Expenditure 2002–2004.*

any case have been always been poorly and unevenly financed.[23] Although PA lending to municipalities does show on the PA budget, the arrears and commercial borrowing of local government units (for which it is ultimately responsible) do not.

In examining the sectoral composition of the PA budget, several elements stand out. One is the very large proportion of government expenditure on the security services (29 percent in 2002). Some of this was certainly underpinned by security needs. As discussed below, much of this employment, however, was attributable to the web of political patronage that developed under Arafat.

This latter factor also helps to explain another noteworthy aspect of the budget, namely the large allocations to the office of the president. At 11 percent of PA expenditures, this was equal to almost one-third of all social service expenditures, or almost three times the combined expenditures of the "economic" ministries (such as agriculture, planning, public works, housing, energy, and natural resources). Again, the reasons for this can be found in Arafat's use of discretionary expenditures to consolidate his base of support, an aspect of expenditure policy that will be more fully explored later. The presidential budget was later slashed under domestic and international pressure for reform.

In theory, the process of developing budgetary allocations was similar to that of most legislative democracies, with the minister of finance required to present a budget bill to the Palestinian Legislative Council (PLC) for approval. Through much of the Oslo era, however, the PLC had little influence over the content of the budget, which was often presented late, if ever. Moreover, weak expenditure controls, the impact of donor-financed projects, and a highly unpredictable economic environment meant that budget figures were only loosely related to actual expenditure levels.

As a consequence of financial reforms, the transparency of the budget process was later improved, with budget documents and monthly reports posted to the Ministry of Finance website (http://www.mof.gov.ps). PLC input remained relatively weak, however, as did that of civil society groups, and there remained room for a more effective government outreach on budget issues. Moreover, the Ministry of Finance tended not to implement costly government decisions (such as public-sector pay increases or changes in the pension system) when these seemed fiscally unsustainable—a boon to financial prudence, perhaps, but somewhat undermining efforts to improve transparency and accountability.

Expenditures and Fiscal Sustainability

Even before the devastating economic and fiscal impact of the intifada era, the World Bank characterized the fiscal outlook of the PA as "fragile" (World Bank 1999c, 88).[24] Although the diversion of PA revenues (and ensuing liquidity crises) was part of the reason for this, an even larger structural problem was posed on the expenditure side of the budget. With the fiscal pressures created by Israeli mobility restrictions and economic recession during the uprising and after, these challenges intensified.

First (and least important) was the issue of debt-financed development expenditures. In 2000 the World Bank highlighted concerns that a significant portion of donor assistance had been offered as credits or loans. The PA had only a weak system at the time for monitoring and managing its debt obligations, and were it to fully take up the credit on offer, it might well "squander its 'debt-free beginning' by taking on unsustainable levels of future borrowing" (World Bank 2000, xix). In practice, this issue was soon overshadowed by the intifada and the ensuing fiscal crisis. The Ministry of Finance also adopted the United Nations Conference on Trade and Development (UNCTAD) Debt Management and Financial Analysis System (DMFAS). Today, it is unclear what the PA's real level of external debt is but for political rather than technical reasons: the PA's "hard" debt is quite small, and other debts, such as International Development Bank "loans" for budget support, may well eventually be forgiven should the peace process advance (or, for that matter, once more sink into crisis).

Second, the PA budget has—even in the "good" years of the Oslo era—tended to include inadequate provision for the maintenance cost of existing capital stock. The budgetary process has also failed to address the downstream recurrent costs of current development investments.[25] During the late Oslo years the PA did attempt to require that ministries calculate such operating costs when submitting investment projects for inclusion in a Palestinian Development Plan (PDP). It was never clear, however, how these estimates were developed and how they were used (if at all) in the process. With the intifada, moreover, these planning and prioritization activities faded amid the weakening of central government institutions and the more pressing need for emergency and humanitarian measures.

Despite their good intentions and their invaluable work in promoting capacity building and policy reform, donors often tended to complicate some aspects of the fiscal picture. At times, inadequate attention was paid to the long-term sustainability of projects given the PA's financial resources. In one (in)famous example of this, the PA was initially unable to accept delivery of a modern EU-financed hospital in Gaza because it could not afford the running costs involved (Brynen 2000b, 196). Donors often ignored the PDP, in tacit cooperation with recipient PA institutions, thus undercutting any PA effort to monitor the cumulative long-term costs of donor-financed investments. Indeed, the lure of donor money could encourage administrative rent-seeking behavior, with elements of the PA pushing projects not because they were a real priority but because they seemed most likely to attract some external funding.

Donor activities had fiscal costs in other ways. The political tendency of donors to inflate their aid pledges could result in excessively high Palestinian expectations of what resources would be made available and hence what resources could be spent. Aid and multilateral agencies tended to drive up local wage costs for qualified Palestinian personnel as well as luring them away from possible PA employment. Donor-supplied technical assistance in the form of staff positions distorted the growth of PA agencies and sometimes created a situation in which the PA had to pick up the bill (or lose the newly built capacity) once donor financing ended. Having to meet with the constant stream of foreign visitors, donor delegations, technical missions, and others sapped enormous amounts of the time of senior PA officials, an operational and financial cost that has never been calculated but which must have run to millions of dollars per year.

All of these issues, however, pale in comparison to the most serious challenge to fiscal sustainability: the very substantial growth in the public-sector payroll since 1994 (see Figure 7.3). By 2003, employment had reached more than 130,000 persons (representing fully 16.4 percent of the labor force), and the annual PA wage bill totaled US$747 million (constituting almost two-thirds—65.5 percent—of all current central government expenditures and 23.8 percent of GDP) (calculated from IMF 2003c; World Bank 2004c; World Bank 2004e; and Palestinian Ministry of Finance, *2004 Budget* and *2005 Budget*). This was a very high proportion, even by the (large public sector) standards of the region.[26] It was also clearly more than the PA could afford, crowding out

Figure 7.3   PA Employment and Wages, 1995–2004

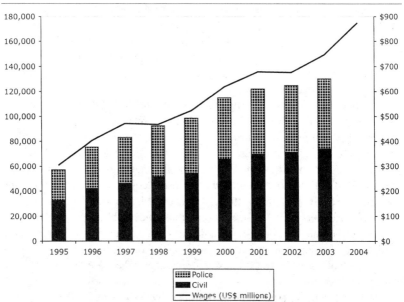

Sources: International Monetary Fund (2003c); Palestinian Authority Ministry of Finance, *2004 Budget* and *2005 Budget*.

critical nonwage expenditures in the areas of education, health, social welfare, and public capital investment.

There were several reasons for this. Growth in civil service employment was spurred, in part, by the very rapid rate of population growth in the WBG—at over 4 percent annually, one of the highest in the world. This alone created the need for some 4,000 new hires per year in the health and education sectors.

Civil service and security force employment also acted as an important social support mechanism as well as an economic buffer during the Palestinian post-2000 economic crisis. Although the bulk of civil service salaries likely went to middle-income groups, much of security sector employment was concentrated among otherwise low-income households. Public employment provided a critical source of income to many households at a time of sharply reduced employment in Israel and severe recession, hence making it difficult for the PA to engage in any sort of downsizing of the public sector.[27] Although it did attempt to keep salary rates down (and even applied a payroll surtax to fund relief activities), by 2003 political pressures and the modest inflationary erosion of public-sector employees' purchasing power, coupled with partial implementation of the new civil service law, had resulted in a roughly 15 percent pay increase.

The growth of the security forces can be seen as serving a strategic purpose, especially during the Oslo era. A large security force might have been seen by Arafat as a potential deterrent to any Israeli retreat from the peace process and as a deterrent to Israeli reoccupation of PA-controlled areas. During this period, the security services also often acted against rejectionist groups, such as Hamas—a key reason why Israel usually tolerated their growth prior to the intifada, despite their numbers' exceeding those authorized in the interim agreements. With the intifada, however, it soon became clear that the poorly trained and led PA security forces were little deterrent to Israel, ineffective at maintaining internal security or law and order, and that some of their individual members were complicit in acts of violence or lawlessness.

All of this points to perhaps the single most important explanation for the growth of a bloated PA public service: political patronage. Hiring, as with many other aspects of PA public policy under Arafat, was often driven by the use of public finance for purposes of political consolidation. The legacies of this system, moreover, would outlast Arafat, creating significant challenges and constraints for his successor.

Politics and Public Finance: The Neopatrimonial Imperatives

Neopatrimonial politics—the use of public resources to sustain informal political networks of patronage and clientelism—has a long history in Palestine. It was an important mechanism of Ottoman, British, and Jordanian social control and was also used by Israeli authorities. The Palestine Liberation Organization (PLO)—relatively wealthy from Arab petrodollar support in the 1970s—also made extensive use of neopatrimonial politics under Arafat. This was especially true in Lebanon, a sociopolitical environment with its own very rich history of clientalism, where the PLO established a near "state within a state" in the anarchic period between the start of the Lebanese civil war and Israel's 1982 invasion.[28]

In the WBG, Arafat used patronage as a way of maintaining control within the ranks of his own Fateh organization, as well as a way of co-opting others. For many years, both Israel and the United States tolerated this, believing consolidation of Arafat's control was conducive to political stability and hence the peace process.[29] Political loyalists (many returning from exile) were placed in positions within government ministries. Street activists from the first intifada (1987–1991) were often recruited into the security forces, and many Fateh cadres drew a security force paycheck without actually reporting for duty. The General Personnel Council, responsible for all PA hiring and promotion, operated at Arafat's behest, was riddled with cronyism, and was not subject to any effective oversight.

In addition to spurring a bloated public sector, neopatrimonial politics also explain many other aspects of Palestinian public finance during the Arafat era. The large presidential budget, for example, provided a ready source of patronage funds, which could be used to finance everything from scholarships for the children of senior Fateh officials, to medical care abroad for loyal petitioners, to development projects in small villages. The diversion of revenues via the Palestinian Commercial Services Company, other commercial activities, and offshore accounts all seemed intended by Arafat not for personal enrichment (at least, not his own) but rather to maintain a reserve fund and income stream that could be used to finance patronage independent of oversight or interference by donors, Israel, or Palestinians themselves. When money is power, in Arafat's view, it paid to have some set aside for a rainy day.[30]

Neopatrimonialism also had highly corrosive effects on public financial management and good governance. Multiple rival power centers were encouraged (particularly in the security services) to blunt any particular challenge from ambitious subordinates, with client often being played off against client. Corruption or incompetence by senior officials was often overlooked in the interests of fealty and political power. Reform was unattractive to Arafat, for the simple reason that it threatened to constrain key instruments of political influence upon which he had come to rely. The PA's supposed independent audit institution, the General Control Institute, issued only one public audit report in 1997, and within the PA whatever other reports it might have produced seem to have gone to Arafat alone.

Still, it is important to stress that the Palestinian administration that evolved after 1994 was not a fully dysfunctional creature. On the contrary, in some areas its performance was quite impressive. Many highly skilled, dedicated, and hardworking officials could be found throughout the PA. Prior to the intifada, public opinion polls showed that Palestinians had high levels of satisfaction with the education sector and had perceptions of real improvement in health conditions under the PA (World Bank 2000, 65).[31] The Ministry of Education had a particularly good reputation for transparency and openness to civil society. Both education and health services were maintained despite the pressures and chaos of the intifada, with Palestinian schoolchildren outperforming many of their regional counterparts in standardized tests despite recession, mobility restrictions, austerity, trauma, and violence.[32] Indeed, a substantial majority of Palestinians continued to report satisfaction with basic government health (63.9 percent) and education (71.9 percent) services (Palestinian Central Bureau of Statistics 2005). In the financial sector, the Palestinian Monetary Authority has done an effective and reliable job of bank supervision.

Even with regard to public corruption, which is undoubtedly present (and much remarked on, and criticized, by Palestinians), it appears to have been much less common in everyday life during the Oslo era than in many (or most) other developing countries.[33] Petty corruption likely increased, however, amid the substantial decline of the rule of law during the intifada.

Ironically, the very neopatrimonial measures taken to consolidate Arafat and "his" PA ultimately undermined the legitimacy of both, especially when many more inefficient government institutions ceased to function amid the pressures and chaos of the intifada. According to one March 2004 poll, 77 percent of Palestinians in the WBG believed that public-sector jobs were largely obtained through "connections" (*wasta*), 84 percent believed that there was corruption in the PA, 57 percent felt that this was likely to get worse, and 87 percent supported or strongly supported calls for reform (Palestinian Center for Policy and Survey Research 2004). Moreover, although neither PA revenue collection nor expenditure policy was particularly socially regressive, there developed a common view that the Fateh "old guard" and their social allies had reaped the predominant benefits of public expenditures. It is interesting, however, that this did not translate into a significant correlation between social class and political outlook—opinion surveys suggested that the poor or unemployed were not significantly more likely to support opposition parties than any others.[34] Instead, support for reform was widespread across social groups.

Reform was a key issue in the Palestinian (post-Arafat) presidential and local elections in 2005, with opposition Hamas candidates successfully positioning themselves as untainted by past corruption. Conversely, Fateh found its reputation steadily eroded owing to its involvement in past abuses. Opinion polls correctly predicted that corruption would be the leading issue in legislative elections, too, setting the stage for the Hamas victory and the institutional and fiscal crises that it provoked.[35]

Conclusion

Palestinian Challenges

This chapter has shown how the evolution of Palestinian public finance in the Oslo and intifada era was heavily shaped by three sets of factors: economic instability and acute dependence on Israel, coupled with a neopatrimonial approach to PA regime consolidation under Arafat, all set against the backdrop of an as-yet-unresolved Palestinian-Israeli conflict. The WBG suffered a series of economic shocks, especially after the onset of the intifada in September 2000, owing to Israeli mobility restrictions and a two-and-a-half-year withholding of tax clearances. This resulted in a severe downturn in PA revenues. At the same time, Arafat's widespread use of political patronage led to the diversion of needed revenues as well as the growth of a bloated and unsustainable PA public sector, many parts of which were afflicted by corruption and cronyism.

In the latter part of this period there was some significant reform of PA public finances, with a combination of international pressure and domestic discontent with corruption helping to buttress the position of Finance Minister Fayyad and other Palestinian reformers. Diversions were ended, new structures for managing public investments were established, revenue accounts were consolidated, expenditure monitoring and control were improved, monopolistic practices by the PA were curtailed, payroll systems were strengthened,[36] a new unified income tax law was adopted, and overall transparency and accountability were enhanced. The system of government accounting was unified between the West Bank and Gaza and strengthened. The General Personnel Council was brought under Ministry of Finance auspices, thereby strengthening payroll management. A Wage Bill Containment Plan was agreed upon with donors. In view of the failing of the General Control Institute, the Ministry of Finance developed its own internal audit capacity.

Indeed, in its 2004 Country Financial Accountability Assessment (CFAA), the World Bank assessed the Palestinian public financial management system as posing only "significant" risks, with the likelihood that it would achieve a rating of "moderate" on the CFAA four-point rating system (low/moderate/significant/high) by 2005. Given that fourteen of twenty-six states assessed by the World Bank in 2003 had ratings of "high" risk—and that only four had ratings of "moderate" or "low"—this would suggest that the management of public finances in the PA had become the same as or better than that of most other well-established developing countries (World Bank 2004f).

Nonetheless, key challenges to sustainable Palestinian public finance remain. These include the legacies of past neopatrimonialism, ongoing political pressures on Abbas, and the overall evolution of Palestinian-Israeli relations.

Years of past patronage and cronyism created a legacy of substantial entrenched resistance to reform. Efforts to eliminate "ghost" employees from the security force payroll, restructure the security services, or retire old-guard officers, for example, were sometimes met by resistance and even protests by armed security personnel.[37] In an attempt to overcome resistance to early retirements, the PLC ultimately passed a generous Security Services Pension Law in January 2005 that offered 100 percent salaries to personnel aged forty-five and over, at a hefty cost of around $40 million per year.

Past practices also engendered a sense of entitlement on the part of Fateh gunmen, who clearly expected that if they suspended armed attacks against the Israeli occupation at the behest of the Abbas government, then they ought to be rewarded (as were veterans of the 1987–1991 intifada) by public-sector employment, especially within the security forces. Moreover, these activists did not see such employment as patronage but rather as the appropriate and dignified way of compensating them for their sacrifices in the struggle for Palestinian self-determination.[38]

Conversely, the lack of such employment was often blamed on the "corrupt" PA elite's stealing the necessary resources. Disgruntled armed cadres were known to seize government offices (and even the prime minister's house) in protest at their poor treatment. Although the PA indicated its desire to reduce the overall size of the security sector, it also moved to hire thousands of new personnel ("PA Recruiting 5,000 Police Officers for Gaza Pullout" 2005)—nominally, to assist in providing security during Israel's withdrawal from Gaza but equally likely as part of its efforts to demobilize activists.

Politically, Abbas faced considerable criticism from a divided and dysfunctional Fateh, coupled with a growing challenge from Hamas. In the case of the former, such weakness made the Palestinian leader understandably skittish about undertaking reforms too enthusiastically, for fear of further undercutting his support base. In the case of the latter, a very strong Islamist showing in local government elections in the WBG in December 2004 and May 2005 led to mounting fears that Hamas could win subsequent elections for the Palestinian Legislative Council. This made the PA even more loath to adopt unpopular austerity measures. The PA cabinet thus agreed to teachers' demands for a public-sector pay increase, undercutting its efforts to slow the growth of the PA wage bill. The 2005 PA budget also called for the establishment of a Social Safety Net Scheme, which would provide direct cash payments to the poor. Although high rates of poverty and uneven social welfare coverage make poverty alleviation an important task, the primary purpose of this proposal seemed to be to compete with Islamist welfare institutions and win political support for the PA. The establishment of such a large entitlement program (up to US$240 million per year) clearly had substantial fiscal implications, even if it was supposed to be financed by earmarked donor contributions. Indeed, overall the entire 2005 budget looked rather like an "election budget," with substantial expenditure increases and excessively optimistic assumptions about revenues and external budget support.

Finally, there was the question of relations with Israel. As long as Israeli mobility restrictions hampered Palestinian economic activity, the PA continued to suffer from substantially depressed revenues, no matter what improvements were made in revenue collection. Although donors hoped that Gaza disengagement might create new opportunities for the Palestinians to develop a robust economy and proto-state institutions, this failed to materialize. On the contrary, Gaza's access to the outside world actually deteriorated sharply following disengagement. In the longer term, it was difficult to see how a stable political-security (and hence economic-fiscal) environment could be maintained in the West Bank and Gaza under the shadow of Israeli military occupation and in the absence of substantial and meaningful progress toward a mutually acceptable Palestinian-Israeli peace agreement. Put simply, for the Palestinians to successfully meet the challenges of "postconflict public finance," they most fundamentally needed to reach the end of the conflict.

The Hamas Earthquake

It was in this context that, in January 2006, the Palestinian Authority experienced a political earthquake: a Hamas victory over Fateh in elections for a new Palestinian Legislative Council. Hamas's Ismail Haniya was subsequently designated as prime minister at the head of a Hamas-dominated cabinet, and Fateh's Abbas retained his position as the elected PA president.

This stunning political turnaround was rooted, in large part, in many of the issues discussed herein: weak governance, lack of transparency and accountability, and widespread perceptions of Fateh corruption.[39] Its immediate effect, however, was to dramatically worsen the fiscal position of the PA. As soon as the new Palestinian government took power, Israel announced that it would no longer remit tax clearances to the PA, totaling some US$65 million per month. Western donors also announced that they would no longer provide budget support to the PA now that Hamas controlled Palestinian ministries. According to a statement issued by the Quartet shortly after the election, "it was inevitable that future assistance to any new Government would be reviewed by donors against that Government's commitment to the principles of non-violence, recognition of Israel, and acceptance of previous agreements and obligations, including the Road Map" (Quartet 2006a).

Such moves, coupled with heightened post-disengagement Israeli restrictions on Palestinian trade and mobility, severely aggravated the existing fiscal crisis that Hamas had inherited from Fateh. Compounding things still further, Palestinian, Israeli, and international banks grew increasingly fearful that any contact with a Hamas-led PA would render them vulnerable to civil litigation from terrorism victims or legal sanction from the United States (which lists

Hamas as a prohibited terrorist organization). As a result, the PA's single treasury account was closed by the Arab Bank, other banks refused to handle PA payments, and Israeli banks stopped clearing all Palestinian checks and money transfers.

In a May 2006 report the World Bank suggested the dire consequences of all this:

> If today's strictures remain or intensify, the PA may be looking at no more than US$25 million in domestic revenues per month, and no banking system with which to distribute them. Under such circumstances, with current monthly wage bills running at c. US$95 million, those Palestinians employed by the PA or dependent on PA salaries (estimated at 30 percent of the population) will suffer major income reductions—while the PA is unlikely to be able to provide basic services or maintain law and order. (World Bank 2006b, 3–4)

The end result, it warned, could be a humanitarian crisis (with poverty rates exceeding 74 percent by 2008), violence, and the dissolution of those Palestinian public institutions that had been built since 1994.

As the PA struggled to make partial and delayed wage payments to some public-sector workers (using domestic tax revenues and cash carried by hand across the Gaza-Egyptian border), the Quartet eventually agreed to an EU proposal to establish a Temporary International Mechanism of limited scope and duration that would provide funds for essential equipment and medicines and some welfare payments for the very poorest (Quartet 2006b). Owing to US objections, however, the mechanism would not provide salary support to PA employees. Several donors also attempted to find ways of channeling funds through Abbas and the Fateh-controlled presidency rather than the Ministry of Finance or other Hamas-controlled ministries—an ironic shift in policy, given many years of donor efforts to weaken the (Arafat) presidency and to support a more transparent, accountable, and effective system of public resource management.

Such international pressures were intended to either encourage Hamas moderation or, more cynically, to force the elected Hamas government from power.[40] Although Hamas popularity had faded somewhat in the West Bank and Gaza by the summer of 2006, however, most Palestinians seemed to blame Israel and donors, rather than Hamas, for the fiscal and economic crisis.

Broader Lessons

Despite the unique characteristics of the Palestinian case, it is possible to draw from it some broader observations about the dynamics of public finance in (post)conflict countries.

The first and most obvious of these is that although public finance management is a technical matter, actual public finances are profoundly political. Budgets do not exist solely to be balanced, nor are they used exclusively to provide services in some theoretically optimal way. They are critical elements of political stabilization, of consolidating state power, and of winning support for incumbent political elites. This reality is now well understood, not only by politicians and diplomats but increasingly by international financial institutions as well.

This rather obvious point leads to a somewhat more difficult one, however: How much budget politics is too much? What is the right balance between financially expensive political stabilization and fiscal prudence? Who decides, and how?

There are simply no obvious answers to these questions, as central as they are to the challenges of postconflict public finance.[41] Yet clearly there has to be a balance between two equally undesirable extremes. On the one hand, there are local political elites who consolidate their personal hold on power through massive patronage expenditures that cripple the long-term sustainability of government finance and the broader economy. On the other hand, there is donor-enforced fiscal restraint that wins kudos from the IMF but propels a shaky postconflict government toward collapse amid resurgent violence and a failure to establish its influence and authority.

Perhaps part of the problem is to think not so much about whether governments will use public finance in political ways—they always have, and always will—but *how* they do so. Are there ways of winning support through public expenditures that are more or less corrosive of long-term institution building? Rather than turning a blind eye to patronage, perhaps donors need to give some thought to how host countries can be encouraged to do it in ways that do not result in a bloated public service, excessive cronyism, diversion of funds, and corruption. Part of the answer may be in accepting that it is appropriate that political considerations shape some key development decisions by local governments (where to build a road or clinic, for example) while at the same time promoting a legal and regulatory environment and governance arrangements that create disincentives for excessive neopatrimonial behavior. In this respect, democratic institutions, active and effective civil society institutions performing a watchdog role, a free press, and rule of law may all be important contextual elements for sound public finance management, in addition to the more usual technical approach of accounting systems and audit institutions.

A second set of observations arising from the Palestinian case concerns the role of donors. Clearly, both donor pressure and donor support for capacity building were very important to reform of the public finance management system in Palestine. They were most effective when donors spoke with a clear and coherent voice and in tandem with parallel pressures for reform from local society, technocrats, and government officials, when innovative long-term thinking was encouraged, when attention was paid to establishing appropriate "rules of the game" (rather than focusing simply on structures and organograms), and when genuine dialogue and partnership were encouraged. In all of this, local political leadership was essential (World Bank 2000, 105).

This, of course, is not a new set of findings but rather has become broadly accepted in the literature on aid effectiveness and policy reform.[42] What perhaps deserves more attention, therefore, is not so much donor *best practices* but rather donor *worst practices*—that is, a catalogue of how usually well-intentioned donor actions can actually aggravate challenges of sound public finance and public finance management in postconflict and other developing countries.

And what of the heavy stick of donor financial sanctions and consequent fiscal and economic crisis as a way of reshaping local politics? As of the end of 2006, the situation in the Palestinian territories remained too fluid to draw any definitive conclusions. It was clear, however, that most of the local population was highly resentful of donors' using a suspension of aid to try to overturn the results of a democratic election—and that, as a consequence, donor sanctions had much less than the desired political and attitudinal effects. Poor donor coordination, mixed donor motives, and poor donor messaging only further compounded this. It is also clear that whatever the eventual outcome of the crisis, it will leave a legacy of institutional damage to the PA and economic damage to the West Bank and Gaza that will substantially impede future statebuilding and the search for peace.

Notes

1. These agreements comprised the April 1994 "(Paris) Protocol on Economic Relations"; the May 1994 "Agreement on the Gaza Strip and Jericho Area," which outlined Israel's withdrawal from these two areas; the August 1994 "Agreement on the Preparatory Transfer of Powers and Responsibilities" and the August 1995 "Protocol on Further Transfer of Powers and Responsibilities," both of which transferred additional civil administrative functions to the PA; the September 1995 "Palestinian-Israeli Interim Agreement," which extended the scope of Israeli withdrawals and PA geographic authority in the West Bank; the January 1997 "Protocol Concerning Redeployment in Hebron"; and the October 1998 "Wye River Memorandum," which called for additional Israeli redeployments (which were only partially implemented).

2. The costs of closure between 1994 and 1996 were estimated by the United Nations and World Bank at up to US$2.4 billion in employment and trade losses. For a more detailed account see Brynen (2000b, 64–68).

3. I have assumed a population growth rate of 3.8 percent per year. Previous estimates put annual GDP growth in 1994–1999 at around 1.2 percent, representing a decline in GDP per capita of around 2.5 percent each year. The very substantial gap between the original data and later estimates should sound a cautionary note about the quality of underlying data used for economic analysis during war-to-peace transitions, especially given the extensive, high-quality Palestinian and international analytical resources available in the WBG. In this case, the original underestimation of GDP was

detected and corrected by the Palestinian Central Bureau of Statistics. Many analysts also feel that Palestinian population data may slightly overestimate the current population of the WBG.

4. There were some cautious discussions between Israeli and Palestinian officials in the spring of 2000, followed by the ill-prepared and unsuccessful Camp David summit in July. Thereafter, a series of meetings was held in Jerusalem, Washington, and elsewhere. The final round of negotiations took place in Taba, Egypt, in January 2001. On this period, see Agha and Malley (2001), together with the later comments by Ehud Barak in Morris (2002) and Agha and Malley (2002); Enderlin (2002); Pressman (2003); Ross (2004); and Swishers (2004).

5. During the period of the Oslo peace process (1993–2001), the number of Israeli settlers in the West Bank and Gaza almost doubled, from approximately 120,000 to 208,000 in 139 settlements. Such figures exclude occupied East Jerusalem and areas of the West Bank illegally annexed to Israel after 1967, where approximately 170,000 Israeli Jews resided by 2001. This growth continued after the intifada, with settler numbers growing by 5.3 percent in 2003 to approximately 232,000 (excluding East Jerusalem)—almost three times the rate of Israel's general population growth (1.9 percent). With East Jerusalem included, this represents a continuing increase of around 15,000–20,000 settlers per year in the occupied Palestinian territories. Information taken from the Israeli Central Bureau of Statistics website, http://www.cbs.gov.il/population/l popul_eng.htm; and the Foundation for Middle East Peace website, http://www.fmep .org/reports/2003/v13n2.html#chart 1.

6. Prior to the establishment of the PA, more than 111,000 Palestinians worked in Israel, representing 28 percent of the employed labor force (1991). This number fell as low as 22,000 in 1996. Israel also accounted for 89.7 percent of all Palestinian imports and 85.4 percent of all exports (1992) (Brynen 2000b, 40, 65–66).

7. As argued later, the budget contained inadequate provision for maintenance and capital expenditures and so could not be considered truly "balanced."

8. The West Bank (which had been annexed by Jordan before Israeli occupation in 1967) was governed by 1964 Jordanian tax laws, whereas Gaza (previously administered by Egypt) operated under Egyptian laws dating to 1947.

9. Corporate income taxes were reduced from 38.5 to 20 percent, and personal income tax rates were lowered from 5 percent to 48 percent to a new scale of between 5 percent (on income less than 27,500 shekels) and 20 percent (on income more than 110,000 shekels) (Palestinian Investment Promotion Agency n.d.). For a more detailed discussion of Palestinian tax policy in the pre-intifada era, see Fjeldstad and Zagha (2004).

.10. As discussed later in this chapter, some of the monopolies formed part of the web of neopatrimonial resource-generation and control exercised by Arafat. Other monopolies seem to have been sanctioned for strategic economic policy reasons, however. For a detailed discussion, see Nasr (2004).

11. Seignorage is the net revenue arising from the difference between the face value of currency and the cost of producing and distributing it.

12. According to the European Anti-Fraud Office (OLAF), some US$238 million was moved to Swiss bank accounts between 1997 and early 2000 (European Anti-Fraud Office 2005).

13. Bush declared that "if they energetically take the path of reform, the rewards can come quickly. If Palestinians embrace democracy, confront corruption and firmly reject terror, they can count on American support for the creation of a provisional state of Palestine" (White House 2002).

14. The Palestinian Investment Fund, as now constituted, manages the PA's commercial investments with an independent board of directors and at (partial) arm's length

from the PA. Although its profits can be transferred to the PA for public purposes, its capital cannot, thereby reducing the risk that its resources could be "raided" for political purposes. For more details, see the Palestine Investment Fund website at http://www.pa-inv-fund.com.

15. For a detailed account of the economic damage wrought by closures and the intifada, see World Bank (2004c).

16. Israel also paid previously suspended arrears, although sometimes not before deducting moneys owed to Israeli enterprises by Palestinian public institutions.

17. In 2002, the Arab League agreed that its members would contribute a total of US$55 million per month to support the PA budget, although in practice the PA received half or less of this amount in most months.

18. These charges were eventually investigated by the European Anti-Fraud Office, which found "no conclusive evidence of support of armed attacks or unlawful activities financed by EC contributions to the PA budget. However, there are consistent indications to support the hypothesis that it cannot be excluded that some of the assets of the PA may have been used by some individuals for other than the intended purposes" (European Anti-Fraud Office 2005).

19. Some budget support funds were also provided through the Holst Fund in the early days of the PA.

20. See also World Bank, Operations Evaluation Department (1999).

21. The EU contributed more than half this amount (US$80 million).

22. UNRWA, *UNRWA in Figures*, December 31, 2002. By 2004 the regular UNRWA budget for the WBG had grown to US$164 million, excluding emergency projects. Should Palestine gain its independence, these services would eventually be assumed by the new Palestinian state, representing a substantial fiscal burden. For further discussion, see Brynen (2000a).

23. This chapter does not examine public finance at the local government level in the WBG, despite its importance. In general, however, it can be said that municipalities have only a weak local property tax base and have instead been reliant on earnings from local utilities, together with fees and profits from local publicly owned enterprises (World Bank 1999c, 50).

24. A similar characterization is offered in World Bank (2000, 29).

25. On this issue, see World Bank (2000, 89); and International Monetary Fund (2003c, 94).

26. Among Palestine's immediate neighbors, the central government wage bill in 2001 constituted 7 percent of GDP and 31.2 percent of current expenditures in Egypt; 6.3 percent of GDP and 21.2 percent of current expenditures in Jordan; 9 percent of GDP and 54.0 percent of current expenditures in Syria; and 8.6 percent of GDP and 25.2 percent of current expenditures in Lebanon. Relative to the labor force, Palestinian central government employment was also much higher than that in 1987 of Egypt (12.4 percent), Jordan (10.1 percent), and Lebanon (4.2 percent) (IMF 2003c, 92; World Bank 1999c, 55).

27. Even the World Bank, a constant critic of PA payroll growth, noted that "reducing the wage bill, by reducing the payroll or cutting salaries, could prove to be highly destabilizing; the PA derives its legitimacy from its ability to provide jobs in a context of economic crisis" (World Bank 2004c, xix).

28. For further discussion of this, see Brynen (1995).

29. Martin Indyk, the former US ambassador to Israel, noted that "the Israelis came to us and said, basically, 'Arafat's job is to clean up Gaza. It's going to be a difficult job. He needs walking-around money'" ("Arafat's Billions" 2003).

30. Arafat's experience of the aftermath of the 1990–1991 Gulf war—when the Gulf states, angered at perceived PLO support for Iraq, cut off financial support and drove the organization into near bankruptcy—may have loomed large in this respect.

31. See also pp. 37–46 in World Bank (2000) for objective measures of performance in this area.

32. In the 2003 Trends in International Mathematics and Science Study, Palestinian eighth graders placed third among nine participating Arab countries in science and sixth in math. In both areas they outperformed schoolchildren from Chile, the Philippines, and South Africa (Gonzales et al. 2004).

33. For example, in one World Bank study, Palestinian businesspersons pointed to corruption as the second greatest impediment to private-sector activity (after political instability/uncertainty), although 79 percent reported seldom or never having to pay a bribe. On a comparative 6-point scale of bribery (1=never, 6=always), the WBG scored 1.7, compared to an average of 2.7 for Latin America, 3.7 for India, 4.3 for ex-Communist Europe, and 4.8 for neighboring Egypt (Sewell 2001). The WBG fared poorly on Transparency International's widely reported index (in which the PA ranks 108 of 146 countries in 2004), but this was based on *perceptions* of corruption rather than its actual frequency or magnitude ("Transparency International Corruption Perceptions Index" 2004).

34. For a discussion of the weak connections between socioeconomic circumstances and political outlook in the WBG, see Brynen (2005).

35. According to a June 2005 survey by the Palestinian Center for Policy and Survey Research, Palestinians rated the leading issues in the PLC elections as "(1) the ability to fight corruption, (2) ability to reach a peace agreement with Israel, (3) ability to improve economic conditions, (4) ability to maintain national unity, (5) ability to protect refugee rights in negotiations, (6) the name or affiliation of the list, (7) ability to enforce law and order, and finally (8) ability to insure the continuation of the *intifada*." See *Public Opinion Poll no. 16*, June 9–11, 2005. Available at http://www.pcpsr.org/survey/polls/2005/p16a.html.

36. In particular, the old system of paying security force salaries in cash—a system highly vulnerable to abuse—was replaced by a system of direct bank deposit.

37. According to a July 2005 comment by US security envoy Lt. Gen. William Ward, only 22,000 of 58,000 Palestinian security personnel "actually show up for work" (Curtius 2005).

38. Although this sort of employment can be seen as a Disarmament, Demobilization, and Reintegration (DDR) program of sorts, there has been little discussion of applying a typical postconflict DDR program to the WBG. The major reason for this is that Palestine is not in a "postconflict" situation, and a majority of the Palestinian public opposes the collection of arms from armed groups as long as the Israeli occupation continues.

39. Polls showed governance issues were far more important to Palestinian voters in the election than were "peace process" issues, with corruption being cited as the primary issue by the largest share of voters (29 percent), followed by law and order (20 percent). See US Department of State, Office of Research (2006).

40. The donors were not fully agreed on this and as a result sent rather mixed messages. Arab and EU officials and Quartet statements seemed to be encouraging Hamas to moderate, whereas most Western donors barred contact with even democratically elected Hamas officials. Moreover, US officials were privately telling the press that the purpose of the aid cutoff was to bring about the collapse of the new Palestinian government.

41 For some additional—albeit inconclusive—reflections on this issue, see Brynen (2005).

42. See, for example, World Bank (1998); World Bank (1999a).

8

Currency and Sovereignty: Why Monetary Policy Is Critical

Warren Coats

The core monetary and financial requirements for economic activity and growth are a stable unit of account, means for payments, and financial intermediation (borrowing and lending). An economy cannot function well without a currency, whether its own or that of another country. If the state issues currency, it must have policies and capacities to control its value. The economy must have the facilities to receive, pay out, and keep safe money, services that generally are provided by banks, which also provide noncash payment and financial intermediation services.

Monetary arrangements and policies potentially contribute to postconflict statebuilding in several important ways. The provision of currency and overseeing the banking system and the means of payment are traditional state functions. A single national currency can contribute to a sense of national identity. A stable currency and efficient payment systems facilitate the efficient allocation of resources and the ability to engage in commerce.[1] Failure to achieve these objectives not only undermines economic recovery and development but also jeopardizes efforts to establish or reestablish a credible state.

Drawing mainly on the experiences of Bosnia and Herzegovina, Kosovo, and Afghanistan, this chapter sets out the key issues that need to be addressed when restoring and reforming monetary and financial functions in postconflict economies. A summary of the monetary and financial issues that must be dealt with in postconflict economies is followed by case studies of Bosnia and Herzegovina, Kosovo, and Afghanistan. A concluding section draws lessons from these experiences for future assistance in rebuilding the monetary and financial systems of postconflict economies.

Monetary and Financial Issues in Postconflict Reconstruction

Initial postconflict efforts must focus on the most urgent needs. Emergency measures may be needed to provide the public with food and water or the financial means to acquire them. Measures may also be needed to restore electricity, sewage and waste disposal, and telecommunications. In the monetary and financial areas, the urgent needs are to have a currency and the means to use it. If the state cannot meet its payment obligations to its employees and the public, the economy will suffer, as will the credibility of the government. Decisions about how best to fulfill the urgent need to make payments during the emergency phase will heavily influence the options available for subsequent reform and development of the monetary and financial systems. These issues are elaborated below with regard to the choice of currency, monetary policy, and the development of the payments and banking systems.

Currency Choice

Initial Currencies

In the medium term, statebuilding is best served by the adoption of a currency with a value that can easily be stabilized and maintained. This might be a foreign currency with a historically stable value or a national currency issued and controlled by a central bank in accordance with well-defined and predictable rules. In the initial months following the end of hostilities, the authorities have no choice, however, but to use whatever currencies are already available and being used. These currencies generally bridge the gap until new currencies can be designed, printed, and issued.

In Kosovo, where the vaults of the regional branch of the National Bank of Yugoslavia had been seriously damaged and were not accessible, the authorities and public initially had to rely on German marks (DMs), which were very widely used anyway. The strong political desire of the Albanian majority to replace the Yugoslav dinar (YUD) with a currency of their own could not be permitted by the UN administration, because Kosovo formally remained a province of Serbia. Similar considerations keep the Palestine Monetary Authority from issuing its own currency. In Bosnia and Herzegovina, too, the German mark was widely used. The Croat majority region also used the Croatian kuna and the Serbian majority area also used the Yugoslav dinar, whereas in the Bosniac majority region a central bank also had issued a currency fixed to the German mark.

Afghanistan had several currencies in use: older and newer afghani notes issued by the central bank in Kabul and by the central bank in exile in the north, as well as unauthorized notes issued by Abdur Rashid Dostum, a northern warlord. An extensive network of money changers provided payment services in a variety of other currencies (US dollar, Pakistani rupee, Iranian rial, and the afghani). Counterfeiting was a concern. The government sold dollars to buy existing afghanis for its budget expenditures and issued a new national currency in 2002.

New Currencies

The main motivation for a new currency is often political rather than economic. In Afghanistan and in Bosnia and Herzegovina, new currencies were chosen to establish a clear national symbol and identity. At the same time, a new currency was desirable to improve monetary control and economic integration.

If a new currency is desired, one option is to use a foreign currency, sometimes called "dollarization."[2] This can establish currency stability immediately, without the need for domestic monetary policy capabilities. Adopting a foreign currency also has the advantage of speed: it can be introduced within days or weeks, though the logistics of importing it can be formidable. If there is an existing currency that would need to be redeemed for the foreign currency, only modest time is needed to develop the redemption and exchange rules and arrangements. The existing and foreign currencies could coexist as legal tender for some time at a fixed rate of exchange.

The choice of a foreign currency carries with it the monetary regime of the country that issued the currency. The use of the dollar or euro would ensure a stable value for the currency, even with a lack of domestic data and/or capacity in the central bank. Dollarization also removes any possibility for financing government expenditures by printing money. This constraint is almost universally considered an advantage (except sometimes by finance ministries or parliamentarians) because historically the possibility of central bank lending to the government has often proven an irresistible temptation with inflationary consequences.

There may be occasions, however, when economic shocks could be mitigated if the monetary authorities had the capacity to adjust the money supply rather than forcing a general adjustment in the price level. In a dollarized economy, the government does not have the option to adjust the money supply in response to fluctuations in international oil prices, weather-induced variations in agricultural production, or other unforeseen events. Postconflict countries may be particularly prone to supply shocks arising from damaged infrastructure and in some cases (as in Afghanistan) from continuing insurgency.

A further drawback of dollarization is that it is expensive in two ways. Its initial introduction must be paid for with "real" money; that is, it cannot just be printed by the country that wants to use it. In addition, the country loses the seignorage income from printing its own currency—the difference between the value of the currency and the cost of printing it.

The Politics of Banknote Design

The Dayton agreement provided for a single central bank with "the sole authority for issuing currency and for monetary policy throughout Bosnia and Herzegovina."[1] The negotiations of the International Monetary Fund with the tripartite political leadership in Bosnia and Herzegovina over the new Central Bank Law compromised on the meaning of a single currency and accepted that two versions of the currency would be issued. The two versions would have "common design elements as well as distinct design elements for the Federation of Bosnia and Herzegovina and the Republika Srpska," according to Article 42.3 of the Central Bank Law.

Discussions of note designs got underway soon after the adoption of the Central Bank Law in May 1997. Each "side" submitted designs for their entity's version. The first Republika Srpska (RS) designs, which were rejected by the CBBH board, had Serb patriots on one side. As explained by then CBBH governor Peter Nicholl: "On the reverse of that set was a very attractive painting— the famous Serb painting of 'the Retreat from Kosovo' in 1389. When RS president Momcilo Krajisnek told me what it was, I pretended to be naive about regional geography and said I hadn't realized Kosovo was part of Bosnia. He said, of course, that it wasn't, to which I replied, 'So why on earth do you think we will agree to put it on a CBBH Bosnian banknote when it isn't even part of the country?' He reluctantly removed the painting. But at a meeting in Pale a few weeks later, attended by the High Representative in order to try to make progress on the design issue, Krajisnek reintroduced the painting. I said that this had already been rejected as it had no relationship to Bosnia. To my surprise, and even more to Krajisnek's surprise, the High Representative stood up and said the president clearly didn't want to negotiate seriously—and he walked out." Meanwhile the Federation members first submitted simple designs, with

Banknote designs submitted by representatives of the Republika Srpska and rejected by the CBBH.

continues

Continued

pictures of plants and so on. These too were rejected by Governor Nicholl because the designs bore no resemblance to each other.

Eventually the Serbs proposed portraits of a set of writers on their design. In late December 1997, the Federation's board members tabled a set of writers too, one of whom, Mesa Selimovic, also appeared in the Serb design. At that point, the Serb member said they would remove the writers from their design—as they wanted the designs to be different.

In January 1998, President Krajisnek said he would agree to the designs that had been unilaterally developed by Governor Nicholl, as long as the RS version had the entity's coat of arms on it. The Federation presidents didn't want the entity coats of arms, but they said that if the RS had it on theirs, they would have it on the Federation's version, too. This would have defeated the purpose of trying to get the two designs to be as similar as possible. Thus the High Representative took the decision not to include the entity coats of arms.

Final designs of bank-notes issued by the CBBH.

The final versions, illustrated here with the 100 convertible markka (KM) notes, were notes that looked very much alike except that they carried portraits of different writers. In addition, the Cyrillic name of the central bank was on top for the RS version, and the Latin version was on top for the Federation version.

The joint presidents accepted the writer Mesa Selimovic, who had been submitted earlier by both the RS and Federation, on both the RS and Federation versions of the five dinar notes.[2] The other writer initially on both lists was Ivo Andrić, who received the Nobel Prize for Literature in 1961.[3] When a 200 KM note later was added to the initial denominations, there was one version for the whole country with Andrić's face on it.

continues

Continued

Notes

---

1. This discussion of banknote design is based on material provided in personal correspondence from Peter Nicholl, former governor of the Central Bank of Bosnia and Herzegovina (CBBH).

2. Mesa Selimovic was born in Tuzla on April 26, 1910, and lived at different times in Belgrade and Sarajevo. His first novel, *Insulted Man,* was published in 1947. Other novels included *Silences,* published in 1961, *Dervish and Death* in 1966, *Island* in 1974, *Memories* in 1975, and *Circle* in 1983.

3. Ivo Andrić was born on October 10, 1892, in Dolac near Travnik, but his parents lived in Sarajevo. He studied in Zagreb and lived at various times in Belgrade, Trieste, Marseille, Paris, Berlin, Brussels, and Geneva.

Moreover, dollarization is not easy to reverse once established, though the move to a currency board (which firmly fixes the exchange rate, fully backs its currency with foreign currency, and passively supplies the amount of currency demanded by the market) is a relatively easy step from dollarization. A currency board has virtually the same inflation/discipline advantages as dollarization but allows the country to capture seignorage profits and to gain the political advantages that come from a currency as a symbol of national unity.

The only countries that have dollarized in recent years are Ecuador, El Salvador, and Timor-Leste. In addition, Kosovo and the West Bank and Gaza Strip remain dollarized because they are not yet sovereign states legally able to issue their own currencies.

The introduction of a new national currency, issued by the central bank, provides a symbol of national identity. In addition, it generates profits (seignorage) from the monopoly issue of bank notes (or more broadly, "base money") and provides the monetary authority with the possibility of manipulating its supply to achieve price stability or other objectives (monetary policy). The latter can be an advantage if the central bank is independent of political pressures and has the capacity to formulate and implement monetary policy—conditions that often are not met in postconflict countries.

When time permits, the process of agreeing on the design of a new currency can be an important integrating and statebuilding undertaking. Other important issues include security features, note denominations (1, 5, 10, 20, 50, 100, 500, and so forth) and the number of each to print, the initial value of one unit in relation to typical domestic household purchases, whether to issue coins, and the breaking point between the highest-value coin and the lowest-value bank note.[3]

Some security features help the general public identify the authenticity of the notes, some are designed for people more specialized in detecting counterfeits (bank tellers), and others are known only to the central bank itself. Appropriately designed and targeted education programs in these features must be developed and implemented. The general public needs information not only on how to recognize the new currency but also on how the central bank will control its supply and value.

Introducing a new currency involves the exchange of the existing currency (or currencies) for the new one. The easiest way to introduce a new currency is for the government to start using it for all of its salary and pension payments and for banks to pay out deposit withdrawals in the new currency, exchanging the old for the new in their vaults. Designated exchange points and rules for direct exchanges are also required. Exchange points might be limited to banks and post offices or might also include temporary storefront locations or mobile teller facilities. Clear rules for the exchange must be developed and communicated effectively to the public.[4]

It goes without saying that existing banking facilities, staff, and procedures should be relied upon to the extent possible. In Bosnia and Herzegovina, the introduction of the new currency was handled with comparative ease by the existing, fully functioning payment bureaus of the previous regime, as described below. In the absence of a functioning banking system, Afghanistan used the services of money changers.

In some cases, as in Afghanistan, the security situation has posed serious challenges to every aspect of the exchange from the transportation of the bank notes from the printer to the central bank's headquarters, to the distribution of cash from the central bank's headquarters vaults to its branches and from its branches to exchange centers. The security of the cash at every point required considerable military assistance.

Monetary Policy Objectives and Regimes

In addition to the choice of currency, postconflict governments face two key questions: (1) what the objective of monetary policy should be, and (2) how that objective can best be achieved. Historically, many central banks were seen as a convenient source of government funding. In the developed world of an earlier day, central banks were often assigned the task of maintaining full employment. In pursuit of these objectives, central banks were often engines of inflation and occasionally hyperinflation.

In the last decade, a strong consensus has emerged at the international financial institutions and elsewhere that the overriding goal of monetary policy should be price stability and that the central bank should be left free to determine how best to achieve it. Smoothing macroeconomic shocks and fostering financial sector development are important but secondary objectives: they should influence the manner and pace of pursuing price stability but should not override that long-run objective.[5] This consensus reflects (1) the theoretical argument, supported by considerable empirical evidence, that in the long run monetary policy cannot affect gross domestic product (GDP) and economic growth (beyond providing a stable price environment); (2) the very short-run nature of the once famous Philips curve, representing a trade-off between unemployment and inflation, which is now understood to apply only to unanticipated inflation; (3) the historical experience of harmful inflations at the hands of politically dominated central banks; and (4) the technical difficulty of fine tuning monetary policy even when it might be theoretically justified.

To overcome the inflation bias that derives from the short-run preference of governments to print money to finance their expenditures or to temporarily stimulate employment, almost all current central bank laws forbid it to lend directly to the government, mandate it to seek price stability, and make it independent from government interference (while holding it accountable for achieving this objective).

Several special considerations often come into play in the postconflict situation. The need for reconstruction expenditures is high and the capacity of the government to raise revenue (other than by printing money) is very limited. Although a policy of deliberate inflation (above, say, 4 or 5 percent) cannot be justified on the grounds of long-run economic growth and development, it might be justified on the grounds that it is the only way to increase the revenue of the government needed for crucial expenditures. There may be validity to this argument, but it is a tool that can be difficult to control. The capacity of the central bank to resist government pressure for financing may be low and its capacity to implement an effective monetary policy may be very limited. Given the importance of price stability for both economic development and the credibility of the new government, the international community generally has supported central bank independence while to various degrees across countries providing supplemental reconstruction funding.[6]

Dollarization has the virtue of combining price stability and low technical requirements from the central bank. If a country issues its own currency, it faces a range of policy options from hard exchange rate pegs to free floating rates with some other policy anchor. The hardest peg, with the highest credibility and least demands on data and analysis by the central bank, is a currency board. Its main prerequisites are acceptance by the government that there will be no central bank financing and sufficient domestic price flexibility to adjust to any trade shocks. Bosnia and Herzegovina has a successful currency board. The fact that it provides for no discretion over monetary policy made it easier to accept for the Bosniac, Croat, and Serb representatives at the Dayton peace negotiations, among whom mutual trust was almost nonexistent.

Soft or managed pegs potentially anchor the system in the same way as a currency board without any legal commitment to maintain the exchange rate if external conditions change. This introduces some scope for domestic liquidity management by the central bank (i.e., some sterilization of the monetary effects of foreign exchange transactions).[7] This flexibility can be useful in some circumstances but has often been misused, resulting in domestic conditions inconsistent with the exchange rate and sometimes in an exchange-rate crisis.

Free floating or lightly managed exchange rates require an alternative anchor for monetary policy. In some well-developed economies, inflation is directly targeted in so-called inflation targeting regimes (e.g., England, Canada, New Zealand, Poland, Czech Republic). Such a sophisticated approach generally is well beyond the capacity of postconflict countries.[8] Thus some variant of an intermediate monetary aggregate target is the most common anchor for monetary policy (and the public's inflation expectations) when the exchange rate is market determined. As with any successful monetary policy regime, monetary targeting requires sufficient central bank autonomy (e.g., zero or very limited lending to government) for the central bank to control its own balance sheet.

Banking and Payment Systems

In the immediate postconflict period, banks may not be functioning, and yet the ability to safeguard and disburse cash needs to be restored rapidly, as it is critical for both economic recovery and political stabilization. Banking offices and staff are likely to be needed from the outset to facilitate government and enterprise payments for wages and pensions. Their vaults, cash handling procedures, security, and teller window staff are essential for the quick restoration of these payments.

In the emergency "triage" environment of early postconflict economies, banks and certainly noncash payment systems take second place. For some months, banks can be left to carry on whatever limited activities they might be performing without much official intervention. As soon as feasible, however, governmental decisions should be taken with regard to banks: Who will supervise them? Are the supervisor and the underlying legal provisions for banking supervision in place, or do they need to be developed? Should existing banks be allowed to resume full operations, or should they be required to be recertified? What should be done with state banks?

Supervision

The postconflict economies reviewed in this chapter all adopted new banking laws and undertook multiyear training programs to develop modern banking supervision capabilities. In Afghanistan and Kosovo, new licensing requirements were established, and all existing banks were required to reapply. In Afghanistan, three of the six state banks have been provisionally licensed, and by the end of 2006 four foreign-owned banks, five branches of foreign banks, and two new domestically owned banks had been licensed. In Kosovo, none of the existing banks qualified to be relicensed. Within two years enough banks were in operation in all major cities, however, to allow the Banking and Payment Authority of Kosovo (BPK) to terminate its temporary banking services for the public. At the end of 2006 there were seven foreign and domestically owned banks licensed in Kosovo.

In Bosnia and Herzegovina, banks in the country's two "entities"—the Federation and the Republika Srpska—were licensed separately and supervised by banking agencies established in each entity. Initially, banks licensed in one entity operated only within that entity. At the end of 2006, twenty-eight licensed banks were in operation—nineteen in the Federation and nine in the Republika Srpska—and branching across entities had become common.

Ownership

The cases in this study all had state-owned banks as well as some privately owned banks. As in other developing countries, the International Monetary Fund and World Bank strongly advised downsizing and privatizing state banks, as they were notoriously inefficient and almost always corrupt (hiring friends and extending noncommercial lending to state-owned enterprises and cronies).

Under the new banking laws adopted in Bosnia and Herzegovina and in Kosovo, foreign ownership was permitted. Over time, some foreign banks were established, and some domestic banks were purchased by foreign entities (generally foreign banks). The entry of foreign banks into the domestic market has strong benefits, as badly needed banking services are provided more quickly and efficiently, and international standards and expertise are brought into the local market and more rapidly disseminated.

The entry of foreign banks is often opposed by the existing banking interests, however, who are often closely allied with political interests. Moreover, reduced corruption opportunities limit the means for paying for political support, which can be an important part of reconciliation or of gaining acceptance of the new state. In addition, cleaning up the state banks invariably means reducing employment by these banks, which can produce a loss of political support among a broader segment of the public.

For these practical reasons, addressing the state bank problem is not the first priority. It needs to be carefully planned and executed and will almost always be implemented late in the reform process and take considerable time to complete. In the interim, it will be important to prevent the state banks from extending new loans to political insiders or for unpromising state projects. If banks are privatized, it is also important that the sales be at fair prices, both for reasons of efficiency and for public acceptance of the process as fair.

Payment Systems Modernization

Payment systems include interbank settlements and retail business and household noncash payments using checks, payment orders, debit cards, credit cards, and so on. In the cases in this study, payment systems modernization invariably focused first on establishing the capacity for efficient electronic interbank payments—so-called large value transfers—that are important for the development of interbank lending and trading markets and for the transmission of monetary policy.

Donors often rushed to finance expensive Real Time Gross Settlement (RTGS) systems before they could be cost-justified and before the stakeholders in the market had a clear understanding of what was needed. RTGS systems permit quick and low-cost (per message) electronic payments between banks and are the backbone of modern payment systems. They were often established alongside electronic payment order clearinghouses (Automated Clearing House network and Giro systems). These systems are attractive to donors because they are discrete, well focused, and attention getting and because much of the cost is spent on foreign vendors.

The payment system reforms in Bosnia and Herzegovina and other former Yugoslav republics were especially challenging because of the unique system of domestic payments that was in operation there. The Social Accounting Service (SDK) had a technical and legal monopoly on noncash domestic payments.[9] Although transferable deposits were technically with banks (the liabilities of banks), deposits and withdrawals and transfer (payment) orders were made at offices of the SDK, which transferred funds and maintained accounting records on behalf of all banks. The SDK had an extensive branch network, employed more people than the commercial banking sector, and was politically very powerful.

Replacement of these organizations in the three regions of Bosnia and Herzegovina by modern, bank-based payment systems and tax collection required more than two years of concentrated and coordinated effort by the IMF, the US Agency for International Development, the World Bank, the US Treasury, and other donors. The new clearing house and RTGS systems in Bosnia and Herzegovina, owned by the Central Bank of Bosnia and Herzegovina (CBBH), came into operation in 2002. They fully reintegrated the domestic noncash systems of the three regions of Bosnia and Herzegovina, based on the central bank's new currency, the convertible markka (KM).

Banking Services for Government

Although modern central banks are almost universally forbidden to lend directly to the government and to the nonbank public, virtually all central banks accept government deposits and most perform some payment services for the government. It is in these areas that the government and the central bank are most interdependent, especially in the early postconflict days when banks and payment systems may not be functioning well.

A proper division of labor and accountability between the Ministry of Finance (MOF) and the central bank assigns government expenditure, cash, and debt management to the MOF and monetary policy, foreign exchange reserves management, and often banking supervision to the central bank. The first domestic financial requirement of government following the end of conflict is the resumption of its payments of government wages and pensions. These payments are most often in cash and require the services of a large number of people to verify the rolls of payees and the amounts due them, to distribute and safeguard the cash needed for payments, to administer the actual disbursements, and to verify the identity of the recipients and otherwise minimize fraudulent payments.[10]

In many instances, the new postconflict government is not well informed about existing systems or in good contact with existing government personnel. But there is no faster or surer way to resume payments than to take up previously existing staff and systems, so the starting point must be an assessment of the previous systems of payment and monitoring and of their capacity to restart. In some instances new programs, such as the National Solidarity Program and National Emergency Employment Program in Afghanistan, will build their own lists of payments and payees, but they still need to rely on the banking and payment systems in place for actual disbursements.

Bosnia and Herzegovina functioned very smoothly in this regard. The successors of the Yugoslav SDK continued to function without much change for several years following the war, ensuring continuity and a degree of efficiency in carrying on basic government payment functions. Kosovo, on the other hand, posed more difficult challenges. Yugoslav dinar payments were replaced with German mark payments and these were almost totally in cash. Thus the Kosovo offices of the Yugoslav SDK became German mark cash storage and distribution centers. Efforts were made to install new accounting systems and procedures from the start. Staff training and acceptance of the new systems were inadequate. As a result, the newly established Finance Ministry opened its own accounts abroad and continually complained of inadequate records and service from what became the BPK. For almost a year, the BPK was not able to produce accurate records on the cash in its vaults. This experience drove home the lesson that changes should be minimized and that any new procedures need to be implemented with considerable training. Afghanistan was able to draw on the extensive branch network of the central bank to make government payments. More important, the MOF used the highly developed network and payment services of money changers and the *hawala* system, as discussed below.

Bosnia and Herzegovina

Background

Bosnia and Herzegovina was one of six republics that made up the Socialist Federal Republic of Yugoslavia (FRY). Following Slovenia and Croatia, which declared independence in the summer of 1991 (and later Macedonia), the Republic of Bosnia and Herzegovina (BH) declared its independence from the FRY in March 1992. The UN and most of its members quickly recognized BH, but its independence was promptly challenged by the Yugoslav National Army and local Serb militia, who launched a war in April 1992 that continued until the last of many cease-fires on October 10, 1995. Armed conflict also erupted between Bosnian Croats and Bosniacs (Muslims), and this lasted from early 1993 until February 25, 1994. The death toll from these conflicts is estimated at about 250,000, and about 3 million of the country's 4.4 million inhabitants were displaced from their homes (about one million became refugees abroad).

During the Balkan wars, the common currency of Yugoslavia (the Yugoslav dinar) gave way to the newly independent republics' own currencies (e.g., the kuna in Croatia and the Bosnian dinar in Bosnia and Herzegovina). The Bosnia and Herzegovina dinar (BHD) was issued by the National Bank of Bosnia and Herzegovina (NBBH). During the war, the Bosniac-majority area used the BHD, the Serbian-majority area (which would become the Republika Srpska, or RS) used the Yugoslav dinar, and the Croat-majority area began to use the Croatian kuna. Each of the three regions also gave some quasi-official status to the German mark, which was widely used for making domestic payments during and following the war and for payments across regional boundaries.

The country's main governmental structures broke into three as well. This was true for the armies, of course, but also for the MOF and other government ministries, the central bank, and the SDK payment system. The banking system broke up as well, with branches of the same bank separated across ethnic/regional boundaries.

In the monetary area, the SDK in many respects was a more critical institution than the central bank, as noted above. The SDK was designed to maximize state control over economic activities in a centrally planned economy. All domestic noncash payments (deposit transfers) were made through the SDK, which had a legal monopoly on such payments. All enterprises were required by law to make all domestic payments through the SDK, except for wage payments, which they made in cash withdrawn from the SDK by debit to their accounts with their bank. Since the payments made through the SDK were really transfers of balances that enterprises and others kept with their respective banks, the payment bureau was really an accounting and payment instruction processing entity. Cash was generally deposited and withdrawn from SDK offices, which outnumbered the offices of banks.

One of the first steps by each republic upon independence was to separate its SDK operation from the broader Yugoslav system. One of the first steps within Bosnia and Herzegovina after the onset of its internal war was the similar separation of its payment bureaus into three separate systems that no longer interacted with each other. The Bosniac region of the SDK, headquartered in Sarajevo, became the Institute for Payments Transactions (ZPP). The Croat region, headquartered in Mostar, became the Institute for Payments Transactions (ZAP) (although not technically or legally related to the Croatian payment bureau of the same name). The Serbian region payment bureau, headquartered in Banja Luka, became the Serbian Payment Bureau (SPP), which remained technically linked with what was left of the Yugoslav system, so that payments cleared through it ultimately were settled on the books of the National Bank of Yugoslavia in Belgrade. As a wartime measure, all three payment bureaus accepted deposits of German mark cash (which was kept in their vaults) and allowed domestic payment through their clearing systems in German marks.

The NBBH became, as a practical though not legal matter, the central bank only of the Bosniac area. The Republika Srpska had its own branch of the National Bank of Yugoslavia, which became the National Bank of Republika Srpska (NBRS). The Croat majority area did without a central bank and relied on its regional payment bureau, the ZAP, to perform quasi–central bank functions. Only the NBBH issued its own currency, which it did in accordance with informal currency board rules. The exchange rate of the BHD was fixed to the German mark at 100 to 1, and all notes issued were fully backed by German marks.

When international technical assistance began in 1996 following the Dayton Peace Agreement, each of Bosnia and Herzegovina's three ethnic regions had currencies and functioning payment systems. Each had established finance ministries and other administrative bodies of government. For a time government revenues would come largely from donor financial support. There were no immediate technical difficulties in making payments in any region of the country.

Monetary Policy

On the eve of the Dayton negotiations, the IMF's first deputy managing director, Stanley Fischer, met with the IMF's executive directors from the Group of Seven (G7) member countries to discuss issues related to Bosnia and Herzegovina and its possible future membership in the fund. On behalf of the G7 (the United States, Germany, Japan, UK, France, Italy, and Canada), the directors requested the IMF to prepare a brief note for the upcoming Dayton peace talks outlining the requirements of viable fiscal and monetary structures in confederacies.

The goal was to find an arrangement for satisfying the monetary and payment needs of Bosnia and Herzegovina that would be acceptable to the warring factions. At the same time, the monetary arrangements would also contribute to the economic reintegration of the divided country.

The IMF advised that these objectives would be best served by a unified monetary system. The essential requirement for a viable monetary system is that the money supply is under proper control (an uncontrolled supply of money would result in uncontrolled inflation). This requires, first and foremost, that there be no more than one monetary policy. If there is more than one monetary authority, there must be very clear and binding rules that link their activities together to ensure that the quantity of money is well determined and controlled.

The IMF recommended a single currency issued by a single central bank in accordance with strict currency board rules. Such provisions were adopted in the Dayton Peace Agreement in Article VII of the new constitution, with the further requirement that the governor must be a foreigner selected by the IMF for the first six years.[11]

New Central Bank Law

The members of the CBBH board were appointed by the joint presidency of Bosnia and Herzegovina and were the direct counterparts to IMF advisers in developing the text of the central bank law. Key issues in these discussions were the role and powers of the branches of the central bank and the name and design of the currency notes.

The role of CBBH branches was hotly debated. Having relaxed somewhat their initial position that there should be separate central banks in the two entities, the Bosnian Serbs sought to preserve as much autonomy as possible by assigning important powers to the branches. The law as finally adopted clearly established one nationwide central bank to which the main units are fully subordinated.

The name of the new currency, convertible markka, and the general principles guiding the design of the new notes were agreed upon so that the new central bank law could be adopted and the institution established. Gentle but persistent international pressure played a key role in reaching an agreement.

The details were put off until later. Each ethnic group put forward its proposed design, which was knocked down by one of the other groups. In February 1998, the new CBBH governor, Peter Nicholl, considered the latest set of objections from each side, unilaterally decided which he felt were justified and which were not, and made his own proposal to his board. When the board could not agree to act, he submitted the resulting designs to the international

Office of the High Representative (OHR).[12] The high representative approved the design and presented it to the joint presidency.

This proved to be a well-timed intervention. No one objected strenuously. Indeed it would not have been possible to force any of the political leaders to take actions they strongly opposed. There were times when it was politically difficult for the three groups to explicitly agree to something they might otherwise find acceptable. At these times, an externally imposed decision could be acceptable (and even welcomed). This was one of those times.

Payment System

Because of the use of foreign currencies and the continued functioning of the three regional payment bureaus, payments within each region could be made without difficulty. The most immediate need was to establish the means for interregional settlements. For the first few years following the end of the war, such payments were made by sending fax payment orders on one of the telephone lines that had been established for the OHR. Settlement took the form of driving German mark cash in the trunk of a car from the payment bureau of one region to the border with the other region, where it was transferred to the receiving payment bureau.

The most difficult challenge technically, and to some extent politically, was the transformation and phasing out of the three payment bureaus, and in the case of the Bosniac and Serb regions the liquidation of their central banks. Each of the three majority ethnic regions had unique and challenging problems, but the common problem was that the payment bureaus were politically powerful organizations. They employed large numbers of people who did not want to lose their jobs or power and who were well connected with the ruling political parties.

On January 5, 2001, the old SDK-based systems closed down. In their place, the CBBH operated an RTGS system and a small-value, Giro, net settlement clearinghouse system. In both, payment instructions originated directly from banks and were settled on the banks' clearing accounts with the CBBH. Getting to that revolutionary place took almost three years of intensive work by the IMF, World Bank, US Treasury, USAID, and other international donors. The work was very political as well as highly technical. The interregional payment clearing and settlement aspects brought payment bureau staff from the three regions together for the first time since the beginning of the wars and made its small contribution to national healing. This work was led by the CBBH and the IMF adviser assigned to CBBH for this purpose, Kim Rhee. The transitional problems in each region are discussed below.

In Sarajevo, the insolvency of the National Bank of Bosnia and Herzegovina and its continued use by government institutions almost sank the currency board arrangements of the new central bank and thus almost destroyed its credibility. The hole in the NBBH's balance sheet (the source of its insolvency or at least of its lack of German mark cover) resulted from a wartime loan to the Bosniac government, presumably to finance the war. This loan had not been repaid, and there was no way that the Croatian municipalities were going to contribute to repaying it, now that they were part of the Federation of the Croat and Bosniac majority regions. All nongovernment deposits with the NBBH were transferred to banks, but government institutions in the Federation (municipalities mainly) continued to maintain their accounts with the NBBH and to use these to make and receive payments. The NBBH did not have a German mark–backed reserve account with the new CBBH. If deposits flowed from the NBBH into other banks, the reserve accounts of these other banks at the CBBH went up, increasing the monetary liabilities of the CBBH without any increase in its German mark assets, thus violating the currency board rules.

The first steps toward resolution of this problem were for the NBBH to open a reserve account with the CBBH (by transferring additional German marks to the CBBH) for use in settling net payments with other banks and for the ZPP to agree not to process payment orders drawn on the NBBH for which there were not sufficient funds in the new reserve account at the CBBH. These arrangements were not in place until May 1998, more than six months after the first violation of the currency board rules.

Full resolution of this problem required the liquidation of the NBBH and the reform of the payment system and the old payment bureaus. Liquidation of the NBBH required an agreement among the Bosniac-majority cantons for covering losses that resulted from the wartime loan to the Bosniac government. A freezing of municipality deposits with the NBBH and related steps to protect the CBBH were not successfully implemented until December 1998. The NBBH was not fully liquidated until late 1999. The process of resolution was slow, and it required patience with political sensitivities, coupled with steady and increasing pressure from international donors, especially the IMF.

In Mostar, the Croat-majority region had no central bank, but its payment bureau (ZAP) had taken on limited central bank functions by accepting in its own name banks' clearing accounts (a liability), against which it held the equivalent value of German marks and kuna as cash in its vaults. It also required banks to deposit with it the equivalent of 45 percent of their deposit liabilities, which were all in kuna. There was some risk that the termination of kuna deposits and payments through the ZAP could result in the public's exchange of kuna for KM more rapidly than banks could convert their kuna assets.

The first and easiest step for the payment bureaus in all three regions was to terminate the German mark payments. All German mark deposits with the payment bureaus were fully backed with cash. These deposits and related payment activities were terminated on October 1, 1999, and in the case of the ZAP, the potentially more difficult step of terminating the similar payments and cash-backed deposits in kuna was accomplished on the same date without difficulty.

In Banja Luka and Pale, the dominant currency was the Yugoslav dinar, issued by a foreign central bank, rather than by the NBRS, which had been a branch of that foreign central bank. This meant that the YUD in circulation in the RS were not really the liabilities of the NBRS, nor did the NBRS have the German mark assets to cover them. Furthermore, the YUD was not freely usable, as it was overvalued and subject to exchange controls. These facts meant that it was not possible to replace YUD with KM as had been done with the Bosnian dinar in the Federation. Instead, the public and depositors in the RS gradually increased their use of KM as they chose to exchange DM for the new currency.

The stable value and free convertibility of the KM became a strong incentive to hold and use it in the region. During this early period, the RS government pressed ahead with steps to encourage the use of KM. It issued an instruction that, effective from July 1, 1998, the KM was to be the official means of payments in the territory of the RS. The portion of the RS government staff's salary paid in KM was 50 percent in December 1998, 70 percent in January 1999, and became 100 percent soon thereafter.[13]

In November 1998, the RS government abandoned the FRY official exchange rate of 6.0 YUD = 1 DM and moved instead to 7.5 YUD = 1 DM, broadly in line with the prevailing market rate at the time. In response, the Belgrade authorities closed the access of the RS payment bureau to the National Bank of Yugoslavia (NBY) and to banks in the FRY.[14] As a result, it became impossible to make payments between the RS and the FRY by submitting payment orders to Serbian payment bureaus (SPP and SDK), and efforts to shift to cash payments were frustrated by an increasing shortage of YUD banknotes in the RS.

The efforts of the public to convert their YUD deposits into cash in order to make payments in the FRY confronted the inability of banks to pay out banknotes both because of the limited supply and because of banks' own lack of liquid assets. These developments forced the insolvency of the NBRS and many RS banks into the open.

The RS authorities were generally more proactive than their counterparts in the Federation. Anticipating the need to liquidate the NBRS and to dismantle its payment bureau (SPP), the RS merged the SPP and the NBRS into the Serb State Bank (SSB). The other banks in the RS were furious over the unfair competition from this new state bank, which also continued to have a domestic payment monopoly.[15] The IMF made the dismantling of the payment bureau operations a condition for further lending. The RS gradually came into line with the new countrywide currency, and the new bank-based countrywide RTGS and Giro clearinghouse.

Banking Agencies

The IMF's original proposals to the peace negotiations in Dayton were for a single banking supervisor within the new central bank. This was rejected, and the Dayton agreement provided for two banking agencies to supervise banks, one for the RS and one for the Federation. Thus initially there were two banking systems. The international advisers succeeded in convincing the RS and the Federation governments to adopt virtually identical banking laws, however. These laws also established rules for "cross-border" branching and licensing that integrated the two banking systems as much as possible. Furthermore, foreign advisers helped the two banking agencies draft virtually identical licensing and prudential regulations. Within a year or two of adopting these laws, banks in each entity began operating branches in the other, and a national banking system began to take root. It is expected that the two banking agencies will eventually be merged into the CBBH.

Kosovo

Background

Kosovo, a majority Muslim Albanian province of Serbia, has been an emotional center of Serbian nationalism since the defeat of Serbian Prince Lazar by the Turks on June 28, 1389, in the Battle of Kosovo, outside of Pristina. Following centuries of Ottoman rule, Kosovo became a part of Serbia in 1912. It was briefly part of Albania during World War II but has been part of Serbia since 1945, with autonomous provincial status from 1968 until 1989.

Soon after the 600th anniversary of the Battle of Kosovo, Slobodan Milosevic, then president of the Republic of Serbia, rescinded Kosovo's autonomy and imposed martial law on the province. Albanian Kosovars in management positions were replaced by Serbs, their schools were closed, and a decade-long period of underground Albanian Kosovar government began. During this period, the League for a Democratic Kosovo (LDK) had offices in several European cities, and in May 1992 Ibrahim Rugova was elected president of the self-proclaimed and internationally unrecognized Republic of Kosovo. This "shadow" government collected voluntary taxes from Albanian Kosovars, operated schools for Albanian children, and provided other basic governmental services outside the Serb-run official administration.

By 1993, 400,000 ethnic Albanians had left Kosovo in response to political tensions and deteriorating socioeconomic conditions. Violence escalated as the Kosovo Liberation Army (KLA) insurgency grew and Serb ethnic cleansing spread in response. The North Atlantic Treaty Organization (NATO) intervened militarily with aerial bombing starting on March 24, 1999. On June 9 the FRY (now consisting of Serbia and Montenegro) accepted the terms of peace with NATO, and on June 10 the UN Security Council approved Resolution 1244, which endorsed the peace agreement and placed Kosovo under direct UN administration, establishing the United Nations Interim Administration Mission in Kosovo (UNMIK).

At the end of conflict, legal tender in Kosovo was the Yugoslav dinar. Nonetheless, DM had been in widespread use in Kosovo for many years, despite legal restrictions against their use. After the war, this preference for DM became almost absolute. Cash in the street was generally limited to DM, with dinars only used for small change.

Until the breakup of the former Yugoslavia in the early 1990s, the national bank system was decentralized into a network of republican and autonomous regional national banks, one of which was the National Bank of Kosovo (NBK). The national bank system was accompanied by a parallel, countrywide network of republican and autonomous regional payment bureaus, one of which was the Payment Bureau of Kosovo (the SDKK[16]). In the early 1990s a more centralized system emerged, when the payment bureau system of the former Yugoslavia was replaced by the NBY Department of Settlements and Payments.

The NBK headquarters in Pristina had been severely damaged in NATO bombings in April 1999, and the modern vaults in the building's basement could not be used. The supply of Yugoslav dinars in its other vaults was very limited and declining. NBK's remaining staff of banking supervisors had ceased any activity.

In June 1999 the offices of the SDKK were operational, though hampered somewhat by broken telecommunications linkages. Cash withdrawals were rationed to stretch available inventories of dinar notes. The online connection to Belgrade was still used but only for conveying outgoing payment orders for customers to make use of their dinar balances. These offices were performing payment transactions at about 5 percent of the level prior to March 1999.[17]

Money and Payment System Issues

As Kosovo remained part of Serbia, it could not issue a currency of its own. However, UNMIK quickly decided that the use of DM should be made legal and facilitated. Thus there were no issues of monetary policy to resolve. There were issues, however, with regard to what formal support would be provided for both cash and noncash payments in DM and how to address an acute shortage of DM coins.

There was an urgent need to initiate payments for UNMIK and enterprises and to provide safekeeping and other payment services in DM. There was a strong desire on the part of the international community to replace the SDK throughout the former Yugoslavia, and this was proving difficult everywhere it had existed. Until a new authority could be legally established, UNMIK provided for the urgently needed monetary services (e.g., safekeeping of border taxes and making pension payments) by hiring the staff and management and leasing the facilities and equipment needed from the SDKK.

The use of DM was made legal (alongside the Yugoslav dinar) on September 2, 1999. A regulation formally giving UNMIK control of the SDKK was adopted on October 15. Following a big debate in Washington about whether to create separate banking supervision and payment institutions, the IMF, World Bank, and USAID quickly prepared legislation to establish one new institution, the Banking and Payment Authority of Kosovo, to take over the SDKK's payment functions and to license and regulate banks. The BPK was to be an autonomous authority with most of the powers of a central bank, including bank licensing, supervision, and regulation. It could not, however, issue its own currency or extend credit.

Temporarily, the new institution was allowed to accept deposits from the public, provide payment services with those deposits, inventory DM banknotes and coins, and provide local DM settlements for banks. As a practical matter this more or less continued the existing practice of the SDKK. This was a controversial measure, as it ran the risk of building up (or prolonging) commercial functions that many thought it should shed as quickly as private banks could be established to take them over. In fact, the first IMF-funded managing director of the BPK was replaced because of his enthusiasm for building up these commercial functions.

Foreign advisers prepared the BPK Regulation (UNMIK's laws were called *regulations*). The first draft was prepared in the summer of 1999 in Washington by the IMF, in consultation with the World Bank, the US Treasury, and USAID advisers. After being reviewed and modestly amended by the UN's New York lawyers, it was presented by the UN High Representative to an Economic Policy Review Committee of local leaders. An IMF team traveled to Pristina and spent many hours answering questions about the draft. The draft was revised on the basis of that meeting and written comments from Kosovars, and the law was issued by UNMIK on November 15, 1999. This procedure fell short of the minimum amount of local consultation the IMF considered desirable, but it seemed acceptable in that environment. A similar procedure was followed with the Regulation on Bank Licensing, Supervision, and Regulation, which reflected the UNMIK decision that banks operating in Kosovo would be licensed and supervised there rather than in Belgrade.

Training in new equipment and procedures was provided, but local staff expressed unwillingness or unease at adopting the new system. The foreign advisers concluded that this reflected, to some extent at least, the desire of local managers to slow down or resist the changes imposed by the transformation of the payment system. In addition, some local managers had an interest in maintaining a certain degree of chaos as a smokescreen for activities that the foreign advisers were not supposed to see.[18]

To some extent, however, foreign advisors also underestimated the difficulty of the task of installing these new systems. The Kosovo branches of the SDK had been managed by ethnic Serbs. The previous managers had been removed when Kosovo lost its autonomous status in 1989, and most of them had moved to Albania or Macedonia. When the Serbian army withdrew on June 11, 1999, Serbian managers and staff fled as well, leaving neither operating manuals, vault keys, nor currency needed for recovery. The remaining Albanian staff members were jubilant, but lost. When the old Albanian managers and staff returned, they were almost a decade removed from current operations. They came back to empty, looted shells of buildings and blank-faced employees expecting an immediate return to their old jobs. This feeling of entitlement was exacerbated by the harsh deportation measures that had been taken by Serbian authorities, including police eviction, confiscation of passports and other legal documents, and loss of all personal property. Open hostility and outbreaks of physical violence between ethnic groups continued for many months.

After fruitless appeals to the National Bank of Serbia for support, the SDKK was forced to start payment operations from scratch—an exercise in the "blind leading the blind," literally as well as figuratively, as there were frequent outages of power, heating, and water service. Its only source of income was from customs receipts trickling in from the border entry points. Lacking a formal processing system and accounting controls, the cash was stored in a small vault in the IMF office at UNMIK headquarters. This continued for several months with the IMF resident representative riding on military convoys having cash aboard.[19] Meantime, Kosovar staff returned to their old posts, signing duty rosters at 8 AM, and chatting, snacking, and smoking until signing out in the early afternoon. The noncash payment system collapsed, and public commerce largely reverted to barter and cash using German marks or US dollars.

Assessment

The basic strategy followed in Kosovo—establishing a new organization (the BPK) rather than restructuring the existing ones (the NBK and SDKK)—was sound, but its requirements were underestimated in several respects. The existing staff of the NBK and SDKK initially did not accept the idea of applying for positions in the new organization, which would occupy what they considered their worker-owned property. The existing SDKK accounting software had to be used initially, with adaptations to add the DM, and the installation of a new package was plagued with problems. The existing software was owned by the NBY, whose permission was required for upgrades and proper maintenance. The boundaries of the law were stretched in several areas. The NBY hardware was plagued by component failure; in October 1999, only one of four processors in the system mainframe was still in operation. Spare parts were not readily available. The system was operating in a language and a character set not very transparent for external consultants.

Political considerations tempered economic judgments. The initial size of BPK staff was set higher than justified by its needs in order to soften the employment impact on existing NBK/SDKK staff. The "governor" of the NBK, who had been "appointed" by the previous shadow government, was made chairman of the board, in order to gain his agreement not to be appointed managing director (a position that went to foreigners for some years). Foreign advisers recommended that the multiple-teller window organization of services used by the SDKK should be replaced by a single-stop universal teller window. Because of inadequate training and local staff resistance, this change proved much more difficult than expected.

The failure of the BPK to provide reliable and timely account information on MOF balances created tensions between the BPK and MOF. To some extent, management and adequate operational control were hampered not only by a lack of continuity in the senior management of the BPK but also by differing opinions among advisers (notably between the BPK's managing director, who was an IMF consultant, and its deputy managing director, who was a BearingPoint/USAID consultant). As but one example, the World Bank and USAID prepared a draft banking law for a separate banking supervision institution, whereas the IMF prepared draft banking and payment laws that envisaged a single institution performing both sets of functions.

On the other hand, the development of the BPK's banking supervision functions, under the supervision of a USAID contractor (BearingPoint), was an unqualified success. Banks were licensed, regulations adopted, and supervisors trained on schedule. It took about two years longer than planned for the BPK to close branches, reduce staff to about 100, and operate with an acceptable degree of efficiency. Once the task was undertaken in 2002, however, it was accomplished effectively, reflecting careful planning and communication with staff at every step of the way. Severance packages and serious help with relocation to new jobs were given to those who lost their jobs.

Afghanistan

Background

In Afghanistan, civil strife has raged on and off for decades, largely among the country's different ethnic groups and regional leaders, backed by various foreign actors, notably the former Soviet Union and the United States. In 1995 the Taliban began a campaign against one warlord after the other, until by 1997 they controlled what was left of Kabul and 95 percent of the countryside. During the quarter century of conflict, it is estimated that 4 million to 7 million Afghans fled the country, mostly to neighboring Pakistan and Iran.

Even before the 1979 Soviet invasion, Afghanistan's private banks had been nationalized in the 1974–1976 period. Under Soviet control in the 1980s, the banking system was further transformed into the Soviet model of specialized monobanks. Da Afghanistan Bank (DAB), the central bank that had been established in 1939, also performed many commercial banking functions through its large branch network. Banking was practically dormant during the Taliban rule. Interest on existing loans was canceled, and interest was not allowed on new loans. Deposit mobilization dropped to very low levels, banks halted lending, and their loan portfolios deteriorated as large numbers of borrowers defaulted. Payment services were increasingly provided by money changers and the unregulated *hawala* system rather than by banks.

When US military forces toppled the Taliban regime in November 2001, following the September 11 terrorist attacks on the United States, Afghanistan's financial system consisted of DAB, three state-owned special purpose development banks, and three state-owned commercial banks.[20] There were about 400 registered money changers operating in Kabul, and a larger but unknown number operating in the rest of the country.

The economy was heavily dollarized. The US dollar, Pakistani rupee, Iranian rial, and the currencies of other neighboring countries were used widely. The central bank was not even in control of "its own" currency. In addition to older issues still in circulation but no longer printed,[21] the Rabbani afghani, issued since 1992, was the official currency issued by DAB. The Rabbani afghanis had no human faces on them, and thus had been acceptable to the Taliban regime, which continued to issue them from existing stocks. The internationally recognized government in exile in the northern areas of Afghanistan, which also claimed to control and operate DAB but from northern offices, had ordered additional printings of the Rabbani notes from the Russian printer Mezhdunarodnaya Kniga. When this came to light, the Taliban regime outlawed those notes, which had higher serial numbers than the earlier issues held by DAB in Kabul. The northern government then ordered additional printings using duplicates of older existing serial numbers and circulated these in the north. It is suspected that more than one duplicate printing was made, and there are many rumors about where many of these notes wound up. The Afghani note situation was further complicated by high-quality counterfeits printed abroad and issued by two warlords in the north to pay their troops. General Dostum issued notes printed from plates prepared by Thomas de la Rue at the instruction of a previous government official, who had the authority to place the order at the time.

Currency and Payment Issues

The Interim Authority installed by the UN on December 22, 2001, faced the critical problems of meeting its financial obligations (payments for salaries and pensions and to suppliers), providing a currency with which to do so, and establishing the means for preserving its value. The remaining stock of "official" Rabbani afghanis in the vaults of the central bank in Kabul was very low. In addition, "President" Rabbani of the Northern Alliance received shipments of notes his government had ordered, some of which were issued. General Dostum's notes were used in the Uzbek regions he controlled, where they traded at or above par (relative to "official" notes), but traded in Kabul with an approximately 50 percent discount.

In these circumstances, the Interim Authority needed to decide on an existing currency for immediate government wage and pension payments and to determine what its currency and monetary policy regime would be in the medium term. These choices had important consequences for establishing the credibility of the new government. The IMF outlined three options: (1) immediate full dollarization, (2) partial dollarization by the government and continued use of the official afghani by the public, and (3) issuing a new currency as quickly as possible.

The Afghan authorities chose to issue a new currency quickly. They saw this as an important contribution to the credibility of the new government and thus to statebuilding. The period until a new currency could be designed, printed, delivered, and issued would pose some very difficult choices, however. This period was kept to nine months, thanks to a clear focus on this objective by President Hamid Karzai and Finance Minister Ashraf Ghani, good advice, hard work, and some good luck. During this nine-month period, the government sold aid-provided dollars to the market in order to acquire existing afghanis (hopefully legitimate ones) to use for government expenditures until the new currency was available.

Taking advantage of an existing contract and preliminary work on the design of new currency notes undertaken between the Taliban regime and Gieseck and Devrient, a reputable German note printer, new notes were designed and printed in an extraordinarily short time. For a period there was discussion of issuing some of the new ("German") notes before the official conversion period started. But the authorities were concerned that without an adequate public information campaign, which was not feasible in such a short period of time, public confusion could undermine the reputation of the new currency.

The greater challenge was developing and implementing sound plans for the safekeeping and distribution of 500 tons of new notes and for the safekeeping and destruction of even larger amounts of redeemed old notes. This required decisions on rules and locations for note exchange, the education of the public with respect to them, and the training of 2,500 DAB staff to carry out the plans.

The logistical challenges of putting together and managing such a large one-off undertaking should not be underestimated. The political challenges of obtaining support from regional commanders and warlords and public cooperation were great as well. The very tight timetable did not allow for fully adequate preparation, but with only a modest delay the new currency was introduced on October 7, 2002.

The decision to utilize the services of money changers, known as *hawala* dealers, was critical. The *hawala* dealers had an established network for dealing in cash throughout Afghanistan (and the Middle East) that the barely functioning banks did not. The public requires payment services for both good and bad purposes. Like the US dollar itself, *hawala* dealers were presumed to facilitate the laundering of opium money and the financing of terrorism as well as remittances of money earned by Afghans abroad to family members at home and other normal payments. Initially, the US government opposed the use of *hawala* dealers, who by the nature of their operations could not be closely monitored or controlled. This opposition was overcome in light of the lack of viable alternatives. The *hawala* dealers were formally brought into the exchange process, and they were essential to its success.

Approximately 19 trillion old afghanis were exchanged for new ones, compared with an estimated 13 trillion outstanding at the start of the exchange program. The difference is attributed to the exchange of counterfeit notes and to some amount of double exchanges (exchanging old notes more than once). It is also possible that the number of duplicate serial-numbered afghanis was somewhat underreported from the outset. The lack of adequate preparations resulted in a relatively high loss rate from corruption of one sort or another, but the achievement of a quick and successful exchange swiftly improved DAB's control over its currency, provided the government with a reliable currency for its budgetary operations, and provided an important symbol of the existence and capacity of the new government.[22]

Monetary Policy

The decision to issue its own currency meant that Afghanistan also would need to adopt a policy regime to ensure the stability of the value of its currency. Traditionally the afghani had traded freely at market-determined exchange rates, and the government, with IMF support, wished to continue this policy. Thus the policy regime would need to aim to control the growth in the supply of afghani to match the growth in its demand at stable prices. This required data, analysis, and policy instruments to enable DAB to determine and achieve an appropriate growth rate for money. These capacities take some years to develop.

In the interim, the government adopted a policy of no-deficit financing in order to remove the usual source of money creation and inflation. As emphasized in Chapter 6 on Afghanistan, this was an essential step and a break from the past. The central bank law adopted on September 18, 2003, restricted DAB from lending to the government. This is now a common feature of independent central bank laws. For all practical purposes, there was no banking sector to which DAB could lend, either. The source of monetary growth came from the sales of donor-provided foreign exchange to DAB for afghanis. DAB in turn auctioned dollars in the market as a means to withdraw excess liquidity and to stabilize (but not fix) the exchange rate. As part of a Staff Monitored Program with the IMF, DAB targeted the growth of currency in circulation, using its foreign currency auctions as the primary instrument of control.

These weekly auctions of dollars to the market were initially conducted only with money changers. In 2005 they were broadened to allow banks to participate, and in the future it is expected that money changers will need to participate through banks. The government quickly agreed to make DAB independent, but it was very slow in adopting the new central bank law. USAID financed a large-scale project with BearingPoint to modernize the structure, systems, and staffing of the central bank. One aspect that was very effective, but not without its problems, was recruiting young, well-educated Afghans as BearingPoint employees in the central bank on whom training efforts were focused (they were often resented by regular DAB employees). In mid-2005 most of these BearingPoint local employees became regular DAB employees, although some were hired away by private banks.

Banking and Payment Systems

As with most postconflict economies, banking-sector rehabilitation and reform was a second-order priority. Technical assistance in drafting a new banking law, which provided for the establishment of branches of foreign banks and for foreign ownership of Afghan banks, was provided in mid-2002 and the new law was adopted in early 2003. Under the new law, all existing banks were required to seek new licenses.

Three of the state banks were relicensed (Bank Millie Afghan, Pashtany Tejaraty Bank, and Export Promotion Bank), and six banks (Afghanistan International Bank, First Micro Finance Bank, Kabul Bank, Arian Bank, Azizi Bank, and Brac Afghanistan Bank) and five branches of foreign banks (Standard Chartered Bank, National Bank of Pakistan, Habib Bank, Punjab National Bank of India, and Bank Alfalah) were licensed.

By the end of 2006, nothing had really been done to wind up the three state banks that had not been relicensed, nor to restructure the three that had been. There was little political appetite to address their work before the parliamentary elections in September 2005. As these banks had been largely dormant for a long time, neglect for a period was not unreasonable (as long as they were not making new loans). In this environment, the new foreign banks and branches were growing rapidly, and the money changers and *hawala* continued to provide the backbone of the payment system. Though DAB was gradually shedding its commercial bank functions, it would not be feasible to end all of them (notably payment services for the government) until the state banks have been fully resolved.

Conclusion

A new government must have a currency and the ability to make payments. The solutions to these immediate needs must be considered in light of the requirements of the long-run development of the monetary and banking system. The most important short-term decisions with long-run implications are the choice of a currency and monetary policy regime; the extent to which existing institutions, facilities, and laws will be used, at least initially; and the degree of modernization of state banks. Four major lessons can be drawn from the foregoing review of experiences in Bosnia and Herzegovina, Kosovo, and Afghanistan.

1. There Are No Blank Slates

Every society has a legacy of existing institutions, customs, and attitudes. These are ignored at the new government's (and its advisers') peril. For example, the Central Bank of Bosnia and Herzegovina was legally a new institution, but it took over the buildings, systems, and some of the staff of predecessor central banks. The Banking and Payment Authority of Kosovo was a radically new institution, but it too took over the buildings, systems, and some of the staff of the National Bank of Kosovo and of the Kosovo branch of the Yugoslav payment bureau. Afghanistan's new monetary and payment systems built not only on preexisting state institutions but also on the informal *hawala* system.

New systems and ways of operating are not constructed on a blank slate. Dealing with existing staff can pose many serious challenges. In some instances a new institution may be easier to develop than reforming an existing one. In all cases, the management of the new (or old) institution will be working with the available human capital and experience; developing new knowledge takes time, and institutional change is always highly political. Outsiders often underestimate the time and resources required to understand and address political sensitivities and conflicts.

2. Planning and Donor Coordination Are Required

Donor resources available for postconflict reconstruction are limited and need to be used effectively. In most cases, financial policy leadership is provided by the international financial institutions in accordance with well-established competencies. Broad agreement on the assignment of leadership responsibilities has generally made it possible to settle rather quickly and easily the turf battles that inevitably exist at the beginning of each postconflict reconstruction effort. Mechanisms for coordination, such as Donor Consultative Groups, are very important, because policy advice and reform strategies are less likely to be implemented if the donor community does not speak with one voice. In spite of extensive experience with such mechanisms over the past fifteen years, they remain ad hoc, and they need to be built anew with each new post-conflict case.

A successful example of donor coordination, somewhat outside of the ordinary, is the reform of the payment system in Bosnia and Herzegovina. Two and a half years after the Dayton Peace Agreement, donors started to apply considerable pressure on the entity governments to dismantle the payment bureau successors of the Yugoslav SDK. Though technically efficient, the payment bureaus of the three regions had been powerful instruments of state and political control of the economy and were thought to be slowing the economic reform and integration necessary for the development of new political arrangements. The payment bureaus also undercut the development of private banks, which in other countries provide payment services more efficiently.

Many donors were eager to contribute to this effort, but sharp differences of view emerged over how to proceed. The main difference, more among individuals than donor organizations, was with regard to the relative extent of donor versus local control of the process. Some pushed for a donor steering group to control the process to ensure that the reform was expeditious. Others advocated national authority over implementation supported by a donor advisory group, arguing that a smooth transition was not likely without local ownership. The IMF took the lead in preparing a draft strategy document that proposed the elements of the future payment system, the means for developing them, and the requirements of dismantling the existing payment bureaus. The document was revised following discussions among donors (World Bank, EU, USAID, US Treasury, and others), and it was then discussed in a series of meetings of the Bosnia and Herzegovina Payment System Council, which had representatives from all three ethnic regions. The document became the blueprint for reform, with control resting with the local authorities (the Central Bank, three regional payment bureaus, and respective entity finance ministries), and the donors establishing an International Advisory Group on Payment Bureau and Payment System Reform.

3. Policies Must Reflect Capabilities

Some policies are more demanding than others. What is possible will depend on what is already in place and what new resources can be drawn on. The design and introduction of a new currency is a one-time undertaking for which relevant local experience is not likely to be found, making foreign assistance necessary.

Dollarization can be implemented quickly and easily, but with its own limitations and political drawbacks. Bosnia and Herzegovina relied extensively on existing institutions for several years, and the currency board arrangements minimized the demands on the new central bank while it focused on its institutional development and reintegrated the monetary and payment systems. This was as much a political as a technical challenge, and time was needed for the gradual reestablishment of interregional trust.

The monetary regime adopted in Afghanistan is much more demanding, with little usable existing infrastructure to draw on. Serious errors in monetary policy have been avoided by the new law against the central bank's lending to government and by the current adequacy of donor-provided international reserves with which to stabilize the exchange rate.

4. Local Support and Leadership for Reforms Are Needed

Reforms in the financial sector are difficult to implement without local understanding and support. Even with the presence of NATO troops, the local political leadership in Bosnia and Herzegovina did not accept a new countrywide currency for over two years after the signing of the Dayton Peace Agreement in December 1995. The three joint presidents did not agree on a new central bank law creating the Central Bank of Bosnia and Herzegovina until May 1997, and the new banknotes were not issued until June 22, 1998. The slow pace of these changes allowed for the development of sufficient local support. Though more heavy-handed compared with Bosnia and Herzegovina, the process by which the central bank and banking laws were adopted in Kosovo by UNMIK also included consultations with and among Kosovars. The difficulties in implementing the universal teller window systems and new accounting systems in the province suggest, however, that these consultations failed to create sufficient local support for the reforms.

The goal of government and enterprise efficiency often conflicts with short-term needs to maintain household income and security. The former is important for economic development and thus the financial viability of state administration, but the latter is important for maintaining public support of the state. For this reason, in spite of inefficiencies associated with padded staffs and poor work ethics, steps to shed redundant workers and make institutions more efficient were often implemented slowly. Such "suboptimal" decisions derive from the tension between short-term and long-term considerations in environments where peace (as well as price stability) is at stake.

Notes

This chapter draws on my experiences in Bosnia and Herzegovina, Kosovo, and Afghanistan. I gratefully acknowledge the help with background information from Andrew Hook, Len Fernelius, Peter Nicholl, Kim Rhee, Marko Skreb, and Jan Waaler.

1. Payment systems are the means by which the ownership of monetary value ("money") is transferred from one person to another. These include the clearing and settlement of checks, payment orders, money orders, credit or debt transactions such as with VISA or American Express cards, automated teller machine transactions, direct deposits of payrolls and pensions, and so on.

2. The term *dollarization* is commonly used to refer to adoption of any foreign currency, be it the US dollar, euro, or others.

3. These and other aspects of note design are reviewed in more detail in Abrams (1995).

4. For a more detailed discussion, see Abrams and Cortés-Douglas (1993).

5. Developed market economies have tended to define price stability as an inflation rate in the 1 to 2 percent range. Developing or emerging market economies more often define price stability as an inflation rate in the range of 2 to 4 or 5 percent, because the large structural and relative price changes in such economies can more easily be absorbed at the somewhat higher inflation rate.

6. Donor funds can finance imported goods and services without limit. There are limits, however, on the amount of external funds an economy can absorb to finance domestic expenditures without inflationary consequences. Beyond some modest point, increased government domestic expenditure needs to come from the diversion of domestic resources from other uses. Generally, taxation is preferable to inflation for such purposes.

7. Central banks control the money supply and monetary conditions primarily by controlling the amount of their liabilities held by the public, including banks. When a central bank buys (or sells) foreign exchange in the market, usually to influence the exchange rate, it increases (or reduces) domestic liquidity, that is, the public's holdings of domestic currency and deposits with the central bank. If these liquidity effects are not desired by the central bank, it can undertake offsetting "sterilization" transactions in domestic assets by issuing (or repurchasing) bonds.

8. Targeting inflation directly (rather than indirectly via the exchange rate or money growth rate) requires adequately developed financial markets through which the central bank's policies are transmitted to economic activity and inflation, reliable data on key economic and financial magnitudes, and the capacity of the central bank's staff and management to model the relationship between its policy instruments and inflation.

9. Služba Društvenog Knjigovodstva, or SDK, translates loosely as the Social Accounting Service. The SDK was actually much more than a payment system, encompassing statistical and financial police functions as well for the Ministry of Finance (MOF).

10. Foreign payments for debt service are often suspended for a period following the end of conflict. Payments for new imports are often made by donors for a period. Nonetheless, the technical capacity to make payments abroad and to manage foreign currency assets abroad (authorized operators of the Society for Worldwide Interbank

Financial Telecommunications [SWIFT], the standard international payment messaging system) needs to be addressed fairly early.

11. At the end of the six-year period, the state government (joint presidency) approved the continuation of the currency board rules and extended the term of the foreign governor (Peter Nicholl from New Zealand) one extra year. His term expired December 31, 2004, and a Bosniac, Kemal Kozarić, became governor.

12. The Office of the High Representative (OHR) is an ad hoc international institution created under the Dayton Peace Agreement that was signed in Paris on December 14, 1995. The OHR is responsible for overseeing the implementation of civilian aspects of the Dayton accord.

13. The amount was limited by the government's holdings (and receipts) of KM (or of DM with which to purchase KM).

14. Until that moment, a payment from an RS enterprise or bank to an FRY enterprise or bank could be made by debiting the payer's account with the SPP and crediting the payee's account with the SDK. The reserve accounts of the payer's and payee's banks with the NBY were debited and credited respectively.

15. The new state bank advertised that depositors might as well open their deposit accounts with the SSB because they would have to go there to make a payment anyway.

16. The Sherbimi I Kontabilitetit Shoqeror I Kosoves, or literally the Public Accounting Service of Kosovo.

17. The number of staff reporting for work at the Pristina office at that time was estimated at about fifty-five to sixty (about 10 percent of previous levels). Although the operating hours of the office remained the same, staff were idle throughout most of the day. This was also true in all of the other offices of the SDKK.

18. Local examinations conducted after the new system was put in place encountered literal "shoe box" cash deposits that were not on record. These were presented as "safe-keeping" storage but were clearly unauthorized by the official management.

19. This IMF employee, Scott Brown, was later seriously injured in the bombing of the UN headquarters in Baghdad.

20. Two institutions that were licensed by the Taliban regime to perform banking service based on Islamic principles never started operations.

21. These were the so-called shah afghani versions I and II, issued before 1974; the Daud afghani, issued from 1974 through 1978; and the Najibullah afghani, dating from the 1980s through 1991.

22. For further discussion of the currency issue, see Chapter 6 by Ashraf Ghani, Clare Lockhart, Nargis Nehan, and Baqer Massoud.

9

Postwar Debts: Time for a New Approach

Patricia Alvarez-Plata and Tilman Brück

Debt has been a core element in the development strategies of almost all low-income countries, including war-affected developing countries.[1] External borrowing can be used to finance public spending aimed at increasing growth and development. Loans can also be used, however, for private gains or to finance warfare. Postwar countries often have large debt arrears, even as they are in need of additional external resources for humanitarian relief, economic recovery, and long-term reconstruction. Despite the common recognition that postwar economies have above-average financing requirements, creditors have been slow to grant exceptional debt relief, either on the basis of future financial requirements or on the basis of the "odious" nature of debts incurred in the past.

This chapter addresses two related issues. First, we analyze the nature and the circumstances of postconflict debt management, including the causes and scale of debt accumulation, the issue of odious debt, and the endogenous nature of debt and war. Second, we examine choices in postconflict debt management, including the institutional relations between donors and borrowers, debt management capacity, debt sustainability indicators, conditionality, and the additionality of debt relief.

Postconflict environments pose special challenges, yet our analysis suggests many similarities between developing countries with or without a history of violent conflict. War sharpens the twin challenges of debt and development, raising the stakes and requiring more focused policy responses. Put simply, we argue that what is good debt policy for war-affected countries may also be good debt policy for other developing countries, but that the reverse is not always true.

The chapter reviews types and modalities of debt relief, considers the arguments for according special treatment to postconflict economies, and discusses the experiences of Mozambique, Uganda, and Democratic Republic of Congo (DRC). We conclude with some policy recommendations.

Debt Relief Strategies

The term *debt relief* refers to steps that reduce the debt stocks or debt service (that is, principal amortization and interest payments) paid by an indebted country to its creditors. Debt relief takes two main forms: rescheduling and forgiveness.

Debt rescheduling involves an agreement on new repayment terms that shifts debt service into the future, lowering payments in the short run. Debt can be rescheduled both by private creditors and by official bilateral creditors; as a rule, multilateral creditors do not reschedule debt. Debt rescheduling does not decrease the value of the debt stock, and it might even increase the future flows of interest paid.

Debt forgiveness, as the name implies, involves a write-off of some or all of the debt. It is simply erased from the books, with the creditors taking the loss on their balance sheets. Debt can be forgiven by private creditors, bilateral official donors, and multilateral donors. The line between debt forgiveness and debt rescheduling is sometimes fuzzy, since rescheduling agreements may reduce total interest payments over the lifetime of the loan below those set forth in the original loan agreement.

Creditors may act individually, or they may coordinate their actions. The main institutional arrangements for coordinated debt relief in the cases of commercial banks, bilateral creditors, and multilateral creditors are the London Club, the Paris Club, and the Heavily Indebted Poor Countries (HIPC) initiative, respectively. In these forums, the creditors and the debtor government reach agreements on the type and amount of debt relief and its distribution among creditors. In cases where countries have suspended debt-service payments to multilateral creditors, and accumulated arrears therefore prevent new lending by these institutions, special arrangements for clearing these arrears also may be devised.

The London Club

The London Club has provided an ad hoc forum for the negotiation of private commercial bank debt between individual sovereign debtors and their creditors since the 1970s (International Monetary Fund 2000b). The aims of the club are to ensure the equal treatment of private bank lenders by the borrower and to allow the borrower to regain credit worthiness in international financial markets. Usually this process is initiated by the debtor, often in parallel with the Paris Club negotiations. Over time, London Club bankers increasingly have accepted terms that include partial forgiveness in exchange for improved performance in repayment of the remaining debt.

Independent of London Club negotiations, private creditors can sell debt at discounted values on the secondary market. Various "buyback" schemes financed by bilateral or multilateral donors sometimes have enabled debtor countries to retire commercial debt at a fraction of its face value, as in the cases of Mozambique and Uganda, discussed below.

The Paris Club

The Paris Club, the most important institution for restructuring sovereign debts of low-income countries to Organization for Economic Cooperation and Development (OECD) creditor governments, has functioned since the mid-1950s. In exceptional circumstances (as, for example, in the case of Uganda), the Paris Club also provides grants to help countries service their multilateral debts. Individual members of the Paris Club sometimes forgive debt unilaterally, as well.[2]

The Paris Club is effectively a cartel of the most important bilateral lenders, allowing them to formulate common positions toward a given debtor country. Conditionality is implemented by insisting on the existence of an International Monetary Fund (IMF) agreement, in the absence of which the Paris Club does not provide debt relief. Smaller lenders benefit from the common sanctions mechanisms that the Paris Club imposes on borrowers. The existence of the Paris Club also offers some advantages to borrowers, providing a one-stop shop for debt restructurings and predictable terms over time. The Paris Club reschedulings are asymmetric, however, in that there is no club of borrowers that could pool the costs of negotiations and improve the terms that developing countries manage to reach.

The recent emergence of alternative lenders, such as China and Libya, complicates bilateral debt negotiations.[3] On the one hand, borrowers who fall out of favor with the Paris Club have alternative financing sources, which Sudan, for example, has tapped. On the other hand, these nontraditional lenders have to find new forms of sanctions (such as withholding future loans or investments) to enforce debt repayment, as they cannot rely on traditional, collective methods.

The frequency of Paris Club meetings is driven by indebted countries' need and perceived institutional capacity to negotiate and implement a debt agreement. These may in part be a function of the generosity and scope of past Paris Club agreements. In some cases, Paris Club negotiations can be quite frequent, with only the small part of the debt stock on which payments fall due within a specific time period being settled each time, leaving the rest for future negotiations. In theory, it would be possible to avoid repeated meetings by agreeing much earlier upon a final settlement, or "exit rescheduling." In practice, however, several considerations favor the piecemeal approach. First, the donors have become more generous over time, a trend driven in part by pressures from civil society in both North and South. Second, and related to the first point, the definition of debt sustainability has changed over time, as discussed below.

Third, donors are concerned that moving to generous terms too quickly would raise "moral hazard" problems by encouraging imprudent borrowing. Fourth, exogenous shocks (including renewed wars) may push debt indicators beyond a previously overcome threshold. Fifth, growing recognition of the special circumstances of postwar economies may make new deals possible in countries where the postwar institutional and governance framework is perceived by the donors to be significantly different from the wartime framework. Finally, the Paris Club expertise of indebted countries may be built up over time, allowing repeated participants to achieve better deals.

From the late 1980s onward, the Paris Club creditors have granted debt relief on increasingly generous terms for debts contracted before 1981 (see Table 9.1). The Toronto terms introduced by the Paris Club in 1988 provide for debt cancellation (that is, forgiveness) of up to one-third of the debt stock. Current options include the Naples terms, with cancellations of up to 67 percent, and most recently the Cologne terms, with cancellations of up to 90 percent for countries that reach the completion point defined by the HIPC initiative.

The HIPC Initiative

The HIPC initiative was launched in 1996 by the multilateral creditors to provide debt relief to the most indebted and poorest developing countries (Addison, Hansen, and Tarp 2004). HIPC assistance is designed to bring the net present value of external public debt down to a critical threshold, specified initially as a debt-to-export ratio of between 200 and 250 percent.

Debt relief under HIPC is a variant of debt forgiveness: debts to the World Bank and other multilateral creditors are repaid by the HIPC Trust Fund, which is financed by the creditor governments, and debts to the IMF are repaid by grants from the IMF's special Poverty Reduction and Growth Facility, again financed in large part by the creditor governments. Strictly speaking,

Table 9.1   Paris Club Terms

Terms	Year of Agreement	Debt Cancellation?	Still in Current Use?
Classic terms		No, but longer repayment period	Yes, standard treatment
Toronto terms	1988	Up to 33.3%	No
Houston terms	1990	No, but longer repayment period	Yes, for highly indebted lower-middle-income countries
London terms	1991	Up to 50%	No
Naples terms	1994	Up to 67%	Yes, for highly indebted poor countries
Lyon terms	1996	Up to 80%	No
Cologne terms	1999	Up to 90%	Yes, for countries eligible for the HIPC initiative

therefore, these debts are not written off by the multilateral institutions; instead they are paid off by the governments that back the initiative. This relief is conditional on the preparation of a Poverty Reduction Strategy Paper (PRSP) and steps taken by the indebted country to improve its macroeconomic policies, financial accounting, and public services. The "decision point" for participation in the HIPC initiative comes when the country achieves a track record of macroeconomic stability and agrees to adopt a reform program, at which point a small package of interim debt relief is given. Upon implementing these reforms, the country attains the "completion point" and receives the full HIPC debt relief package.

The initiative was revised in 1999 as a result of ongoing controversies over its modes of operation and its effectiveness.[4] The "enhanced" HIPC initiative allows for broader and deeper debt relief (covering more countries and cutting more debt) and strengthens the link between debt relief and poverty alleviation by specifying that freed resources should be budgeted on the basis of poverty reduction strategy papers. Broader debt relief was made possible by defining a greater safety margin for debt sustainability, thereby increasing the number of countries potentially eligible for the HIPC initiative assistance. Deeper debt relief was provided by lowering the threshold for the ratio of the net present value of debt to exports from 200–250 percent to 150 percent.[5] In addition, faster debt relief was made possible by granting interim relief between the "decision point" and the "completion point" and by introducing *floating* completion points based on specific outcomes on policy reform and the maintenance of macroeconomic stability, rather than the length of the track record.

The enhanced HIPC initiative did not account for the special circumstances of war-affected countries. In conflict-affected HIPCs, the export sector is typically less productive. The state's ability to mobilize domestic revenue is typically lower. And debt-service burdens that are high, relative to total spending, reduce the fiscal peace dividend and hence the prospects for both economic recovery and political stability. For countries emerging from violent conflict, the HIPC initiative's requirement for a stable, three-year track record of good policy is problematic, and there may be a case for reducing the time lag between the decision and completion points and for front-loading debt relief to provide the government with additional resources for immediate postwar needs (Addison and Murshed 2003). More generally, the assessment of track records in postconflict countries should extend beyond macroeconomic stability and also pay attention to consolidating peace, security, and poverty reduction (International Monetary Fund and World Bank 2001).

Arrears to Multilateral Donors

Countries cannot obtain new concessional development financing from multilateral creditors—the World Bank, IMF, and regional development banks—as long as they are in arrears in servicing past debts to these institutions.[6] Bilateral donors generally respect the primacy of multilateral donors in this respect, treating arrears to multilateral creditors as a signal that contracts with bilateral creditors will not be honored either.

Normalizing relations with multilateral donors involves five steps. First, the indebted country must establish the political will to normalize relations and some minimal managerial capacity for debt management. Second, assisted by the international community, the government must undertake a stocktaking exercise (called "debt reconciliation") to ascertain the level, the terms, and the lenders of the outstanding stock of foreign debt. Postwar countries may face problems in completing this step if records were lost during the war, as happened in Liberia. Third, the country must formally reestablish its relations with the IMF and other international donors and start to build some trust, possibly by initiating nominal but regular payments on the arrears. Fourth, the government has to develop and start implementing national debt management policy, which should address in particular the issue of arrears. Finally, having cleared the arrears, the government can enter into debt relief negotiations with its Paris Club and other official creditors.

The clearance of arrears to international financial institutions often is accomplished by means of bridge loans from bilateral official creditors. These are very short-term loans, sometimes lasting only a few days, given by bilateral lenders specifically to allow the government to clear arrears to multilateral institutions. Multilateral assistance resumes upon receipt of the bridge loan, and loans (or grants) from the multilaterals can then be used to repay the bridge loan. If the bridge loan is repaid with a new multilateral loan, the indebted country has, in effect, rolled over its multilateral debt. If it is repaid with a grant from the World Bank's International Development Association (IDA), this is equivalent to cancellation of that portion of the country's outstanding arrears.[7]

There are two key conditions for such an operation to take place. First, arrears clearance must be done at a global level by all multilateral creditors, since they all have preferred creditor status. Second, the government must present a credible policy framework and macroeconomic program, supported by the international community. The rationale for such conditionality is to ensure that the country will not fall back into arrears again.

Additionality

Debt relief is "additional" if it does not lead to lower levels of other aid to the debtor. It is difficult to assess additionality, since this requires knowledge of what would have happened to aid volumes in the absence of debt relief. Data on debt relief and aid flows for Uganda, Mozambique, and Democratic Republic of Congo for the years 1989 to 2003, to be presented later in the chapter, indicate that in these cases debt relief tended to be positively correlated with aid; at least in this sense, debt relief appears to have been additional.[8]

Should Postconflict Economies Receive More Debt Relief?

Surprisingly few studies have focused on the external debt of postwar economies. Given the special problems faced by war-torn countries, it is useful to consider whether a case can be made for debt management strategies specifically oriented to these economies. The arguments for more debt relief for postwar economies include their exceptional burdens and needs, the obstacle that debt overhang puts on renewed investment, and the odious nature of the debts.[9]

Exceptional Burdens and Needs

Postwar countries typically have lower output and lower exports than otherwise similar countries. This has two effects. On the one hand, there is less domestic scope for financing development. On the other hand, debt sustainability indicators will be worse for any given debt levels. Many postwar countries also inherit higher absolute levels of debt, as conflicts are at least partly funded by loans; if so, this further worsens the debt sustainability indicators. Postconflict countries also have weaker capacities for negotiating external financial support and coordinating aid than do other developing countries. Comprehensive debt restructuring would remove the burden of constantly renegotiating debt service in future years.

Furthermore, postwar countries have high financing needs for the (re) construction of public goods, public infrastructure, and current expenditure. These include both the direct costs of making peace, such as demobilization programs, and the costs of reestablishing working institutions. These countries hence have higher financing needs than other developing countries with similar levels of output that are not carrying the burdens of previous war. Debt forgiveness could increase the chance of peace by freeing resources for these needs.

Although debt relief may reduce political grievances through broad-based public spending or free resources to buy off belligerent parties, the fiscal system may be too degraded to achieve the promised transfers (Addison and Murshed 2003). The timing of debt relief is critical to maximizing its impact. In some cases, debt relief a few years after the conflict has ended might be more efficient than debt relief immediately after the conflict.

Table 9.2 compares debt indicators for the year 2002 for low-income countries at war, postwar low-income countries, and for low-income countries that had not experienced war in the preceding twelve years. The data refer to thirty-

Table 9.2   Summary Debt Indicators, 2002

	Number of Cases	Debt/GNI[a] (%)	Debt/Export (%)	Aid/GNI (%)
LICs[b] (all)	38	127.3	432.7	15.4
LICs (no conflict)	18	116.0	328.0	13.2
LICs (in war)	3	116.4	1,292.1	11.2
LICs (postwar)	17	161.1	436.0	21.6

Sources: World Bank (2004d); World Development Finance; World Bank; and authors' calculations.

Notes: a. GNI = gross national income. b. LIC = low-income country. Only severely and moderately indebted low-income countries for which data were available are taken into account.

eight moderately and severely indebted low-income countries (LICs) for which data are available from the World Bank. Both wartime and postwar LICs have higher debt-to-export ratios than peacetime economies. In relation to their gross national income, postwar countries receive the highest amount of aid on average, whereas countries currently affected by war receive the least.

Debt Overhang Effects

A country suffers from "debt overhang" if its expected debt service costs discourage domestic and foreign investment (Sachs 1989). Debt relief can promote growth not only by making additional resources available for public investment but also by reducing the debt overhang effect. On the other hand, the main obstacle to investment and growth in postwar countries might derive from a lack of basic economic institutions. If so, the resources devoted to the HIPC initiative might be more effectively employed as direct foreign aid (Arslanalp and Henry 2004).

Kanbur (2000) posits that in the African context, high stocks of debt act as a drag on private investment. Furthermore, the pressures of continual debt rescheduling and negotiations to maintain sufficient gross inflows to fund debt service absorb the scarce time, energy, and political capital of key policymakers and technocrats. For these reasons he recommends that peacebuilding governments should receive faster debt relief, ensuring that peace is not delayed by the difficulties that postwar governments face in meeting donor policy conditionality.

Odious Debt

Odious debt can be defined as debt incurred by a dictator, not in the interest of the country but instead to strengthen the despotic regime. This debt can be considered a personal debt of the regime, as opposed to an obligation of the nation.

Legal and moral scholars have advanced numerous approaches to formulate a doctrine of odious debt (Hanlon 2006). Our study proposes three criteria for debt to be considered odious. First, the regime must use the loan contrary to the interest of the population. Second, there must be some degree of awareness, or potential for awareness, by the creditor of the possible or actual (mis)use of funds by the regime. Third, the debt must pass a certain threshold of harm to the country's future economic development.

There are both *ex ante* and *ex post* aspects to the problem of odious debts. *Ex ante*, there appears to be a lack of mechanisms in the international financial markets and donor practices to prevent the buildup of odious debt. In other words, there are insufficient incentives to deter creditors from lending to odious regimes. *Ex post,* there are insufficient mechanisms to achieve significant reductions of existing odious debt levels. In a study of DRC, Ndikumana and Boyce (1998) made a case for *ex post* debt relief based on the doctrine of odious debt. They reviewed evidence that the official and private creditors of the regime of Mobutu Sese Seko knew, or should have known, that there was a high risk that their loans would not benefit the Congolese people. Ndikumana and Boyce presented evidence that a sizable portion of loans fueled capital flight, and they concluded that between 1968 and 1990 the country was in fact a net creditor to the rest of the world, exporting more capital than it imported. Perhaps the relatively generous stance of the international donor community in forgiving the DRC debt has been based implicitly on the belief that much of this debt was odious.

There are some historical precedents of debt relief based explicitly on the doctrine of odious debt. After the Spanish-American War of 1898, for example, the United States proclaimed that neither Cuba nor the United States would be responsible for repaying the debt incurred by the previous Cuban government under Spanish colonial rule, as it did not benefit the people of Cuba but instead only strengthened the oppressive regime. After the Russian revolution in 1919, the Soviet government repudiated czarist debts on the same grounds. Similarly, in the Treaty of Versailles that same year, Polish debts to Prussia were also repudiated under the odious debt doctrine (Khalfan, King, and Thomas 2003). There is no international institution, however, with the authority to assess or declare the "odiousness" of sovereign debt.

To prevent odious debt from being contracted in the future, granting an institution (such as the UN Security Council) the authority to rate *ex ante* a sovereign state "odious" should be considered (Jayachandran and Kremer 2004). Any debt accumulated after this point would be subject to repudiation, decreasing creditors' incentive to lend to sanctioned regimes.

Uganda: The Slow Road to Debt Reconciliation

Uganda has suffered a series of internal and international conflicts and political coups in recent history (see Chapter 2 by Léonce Ndikumana and Justine Nannyonjo). The current president, Yoweri Museveni, led a rebel group that came to power in 1986, ending years of chaos and widespread civil war. He has cautiously moved the country to a managed form of democracy and cooperates closely with multilateral and bilateral donors. Uganda's per capita income rose from US$974 in 1989 to US$1,370 in 2002 (in constant, purchasing power-adjusted dollars; see Table 9.3). Domestically, fighting continues with rebel groups (including the Lord's Resistance Army) in the north of the country (Nannyonjo 2005). Internationally, Uganda has been actively involved in the wars in DRC and Sudan.

Origins of Debt

Uganda's external debt grew in the 1970s, but the rapid rise of the country's debt stock to unsustainable levels began in the early 1980s, propelled in part

Table 9.3   Debt Summary—Uganda (US$ million, unless otherwise indicated)

	Last Prewar 1980	First Postwar 1989	Most Recent 2002
Total debt stocks	687	2,177	4,100
Long-term debt outstanding	535	1,846	3,690
Short-term debt outstanding	63	105	153
of which interest arrears, official creditors	10	22	79
of which interest arrears, private creditors	9	33	2
Principal arrears, official creditors	30	51	200
Principal arrears, private creditors	52	83	28
Total debt flows			
Disbursements	83	312	162
Disbursement multilateral %	8.2	46.4	84.0
Disbursement bilateral %	13.3	40.4	12.8
Disbursement private %	78.4	13.1	3.3
Net transfers on debt	118	187	93
Debt indicators			
Total debt/exports of goods and services (%)	207.8	783.8	369.7
Total debt/GNI[a] (%)	4.1	41.8	71.4
Total debt service (% of GNI)	0.3	3.6	1.4
Debt composition			
Multilateral debt/total debt (%)	12	45	77
Bilateral PPG[b] debt/total PPG debt (%)	39.6	28.7	10.5
Private PPG debt/total PPG debt (%)	45.6	18.1	0.8
Aid and GNI			
Aid (% of GNI)	9	9	11
Aid per capita (current US$)	9	27	26
GNI, PPP[c] (real 2002 million $)	—	16,288	33,819
GNI per capita, PPP (real 2002 million $)	—	974	1,370

Source: World Bank (2004d).

Notes: a. GNI = gross national income. b. PPG = public and publicly guaranteed debt. c. PPP = purchasing power parity-adjusted.

by government borrowing to finance the civil war (Barungi and Atingi 2000). After an economic crisis at the end of the 1970s, an economic recovery program was implemented from 1981 to 1984, financed through heavy borrowings that marked the beginning of Uganda's debt problems. The program succeeded in reviving the economy, but it was abandoned in 1984 in the midst of the civil war, after the World Bank cut off adjustment lending.

In 1987 a second economic reform program was launched by the Museveni government. Once again the country relied heavily on external assistance, contributing to further rapid growth of the debt burden, with multilateral creditors accounting for most of the increase. Meanwhile, a decline in coffee export earnings reduced Uganda's capacity to service its external debt (Mijumbi 2001). The external debt-to-export ratio soared to more than 1,400 percent in 1990.

Postwar Debt Management

When Uganda emerged from civil war in 1986, the country had built up significant arrears on its commercial and bilateral debt repayment obligations. Commercial creditors accounted for the largest part of the arrears, followed by non–Paris Club bilateral creditors such as India, Tanzania, and Yugoslavia. Compared to many conflict-affected countries, however, the arrears were not huge.

In 1990, using resources from World Bank technical assistance projects, the government recruited a team of international financial advisers to undertake an inventory of Uganda's external debt by individually contacting every major creditor. The process of debt reconciliation with the IMF, World Bank, Paris Club creditors, and some non–Paris Club bilateral creditors—covering about 80 percent of all outstanding debt—was completed only in 1997, seven years after the effort was initiated.

Meanwhile, work commenced in 1991 on developing an external debt strategy with the following aims: first, to restore normal working relations with creditors; second, to stop the increase in outstanding debt resulting from the accumulation of penalty and late interest charges; and third, to reduce annual contractual debt to a level commensurate with Uganda's ability to pay. It was agreed that all creditors should be treated fairly, but that priority in debt service payments would be given to multilateral creditors.

Debt Relief

Commercial debt. The government restructured its commercial debt by converting some debt into equity, rescheduling a portion of the debt, and discharging the remainder in a buyback operation at a significant discount to face value. The latter operation was financed by the World Bank's Debt Reduction

Facility for IDA-only countries, established in 1989 to provide grants for the cash buyback of commercial debt, with cofinancing from the governments of Germany, the Netherlands, and Switzerland.

When it became clear that a critical mass of commercial creditors was willing to participate in the buyback, the government formally requested the World Bank to initiate the process of mobilizing resources. The government of Uganda was able to buy back its uninsured commercial debt at a very large discount—retiring debt at only 12 percent of its face value—with a participation rate in excess of 80 percent (Kapoor 1995). The operation thereby eliminated about one-third of the total external arrears of the country and more than 7 percent of the total stock of debt.

Sometimes concern is expressed that buy-back operations at a deep discount could affect a country's future access to short-term credit on reasonable terms. In the case of Uganda, this was not a major worry, if only because the magnitude of these arrears, and the government's inability to settle them, had already reduced the government's access to short-term and trade credit lines.

Bilateral debt. The first debt agreements between Uganda and the Paris Club took place during its civil war, in 1981 and again in 1982, rescheduling US$59 million under classic terms. These were followed by larger reschedulings on ad hoc terms in 1987 and on Toronto terms in 1989 (see Table 9.4). Four subsequent operations, from 1992 to 2000, rescheduled eligible debt on increasingly generous terms. The authorities have sought to settle arrears to non–Paris Club bilateral creditors on comparable terms.

Multilateral debt. By the mid-1990s, Uganda had benefited from debt relief from commercial and bilateral Paris Club creditors. This had only a modest impact on the country's overall debt position, however, as by that time 70 percent of Uganda's debt was owed to multilateral creditors.

In 1995 a number of bilateral donors set up a Multilateral Debt Fund for Uganda, into which they paid funds in order to help Uganda meet its debt repayment obligations to multilateral creditors. With funding from the governments of the Netherlands, Denmark, Sweden, Switzerland, Norway, and Austria, this operated through 1998, when it was superseded by the HIPC initiative.

Uganda was the first country to qualify for debt relief under both the first HIPC and the enhanced HIPC initiatives. In April 1997, the executive boards of the World Bank and the IMF decided in principle that Uganda could qualify for assistance under the HIPC initiative with only a one-year interval to reach the completion point, instead of the standard six-year qualifying period, and as a result Uganda first received debt relief under the HIPC initiative in 1998. It received further relief under the enhanced HIPC initiative in 2000 (see Table 9.5). In total, as a result of both initiatives, Uganda was granted debt relief amounting to almost US$2 billion in nominal terms (or roughly US$1 billion

Table 9.4 Paris Club Reschedulings: Uganda, Mozambique, and DRC

	Uganda Cut-off Date: July 1, 1989			Mozambique Cut-off Date: February 1, 1984			Democratic Republic of Congo Cut-off Date: June 30, 1983		
	Amounts Treated (in US$ million)	Amounts Treated as Percentage of Total Amount of Debt	Terms of Treatment	Amounts Treated (in US$ million)	Amounts Treated as Percentage of Total Amount of Debt	Terms of Treatment	Amounts Treated (in US$ million)	Amounts Treated as Percentage of Total Amount of Debt	Terms of Treatment
1980									
1981	40	5.69	classic				600	11.78	classic
1982	19	2.18	classic						
1983							1,490	27.93	classic
1984				142	9.87	classic			
1985							322	5.21	classic
1986							350	4.87	classic
1987	256	13.33	ad hoc	612	14.83	ad hoc	883	10.06	ad hoc
1988									
1989	90	4.13	Toronto				NA	NA	Toronto
1990				707	15.21	Toronto			
1991									
1992	38	1.30	London						
1993				440	8.44	London			
1994									
1995	110	3.07	Naples						
1996				663	8.76	Naples			
1997									
1998	147	3.75	Lyon	NA	NA	Lyon			
1999				1,860	26.66	Lyon			
2000	147	4.20	Cologne						
2001				2,800[a]	61.35	Cologne			
2002							8,980[b]	89.27	Naples

Source: Paris Club website.

Notes: a. Out of the US$2,800 million treated, US$2,270 million were cancelled and US$530 million rescheduled. b. US$4,640 million were cancelled, and US$4,340 million rescheduled. Cologne terms given for maturities falling due from July 2003 through June 2005. NA = details on the amounts rescheduled in these years are not available.

Table 9.5   HIPC Relief: Uganda, Mozambique, and DRC[a]

| | Original HIPC Initiative | | | | | Enhanced HIPC Initiative | | | | |
| | Nominal Debt Service Relief | | | | | Nominal Debt Service Relief | | | | |
	US$ Million	as Percent of Total Debt	as Percent of GNI[b]	Decision Point	Completion Point	US$ Million	as Percent of Total Debt	as Percent of GNI	Decision Point	Completion Point
Mozambique	3,700	44.6	101.0	April 1998	June 1999	600	8.5	17.4	April 2000	September 2001
Uganda	650	16.8	10.4	April 1997	April 1998	1,300	37.1	22.6	February 2000	May 2000
Democratic Republic of Congo	—	—	—	—	—	10,389	93.0	192.9	July 2003	Floating

Source: International Monetary Fund decision point documents and completion point documents, and International Monetary Fund and International Development Association "Statistical Updates on the HIPC Initiative."

Notes: a. Status as of March 2005. b. GNI = gross national income.

in net present value terms) to be delivered over a period of twenty years. The resulting cash savings averaged US$60 million per annum in 2000–2003, equivalent to almost a quarter of the total budget support the government received over this period.

Looking at the timing of debt relief and grant aid to Uganda, it seems that debt relief was generally additional (see Table 9.6). Although grants dipped in 1993 and 1998, the overall trend has been an increase in the provision of grants. The case of Uganda shows, however, how slow and painstaking the debt reconciliation and relief processes can be for postconflict countries, even under relatively favorable circumstances.

Mozambique: High Debt and High Aid

Mozambique became independent in 1975 following years of warfare and then suffered a devastating civil war from the early 1980s until the 1992 peace accord between the government of the Front for the Liberation of Mozambique (FRELIMO) and the South African–backed rebels (Newitt 1995). The aim of the rebels was to destroy the capacity of FRELIMO to govern the country, and in many rural areas they fulfilled that objective. After the war, Mozambique turned to multiparty democracy. The FRELIMO party has won successive presidential and parliamentary elections, ensuring a high degree of political consistency internally and in dealings with the international aid donors.

The economy was badly damaged by both the independence struggle and the civil war (Colletta, Kostner, and Wiederhofer 1996b; Addison and de Sousa 1999). In the mid-1990s, income per capita was US$550, or less than two dollars per day, and the national poverty headcount of Mozambique was nearly 70 percent (Government of Mozambique 1998). Since then, Mozambique has experienced sustained growth resurgence, with an average annual gross domestic product (GDP) per capita growth rate for the period 1995 to 2002 of 5.6 percent (World Bank 2005f). Income per capita rose to US$990 in 2002, and the poverty headcount dropped to 54 percent (Government of Mozambique 2004).

Mozambique's exports of goods and services increased slowly in the 1990s and then accelerated. Much of the increase was based on exogenous improvements in export prices for prawns, cotton, and cashews and on the start of electricity exports from the Cahora Bassa dam to Zimbabwe in 1998 (Falck 1999). Nevertheless, the external financial balance of Mozambique since the end of the war has been supported by high levels of foreign aid.

Origins of Debt

Mozambique did not accumulate noteworthy amounts of external debt until the late 1970s. During the first years of independence, the drawdown of foreign

Table 9.6 Debt Relief and Aid Grants: Uganda, Mozambique, and DRC (US$ million, unless otherwise indicated)

	1989	1990	1991	1992	1993	1994	1995	1996	1997	1998	1999	2000	2001	2002	2003
Uganda															
Total rescheduling	28.80	4.50	6.40	91.80	34.40	0.00	172.00	0.00	0.00	158.40	18.40	37.50	0.00	1.20	19.00
Total forgiveness (including interest forgiven)	0.30	51.20	1.00	14.40	156.40	6.90	40.50	0.00	0.00	626.70	11.00	189.10	33.30	128.30	39.70
Total debt relief	29.10	55.70	7.40	106.20	190.80	6.90	212.50	0.00	0.00	785.10	29.40	226.60	33.30	129.50	58.70
Total debt relief as % of debt stock	2.8	2.6	0.4	3.9	6.4	0.2	5.9	0.0	0.0	19.8	0.9	6.4	0.9	3.2	1.4
Total debt relief as % of GNP[a]	0.56	1.32	0.23	3.83	6.02	0.18	3.73	0.00	0.00	12.03	0.49	3.94	0.60	2.26	0.95
Grants (including technical cooperation)	264.15	348.35	419.67	454.75	381.32	439.76	547.71	467.44	492.23	483.00	489.11	658.73	512.30	576.81	694.04
Grants as percentage of GNI	5.07	8.24	12.86	16.41	12.02	11.19	9.61	7.79	7.87	7.40	8.22	11.46	9.25	10.04	11.26
Mozambique															
Total rescheduling	0.00	343.20	141.40	375.60	134.20	135.70	218.90	186.70	114.30	229.00	469.40	1.60	268.90	0.00	0.00
Total forgiveness (including interest forgiven)	0.00	1,174.10	236.70	23.50	35.80	63.30	322.80	130.80	223.10	27.90	535.50	46.20	2,556.00	34.80	83.40
Total debt relief	0.00	1,517.30	378.10	399.10	170.00	199.00	541.70	317.50	337.40	256.90	1,004.90	47.80	2,824.90	34.80	83.40
Total debt relief as % of debt stock	0.0	33.6	9.3	13.6	4.0	3.6	5.2	4.3	4.7	7.5	17.3	0.7	62.4	0.7	1.7
Total debt relief as % of GNI	0.00	65.39	16.48	23.75	9.38	10.03	25.40	11.88	10.49	7.01	26.61	1.38	90.24	1.02	2.03
Grants (including technical cooperation)	672.13	841.48	1,001.08	920.29	860.93	876.20	1,003.15	630.57	680.13	824.44	781.60	898.80	822.20	1,871.68	829.69
Grants as percentage of GNI	31.55	36.27	43.64	54.77	47.49	44.16	47.04	23.59	21.14	22.51	20.70	26.03	26.27	54.90	20.20

continues

Table 9.6 Continued

	1989	1990	1991	1992	1993	1994	1995	1996	1997	1998	1999	2000	2001	2002	2003
Democratic Republic of Congo															
Total rescheduling	975.60	390.10	0.00	0.00	0.00	0.00	0.00	0.00	0.00	0.00	6.90	0.00	0.00	3,518.30	79.00
Total forgiveness (including interest forgiven)	152.90	24.10	0.00	0.00	0.00	0.00	0.00	0.00	0.00	0.00	1.60	0.00	0.00	3,553.30	101.80
Total debt relief	1,128.50	414.20	0.00	0.00	0.00	0.00	0.00	0.00	0.00	0.00	8.50	0.00	0.00	7,071.60	180.80
Total debt relief as % of debt stock	15.43	4.58	0.00	0.00	0.00	0.00	0.00	0.00	0.00	0.00	0.01	0.00	0.00	83.13	0.91
Total debt relief as % of GNI	13.48	4.83	0.00	0.00	0.00	0.00	0.00	0.00	0.00	0.00	0.20	0.00	0.00	134.72	3.36
Grants (including technical cooperation)	364.76	519.68	584.09	196.45	131.32	258.88	216.26	182.12	161.91	137.12	152.09	191.39	269.43	565.63	4,934.43
Grants as percentage of GNI	4.36	6.06	7.01	2.39	1.32	5.05	4.43	3.37	2.84	2.36	3.52	4.89	6.03	10.78	91.63

Source: World Bank (2004d) and authors' calculations.

Notes: GNI = gross national income. Total forgiveness corresponds to the change in debt stock due to debt forgiveness or reduction, including principal and interest arrears forgiven. Total debt relief includes total debt rescheduling in addition to forgiveness.

reserves was sufficient to finance the current account deficit. Soon after the onset of the civil war, however, Mozambique's external debt increased rapidly. In contrast to some conflict-affected countries, Mozambique did not entirely stop servicing its debt during the war, but significant arrears vis-à-vis official creditors accumulated during this period. By 1993, Mozambique's debt–to–gross national income (GNI) ratio reached nearly 300 percent, and the external debt-to-exports ratio reached 1,400 percent (Table 9.7). These very high ratios reflected not only increased debt but also reduced output.

The initial loans were given primarily by the Eastern bloc and by oil-exporting countries. The Soviet Union, for example, was one of the main

Table 9.7   Debt Summary—Mozambique (US$ million, unless otherwise indicated)

	Last Prewar 1984	First Postwar 1993	Most Recent 2002
Total debt stocks	1,438	5,212	4,609
Long-term debt outstanding	1,354	4,859	4,039
Short-term debt outstanding	84	164	371
of which interest arrears, official creditors	4	145	243
of which interest arrears, private creditors		3	2
Principal arrears, official creditors	46	731	189
Principal arrears, private creditors	1	49	2
Total debt flows			
Disbursements	834	186	270
Disbursement multilateral %	0.6	77.5	89.1
Disbursement bilateral %	75.3	20.3	10.2
Disbursement private %	24.1	2.3	0.0
Net transfers on debt	817	20	41
Debt indicators			
Total debt/exports of goods and services (%)	673	1,402	363
Total debt/GNI[a] (%)	43	287	135
Total debt service (% of GNI)	1	7	2
Debt composition			
Multilateral debt/total debt (%)	4	15	32
Bilateral PPG[b] debt/total PPG debt (%)	78.3	80.5	44.2
Private PPG debt/total debt PPG (%)	17.1	3.0	0.1
Aid and GNI			
Aid (% of GNI)	8	65	60
Aid per capita (current US$)	19	79	112
GNI, PPP[c] (real 2002 million $)	7,647	9,793	18,293
GNI per capita, PPP (real 2002 million $)	565	652	990

Source: World Bank (2004d).
Notes: a. GNI = gross national income. b. PPG = public and publicly guaranteed debt. c. PPP = purchasing power parity-adjusted.

lenders. After the ruling FRELIMO party formally abandoned Marxism in 1989 and a new constitution paved the way for a free-market economy, multilateral institutions, particularly the World Bank and the IMF, became the main lenders. The multilateral debt stock doubled between 1989 and 1993 to nearly US$800 million. Mozambique became both highly indebted and highly aid dependent.

Postwar Debt Management

When the civil war ended in 1992, the largest share of Mozambique's debt was owed to bilateral official creditors. Paris Club creditors formed the largest group, accounting for more than 70 percent of total debt, with Italy, Portugal, and France among the main creditors. A considerable portion was also owed to the former Soviet Union. Brazil was also a major creditor, having lent US$350 million to Mozambique.

The share of multilateral debt was growing quickly, however, and by 2002 this accounted for more than 30 percent of the external debt. Annual disbursements after the war were on average lower than disbursements had been during the war, and at the same time debt service payments increased significantly, decreasing the net flows on debt.

Beginning in 1996, several "like-minded" bilateral donors, including the Netherlands, Denmark, Norway, Sweden, Ireland, and the UK, contributed to a Multilateral Debt Fund (MDF) in order to help Mozambique meet its debt service payments. In contrast to MDFs in other countries, Mozambique's MDF did not place any conditions on public spending or public financial management.

Debt management in Mozambique is the responsibility of the Ministry of Planning and Finance. Public or publicly guaranteed debt can only be contracted with the approval of the ministry. The ministry maintains a database of multilateral debt, whereas the Bank of Mozambique maintains a database of bilateral debt. The technical staff at both institutions is experienced and knowledgeable about debt issues, having carried out numerous debt-restructuring negotiations. The government has received financial support for debt management from the government of Sweden and technical assistance from Debt Relief International and the Commonwealth Secretariat.[10]

Although Mozambique appears to have built strong debt management structures, the frequency of its debt reschedulings (see Table 9.4) suggests that a leaner operation might have saved scarce human capital for other, more productive tasks. Even though the opportunity costs of not having a debt management capacity are large (as discussed below in the case of DRC), devoting much time and effort to debt management capacity in response to donors' demands also entails important opportunity costs for an impoverished developing country.

Debt Relief

In comparison to many postwar economies, Mozambique received generous debt relief. Relief under the HIPC and enhanced HIPC initiatives amounted to US$4.3 billion. After a large amount of debt was forgiven by the Paris Club in 2001, the country's outstanding debt stock fell below its immediate postwar level.[11] Resources freed by the debt relief granted started to be allocated through the fiscal system into basic social expenditures, helping to redress some of the regional inequalities in living standards.

Grant aid flows to Mozambique have been large and fairly stable, declining after the mid-1990s but with a spike in 2002 as a consequence of floods in 2001. The country thus received both substantial aid and substantial debt relief, more or less in parallel. Mozambique thus is slowly moving away from being highly indebted while remaining highly aid dependent.

Democratic Republic of Congo: Fast but Unsustainable Action

Democratic Republic of Congo is a resource-rich country that has suffered from domestic and international mismanagement and corruption and from devastating conflicts. War resulted in an estimated 3 million deaths from 1996 to 2001 (Clément 2004). The regime of President Mobutu Sese Seko relied heavily on Western financial support, which eventually dried up in the early 1990s. In 1997, Mobutu was overthrown by Laurent Kabila, who was assassinated in 2001. His son Joseph Kabila succeeded him and has sought to realign the country with the multilateral donor community. Between 1991 and 2001, DRC's real income per capita dropped by more than half, to US$630 (Table 9.8). The country continues to be characterized by ongoing political instability and extreme poverty.

Origins of Debt

The Mobutu government borrowed more than US$9 billion abroad between 1970 and 1994. Initially, the borrowings were mainly from private creditors. As the private creditors started to shorten their exposure to the country in the late 1970s, official borrowings increased in the 1980s. In 1981 the IMF provided the country with the largest credit it had ever given to an African country. In 1987 another IMF credit was approved under pressure from the US government, in the face of strong objections from senior IMF staff (Ndikumana and Boyce 1998, 210–211). New lending slowed substantially after 1994, but the country's external debt stock continued to rise as interest arrears accumulated. By 2001, DRC's external debt stood at more than US$11.5 billion.

Since 2001, the international community—the IMF in particular—has adopted a very proactive approach in DRC. In February 2001 an IMF mission

Table 9.8 Debt Summary—Democratic Republic of Congo (US$ million, unless otherwise indicated)

	Last Prewar 1996	First Postwar 2001	Most Recent 2002
Total debt stocks	10,840	11,519	8,726
Long-term debt outstanding	9,285	7,587	7,391
Short-term debt outstanding	1,083	3,556	764
of which interest arrears, official creditors	585	2,997	409
of which interest arrears, private creditors	108	178	53
Principal arrears, official creditors	376	4,798	578
Principal arrears, private creditors	674	488	482
Total debt flows			
Disbursements	3	0	415
Disbursement multilateral %	0.0	0	98.7
Disbursement bilateral %	100	0	1.3
Disbursement private %	0.0	0	0
Net transfers on debt	0	0	0
Debt indicators			
Total debt/exports of goods and services (%)	130	—	—
Total debt/GNI[a] (%)	2	241	159
Total debt service (% of GNI)	20	—	17
Debt composition			
Multilateral debt/total debt (%)	20	18	28
Bilateral PPG[b] debt/total PPG debt (%)	66.9	66.3	68.5
Private PPG debt/total PPG debt (%)	9.4	6.4	3.9
Aid and GNI			
Aid (% of GNI)	6	6	15
Aid per capita (current US$)	12	5	16
GNI, PPP[c] (real 2002 million $)	56,977	31,605	32,697
GNI per capita, PPP (real 2002 million $)	1,479	630	630

Source: World Bank (2004d).

Notes: a. GNI = gross national income. b. PPG = public and publicly guaranteed debt. c. PPP = purchasing power parity-adjusted.

visited Kinshasa, and in December 2001 donors met with a Congolese delegation in Paris to gather support from the international community. At the beginning of 2002, the IMF sent a mission to negotiate a medium-term program to be supported by a three-year arrangement under the Poverty Reduction and Growth Facility (PRGF).[12]

Postwar Debt Management

After years of turmoil, more than half of DRC's external debt constituted arrears on debt service payments, including to the IMF and the World Bank (Table 9.8). By the end of 2003, the loan-by-loan debt reconciliation process was completed with most of the country's multilateral and bilateral creditors. This remarkably fast process resulted from good personal relationships between the national and international negotiators. This made it possible to finalize an HIPC decision point document for DRC in July 2003 (Table 9.5).

To build good relations prior to reaching a formal debt agreement, starting in 2001 DRC authorities committed to deposit 100,000 special drawing rights per month into a government account held with the Bank of International Settlements in Switzerland and closely monitored by the IMF. These deposits continued to be part of DRC's international reserves until their eventual use for arrears clearance. The amount chosen was relatively low, given that the stabilization of DRC's arrears to the fund would have implied monthly payments of about 1 million special drawing rights. Recognizing DRC's limited debt service capacity, however, the IMF's board expressed its readiness to accept reduced payments by a postconflict member in arrears. This unusual treatment required that all other multilateral donors to which the DRC was in arrears take comparable action.

Although these measures were implemented fairly quickly and with a high degree of flexibility, on the institutional side DRC's debt management exhibited ongoing weaknesses. The principal agency charged with handling debt issues still did not have the technical and financial means to fulfill its mandate by August 2003 (IMF 2003a). The government failed to develop a coherent debt management strategy. In part, this failure may be explained by the lack of capacity. Given the positive start to these negotiations, it should have been possible to build national capacity with donor support. Yet in the end, the quick progress made in the initial phases of the debt management process was not sustained.

Debt Relief

DRC's arrears vis-à-vis the IMF ultimately were cleared through a one-day bridge loan—financed by the governments of Belgium, France, South Africa, and Sweden—that was repaid with a new loan from the IMF's Poverty Reduction and Growth Facility (Clément 2004). Arrears to the World Bank were cleared through a bridge loan from Belgium and France, which in turn was repaid using the first tranche of an Emergency Recovery Credit that was provided by the Bank on standard IDA terms. The arrears with the African Development Bank and other main multilateral creditors were also consolidated.

In 2001, Paris Club bilateral donors were owed around 69 percent of DRC's outstanding debt, most of which had been contracted before the cut-off date and was thus in principle eligible for rescheduling. In September 2002, the creditors agreed to provide a rescheduling on Naples terms, on pre-cut-off date debt in arrears as of the end of June 2002 and also on further maturities falling due during the PRGF arrangement period (see Table 9.4).

Conclusion

Our analysis suggests that debt in postwar developing countries deserves special treatment in light of the financial needs for reconstruction, the impediments to economic recovery posed by debt overhang effects, and the normative issues surrounding odious debts. Yet surprisingly, the existing debt relief strategies of private, bilateral, and multilateral lenders fail to take account of the special circumstances of postconflict economies.

The HIPC initiative, for example, is not designed to benefit postconflict economies quickly once the fighting ends. In the cases of Mozambique and Uganda, it is not clear why the enhanced HIPC initiative required another "track record" period given that both countries had completed track records before and after their first decision points in the late 1990s. If these two relatively successful economies were required to meet more stringent requirements, then it is clear that weaker postwar economies will find it even more difficult to comply with HIPC conditionality.

We recommend that postwar countries should receive special treatment in debt relief negotiations, including those under the HIPC initiative, with faster and deeper relief linked to broader policy conditionality. Specifically, sustainability criteria should be redefined to include issues of peace sustainability, conditions should be framed to include peace conditionality, and the required track record should be shortened or waived altogether depending on individual circumstances.

Our analysis also points to the lack of an international regulatory framework for the adjudication of conflict-related and odious debt. In the context of the recent high-profile regime changes in Afghanistan and Iraq, discussions of postconflict debt legacies have increasingly focused on the responsibilities of the lenders for ensuring that debt is used sustainably. We recommend two institutional innovations to address this problem.

First, an international institution such as the UN or IMF could be given the power to declare a regime "odious" and thereby deny future lenders the legal right to enforce repayments on debts contracted after that point. This would create incentives *ex ante* to prevent exposure to odious debt. It would signal to creditors that lending unsustainably carries a high risk of default and would impede kleptocratic or oppressive regimes from financing wars with new loans.

Second, to address the *ex post* legacy of odious debts, we recommend the establishment of the financial equivalent of an international truth and reconciliation commission to adjudicate the odiousness of debts incurred in the past. Such a Debt Relief Commission for postconflict HIPCs would be made up of senior global public figures, with its rulings regarded as binding on the participating international donors and the debtor government.

The international donor community may not be well prepared for such comprehensive policies and the monitoring they would require. From the points of view of poverty reduction, growth, and peace, however, these policy innovations merit serious attention.

Notes

1. A few newly independent countries and nonmarket economies, such as Timor-Leste and North Korea, respectively, are exceptions to this rule. .

2. For example, Canada announced bilateral debt write-offs ahead of the 1999 Cologne summit of Group of 8 countries, in an effort to augment the ongoing HIPC initiative and shame other donors into concerted action (Pearson 2005).

3. In part, this phenomenon is driven by the need of borrowers to sell and the need of lenders to buy raw materials, such as oil. Such arrangements can be particularly relevant for conflict-ridden countries. In the case of Sudan and China, for example, Sudan faces constraints in accessing oil markets owing to its ongoing conflicts, and China utilizes this opportunity irrespective of the negative side effects this may have for its international political standing.

4. For modifications, see International Monetary Fund and World Bank (1999). For further discussion, see Fedelino and Kudina (2003); Hjertholm (2003); International Development Association and International Monetary Fund (2001); Sanford (2004); Sun (2004).

5. The debt-to-fiscal-revenue target was also lowered from 280 percent to 250 percent.

6. In 1999, the World Bank's International Development Association (IDA) authorized the limited use of grant financing to support economic recovery in postconflict countries prior to the clearance of arrears. By 2001, only one out of the five postconflict countries in Africa with large and protracted arrears that could have qualified for these IDA grants did indeed qualify, however, namely Democratic Republic of Congo (Michailof, Kostner, and Xavier 2002). For further discussion of arrears as an obstacle to multilateral reengagement, see Birdsall and Claessens (2003).

7. Under the IDA-14 replenishment, which was approved in 2005, debt-distressed countries will be able to receive grants rather than loans from the World Bank. For IDA grants to be used to repay bridge loans for arrears clearance, three conditions must be met: first, arrears clearance on comparable terms must be arranged with all other multilateral creditors; second, the country must refrain from debt repayments to bilateral and commercial creditors until comparable treatment has been agreed; and third, government must present a credible policy framework and macroeconomic program.

8. The correlation coefficient for debt relief and grants for the pooled data is 0.16. In an econometric analysis of 22 donors and 111 developing countries, Ndikumana (2004) examined whether and to what extent debt relief had been accompanied by decreasing aid flows. He found no direct causal link between the volume of debt restructurings awarded and the volume of official development financing disbursed.

9. Moral hazard considerations might suggest that if special provisions for postwar countries were implemented, governments would deliberately risk violent conflict to obtain debt relief. But although it appears to be the case that some countries, such as Mozambique, used external debt to fund ongoing wars, we know of no case of a government starting a war with the objective of winning debt relief.

10. Debt Relief International is a London-based organization founded in 1997 with funding from seven OECD governments to build the debt management capacity of HIPC governments.

11. In addition, a commercial debt buyback operation in December 1991 eliminated US$203 million of debt, of which US$119 million was outstanding interest arrears (Dijkstra 2003).

12. The PRGF is an IMF facility that provides loans to low-income countries in support of programs framed by Poverty Reduction Strategy Papers.

10

Policy Implications: The Economics of Postwar Statebuilding

James K. Boyce and Madalene O'Donnell

The experiences recounted in this book provide valuable insights into the critical role of the public purse in postwar peacebuilding. In this conclusion, we first highlight some key insights from the preceding chapters and then examine eight policy issues that illuminate opportunities for greater synergy among public finance, statebuilding, and peacebuilding.

The first four issues pertain to resource mobilization: How should distributional impacts enter into revenue policies? How can postwar external assistance do more to prime the pump of domestic revenue capacity? Should macroeconomic strictures prescribed for economic stabilization be relaxed to foster political stabilization? How should the benefits of external resources be weighed against their costs?

The second four issues relate to the expenditure side of public finance: How should the dynamics of conflict be factored into public spending policies? Can the pathologies of a "dual public sector"—one funded and managed by the government, the other by the aid donors—be surmounted by channeling external resources through the government with dual-control oversight mechanisms to reduce corruption? How should long-term fiscal sustainability enter into short-term expenditure decisions? Last, is there scope for more innovative solutions to postwar legacies of external debts?

After discussing each of these issues, we close with some thoughts on the challenges of achieving policy "coherence" in the interconnected realms of public finance, statebuilding, and peacebuilding.

Overview of the Cases

In postwar settings, security and public finance are intertwined. As the case studies in this book illustrate, violence and insecurity impede efforts to collect and expend public resources. In Afghanistan, the fact that many customs posts remained effectively under the control of regional strongmen undermined the state's monopoly on the legitimate collection of revenue as well as the legitimate use of force. Yet the government had little success in convincing the international community to help reestablish state control over these facilities. In Palestine, the ongoing conflict has created a deeply problematic environment in which to try to construct new fiscal institutions. After 2000, the second intifada and Israeli responses to it precipitated what the World Bank (2004b, 1) called "one of the deepest recessions in modern history," and Palestinian Authority revenues dropped from more than US$900 million in 2000 to less than US$300 million in 2001. And in 2006, when the electoral victory of Hamas sparked the suspension of international aid and withholding of Israeli-collected revenues, the result was a fiscal as well as a humanitarian crisis.

At the same time, fiscal issues can have important impacts on security. In Timor-Leste, budget allocations that reflected donor preferences to finance the police rather than the military, notwithstanding the popular legitimacy of the former resistance fighters in the latter, contributed to a new eruption of violence in March 2006. In Guatemala, the failure to meet revenue targets is one factor inhibiting the government's ability to respond to elevated rates of violent crime that persist a decade after the peace accords. In Afghanistan, a major crisis lies ahead in financing the Afghan army and police, who were trained and equipped without regard to domestic fiscal constraints.

Postwar states typically are characterized by low levels of domestic revenue mobilization. Among our six case-study countries, the ratio of revenue to gross domestic product (GDP) in the immediate postwar years ranged from approximately 4 percent in Uganda, Cambodia, and Afghanistan to 8 percent in Guatemala. This is not surprising. What is more disconcerting, however, is that this ratio showed only modest improvements a decade or more after the peace accords in Uganda, Cambodia, and Guatemala, where it now hovers around 11 percent, still far below the average for developing countries.[1] Progress in raising revenue in the more recent cases of Palestine, Timor-Leste, and Afghanistan is hard to predict, but signs of problems are already apparent. Palestine briefly achieved revenues equivalent to 20 percent of GDP, but the bulk of these were customs duties collected by Israeli authorities on imports destined for the West Bank and Gaza and, as of this writing, these are being withheld. Timor-Leste's revenue has increased since independence, but this is largely owing to petroleum royalties rather than tax revenues. Afghanistan initially made some progress in revenue mobilization, meeting the targets it negotiated with the International Monetary Fund (IMF), but did so starting from a very low base.

Enhancing the state's capacity to generate revenue is not an easy task. Nevertheless, the poor performance in revenue generation suggests that stronger efforts are needed on the part of both national governments and international actors. Even when national governments are convinced of the importance of expanding their own resources—rather than relying on external assistance—they often fail to provide the improved services that are the quid pro quo demanded by the citizenry. Among international actors, as the chapters on Guatemala, Cambodia, Timor-Leste, and Afghanistan describe, we find a common pattern in which a subset of donors is seriously concerned with generating a stable flow of revenues for the state, whereas others are not, a situation that undermines incentives to pursue this objective. In Cambodia, for example, bilateral donors generally favored liberal tax incentives to attract investors, whereas multilateral donors opposed them in light of the need for higher revenues, a mixed message that contributed to slowing the pace of reforms.

The scale and importance of international aid varied considerably across our cases. As a percentage of national income, aid ranged from nearly 60 percent in Timor-Leste to less than 2 percent in Guatemala. Aid can provide a critical means of financing core government services and operations in a context of poor revenue mobilization. But reliance on international aid to fund government operations has at least two disadvantages over domestic revenue collection. First, aid flows can be highly volatile, as illustrated vividly in the Palestine case. Second, securing and administering aid is a time-consuming undertaking for government officials, a point emphasized in the Afghanistan study. Yet even in the "older" cases of Uganda and Cambodia, the degree of reliance on aid to finance the state budget has not declined substantially over time, suggesting that aid has done little to "crowd in" domestic revenue mobilization.

In all cases, however, international aid to the state budget was dwarfed by aid that bypassed the government, flowing through international agencies, nongovernmental organizations (NGOs), and private contractors. In Afghanistan, the result was an "external budget" roughly twice the size of the government's "internal budget." The phenomenon of a dual public sector creates tremendous challenges for financing peace-related needs in a coherent fashion and for ensuring sustainable political, social, and economic development. It also limits the government's ability to render accounts to its citizens, since its own budget process governs only a fraction of total spending in the country.

The Cambodia chapter referred to two competing mentalities among international aid donors—a "peace and security" mentality that tolerates patronage in the name of political stability and a "developmental" mentality that focuses primarily on the state's role as provider of services. Although admittedly a simplification, this contrast highlights the fact that tensions among political, security, and socioeconomic objectives are a recurring theme of postwar transitions. This theme has particular salience for fiscal policy, for this is the key arena in which *all* operational state objectives—political, security, and socioeconomic—are pursued and reconciled with available resources.

There is a profound interdependence between the state's ability to allocate and manage expenditures and its ability to mobilize domestic resources. On the one hand, the volume of domestic revenue limits the volume of expenditure, a constraint that can be eased but not eliminated by international aid and deficit finance. On the other hand, the willingness of the citizenry to pay taxes hinges on its perception that the state will effectively deliver public goods and services—including infrastructure, public safety, health, and education—in return. If the state fails to uphold its end of this social compact, its ability to raise revenue encounters serious political and administrative constraints. This reality was visible even in Guatemala, despite the fact that its peace accords explicitly mandated substantial increases in revenue and social expenditure.

The international community can help to resolve this chicken-and-egg dilemma by providing external resources. In principle, these can fund expenditures that enhance both the ability to pay taxes (by stimulating economic recovery) and the willingness to pay taxes (by demonstrating the state's capacity to deliver results). In practice, however, as the studies in this book attest, this positive outcome is not automatic. Budget allocation and expenditure management capacities do not spring forth spontaneously in response to resource availability; they must be built painstakingly over time. The legitimacy of the state rests not only on its ability to provide public goods and services but also on its willingness to respond to the expressed needs and demands of the public. If external resources fail to build core public finance capacities, and if the state's attentiveness to the preferences of donors deflects it from responding to the needs and demands of its own people, then the long-run contribution of aid to this crucial dimension of statebuilding will prove marginal at best.

Peace and the Public Purse: Eight Issues

1. Who Pays? Revenue Through a Conflict Lens

In many postwar settings, a central task is to raise domestic revenue to provide sustainable funding for new democratic institutions and for expenditures to improve human well-being, strengthen public security, and ease social tensions. The size of government revenue relative to gross domestic product in war-torn societies typically is far below the average for other countries with similar per capita income.[2] Yet as the contributions to this book attest, the needs for government expenditure are, if anything, greater. Hence concerted efforts are needed to increase revenues.

But size is not all that matters. In addition to the total volume of revenue, the distributional impact of revenue collection matters, too. The issue sometimes is slighted by economists who were taught in graduate school that distributional objectives are tackled most efficiently on the expenditure side of fiscal policy. Inattention to "who pays?" questions in revenue policy is dysfunctional, however, for the three reasons noted in Chapter 1: first, the axiom that distribution can be relegated to expenditure alone rests on a textbook "optimal planner" model that does not fit the real world; second, even optimal planners would need full information on the distributional impacts of revenue policies to achieve their targets; and third, if the public believes that the distributional effects of revenue policies matter, then politically they do.

Economists usually think about distribution in terms of "vertical equity," differences between rich and poor. But "horizontal equity"—differences across population groups defined in terms of ethnicity, race, religion, or region—often figure as much (or more) in the dynamics of conflict.

For this reason, in the past decade scholars and policymakers have begun to pay more attention to intergroup disparities. Researchers have analyzed the role of horizontal equity in the genesis of civil wars (Stewart 2000, 2002; Østby 2004). Economists have begun to think hard about how to measure it, starting with spatial inequalities across regions (Kanbur and Venables 2005). International aid agencies increasingly recognize the need for "conflict impact assessment" as an input into policymaking and project appraisal, and some have begun to put this recognition into practice.[3]

Yet to date, little has been done to bring these insights to bear on revenue policies. The primary revenue goal of postwar government authorities, and of the international agencies that seek to assist them, has been to increase the volume of collections; the secondary goal has been to do so as "efficiently" as possible. To be sure, increasing the volume of revenue is no small task, even in cases where war has not led to state collapse, as Chapter 4 on Guatemala illustrates. And efficiency—if understood in terms of the realities of war-torn societies, as opposed to textbook axioms—is desirable. But neglect of the distributional impacts of taxation can subvert both of these goals.

The starting point for any effort to address this lacuna must be careful documentation of the distributional incidence of revenue instruments both vertically and horizontally. Collecting the necessary data will be a nontrivial task, for today there is a paucity of such information even in "normal" developing countries, let alone in war-torn societies.[4] This can be contrasted with the situation in the industrialized countries, where the distributional impacts of proposed taxes typically are subjected to intense scrutiny by politicians and policymakers alike. Ironically, it is precisely where the need for such analysis is greatest—in societies embarked on the fragile transition from war to peace—that these issues receive the least attention. Technical assistance from the international community could play a valuable role in filling this information gap.

Documentation is only the first step. The second is to incorporate this information into policymaking. In choosing the mix of revenue instruments—the balance between tariffs, value-added taxes, and income taxes, for example—their distributional incidence must be considered alongside their revenue potential, administrative feasibility, and efficiency effects. One option that would be likely to receive much more attention, once revenue is seen through the distributional lens, is luxury taxation. Taxes on items such as private automobiles and private aircraft can combine the attractions of administrative ease, distributional progressivity, and substantial revenue. Yet remarkably, they rarely feature in discussions of postwar revenue policies.

Finally, information on the distributional impacts of revenue instruments, and on the ways that government policies are taking these into account, must be disseminated widely to the public, so as to guard against misperceptions and to facilitate compliance by legitimizing the policies. The importance of this was demonstrated vividly in Guatemala, where the Peace Accords set explicit targets for increasing government revenue and social expenditure. To this end, the first postwar government attempted to increase the tax on large property owners. As described in Chapter 4, this effort was scuttled, however, in the face of protests not only from estate owners but also from small-scale indigenous farmers who thought that the tax would burden them (see also Jonas 2000, 171–172). The lesson is clear: successful revenue policymaking cannot be a purely technocratic preserve; it must be part and parcel of the democratic process.

2. Priming the Pump? External Support for Domestic Revenue Mobilization

Experience has shown that aid can crowd out domestic revenue mobilization, reducing the incentive for the government to tax its own populace.[5] If aid instead is to crowd in domestic revenue, conscious efforts are needed to this end. The international community can support government efforts to mobilize domestic revenue in four ways: by providing technical assistance, by linking some of its aid to progress in domestic revenue performance, by helping to curb extralegal revenue exactions, and by reducing tax exemptions on postwar aid.

Technical assistance. Technical assistance (TA) is the most common type of support. The preceding chapters have documented many instances in which TA from the IMF, World Bank, and bilateral donors has helped to develop revenue capacities, ranging from drafting tax codes in Timor-Leste to setting up Guatemala's Superintendency for Tax Administration, a unit within the finance ministry with special training and higher pay in an effort to insulate it from corruption.

In public finance, as in other arenas, the effectiveness of TA could be strengthened by efforts to adopt technologies and procedures that build on existing capacities, rather than opting for off-the-shelf imported solutions. In Afghanistan, for example, as recalled by Ashraf Ghani and his colleagues in Chapter 6, computerized information systems introduced at the Ministry of Finance were "unsuitable in terms of complexity and language," prompting subsequent efforts to retool with Persian-language systems from Iran. More attention to training local personnel, rather than simply substituting for them, could also foster capacity building. In their study of Timor-Leste, Emilia Pires and Michael Francino remark in Chapter 5 that the concentration on expatriate advisory services was accompanied by "some neglect for formal training programs for national staff." The ultimate goal of technical assistance is to become redundant.

There is also scope for greater conflict sensitivity in technical assistance. In some cases, TA providers have shown an impressive ability to cast aside orthodoxies and adapt their policy advice to local realities. For example, despite the aversion of the international financial institutions (IFIs) to trade taxes, import duties were recognized as the most feasible source of revenue enhancement in Timor-Leste, Kosovo, and Afghanistan. In the case of Timor-Leste, the IMF even supported introduction of a levy on coffee exports (see Chapter 5), a policy that verges on the heretical. In other cases, however, orthodoxy triumphed over pragmatism. In Guatemala, for example, even as the IMF gave rhetorical support to the revenue-enhancement goal mandated by the Peace Accords, the fund's staff urged the government to cut tariffs.[6] Theoretical work and empirical evidence cast doubt on both the efficiency advantages of a shift from tariffs to value-added taxes and the prospects for accomplishing this without a decline in total revenues.[7] Nevertheless, this remains a key plank of IFI policy prescriptions in developing countries. In postwar countries, where administrative capacities are especially weak and the need for revenue especially pressing, the case for departures from orthodoxy is all the more compelling.

Conditionality. Conditionality is a second way that donors can encourage domestic resource mobilization. On the expenditure side of fiscal policy, it is not unusual for donors to require "counterpart funding" by the government as a condition for aid to specific projects, a strategy intended to ensure domestic "buy-in" and to counteract fungibility (whereby aid merely frees government money for other uses). But on the revenue side, conditionality of this type has been rare. It would be a straightforward matter to link certain types of aid—notably budget support—to progress in meeting domestic revenue targets. Such a policy is akin to the provision of matching grants by private foundations. In both cases, the aim is to strengthen incentives for aid recipients to seek further resources, counteracting the disincentive effects of unconditional aid.[8]

Visiting Guatemala in May 1997, a few months after the signing of that country's peace accords, IMF managing director Michel Camdessus took a broad step in this direction when he stated that the fund's only condition for a standby agreement would be that the government comply with its peace accord commitments, including a 50 percent increase in the revenue-to-GDP ratio.[9] Making a tighter linkage, the European Union (EU) conditioned its budget support to the government of Mozambique in 2002 on increases in domestic revenue.[10] One of the benchmarks in the Afghanistan Compact signed in London in early 2006, which sets out the framework for international assistance to that country over the next five years, is to increase the revenue/GDP ratio from 4.5 percent in 2004–2005 to 8 percent in 2010–2011.[11] But conditionality with respect to revenue mobilization remains the exception, not the rule.

Curing extralegal revenue exactions. Curbing extralegal revenue exactions in some cases is a critical postwar task, one that is located on the cusp between public finance and security. When profits from the exploitation of nominally public resources, like Cambodia's forests, flow into private pockets, this not only deprives the state of revenues but also often finances quasi-autonomous armed groups that threaten the peace (Le Billon 2000). When local warlords levy "taxes" on trade, sometimes including trade in narcotics, as in Afghanistan, they undermine the state's monopoly not only on revenue collection but also on the legitimate exercise of force. Curtailing such activities may require the assistance of international peacekeeping forces, which is what prompted the Afghan finance ministry's request for help in securing customs posts (see Chapter 6). Yet peacekeeping forces, even those with a relatively expansive mandate, such as the International Security Assistance Force (ISAF) in Afghanistan, typically have not seen this as a part of their job.

Even more problematic, powerful members of the international community may be reluctant to crack down on extralegal revenue exactions when they regard those involved as political allies. In Afghanistan, for example, efforts to consolidate revenue in the hands of the state and to fight drug trafficking have been complicated—to put it mildly—by the decision of the US government to enlist anti-Taliban warlords as partners in its global war on terror. Such marriages of convenience, reminiscent of US support to the anti-Soviet *mujahadeen* in the 1980s, may serve short-run security objectives but do so only at the expense of the legitimacy and effectiveness of the state—and ultimately security too—in the long run.[12]

Reducing tax exemptions on postwar aid flows. Reducing tax exemptions on postwar aid flows could do a great deal to prime the pump of domestic revenue-collection capacity. In the first postwar years, aid often is the single biggest component of the formal-sector economy. Yet today aid flows, and many of the incomes generated by them, are tax exempt. The incomes of expatriate aid officials and aid workers are often tax free.[13] The incomes of their local staff, quite high by local standards, are often tax free, too. The goods imported by the aid agencies, ranging from Toyota Land Cruisers to cases of Coca Cola and whiskey, are seldom taxed. The rents paid by expatriates for office space and housing—again, exorbitant by local standards—are often tax free. So are other services provided to them, such as hotels and restaurants.

These pervasive exemptions have several adverse consequences. Most obvious is the opportunity cost of forgone government revenues. In addition, scarce administrative capacity is devoted to administering different rules for different people. Goods that enter the country as aid frequently wind up on sale in local markets, undercutting legitimate competitors who pay import duties.[14] Last but not least, the special treatment accorded to expatriates sends an unmistakable message to the local populace: rich and powerful people do not have to pay taxes. The result can be "the creation of a culture of tax exemptions," in the words of a recent IMF review of postconflict experiences (Gupta et al. 2005, 12). This demonstration effect runs precisely counter to efforts to establish effective and progressive revenue collection systems. It also undermines the credibility of international agencies when they argue, as in Cambodia, that governments should reduce tax loopholes and "tax incentives" for local businesses (see Chapter 3).

Efforts to tax aid bonanzas—even with backing from the IMF—have run into adamant resistance from aid donors. In Timor-Leste, efforts to tax the floating hotels in the Dili harbor that accommodated the postwar influx of foreigners were rebuffed by lawyers at United Nations headquarters in New York, on the dubious grounds that diplomatic "privileges and immunities" extend to those who provide services to UN personnel (see Chapter 5). In Afghanistan, the introduction of a tax on rental incomes generated by expatriates in Kabul likewise met resistance; as Ashraf Ghani and his colleagues remark in Chapter 6, "the international community's declarations on the importance of enhancing domestic revenue mobilization have not been matched by willingness to consider new initiatives to tap the revenue possibilities generated by their own presence."

This issue has often pitted the IMF and World Bank, along with national officials, against other donor agencies. Writing in Chapter 5, Emilia Pires and Michael Francino recall "bitter fights between international officials at the Ministry of Finance and international officials of donor organizations . . . with the latter winning." They go on to say that the finance ministry's inability to tax the international presence where there was not an explicit legal basis for their exemption came as a "bitter blow" and that "the donors and the UN, who disagreed about many things, were as one on their inviolable right to a complete exemption from taxes, not only for themselves as individuals or for goods imported for their direct use but also on their contractors and goods imported for reconstruction." Similarly, NGOs "ferociously defended every inch of ground" in resisting taxation of even their local employees: "Even when UNTAET offered to pay the taxes of international staff working with NGOs, provided they were prepared to declare the income they were receiving, the answer was still no."

As Pires and Francino explain in Chapter 5, donor agency staff made three arguments against paying taxes. The first was that this would be equivalent to budget support. This is true. But its implicit premise—that the government cannot be trusted to use tax revenues well—again sends a clear message to the local populace. The second argument was that expatriates were already paying taxes in their countries of origin. In cases where this is so, existing tax treaties allow credits for taxes paid elsewhere, avoiding the problem of double taxation. The third argument was that no other countries where they worked had taxed them, "so why should Timor-Leste be any different?" The answer to this objection is, of course, that desirable changes have to begin somewhere.

Two further points are worth mentioning here. First, income tax payments by expatriate or local aid personnel need not come from their own pockets. Those who pay taxes could be given salary "top-ups" to maintain their after-tax incomes. This is the current practice at the World Bank and IMF headquarters in Washington, D.C., where those employees who are US citizens must pay income taxes (unlike their non-US co-workers) but receive compensating pay increments in the interest of horizontal equity.

Second, initiatives could take the form of payments in lieu of taxes, a solution that has been adopted in a number of college towns in the United States, where municipal governments quite understandably want tax-exempt institutions of higher education to contribute to funding public schools, police and fire protection, and other local services. These negotiated payments maintain the legal privileges of those who make them and open the door for individual donors who are serious about building domestic revenue capacity to act without waiting for across-the-board solutions.

3. Economic vs. Political Stabilization? Balancing the Budget Deficit

An alternative way that governments can mobilize domestic resources—apart from increasing revenues—is to borrow or print money to cover budget deficits. In many postwar settings, a lack of well-developed financial markets means that domestic borrowing is not feasible. Even where this is possible, governments may be reluctant to borrow, since this could push up interest rates and dampen private investment.

Printing money can be a more tempting option. This does not require the institutional capacities for a market in government bonds. Instead the government "borrows" from its own central bank. But this type of deficit finance has costs, too. If printing money fuels rapid inflation, this can disrupt the economy, hit the real incomes of the poor (who generally are least able to "index" their incomes to prices), and spark political unrest.

For these reasons, many economists advocate tight restrictions on budget deficits in general and restrictions on central bank financing of them in particular. One need not be a monetarist economist to appreciate the merits of this position. Yet controlling inflation is not the sole objective of economic policy. In settings with widespread unemployment and slack demand, modest inflation may be a tolerable price to pay for gains in employment and growth.[15] The conventional economic wisdom today holds that inflation cannot boost employment in the long run. In the short run, however, there is no doubt that inflationary finance can provide an economic stimulus.

In postwar countries, short-run concerns have special salience. The macroeconomic goal of price stability must be pursued alongside the peace-building goal of political stability. The former requires efforts to balance the budget, or at least to rein in the gap between expenditure and revenue. But the latter may require expenditures to implement peace accord commitments and to address pressing social needs that surpass the resources available to the government. In such settings, the need for a balanced budget itself must be balanced against the urgent need for peace-related spending.

When confronted with the argument that relaxation of price-stability targets could increase political stability by allowing more expenditures to ease social tensions, proponents of "sound money" counter that price instability fuels social tensions, too. Both sides may be right. Beyond some point, high inflation—and certainly "hyperinflation" at rates of more than 50 percent per month—would harm the economy in general and the poor in particular, exacerbating tensions. At the same time, however, excessively tight money and a complete refusal to finance budget deficits via the "inflation tax" could impede efforts to fund peace-related needs.

If so, the relationship between the macroeconomic stability and political stability may take the shape of an inverted U rather than a straight line. This is depicted in Figure 10.1. The horizontal axis represents price stability, with movement away from the origin denoting lower inflation. The vertical axis

Figure 10.1   Price Stability and Political Stability

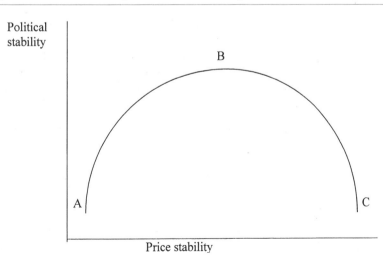

represents political stability, with movement away from the origin denoting lower social tensions. Supporters of stringent anti-inflation policies assume that the country is on the upward-sloping part of the curve, segment *AB*, where greater macroeconomic stability fosters greater political stability. In asserting that there is a tradeoff between the two, critics of these policies assume that the country is on the downward-sloping segment, *BC*.

Both of these scenarios are plausible. Recalling the inflation rates presented in Chapter 1 (see Table 1.2), postwar Cambodia with annual inflation near 100 percent may well have been on the upward-sloping part of the curve, so that anti-inflation efforts were consistent with political stabilization; in postwar Guatemala with only 7 percent inflation, on the other hand, a more relaxed macroeconomic stance might have allowed more fiscal room to maneuver to address peacebuilding needs. Research at the interface between macroeconomics and conflict impact assessment is needed to estimate where the turning point is located in any given time and place. Equally important is to explore policies that might shift the curve, easing potential trade-offs between macroeconomic and political stability. If, for example, there is scope for shifting public expenditure from items that do little to consolidate peace to other uses that are central to this goal, this would help to reconcile the two stability objectives.

Even though some relaxation of budget-deficit targets may be warranted to advance the goal of political stabilization, the scope for financing public spending by this route is limited: at some point, price instability will feed into political instability. Printing money may increase the government's room to maneuver at the margin, but it is not a "soft" substitute for domestic revenue mobilization. As Warren Coats remarks in Chapter 8, "historically the possibility of central bank lending to the government has often proven an irresistible temptation." Opening the door a crack can let in a flood of inflationary finance. Moreover, there are some cases in which very strict monetary policies—or even a straitjacket on the central bank's ability to print money, in the form of "dollarization" or a currency board—can enhance political stability, by taking a bone of contention off the table. Coats argues that that was the case in Bosnia, where a currency board arrangement was mandated in the Dayton Peace Agreement. There may be good arguments for recalibrating monetary discipline in light of the political demands of war-to-peace transitions, but there is no good argument for abandoning it.

4. How Much Aid? Dilemmas in External Resource Mobilization

Government expenditures can be funded by *external* resources as well as by domestic resources—that is, by grants and loans from overseas. In postwar countries, these external resources come mostly from official aid donors: the

Bretton Woods institutions, the regional development banks, and bilateral aid agencies.

For recipients, aid has both benefits and costs. External budget support allows a government to spend money—for example, to pay teachers, healthcare workers, and public security forces—beyond the constraints otherwise imposed by its capacity to mobilize domestic resources. This buys time for the government to increase domestic revenues. The costs to the recipient country include the risk that external resources will crowd out domestic resource mobilization (see above, "2. Priming the Pump?"), the risk that external resources will lead to unsustainable expenditure commitments (see below, "7. Thinking About Tomorrow, Today?"), and the risks posed by exchange-rate appreciation and policies to counter it.

When a government's popularity among aid donors enables it to attract substantial budget support, the IMF sometimes presses for ceilings on the "domestic primary deficit," the extent to which the government uses aid to finance public expenditure. These ceilings are intended to contain the potential adverse macroeconomic effects of aid inflows. The logic is that foreign currency inflows from aid can lead to exchange-rate appreciation, making the country's tradable-goods sector (exports and import substitutes) less competitive, a phenomenon akin to the Dutch disease in which a boom in natural resource exports has the same effect. If the central bank increases the money supply to counter upward pressure on the exchange rate, this can lead to inflation. If the central bank issues bonds to absorb the increased money supply and control inflation (a policy mix known as "sterilization"), this can push up domestic interest rates, adversely affecting private investment. Faced with the trade-offs among exchange-rate appreciation, inflation, and higher interest rates, aid ceilings represent a policy for damage control.

To control the domestic primary deficit in Uganda, the government imposes limits on the share of expenditure in each ministry that can be financed by external resources. As Léonce Ndikumana and Justine Nannyonjo observe in Chapter 2, these aid-intensity ceilings inflict yet another kind of damage, constraining expenditures that could improve social welfare. Uganda's health targets go unmet even as unemployed doctors and nurses emigrate abroad in search of work.[16] When a country has unemployed resources that can be put to work with aid financing—as appears to be the case in this instance—the very elastic supply response means that the impacts of greater aid absorption on inflation and the exchange rate would likely be modest.[17] Moreover, Ndikumana and Nannyonjo argue that aid-intensity ceilings fail to take due account of the fact that much aid is spent abroad on goods and services that do not compete with local production—for example, on technical assistance salaries that are deposited directly into foreign bank accounts. Since such aid does not pose sterilization dilemmas, there is no reason to include it in the calculation of expenditure ceilings.

A recent IMF study echoes these concerns. Instead of real exchange-rate appreciation as aid flows surged, Uganda actually experienced depreciation and low inflation, a scenario that suggests "a rapid supply response to aid expenditures or high import propensities" as well as fiscal and monetary policies designed to counter appreciation (IMF 2005b, 13). "Concerns about inflation," the study cautions, "must be balanced against the dangers of failing to absorb the aid and of crowding out the private sector" (IMF 2005b, 5).[18]

Of course, there may be other good reasons for aid-intensity ceilings, apart from macroeconomic concerns. "Plentiful aid," Bevan (2005, 4) observed, "may induce corruption and other rent-seeking activities in much the same way that resource rents have frequently done." Plentiful aid can lure governments into unsustainable expenditure commitments, a problem discussed below. Plentiful aid can undermine sovereignty: "Countries whose budgets rely heavily on aid flows rather than on their own domestic resources," Heller (2005, 22) observed, "give up significant political autonomy in their capacity to manage and make decisions on budget priorities." Plentiful aid also can undermine democracy, diminishing political accountability to the local populace and tilting the state's attention instead to accountability to donors. And capping the ratio of external resources to total expenditures strengthens incentives for domestic resource mobilization.

Taking into account these costs of aid, as well as its benefits, policymakers again may face an "inverted-U" curve, with aid intensity on the horizontal axis and aid's contribution to the goals of statebuilding and peacebuilding on the vertical axis: aid may advance these goals up to a point, after which its marginal impact turns negative. If so, again there is a need to analyze where this turning point is located in specific times and places and what can be done to shift the curve by enhancing the positive effects of aid and countering its negative effects.

Donor agencies, operating within an overall budget envelope, also face an opportunity cost: aid provided to one country cannot be provided to another. In recent years, donors increasingly have adopted country assessment tools in an effort to channel aid to those countries where it will have the greatest positive impact. The World Bank, for example, uses Country Policy and Institutional Assessment scores in allocating aid (World Bank 2005e). The European Union uses results-based performance indicators, such as vaccination and school enrollment rates, to guide its budget support to developing countries (European Commission 2005). This move toward selectivity has led to a bifurcation between "aid darlings" and "aid orphans"—governments that score well in such assessments and those that score poorly (World Bank and International Monetary Fund 2005, 17). War-torn countries are often in the latter camp.

Two innovations could make selective aid allocation better attuned to the requirements of postwar statebuilding. The first is the incorporation of trends, as well as levels, into existing performance indicators.[19] The second is the development of new indicators that assess progress in conflict resolution and peacebuilding. The latter would apply conflict assessment to the allocation of aid *among* countries as well as within them.

5. Who Benefits? Expenditure Through a Conflict Lens

Turning to the expenditure side of public finance, policymaking in postwar settings requires careful attention to questions of *to whom* as well as *what*.

The "what" question is about priorities. Faced with many pressing needs—for spending in areas such as public safety, the demobilization and re-integration of ex-combatants, health, education, and the rehabilitation of economic infrastructure—how should scarce resources best be allocated? The key point here is that the aim must be not simply to maximize returns defined in terms of conventional development indicators but also to get the most "non-bang for the buck" in terms of building a durable peace.

Making the same point, the synthesis report emerging from the World Bank's research program on violent conflict observed that this "creates the potential for trade-offs between policies that promote growth and those that promote peace." In particular, a strategy focused exclusively on short-term economic returns might concentrate spending on the capital city and developed regions, leading to "a trade-off between the growth-maximizing geographic distribution of public expenditure and a distribution that might be regarded as fair." Where such trade-offs exist, the report concluded, "the government may need to give priority to policies for peace building" (Collier et al. 2003, 166).

When viewed through a conflict lens, the "what" question in public expenditure cannot be divorced from the "to whom" question. Two sets of issues are particularly relevant. The first is how to incorporate vertical and horizontal equity concerns into spending decisions, the importance of which has already been noted in relation to revenue policy (see above, "1. Who Pays?"). The second is how to allocate expenditures across the political landscape so as to bolster incentives for the implementation of accords and the consolidation of peace.

Conflict impact assessments could address both sets of issues. These are analogous to environmental impact assessments, first introduced in the 1970s, with the difference that here the concern is the social and political environment rather than the natural environment. Just as environmental impact assessment aims to incorporate "negative externalities" of pollution and natural resource depletion into expenditure policies, so conflict impact assessment aims to incorporate the "negative externalities" of social tensions and violent conflict.[20]

Today, efforts to incorporate equity impacts into expenditure decisions are still in their infancy. Information on vertical equity—the distribution of benefits across the poor-to-rich spectrum—is sometimes collected and sometimes used as an input into policymaking. For example, the World Bank's 2003 public expenditure review in Cambodia presented data on the distribution of health and education spending (see Tables 3.2a and 3.2b), as did the Bank's 2003 report on poverty in Guatemala (see Chapter 4). In many cases, however, even such basic data are not available.

In the case of horizontal equity—distribution across regions and groups defined on the basis of race, ethnicity, language, or religion—the current lack of information is even more glaring. Collection of regional data on expenditures in administrative units, such as states, provinces, and districts, would seem to be relatively straightforward, both practically (since ministries often allocate their funds across regional units) and politically (since regions often can serve as a proxy for more sensitive categories such as ethnicity). Yet today such data are remarkably few and far between. In Chapter 6, Ashraf Ghani, Afghanistan's former finance minister, and his colleagues recount their experience: "Obtaining the figures on provincial expenditures from line ministries required months of intense discussion and analysis of manual systems of recordings. When the figures were first presented to the cabinet, it came as a shock that the ten poorest provinces of the country were receiving the smallest amounts of allocation." The most unusual feature of this experience is that the finance ministry went to the trouble to request this information. Faced with such paucity of data, conflict impact assessment today is roughly where environmental impact assessment was three decades ago.

In addition to equity, postwar expenditure policy must consider balances of power among and within competing parties. This requires attention not only to community-wide characteristics such as living standards and ethnicity but also to the stances of individual political leaders who often vary in their commitment to peace. Some leaders are enthusiastic about implementing peace agreements, others are lukewarm, and still others are prepared to resume war rather than make concessions for peace. Selective allocation of public spending can be one instrument to reward those who are committed to peace, penalize spoilers, and encourage vacillators to get off the fence on the side of peace implementation.[21] If instead public spending strengthens the hand of hard-liners, this can contribute to an unraveling of the peace process.

Systematic attention to this dimension of the "to whom" question is rare. One exception is the selective allocation of aid to municipalities in Bosnia and Herzegovina, taking into account the stance of local authorities regarding implementation of the Dayton Peace Agreement's key provisions. The "open cities" program of the United Nations High Commission for Refugees, for example, targeted reconstruction assistance to municipalities whose officials agreed to welcome the return of refugees and internally displaced persons. Similarly, the World Bank sought advice from the Office of the High Representative in allocating aid for rehabilitation of municipal infrastructure.[22] To date, however, such conflict sensitivity in expenditure decisions remains the exception rather than the rule.

6. Dual Public Sector or Dual Control?
External Support for Domestic Expenditure

The international community often seeks to help postwar governments to develop fiscal capacity to allocate and manage expenditure by providing technical assistance. More could be done, however, if donors were to channel a greater share of their resources through the state rather than bypassing it. This will require new strategies for combating corruption and ensuring fiduciary responsibility.

In this book, the useful role of technical assistance is illustrated by its contributions to establishing a payments system in Afghanistan, improving procurement procedures in Guatemala, and increasing transparency in public expenditure management in Uganda. These are not purely technical problems: they are political problems, too. The contrast between Afghanistan, where instituting a payments system was pursued as a high priority, and Cambodia, where the cash-based payments system remains subject to significant leakages, is instructive in this regard: lack of a reliable payments system not only harms government employees but also erodes the delivery of services and hence public perceptions as to the effectiveness and legitimacy of the state.

Beyond the "dual public sector." As on the revenue side, there is scope for donors to do more than provide technical assistance. As Ashraf Ghani and his colleagues emphasize in Chapter 6 on Afghanistan, the current practice of routing the lion's share of external assistance outside the government gives rise to a "dual public sector": an internal public sector that is funded and managed by the government and an external public sector that is funded and managed by the donors. In sheer money terms, the latter frequently dwarfs the former.

The dual public sector phenomenon has several adverse consequences. Most evident is the opportunity cost of failing to tap these resources to build state capacities to allocate and manage public expenditure. Less obvious, but no less serious, is the "crowding-out" effect as professionals are recruited into the external public sector, often at salaries that the government cannot match. The situation in Timor-Leste that Emilia Pires and Michael Francino describe in Chapter 5—where the much higher salaries paid by international agencies drew the "best skilled workers" away from the Timorese public service—is repeated again and again during postwar reconstruction.[23] Ironically, aid donors then point to lack of capable government personnel as a rationale for continuing to bypass the state. Again, the failure to route resources through the government has feedback effects on domestic revenue mobilization, insofar as the willingness of citizens to pay taxes hinges on the perception that the state delivers services in return.

The fact that the external public sector is managed by numerous agencies, each with its own priorities, poses enormous coordination problems. This also leads to the waste of scarce administrative resources, as government ministries cope with the different reporting systems of multiple funders. Last but not least, there are no institutional mechanisms that make donor agencies accountable to the local citizenry. No matter how imperfect the degree of democratic governance, the state arguably has a comparative advantage in this respect.

When pressed on this issue, donors maintain that they (and the nongovernmental organizations and private contractors on whom they often rely) do a more effective job than the government in delivering goods and services. This is not an argument that can be dismissed lightly. There undoubtedly are situations in which the short-run advantages of circumventing the state are compelling. But once we recognize that the long-run aim of aid is—or ought to be—to *build state capacities* as well as to deliver services, the argument loses at least some of its force.

Experience shows that the "short run" can last a long time. In Chapter 3, Paul Smoke and Robert R. Taliercio Jr. observe that in Cambodia, where more than a decade has elapsed since the United Nations transitional administration handed power to a new government, the donors' focus on delivering results still leads them to "bypass when possible—and 'capture' when not—the civil service" and that spending on technical assistance remains two to three times greater than the total wages paid to government civil servants. One cannot help feeling that something is wrong with this picture.

The Afghanistan Reconstruction Trust Fund (ARTF) offers an instructive model for how donors can route aid through the government—in effect, helping to internalize external resources. The ARTF, as explained in Chapter 6, is a World Bank–administered account through which donors help to fund the government's recurrent budget. The government allocates these external resources through its internal budgetary process, reinforcing the budget as the central instrument of policy. When the ministries spend the money—for example, paying teachers—an external monitoring agent appointed by the World Bank verifies that the accounting standards of the ARTF and government (which are the same) have been met and releases the funds. The ARTF thus is like a bank account with a fiduciary screen. Approximately two-thirds of the Afghan government's nonsecurity recurrent budget is now being funded by the ARTF, although this amount remains small relative to total external assistance.[24]

Channeling aid through the government in this fashion does not imply that the donors abdicate control or responsibility for how their resources are used. The ARTF does not issue blank checks. Two signatures are required to release funds, one from the government and one from the external monitoring agent.

The result is a dual-control system—a setup analogous to the dual-key system used to prevent an accidental launch of nuclear missiles.

Combating corruption. Corruption saps the delivery of public services, deters private investment, and fuels popular discontent.[25] But efforts to combat it are complicated where corruption helps to maintain political cohesion by distributing resources through informal channels. Not all corruption is equally corrupt or equally corrosive: in some cases it is driven entirely by individual greed, but in others it provides patronage resources for wider networks. An example of the latter is the use of government revenues and profits from state-sanctioned monopolies to lubricate neopatrimonial governance in the Palestinian Authority under Yasser Arafat (see Chapter 7).

Donors often adopt an "avoidance strategy" for dealing with corruption: avoid "leakages" by bypassing the government and avoid public discussion of the topic for fear of ruffling political feathers. This strategy is dysfunctional for two reasons. First, aid that is routed outside the government is insulated from neither the perception nor the reality of corruption.[26] Indeed, the lack of transparency and accountability mechanisms can fuel public perceptions that externally administered projects are even more prone to corruption than are government projects.[27]

Second, the avoidance strategy fails to harness aid to build the state's capacity to budget and manage public expenditure effectively. And just as the refusal of the donor agencies to pay taxes has a demonstration effect—sending a message to the populace of no confidence in the government—so, too, their refusal to route resources through the government sends an unmistakable signal.

An alternative strategy for addressing problems of corruption would have two prongs. The first is the use of dual-control systems, like the ARTF, to build more robust institutions for accountability and transparency along with public expenditure capacities.[28] The second is to devise transitional adjustment assistance programs for people who have been dependent on patronage networks, recognizing that corruption for this purpose differs from personal corruption. Such assistance would be analogous, in a sense, to job training programs for workers displaced by the effects of trade liberalization in industrialized countries, and—closer to home—to the Disarmament, Demobilization, and Reintegration (DDR) programs for ex-combatants that are often implemented in postwar countries.

7. Thinking About Tomorrow, Today?
Getting Serious About Fiscal Sustainability

External resources that are spent today—regardless of whether they are channeled through the state or around it—often have implications for how domestic resources must be spent tomorrow. This is true both for recurrent expenditures, such as salaries, and for capital expenditures that will require spending for operation and maintenance in future years. Hence there is a need to think about the long-term fiscal implications of current decisions.

In the aftermath of war, attention to pressing short-term needs is perfectly natural and perfectly valid. But this does not imply that the future consequences of today's decisions can or should be shunted aside for others to handle later. The long run begins in the short run. Myopia not only postpones getting serious about long-run problems but also can make them worse.

Although much can be done to enhance domestic revenue capacities (see above, "2. Priming the Pump?"), the sky is not the limit. Prudence demands recognition that budget constraints will always be a fact of life. In building new government institutions and infrastructure, this reality must be borne in mind. It would be a mistake to rely on a transitory flush of external funds to create structures that are not fiscally sustainable. The point may seem obvious, but past experience suggests that it is often ignored.

Consider, for example, security spending in Afghanistan, where the Afghan National Army has been built with large-scale funding from the US government. Security-sector expenditures in the three-year period from 2003–2004 to 2005–2006 were equivalent to 494 percent of the Afghan government's revenue, or roughly one-third of the country's GDP.[29] "Total security expenditures will exceed forecast domestic revenues for some years to come," warned a recent World Bank study (2005b, 47) that described the situation as "unaffordable and fiscally unsustainable."

As Ashraf Ghani and his colleagues remark in Chapter 6, "Even under very optimistic projections for domestic revenue, such an expenditure on security would imply a totally inadequate allocation of resources for human capital, infrastructure, and other vital functions of government." Even from a security standpoint, unsustainable expenditures are shortsighted. A well-equipped army that is not getting paid ceases to be a security force. Instead it becomes an insecurity force.

A recent operational note prepared jointly by the United Nations Development Group and the World Bank (2005, 4) drew the clear lesson from such experiences: "It is important to ensure that security issues are treated as an integral part of the national planning and budgetary process, rather than through separate fora which may lead to a lack of transparency or the taking of decisions which are fiscally unsustainable or undermine other reconstruction efforts."

The problem of unsustainable expenditure is not confined to the security sector. Salary supplements for civil servants—including "sitting fees" for attending donor-funded workshops, where "the daily rates can exceed regular monthly salaries" (Moss, Petersson, and Vande Walle 2005, 7)—likewise can create problems for fiscal sustainability. Citing studies showing that additional remuneration to civil servants in Cambodia far exceeds their regular salaries, a United Nations Development Programme study concluded that "the principal incentive to work in public employment is the prospect of access to external salary supplements" (Beresford et al. 2004, 33).

Capital investments with high operation and maintenance costs also generate fiscal burdens down the road. Rex Brynen reports in Chapter 7 that in Palestine, aid donors have often ignored the development plans of the Palestinian Authority (PA), "undercutting any PA effort to monitor the cumulative long-term costs of donor-financed investments." Again he points to the resulting distortion in incentives: the "lure of donor money" encouraged government officials to put forward projects "not because they were a real priority but because they seemed most likely to attract some external funding."

A famous example of a costly, donor-driven project with high "flagpole value" but problematic fiscal implications is the Gaza hospital financed by the European Union (Brynen 2000b, 196–197). "Donor-driven investments in public hospitals are sometimes referred to as 'Trojan horses,'" noted a World Bank report (2005b, 52), "because of their large operating costs which crowd resources out of priority areas such as the basic package of health services."

Closely related to this problem is the bias of many aid-funded projects in favor of excessive reliance on imports. In deciding on the extent to which the goods and services purchased for relief, recovery, and reconstruction should be imported, as opposed to being procured locally, donors face another tension between short-run expediency and long-run capacity building—the capacity in this case being in the private sector. Again there are undoubtedly cases where the former trumps the latter: for example, where local sourcing would require large investments with long gestation periods. But there are also cases where local procurement could do more to stimulate economic recovery, and perhaps save money in the process.[30]

To cite an example of the pervasive bias against local suppliers, during the United Nations Transitional Administration in Timor-Leste, some quarter of a million desks and chairs for local schools were purchased with money from the World Bank–administered Trust Fund for Timor-Leste. At the time, some Timorese officials suggested that some of these be procured locally to spur the growth of small and medium-sized woodworking enterprises. According to Emilia Pires and Michael Francino in Chapter 5, the international officials rejected this on the grounds that local procurement would be too slow. This was not a life-or-death case of emergency food supplies in which time was of the essence; the goods in question were school furniture.[31]

The interwoven challenges of building an effective state, a robust economy, and a durable peace all require thinking about tomorrow, today. Postwar inflows of external assistance cannot be sustained indefinitely. The success of this aid ultimately will rest on whether the structures built with it can be sustained without it.

8. Odious Debts? Facing War's Financial Legacy

Large external debts are often among the baneful legacies inherited by a postwar government. These debts impede the war-to-peace transition in two ways. First, debt-service payments absorb scarce resources that otherwise could be allocated to peacebuilding expenditures. Second, the overhang of accumulated debt deters investment and new lending to the country.

The original loans often were of dubious benefit to the country's people. Indeed, insofar as they financed predatory and oppressive regimes, some of the loans not only failed to benefit the majority of the populace but may even have actively harmed them.

To cite a stark example, after the fall of the Taliban regime the Russian government claimed that the new Afghan government owed it US$10 billion, most of it for aid provided in the 1980s when the Soviet army was fighting in Afghanistan. The Karzai administration refused to accept this obligation, arguing that "the Soviet Union spent the money for its own political and strategic purposes, not to benefit the Afghan people."[32] This argument echoed the stance taken a century earlier by the US commissioners at the Paris peace conference after the Spanish-American War. At issue were the external debts incurred by Cuba under Spanish colonial rule and the question of whether these would be passed to the new Cuban government. The United States repudiated these debts on the grounds that the purpose of the loans had been not to benefit the Cuban people but rather to finance "the continuous effort to put down a people struggling for freedom from the Spanish rule."[33] In international law, this became known as the doctrine of odious debt.[34]

The Russian claims in Afghanistan might be seen as lying at one end of a legitimacy-illegitimacy spectrum, but the legitimacy of many other postbellum debts can be questioned, too. Democratic Republic of Congo, for example, inherited a US$12 billion external debt from the Mobutu regime (Ndikumana and Boyce 1998). Much of this arguably could qualify as odious debt, in that the Congolese people did not benefit and that the creditors knew or should have known that this would be the case. Similar questions can be raised about the wartime debts incurred by the Angolan government, some of them backed by liens on that country's future oil revenues (Boyce 2005).

Yet the principle that external debts are sacrosanct, unless forgiven by the creditors, remains official doctrine today. In the case of the IMF and World Bank, for whom debt write-offs until recently have been taboo, this poses a stumbling block: lending to postwar governments cannot begin until past debt arrears have been cleared. This is usually accomplished by means of bridge loans from bilateral donors, which are used to clear the arrears, opening the door to new loans from the Bank and the IMF that in turn are used to repay the bridge loans.[35] By this stratagem, debts contracted by the ancien régime are recycled as fresh debts of the postwar government.

Today there is renewed interest in the doctrine of odious debt. One recent proposal has been to empower an international body—such as the UN Security Council or an independent commission of jurists—to declare governments to be illegitimate, in which case subsequent loans to such governments would be designated as odious (Kremer and Jayachandran 2003). This might curb lending to noxious regimes in the future, but it would not address the legacy of odious debts created by lending in the past.

The case of Iraq has spotlighted the latter issue. Soon after the US-led invasion that toppled Saddam Hussein's regime, US Treasury Secretary John Snow declared, "Certainly the people of Iraq shouldn't be saddled with those debts incurred through the regime of the dictator who's now gone."[36] In a similar vein, two former US Treasury officials proposed the establishment of an international debt commission for Iraq that would examine all outstanding claims and disallow debt that was used for state security or military aggression (Mulford and Monderer 2003).[37]

Such ad hoc measures, devised on a country-by-country basis, may be better than nothing. A systematic approach to the problem of odious debt, however, could be implemented by establishing an international institution empowered to adjudicate questions of debt legitimacy in postwar countries. The Norwegian government's call in 2005 for the creation of "an international debt settlement court" to hear matters concerning illegitimate debt is a step in this direction.[38] In addition to easing debt-service burdens, an institution with a mandate to review debt claims in postwar countries could function as a financial "truth commission," analogous to truth commissions that aid the reconciliation process by documenting responsibility for crimes of violence. The new Peacebuilding Commission of the United Nations, established at the request of the September 2005 World Summit, might be an appropriate forum to launch such an initiative.[39]

Apart from its benefits to the public purse in postwar countries, such an institution could have a salutary effect on the functioning of international credit markets in the future.[40] The risk that debts could be declared odious would curb the moral hazard problem that arises when creditors believe that they are insured against the risk of debt repudiation, diluting their incentives to guard against it. The existence of an international debt adjudication body would encourage creditors to exercise due diligence in lending decisions, helping to ensure that future loans are used for bona fide public purposes.

Getting Priorities Right

These themes have far-reaching implications for policymaking by governments and international agencies engaged in the interwoven tasks of postwar peacebuilding, statebuilding, and economic development. In the arena of public finance, there is a need for policy reforms aligned to the dynamics of war-to-peace transitions. These include paying more serious attention to distributional impacts on both the revenue and expenditure sides of fiscal policy, weighing potential trade-offs between macroeconomic stability and political stability in setting budget-deficit and aid-intensity targets, and devising innovative strategies to address postwar legacies of external debts.

In the arenas of peace implementation and economic development, there is a need for policy reforms aligned to the public finance requirements of statebuilding. These include devising ways to tap postwar aid inflows so as to prime the pump of domestic revenue collection, moving from the "dual public sector" toward dual control of aid-financed expenditures, and rethinking spending and procurement practices in light of the long-term goals of fiscal sustainability and economic recovery.

Policy Coherence

These reforms would foster greater policy coherence among the many actors engaged in postwar peacebuilding, statebuilding, and development activities. Coherence requires coordination among multiple agencies and institutions with the aim of fostering complementarities rather than duplicating efforts or working at cross-purposes. This is no small task. Although calls for better coordination have become so frequent as to be almost a platitude, efforts to achieve it run up against the familiar obstacles of bureaucratic rivalries and contests for resources.

Coherence also requires agreement on common goals. Getting priorities right presupposes agreement on ends of policy as well as coordination of the means. Policy coherence at this deeper level poses profound challenges, too.

Divergences in policy goals among and within institutions often play out behind the scenes, rather than being debated openly. Sometimes differences in goals are simply ignored, the implicit assumption being that they are complementary—in which case goal coherence is not really a problem. When problems caused by contradictory goals do get raised, they are often blamed entirely on others, and fail to provoke self-appraisal—in which case goal coherence becomes a euphemism for asserting the primacy of one's own agenda.

Policy incoherence is not all bad. Diverse viewpoints within institutions, and diverse mandates across institutions, ensure that a variety of goals enters into the policy decisions. This guards against narrow sorts of coherence that lose sight of important values and trade-offs. But frank discussion of the tensions among policy goals would help clarify these trade-offs and could contribute to more effective policies.

Security and Development

Two central goals in much postwar policy discourse are security and development. The relation between these goals has been a focus of renewed attention in the wake of the September 2001 attacks in New York and Washington, D.C., but the topic has a long history. In Robert McNamara's book *The Essence of Security,* published in the same year that he left the helm of the US Department of Defense to become president of the World Bank, he argued that development is crucial for security. "In a modernizing society security means development," he wrote. "Without internal development of at least a minimal degree, order and stability are impossible. They are impossible because human nature cannot be frustrated indefinitely" (1968, 149).

Yet an operational note on policies in what are now termed "fragile states," prepared jointly by the United Nations Development Group and the World Bank, pointed out that a single-minded focus on economic development "has in cases led to serious shortfalls in funding for critical interventions in the political and security spheres, interventions that are critical to creating an environment for economic and social programs to deliver benefits for the population." Moreover, the UN and the Bank observe that not all development policies are equally supportive of security: "Well designed economic and social programs can contribute to political stabilization; ill-timed or badly targeted programs can undermine it (United Nations Development Group and World Bank 2005, 4)."[41]

Although statebuilding can foster both security and development in the long run, the case studies presented in this book point to possible tensions between these goals in the short run. In Palestine, for example, Brynen depicts the contradiction between a patronage-based political order and the need for an economic environment conducive to investment and growth. In Cambodia, Smoke and Taliercio similarly point to the divergence between the "peace and security" approach to public finance, which sees the existing patronage system as necessary for political stability, and the "developmental" approach, which advocates reform in the name of economic growth and poverty reduction. In Afghanistan, as noted above, we find a tension between fiscally unsustainable security expenditures and long-term development needs.

On the surface, these examples appear to pit short-run expediency against longer-run goals. But there are deeper sources of tension that can be traced to competing visions of security and development. Is security merely the absence of violent conflict—what is sometimes called "negative peace"? Or is it the absence of social tensions that threaten to precipitate conflict—sometimes called "positive peace"? The former can be achieved, at least for a time, by means of repression and intimidation; the latter requires political inclusion and shared perceptions of justice. Similar questions can be asked about development: is this defined simply in terms of economic growth, or to qualify as genuine development must this growth be economically inclusive?

In the international community, a further source of tension arises from the differences between the priorities of donor governments and those of the people on the receiving end of aid. When international actors intervene in the name of security, whose security is paramount—the human security of the populace, the national security of the government, or the security concerns of outsiders?[42] Is development success measured in terms of local livelihoods or of benefits to external commercial interests? When priorities do not overlap neatly, what are the overriding objectives of donor governments? During the Cold War, UN Secretary-General Kofi Annan recalled, "corruption and waste—indeed, results of any kind—were secondary to what donor countries wanted most, namely political allegiance" (2002, 8). It would be comforting, but naive, to assume that with the end of the Cold War this logic has been consigned to history's dustbin.

The issues of the relationship between peace and the public purse with which this book has grappled are situated within this larger context. Once we recognize potential divergence among goals, however, getting priorities right is no longer only a technical challenge. It is a political challenge, too, forcing us to make choices about fundamental values and the kind of world in which we want to live.

Our premise is that in war-torn societies, building a durable peace should be a top priority for public policy—indeed, *the* top priority. Both statebuilding and economic development are central to this goal. We have pointed to ways that peacebuilding operations could support these processes more effectively. At the same time, we have pointed to ways that statebuilding and development strategies could be reframed with the objective of peacebuilding more firmly in mind. In war-torn societies, the soundness of public finance policies must be assessed in terms of their effects on the dynamics of violent conflict. Not all policy conflicts can or should be resolved. But if peace is the ultimate public good, policies must cohere around this goal.

Notes

1. Tanzi and Zee (2000, 8) reported that the average for developing countries as a whole was about 18 percent of GDP in the 1980s and 1990s.

2. Gupta et al. (2004) found a negative relationship between government revenue and conflict in a sample of low- and middle-income countries. Addison, Chowdhury, and Murshed (2004) reported that the intensity of conflict, as well as its presence, negatively affected the tax/GDP ratio.

3. See, for example, World Bank (2002a); Department for International Development (2002); US Agency for International Development, Office of Conflict Management and Mitigation (2005); and Swedish International Development Agency (2006). For an example of an assessment, see Goodhand (2001).

4. For a review of the rather sparse literature on the distributional impacts of taxation in developing countries, see Gemmell and Morrissey (2005).

5. Examining evidence from a large sample of developing countries, Gupta et al. (2003, 2) found that grant aid, in particular, tended to lower revenue efforts; in countries with high levels of corruption, "the decline in revenues completely offsets the increase in grants."

6. Thus at the 1998 meeting of the Consultative Group for Guatemala, the IMF representative urged the government to "resist pressures to increase import duties or delay the scheduled reduction in customs tariffs," arguing that "these actions will have adverse effects on output growth" (quoted in Boyce 2002, 47).

7. For a theoretical critique, see Emran and Stiglitz (2005). For empirical evidence, see Khattry and Rao (2002) and Baunsgaard and Keen (2005).

8. An IMF study (Heller 2005, 4, 21) cited disincentives to mobilize domestic resources as a "moral hazard" of external aid flows, observing that "some African countries with among the highest ratios of aid to GDP are also those that have stubbornly low tax ratios."

9. Boyce (2002, 41–42). Camdessus warned that without a significant increase in the tax effort, Guatemala could not expect to receive substantial international aid, and noted that the IMF would have preferred an even more ambitious revenue target. See also Jonas (2000, 185–186).

10. Thus among dozens of examples of EU budget-support conditionality listed in a report by the European Commission (2005), the Mozambique case is the sole example of revenue-side conditionality.

11. "The Afghanistan Compact," London Conference on Afghanistan, January 31–February 1, 2006, 12. Available at http://www.unama-afg.org/news/_londonConf/_docs/06jan30-AfghanistanCompact-Final.pdf.

12. For further discussion of the Afghan case, see Sedra and Middlebrook (2005) and Ahmad (2006).

13. In the case of United Nations employees, a "staff assessment" is deducted from gross salaries. This is credited to a Tax Equalization Fund, most of which is used as an offset against member states' assessments for the UN budget; in the few cases of member states that tax the incomes of their nationals working for the UN, the fund is used to reimburse income tax payments to the staff member.

14. Emilia Pires and Michael Francino give this example in Chapter 5 from the period of the United Nations Transitional Administration in Timor-Leste (UNTAET): "There was a little shop within UNTAET grounds that sold alcohol and other goods very cheaply to the international staff. These same goods were often bought and then sold outside at a profit, thus creating black market activities."

15. "The neoliberal recommendation to national policymakers is that they should insist on maintaining inflation rates of 3–5 percent," wrote McKinley (2006, 352), "even though there is little empirical evidence to suggest that inflation rates above that level, or even above 10 percent, have an adverse effect on growth." For discussion of alternatives to inflation targeting, based on "real-economy" targets such as employment, see Epstein (2005).

16. See also Bundred and Levitt (2000) and Dovlo (2003).

17. In addition, as Heller (2005, 7) noted, the exchange-rate impact of aid can be lessened if it is "used to remove key bottlenecks to improved productivity and productive capacity in the nontradable goods sector." See also Bevan (2005, 11–12).

18. The IMF study (2005b, 49) attributed excessively restrictive policies on aid absorption to central bank officials, going so far as to suggest that "there is a potential cost to central bank independence in the context of aid-dependent low-income countries."

19. For discussion, see Eifert and Gelb (2005, 27–28).

20. See Note 2.

21. For a discussion of spoilers—including the distinction between limited and greedy spoilers, who are responsive to changing incentives, and total spoilers, who are not—see Stedman (1997, 2002).

22. See Boyce (2002, 16–19) and Boyce and Pastor (1998).

23. In the case of Rwanda, for example, Obidegwu (2003, 20) observed that "with the flood of international NGOs, relief and development agencies into Rwanda after the genocide, the government service could not compete for the few qualified people available." In the case of Afghanistan, Ghani, Lockhart, and Carnahan (2005a, 10) contrasted the salaries of US$1,000 per month paid by donor agencies to the US$50 per month paid by the government and remarked: "Unsurprisingly, there has been a brain drain from the managerial tier of the government to menial positions in the aid system. The people might have judged it to be fair had the disparity in wages resulted from a competitive market; however, the problem is that both bureaucracies are funded from the resources of the aid system and the rules for remuneration are arrived at by bureaucratic fiat rather than by open processes of competition."

24. For details on the ARTF, see Scanteam, "Assessment, Afghanistan Reconstruction Trust Fund: Final Report," Oslo, March 2005. Available at http://siteresources .worldbank.org/INTAFGHANISTAN/Resources/ARTFEvaluationFinalReport.pdf.

25. For a review of the impacts of corruption, see Rose-Ackerman (1999).

26. In the program of the USAID for building schools and health clinics in Afghanistan, for example, "employees of a Maryland-based nonprofit relief agency hired to monitor construction quality demanded a $50,000 payoff from Afghan builders—a scene captured in a clandestine videotape obtained by *The Washington Post*" (Stephens and Ottaway 2005).

27. In Afghanistan, the former planning minister "has become one of the most popular politicians in the country by campaigning against NGOs [nongovernmental organizations], which he has said are more dangerous than al-Qaeda" (Rubin 2005, 101).

28. In exceptional circumstances, dual-control systems can also be applied to domestic revenues (for discussion, see Le Billon 2003). An example is the Governance and Economic Management Assistance Program (GEMAP) instituted in postwar Liberia in 2005.

29. World Bank (2005b, 42). The security-sector expenditures figure excludes counternarcotics expenditures, which would push the ratio closer to 600 percent.

30. The supposed efficiency advantages of foreign sourcing can be illusory. In Afghanistan, for example, where USAID funds for rebuilding schools and health clinics were routed through a New Jersey–based private contractor, press reports revealed inordinate delays, shoddy construction, and "extraordinary costs," in the words of a USAID official (Stephens and Ottaway 2005; see also Rohde and Gall 2005).

31. For discussion of the scope for greater local procurement in postconflict operations, see also Carnahan, Gilmore, and Rahman (2005).

32. Ibrahimi and Saeed (2005). As of mid-2006, the Paris Club was engaged in negotiations for a write-off of the Russian debt in the context of the Heavily Indebted Poor Countries (HIPC) process (Paris Club 2006).

33. Quoted in O'Connell (1967, 460).

34. For discussion, see Hoeflich (1982); Centre for International Sustainable Development Law (2003); and Hanlon (2006).

35. For example, in December 1995 the IMF lent US$45 million to Bosnia—the first loan issued under the fund's newly created emergency credit window for postconflict countries. The IMF heralded this loan as "a new beginning," but its purpose was simply to allow the Bosnian government to repay a bridge loan from the Dutch government, which in turn was used to repay Bosnia's assessed share of the former Yugoslavia's arrears to the IMF. Old Yugoslavian debt was thereby transformed into new Bosnian debt. Similarly, in 2002 the IMF lent US$543 million to DRC, US$522 million of which was used to repay bridge loans from the governments of Belgium,

France, Sweden, and South Africa that had been used to clear IMF debt contracted under Mobutu (International Monetary Fund, "IMF Approves US$750 Million PRGF Arrangement for the Democratic Republic of the Congo," press release no. 02/27, June 13, 2002. Available at http://www.imf.org/external/np/sec/pr/2002/pr0227.htm). For further discussion of arrears clearance operations, see Chapter 9.

36. Quoted in Beattie (2003).

37. The Paris Club of official creditors agreed to write off 80 percent of US$39 billion in Saddam-era debts, not on the basis of a determination of which debts were legitimate but rather on the basis of debt sustainability calculations by the IMF. As of mid-2006, negotiations were continuing on other components of Iraq's US$120 billion in external debts (Chung 2005).

38. See the Soria Moria Declaration on International Policy, October 2005. Available at http://www.dna.no/index.gan?id=47619&subid=0.

39. "2005 World Summit Outcome," September 15, 2005, pars. 97–105. Available at http://www.un.org/summit2005/documents.html.

40. For discussion, see Buckley (2002) and Boyce and Ndikumana (2005).

41. In a similar vein, Smith (2004, 44) warned, "It is, unfortunately, likely that where development cooperation is the default conceptual and planning mode, the specifics of peacebuilding—the war-defined context—will slip out of focus. The results of that could be serious."

42. For an account of the emergence of the concept of "human security" in international relations, see MacFarlane and Khong (2006).

Acronyms

ABC	Abstinence, Be faithful, and use Condom
ACH	Automated Clearing House network
ADB	Asian Development Bank
ADD	Accelerated District Development
AIDS	acquired immunodeficiency syndrome
AMF	Afghan militia forces
APODETI	Timorese Popular Democratic Association
ARG	Afghanistan Reconstruction Group
ARTF	Afghanistan Reconstruction Trust Fund
ASDT	Timorese Association of Social Democrats
AWCC	Afghan Wireless Communication Company
BH	Republic of Bosnia and Herzegovina
BHD	Bosnia and Herzegovina dinar
BOT	Build-Operate-Transfer
BPK	Banking and Payment Authority of Kosovo
CA	Constituent Assembly
CABEI	Central American Bank for Economic Integration
CAP	Consolidated Inter-Agency Appeal
CAR	Council for Administrative Reform
CARERE	Cambodia Resettlement and Reintegration
CBBH	Central Bank of Bosnia and Herzegovina
CC	Constitutional Court
CDC	Commune Development Committee
CFA	Central Fiscal Authority
CFAA	Country Financial Accountability Assessment
CFET	Consolidated Fund for East Timor
CNRM	National Council of Maubere Resistance
CNRT	National Council of Timorese Resistance

CoM	Council of Ministers
CPP	Cambodia People's Party
CS	commune and sangkat
CSB	combined sources budget
CTL	commercial tax levy
DAB	Da Afghanistan Bank
DAC	Development Assistance Committee [of OECD]
DDR	Disarmament, Demobilization, and Reintegration [program]
DfID	Department for International Development
DM	German mark
DMFAS	Debt Management and Financial Analysis System
DRC	Democratic Republic of Congo
DR-CAFTA	Dominican Republic and Central American Free Trade Agreement
ENCOVI	First National Survey of Living Conditions
ENIGFAM	Survey of Family Income and Expenditure
ETTA	East Timor Transition Administration
EU	European Union
FAD	Fiscal Affairs Division [of IMF]
FALINTIL	Armed Forces for the National Liberation of Timor-Leste
FBC	Finance and Banking Committee
FDI	foreign direct investment
F-FDTL	FALINTIL–Timor-Leste Defense Force
FRELIMO	Front for the Liberation of Mozambique
FRETILIN	Revolutionary Front for the Liberation of East Timor
FRY	Federal Republic of Yugoslavia
FTA	free trade agreement
FTP	First Tranche Petroleum
FUNCINPEC	United National Front for an Independent, Neutral, Peaceful, and Cooperative Cambodia
FY	fiscal year
G7	Group of Seven
GCF	gross capital formation
GDP	gross domestic product
GEMAP	Governance and Economic Management Assistance Program
GNI	gross national income
GTZ	German Technical Assistance
HDI	human development index
HIPC	Heavily Indebted Poor Countries
HIV	human immunodeficiency virus
HRMIS	Human Resource Management Information System
HSMF	Holy Spirit Mobile Forces
IADB	Inter-American Development Bank

IDA	International Development Association
IDPs	internally displaced persons
IEMA	Tax on Mercantile and Farm Enterprises
IFI	international financial institutions
IMF	International Monetary Fund
ISAF	International Security Assistance Force
JAM	Joint Assessment Mission
KKN	corruption, collusion, and nepotism
KLA	Kosovo Liberation Army
KM	convertible markka
LDF	Local Development Fund
LDK	League for a Democratic Kosovo
LICs	low-income countries
LOTFA	Law and Order Trust Fund
LRA	Lord's Resistance Army
MBPI	Merit-Based Pay Initiative
MDF	Multilateral Debt Fund
MEF	Ministry of Economy and Finance
MIGA	Multilateral Investment Guarantee Agency
MINFIN	Ministry of Finance
MINUGUA	United Nations Verification Mission in Guatemala
MOI	Ministry of Interior
MOF	Ministry of Finance
MPF	Ministry of Planning and Finance
MTEF	Medium Term Expenditure Framework
NAA	National Audit Authority
NATO	North Atlantic Treaty Organization
NBBH	National Bank of Bosnia and Herzegovina
NBK	National Bank of Kosovo
NBRS	National Bank of Republika Srpska
NBY	National Bank of Yugoslavia
NC	National Council
NCC	National Consultative Council
NDP	National Development Plan
NDPEAC	National Directorate for Planning and External Assistance Co-ordination
NGO	nongovernmental organization
NPDA	National Planning and Development Agency
NRA	National Resistance Army
NRM	National Resistance Movement
OAS	Organization of American States
OCG	Comptroller General's Office
OCHA	Office of Co-ordination of Humanitarian Assistance

ODA	Overseas Development Administration
OECD	Organization for Economic Cooperation and Development
OHR	Office of the High Representative
OLAF	European Anti-Fraud Office
OPIC	Overseas Private Investment Corporation
PA	Palestinian Authority
PAF	Poverty Action Fund
PAP	Priority Action Program
PAYE	pay as you earn
PCSC	Palestinian Commercial Services Company
PDP	Palestinian Development Plan
PDP	Provincial Development Plan
PEAP	Poverty Eradication Action Plan
PER	Public Expenditure Review
PFM	public financial management
PFMRP	Public Financial Management Reform Program
PIDE	International and State Defense Police
PIF	Provincial Investment Fund
PKF	peacekeeping forces
PLC	Palestinian Legislative Council
PLO	Palestine Liberation Organization
PM	provinces and municipalities
PNTL	Timor-Leste National Police Force
PPG	public and publicly guaranteed
PPP	purchasing power parity
PRDC	Provincial Rural Development Committee
PRGF	Poverty Reduction and Growth Facility
PRSP	Poverty Reduction Strategy Paper
PRT	Provincial Reconstruction Team
Quip	Quick Impact Project
RGC	Royal Government of Cambodia
RS	Republika Srpska
RTGS	Real Time Gross Settlement
SAT	Superintendence of Tax Administration
SDK	Social Accounting Service
SDKK	Payment Bureau of Kosovo
SEGEPLAN	Secretariat of Planning
SIAF	Integrated Financial Administration and Control System
SIP	Sector Investment Program
SME	small and medium enterprises
SNEC	Supreme National Economic Council
SPLA	Sudan People's Liberation Army
SPLM	Sudan People's Liberation Movement

SPP	Serbian Payment Bureau
SRSG	Special Representative of Secretary-General
SSA	sub-Saharan Africa
SSB	Serb State Bank
SWG	sector working group
SWIFT	Society for Worldwide Interbank Financial Telecommunications
TA	technical assistance
TFET	Trust Fund for East Timor
TI	Transparency International
UDT	Timorese Democratic Union
UNAMET	United Nations Mission in East Timor
UNCTAD	United Nations Conference on Trade and Development
UNDP	United Nations Development Programme
UNICEF	United Nations Children's Fund
UNLA	Ugandan National Liberation Army
UNLF	Uganda National Liberation Front
UNMIK	United Nations Interim Administration Mission in Kosovo
UNMISET	United Nations Mission of Support for East Timor
UNPOL	UN Police
UNRWA	United Nations Relief and Works Agency
UNTAC	United Nations Transitional Authority in Cambodia
UNTAET	United Nations Transitional Administration in East Timor
UPDA	Uganda People's Defense Army
UPDF	Uganda People's Defense Force
UPE	universal primary education
URA	Uganda Revenue Authority
URNG	Guatemala National Revolutionary Unity
USAID	US Agency for International Development
VAP	Veteran Assistance Program
VAT	value-added tax
WB	World Bank
WBG	West Bank and Gaza
WFP	World Food Program
WTO	World Trade Organization
YUD	Yugoslav dinar
ZAP	Institute for Payments Transactions
ZPP	Institute for Payments Transactions

Bibliography

Ablo, Emmanuel, and Ritva Reinikka (1998). "Do Budgets Really Matter? Evidence from Public Spending on Education and Health in Uganda." World Bank, Policy Research Working Paper no. 1926, Washington, DC.

Abrams, Richard K. (1995). "The Design and Printing of Bank Notes: Considerations When Introducing a New Currency." IMF Working Paper 95/26, Washington, DC.

Abrams, Richard K., and Hernán Cortés-Douglas (1993). "Introduction of a New National Currency: Policy, Institutional, and Technical Issues." IMF Working Paper 93/49, Washington, DC.

Action for Development of Local Communities (2000). "Research and Workshop Report on Feasible, Participatory, Peaceful, and Sustainable Disarmament of the Karamojong." Available at http://www.small-arms.co.za/workshops/.

Addison, Tony, Abdur R. Chowdhury, and S. Mansoob Murshed (2004). "The Fiscal Dimensions of Conflict and Reconstruction." In *Fiscal Policy for Development: Poverty, Reconstruction, and Growth,* ed. Tony Addison and Alan Roe. Basingstoke, UK: Palgrave Macmillan, 260–273.

Addison, Tony, and Clara de Sousa (1999). "Economic Reform and Economic Reconstruction." In *Mozambique—Evaluating Economic Liberalization*, ed. M. McGillivray and O. Morrissey. Basingstoke, UK: Macmillan, 163–185.

Addison, Tony, Henrik Hansen, and Finn Tarp, eds. (2004). *Debt Relief for Poor Countries.* Houndmills, UK: Palgrave Macmillan.

Addison, Tony, and Mansoob S. Murshed (2003). "Debt Relief and Civil War." *Journal of Peace Research* 40, no. 2: 159–176.

Afghanistan Research and Evaluation Unit [AREU] and World Bank (2004). *Guide to Government in Afghanistan.* Kabul: AREU.

Agencia Geral do Ultramar (1974). *Timor: Pequeña Monografia.* Lisbon: Portuguese Government, Agencia Geral do Ultramar.

Agha, Hussein, and Robert Malley (2001). "Camp David: The Tragedy of Errors." *New York Review of Books* 48, no. 13, August 9.

———(2002). "Camp David and After: An Exchange (2. A Reply to Ehud Barak)." *New York Review of Books*, June 13.

Ahmad, Sardar (2006). "Poverty, Drugs, and Corruption 'Fueling Afghan Insurgency,'" Agence France-Presse, February 12.

Aldeia, Alves F. (1973). *Na Hora do Arrangue.* Lisbon: Agencia Geral do Ultramar.

Annan, Kofi (2002). "Help by Rewarding Good Governance." *International Herald Tribune,* March 20, p. 8.

Annual Financial Report and Accounts for Timor Leste (2001–2004). Dili: Democratic Government of Timor-Leste Ministry of Planning and Finance, Treasury Division.

Appleton, Simon (2001). "Education, Incomes, and Poverty in Uganda in the 1990s." Centre for Research in Economic Development and International Trade Research Paper no. 01/22, Nottingham, UK (December).

———(2003). "Regional or National Poverty Lines? The Case of Uganda in the 1990s." *Journal of African Economies* 12, no. 4: 598–624.

"Arafat's Billions" (2003). *Sixty Minutes,* CBS, November 9. Available at http://www.cbsnews.com/stories/2003/11/07/60minutes/main582487.shtml.

Arslanalp, Serkan, and Peter Blair Henry (2004). "Helping the Poor to Help Themselves: Debt Relief or Aid." National Bureau of Economic Research Working Papers, vol. 10230, Cambridge, MA.

Ascher, W. (2002). *Why Governments Waste Natural Resources.* Baltimore, MD: Johns Hopkins University Press.

Asian Network for Free Elections (2002). "Final Statement on Cambodia Commune Council Elections." Available at http://www.forumasia.org/anfrel/news/020220finalcambodia.html.

Atingi-Ego, Michael, and Rachel Kaggwa Sebudde (2004). "Uganda's Equilibrium Real Exchange Rate and Its Implications for Non-traditional Export Performance." AERC Research Paper 140, Nairobi, Kenya.

Ayoki, Milton, Marios Obwana, and Moses Ogwapus (2005). "Tax Reforms and Domestic Revenue Mobilization in Uganda." Study prepared for the project "Macroeconomic Policy Challenges of Low Income Countries," sponsored by Global Development Network. Mimeographed, Institute of Policy Research and Analysis, Nairobi, Kenya.

Barnett, Michael, Hunjoon Kim, Madalene O'Donnell, and Laura Sitea (2007). "Peacebuilding: What Is in a Name?" *Global Governance* 13, no. 1 (January–March): 35–58.

Barungi, B., and Michael Atingi (2000). "Growth and Foreign Debt: The Ugandan Experience." In *External Debt and Capital Flight in Sub-Saharan Africa,* ed. S. Ibi Ajayi and Mohsin S. Khan. Washington, DC: International Monetary Fund, 93–127.

Bategeka, Lawrence (2004). "The Budget Process and Economic Governance in Uganda." Paper submitted to Southern and Eastern Africa Policy Research Network (SEAPREN), June.

Bategeka, Lawrence, Milton Ayoki, and Ashie Mukungu (2004). "Financing Primary Education for All: Uganda." Mimeographed, Economic Policy Research Centre, Kampala.

Baunsgaard, Thomas, and Michael Keen (2005). "Tax Revenue and (or?) Trade Liberalization." IMF Working Paper 05/112, June, Washington, DC. Available at http://www.imf.org/external/pubs/ft/wp/2005/wp05112.pdf.

Beattie, Alan (2003). "US in Push for Iraqi Debt Relief." *Financial Times* (London), April 11.

Bennet, James (2003). "The Radical Bean Counter." *New York Times,* May 25.

Beresford, Melanie, Nguon Sokha, Rathin Roy, Sau Sisovanna, and Ceema Namazie (2004). "The Macroeconomics of Poverty Reduction: The Case Study of Cambodia." New York: UNDP Asia-Pacific Regional Programme on Macroeconomics of Poverty Reduction.

Bevan, David L. (2005). "An Analytical Overview of Aid Absorption: Recognizing and Avoiding Macroeconomic Hazards." Paper presented at the Seminar on Foreign

Aid and Macroeconomic Management, Maputo, Mozambique, March. Available at http://www.imf.org/external/np/seminars/eng/2005/famm/pdf/bevan.pdf.

Biddulph, R., and C. Vanna (1997). *Independent Monitoring and Evaluation of the Seila Local Planning Process: Final Report.* Phnom Penh, Cambodia: UNDP-CARERE.

Birdsall, Nancy, and Stijn Claessens (2003). "Policy Selectivity Forgone: Debt and Donor Behaviour in Africa." *World Bank Economic Review* 17, no. 3.

Blunt, M., and M. Turner (2005). "Decentralization, Democracy, and Development in a Post-Conflict Society: Commune Councils in Cambodia." *Public Administration and Development* 25, no. 1: 77–85.

Boyce, James K. (2002). *Investing in Peace: Aid and Conditionality After Civil Wars.* Oxford: Oxford University Press.

———(2005). "Development Assistance, Conditionality, and War Economies." In *Profiting from Peace: Managing the Resource Dimensions of Civil War,* ed. Karen Ballentine and Heiko Nitzsche. Boulder, CO: Lynne Rienner Publishers, 287–314.

Boyce, James K., and Léonce Ndikumana (2005). "Africa's Debt: Who Owes Whom?" In *Capital Flight and Capital Controls in Developing Countries,* ed. Gerald A. Epstein. Northampton, MA: Edward Elgar, 334–340.

Boyce, James K., and Manuel Pastor Jr. (1998). "Aid for Peace: Can International Financial Institutions Help Prevent Conflict?" *World Policy Journal* 15, no. 2: 42–49.

Brown, F., and D. Timberman, eds. (1998). *Cambodia and the International Community: The Quest for Peace, Development, and Democracy.* New York: The Asia Society.

Brynen, Rex (1995). "The Neopatrimonial Dimension of Palestinian Politics." *Journal of Palestine Studies* 25, no. 1 (Autumn): 26–36.

———(2000a). "The Future of UNRWA: An Agenda for Policy Research." PRRN/IDRC/RIIA *Workshop on the Future of UNRWA,* February. Available at http://www.arts.mcgill.ca/mepp/new_prrn/research/papers/brynen_000219.htm.

———(2000b). *A Very Political Economy: Peacebuilding and Foreign Aid in the West Bank and Gaza.* Washington, DC: United States Institute of Peace Press.

———(2005). "Donor Aid to Palestine: Attitudes, Incentives, Patronage, and Peace." In *Aid, Diplomacy, and Facts on the Ground: The Case of Palestine,* ed. Michael Keating, Anne Le More, and Robert Lowe. London: Royal Institute of International Affairs; Washington, DC: Brookings Institution Press, 129–142.

Buckley, Ross P. (2002). "The Rich Borrow and the Poor Repay: The Fatal Flaw in International Finance." *World Policy Journal* 19, no. 4: 59–64.

Bundred, Peter E., and Cheryl Levitt (2000). "Medical Migration: Who Are the Real Losers?" *The Lancet* 356: 245–246.

Byrnes, Rita M., ed. (1992). *Uganda: A Country Study.* Washington, DC: Federal Research Division, Library of Congress.

Calcott, Gary (2004). *Revenue Service in Timor-Leste—A Strategy for Building the Foundation of Governance for Peace and Stability.* Dili, Timor-Leste: Public Information Office of UNMISET.

Call, Charles T., ed. (forthcoming). *Building States to Build Peace.* Boulder, CO: Lynne Rienner Publishers.

Cambodian Institute for Cooperation and Peace (2004). "Governance in Post-Conflict Situations: The Case of Cambodia." Bergen, Norway: Chr. Michelsen Institute.

Carnahan, Michael, William Durch, and Scott Gilmore (2006). *The Economic Impact of Peacekeeping: Final Report.* New York: UN Department of Peace Keeping Op-

erations, Best Practices Unit. Available at http://pbpu.unlb.org/pbpu/library/EIP_
FINAL_Report_March20_2006doc.pdf.

Carnahan, Michael, Scott Gilmore, and Monika Rahman (2005). *Economic Impact of
Peacekeeping: Interim Report, Phase I.* New York: United Nations Department of
Peacekeeping Operations, Best Practices Unit. Available at http://www.peace
dividendtrust.org/EIPdata/pdf%20downloads/EIP%20Interim%20Report.pdf.

Cely, Nathalie, Rossana Mostajo, and Peter Gregory (2003). "Guatemala: Hacia un
gasto social más eficiente, equitativo y transparente. Retos y recomendaciones."
Association for Research and Social Studies (ASIES), Guatemala City.

Centre for Defence Studies (2000). *Independent Study on Security Force Options and
Security Sector Reform in East Timor.* London: King's College.

Centre for International Sustainable Development Law (2003). "Advancing the Odious
Debt Doctrine." Montreal, QC: CISDL. Available at http://www.cisdl.org/pdf/
debtentire.pdf.

Chandler, D. (1996). *A History of Cambodia.* Chaing Mai, Thailand: Silkworm Press.

Chen, D., J. Matovu, and R. Reinikka (2001). "A Quest for Revenue and Tax Incidence." In *Uganda's Recovery: The Role of Farms, Firms, and Government*, ed.
Ritva Reinikka and Paul Collier. Washington, DC: World Bank, 271–317.

Chung, Joanna (2005). "Iraq's Debt Solution Ruffles Feathers." *Financial Times* (London), December 21, p. 37.

Claessens, S., E. Detragiache, Ravi Kanbur, and P. Wickham (1997). "Analytical Aspects of the Debt Problems of Heavily Indebted Poor Countries." In *External Finance for Low-Income Countries*, ed. Z. Iqbal and Ravi Kanbur. Washington, DC:
International Monetary Fund, 21–48.

Clément, Jean A.P., ed. (2004). *Post-conflict Economics in Sub-Saharan Africa:
Lessons from the Democratic Republic of the Congo.* Washington, DC: International Monetary Fund.

Cohen, Susan A. (2003). "Beyond Slogans: Lessons from Uganda's ABC Experience."
In *Guttmacher Report on Public Policy.* New York: Alan Guttmacher Institute,
1–3.

Colletta, Nat J., M. Kostner, and I. Wiederhofer (1996a). *Case Studies in War-to-Peace
Transition: The Demobilization and Reintegration of Ex-Combatants in Ethiopia,
Namibia, and Uganda.* Washington, DC: World Bank.

———(1996b). *The Transition from War to Peace in Sub-Saharan Africa.* Washington,
DC: World Bank.

Collier, Paul, V. L. Elliott, Håvard Hegre, Anke Hoeffler, Marta Reynal-Querol, and
Nicholas Sambanis (2003). *Breaking the Conflict Trap: Civil War and Development Policy.* Washington, DC: World Bank and Oxford University Press.

Committee for Free and Fair Elections in Cambodia (2002). "The Performance and
Functioning of the Commune Councils." Phnom Penh, Cambodia.

Curtis, G. (1998). *Cambodia Reborn? The Transition to Democracy and Development.*
Washington, DC: Brookings Institution Press; Geneva: United Nations Research
Institute for Social Development.

Curtius, Mary (2005). "US Envoy Says Palestinian Forces Unprepared for Pullout."
Los Angeles Times, July 1, p. A3.

Darling, Linda T. (2002). "'Do Justice, Do Justice, for That Is Paradise': Middle Eastern Advice for Indian Muslim Rulers." *Comparative Studies of South Asia, Africa,
and the Middle East* 22: 3–19.

Deininger, Klaus, and Paul Mpuga (2005). "Economic and Welfare Impact of Abolition
of Health User Fees: Evidence from Uganda." *Journal of African Economies* 14,
no. 1: 55–91.

Democratic Republic of Timor-Leste [RDTL]–Ministry of Planning and Finance (2002). *Annual Financial Report and Accounts 2001–2002.* Dili: RDTL–Ministry of Planning and Finance.

———(2003). *Annual Financial Report and Accounts 2002–2003.* Dili: RDTL–Ministry of Planning and Finance.

———(2004a). *Annual Financial Report and Accounts 2003–2004.* Dili: RDTL–Ministry of Planning and Finance.

———(2004b). *Combined Sources Budget 2004–05*—Budget Paper no. 1. Dili: RDTL–Ministry of Planning and Finance.

———(2005a). *Overview of Sector Investment Programs: Volume 1.* Dili: RDTL–Ministry of Planning and Finance.

———(2005b). "Report on Budget Execution Study." Internal document.

Department for International Development [DfID] (2002). *Conducting Conflict Assessments: Guidance Notes.* London: DfID, Conflict and Humanitarian Affairs Department. Available at http://www.dfid.gov.uk/pubs/files/conflictassessmentguidance.pdf.

DevTech (2001). "Aplicación de mejores prácticas internacionales al desempeño de la administración tributaria de Guatemala: Un estudio de benchmarking." Unpublished study prepared for the Project on Promotion of a Solid and Simple Tax System, financed by the US Agency for International Development.

Dijkstra, Geske (2003). "Results of Debt Relief for Mozambique." Case study prepared for the Netherlands Ministry of Foreign Affairs, Policy and Operations Evaluation Department (IOB) Evaluation of Dutch Debt Relief.

Dillon, K. Burke, C. Maxwell Watson, G. Russell Kincaid, and Chanpen Puckahtikom (n.d.). "Recent Developments in External Debt Restructuring," IMF Occasional Papers, vol. 40, Washington, DC.

Dovlo, Delanyo (2003). "The Brain Drain and Retention of Health Professionals in Africa." Paper prepared for Conference on Improving Tertiary Education in Sub-Saharan Africa, Accra, Ghana, September. Available at http://www.worldbank.org/afr/teia/conf_0903/dela_dovlo.pdf.

Doyle, Michael (1998). "Peacebuilding in Cambodia: The Continuing Quest for Power and Legitimacy." In *Cambodia and the International Community: The Quest for Peace, Development, and Democracy,* ed. Frederick Z. Brown and David G. Timberman. New York: The Asia Society.

Doyle, Michael, and Nicholas Sambanis (2000). "International Peacebuilding: A Theoretical and Quantitative Analysis." *American Political Science Review* 94, no. 4: 779–801.

Dugger, C. W. (2006). "A Cure That Really Works: Cambodia Tries the Nonprofit Path to Health Care." *New York Times,* January 8.

Dunn, James (1983). *Timor: A People Betrayed.* Queensland, Australia: Jacaranda Press.

Easterly, William (2002). "An Identity Crisis? Testing IMF Financial Planning." Center for Global Development, Working Paper no. 9, Washington, DC.

Economic Commission for Latin America and the Caribbean [ECLAC] (2004). "The United States–Central American Free Trade Agreement: Fiscal Implications for the Central American Countries." ECLAC Report no. LC/MEX/l.616, Mexico City.

Eifert, Benn, and Alan Gelb (2005). "Improving the Dynamics of Aid: Towards More Predictable Budget Support." World Bank Policy Research Working Paper 3732, Washington, DC.

Emran, M. Shahe, and Joseph E. Stiglitz (2005). "On Selective Indirect Tax Reform in Developing Countries." *Journal of Public Economics* 89, no. 4: 599–623.

Enderlin, Charles (2002). *Shattered Dreams: The Failure of the Peace Process in the Middle East, 1995–2002.* New York: Other Press.

Eng, N., and C. Rusten (2004). *Fiscal Decentralization: Existing Taxation and Potential Tax Candidates for Reassignment and Sharing Between the Province and the Commune.* Phnom Penh: Cambodia Development Resource Institute.

Epstein, Gerald (2005). "Alternatives to Inflation-Targeting Monetary Policy for Stable and Egalitarian Growth: A Brief Research Summary." Paper presented at the American Social Science Association Meetings, Boston, MA.

Escobar, Rolando (2004). "Principios constitucionales de la tributación en Guatemala." Unpublished paper, Guatemala City.

European Anti-Fraud Office [OLAF] (2005). "OLAF Investigation into EU Assistance to the Palestinian Authority Budget." Press release, March 17. Available at http://europa.eu.int/comm/anti_fraud/press_room/pr/2005/03_en.html.

European Commission (2005). *EC Budget Support: An Innovative Approach to Conditionality.* Brussels: EC Directorate-General for Development. Available at http://spa.synisys.com/resources/2005/EC_GBS_VT_Review.pdf.

European Commission Technical Assistance Office for the West Bank and Gaza Strip. "Budgetary Support to the Palestinian Authority." Available at http://www.delwbg.cec.eu.int/en/cooperatio_development/sector1.htm.

European Union (2003). "EU to Support Reform of Palestinian Authority with New Forms of Aid." Press release, April 30.

Falck, H. (1999). *Mozambique in a Post-Washington Consensus Perspective.* Stockholm: SIDA.

Fedelino, Annalisa, and Alina Kudina (2003). "Fiscal Sustainability in African HIPC Countries: A Policy Dilemma?" IMF Working Paper, vol. 03/187, Washington, DC.

Fiscal Pact Follow-up Commission [CSPF] (2003). "El gasto público en cumplimiento de los principios y compromisos del Pacto Fiscal." CSPF, Guatemala City.

Fjeldstad, Odd-Helge, and Adel Zagha (2004). "Taxation and State Formation in Palestine, 1994–2000." In *State Formation in Palestine: Viability and Governance During a Social Transformation,* ed. Mushtaq Husain Khan (with George Giacaman and Inge Amundsen). London: RoutledgeCurzon, 192–214.

French, L. C. (1994). "Enduring Holocaust, Surviving History: Displaced Cambodians on the Thai-Cambodian Border, 1989–1991." PhD diss., Harvard University.

Galper, Harvey, and Fernando Ramos (1992). "The Incidence of the Guatemalan Tax System." Unpublished paper prepared for KPMG Peat Marwick.

Gauthier, Bernard, and Ritva Reinikka (2001). "Shifting Tax Burdens Through Exemptions and Evasion: An Empirical Investigation of Uganda." Mimeographed, World Bank Development Research Group, Washington, DC.

Gemmell, Norman, and Oliver Morrissey (2005). "Distribution and Poverty Impacts of Tax Structure Reform in Developing Countries: How Little We Know." *Development Policy Review* 23, no. 2: 131–144.

Ghani, Ashraf, Clare Lockhart, and Michael Carnahan (2005a). "Closing the Sovereignty Gap: An Approach to State-Building." Overseas Development Institute, Working Paper no. 253, London. Available at http://www.odi.org.uk/Publications/working_papers/wp253.pdf.

———(2005b). "Stability, State-Building, and Development Assistance: An Outside Perspective." Paper prepared for the Princeton National Security Project.

Gobierno de Guatemala (1997). "Programa de paz: La oportunidad para Guatemala. Informe a la reunión del Grupo Consultivo." Document presented at the Consultative Group for Guatemala meeting in Brussels, January 21–22.

Gonzales, Patrick, et al. (2004). *Highlights from the Trends in International Mathematics and Science Study (TIMSS) 2003.* Washington, DC: US Department of Education, National Center for Education Statistics.

Goodhand, Jonathan (2001). "Aid, Conflict, and Peacebuilding in Sri Lanka." King's College, Centre for Defence Studies, London. Available at http://www.dfid.gov.uk/pubs/files/conflictassessmentsrilanka.pdf.

Government of Mozambique (1998). *Understanding Poverty and Well-Being in Mozambique: The First National Assessment (1996–97).* Maputo: Government of Mozambique, Eduardo Mondlane University, and International Food Policy Research Institute.

———(2004). *Poverty and Well-Being in Mozambique: The Second National Assessment (2002–2003).* Maputo: Ministry of Planning and Finance, International Food Policy Research Institute, and Purdue University.

Gunn, Geoffrey (1994). *A Critical View of Western Journalism and Scholarship on East Timor.* Manila, Philippines: Journal of Contemporary Asian Publishers.

Gupta, Sanjeev, Benedict Clements, Rina Bhattacharya, and Shamit Chakravarti (2004). "Fiscal Consequences of Armed Conflict and Terrorism in Low- and Middle-income Countries." *European Journal of Political Economy* 20, no. 2: 403–421.

Gupta, Sanjeev, Benedict Clemens, Alexander Pivovarsky, and Ervin R. Tiongson (2003). "Foreign Aid and Revenue Response: Does the Composition of Aid Matter?" IMF Working Paper 03/176, Washington, DC, September. Available at http://www.imf.org/external/pubs/ft/wp/2003/wp03176.pdf.

Gupta, Sanjeev, Shamsuddin Tareq, Benedict Clemens, Alex Segura-Ubiergo, and Rina Bhattacharya (2005). "Rebuilding Fiscal Institutions in Postconflict Countries." IMF Occasional Paper no. 247, Washington, DC, December.

Hanlon, Joseph (2006). "Lenders, Not Borrowers, Are Responsible for 'Illegitimate' Loans." *Third World Quarterly* 27, no. 2: 211–226.

Hansen, Henrik (2004). "The Impact of External Aid and External Debt on Growth and Investment." In *Debt Relief for Poor Countries,* ed. Tony Addison, Henrik Hansen, and Finn Tarp. New York: Palgrave Macmillan, chap. 7.

Heller, Peter S. (2005). "'Pity the Finance Minister': Issues in Managing a Substantial Scaling Up of Aid Flows." IMF Working Paper WP/05/180, Washington, DC, September.

Hellman, Joel S., Geraint Jones, and Daniel Kaufmann (2000). "Seize the State, Seize the Day: State Capture, Corruption, and Influence in Transition." World Bank Policy Research Working Paper no. 2444, Washington, DC, September.

Hill, Helen (1976). *The Timor Story.* Victoria, Australia: Timor Information Service.

Hjertholm, Peter (2003). "Theoretical and Empirical Foundations of HIPC Debt Sustainability Targets." *Journal of Development Studies* 39, no. 6: 67–100.

Hoeflich, M. H. (1982). "Through a Glass Darkly: Reflections upon the History of the International Law of Public Debt in Connection with State Succession." *University of Illinois Law Review* 1: 39–70.

Hughes, C. (2003). *The Political Economy of Cambodia's Transition: 1991–2001.* London: RoutledgeCurzon.

Hull, Geoffrey (1999). Paper presented to Conference on East Timor held at Parliament House in Sydney, Australia.

Human Rights Watch (2002). "Cambodia's Commune Elections: Setting the Stage for the 2003 National Elections." *Human Rights Watch Reports* 14, no. 4. Available at http://www.hrw.org/report/2002/cambo0402.

Ibrahimi, Sayeed Yaqub, and Abdul Baseer Saeed (2005). "Outcry over Russian Debt Demands." Afghan Recovery Report no. 185, Institute for War and Peace Reporting (IWPR), London, September 10.

International Development Association and International Monetary Fund (2001). *The Challenge of Maintaining Long-term External Debt Sustainability.* Washington, DC: International Monetary Fund. Available at http://www.imf.org/external/np/hipc/2001/lt/04001/htm.

Inter-American Development Bank [IADB] (2004). *Cooperación de la comunidad internacional 2003: Actualización del documento mapeo de donantes.* Guatemala City: IADB.

International Crisis Group (2004). "Northern Uganda: Understanding and Solving the Conflict." Africa Report no. 77, Nairobi and Brussels, April 14.

———(2005a). "The Khartoum-SPLM Agreement: Sudan's Uncertain Peace." Africa Report no. 96, Nairobi and Brussels, July 25.

———(2005b). "Shock Therapy for Northern Uganda's Peace Process." Africa Briefing no. 23, Nairobi and Brussels, April 11.

International Monetary Fund [IMF] (2000a). *East Timor: A Strategy for Rebuilding Fiscal Management.* Washington, DC: IMF, Fiscal Affairs Department.

———(2000b). "The Logic of Debt Relief for the Poorest Countries." *IMF Issues Brief,* Washington, DC. Available at http://www.imf.org/external/np/exr/ib/2000/092300.htm.

———(2003a). *Democratic Republic of the Congo: Enhanced Initiative for Heavily Indebted Poor Countries—Decision Point Document.* Country Report 03/267, Washington, DC.

———(2003b). "Transcript of a Press Briefing on the West Bank and Gaza by Adam Bennett and Karim Nashashibi of the IMF's Middle Eastern Department with William Murray, Deputy Chief of Media Relations." Dubai, United Arab Emirates, September 20.

———(2003c). *West Bank and Gaza: Economic Performance and Reform Under Conflict Conditions.* Washington, DC: IMF.

———(2004). *International Financial Statistics.* Washington, DC: IMF.

———(2005a). "Islamic Republic of Afghanistan—Sixth Review Under the Staff-Monitored Program and 2005 Article IV Consultation." Kabul, November 22. Available at http://www.imf.org/external/np/ms/2005/112205.htm.

———(2005b). *The Macroeconomics of Managing Increased Aid Flows: Experiences of Low-Income Countries and Policy Implications.* Washington, DC: IMF, Policy Development and Review Department.

International Monetary Fund and World Bank (1999). *Modifications to the Heavily Indebted Poor Countries (HIPC) Initiative.* Washington, DC: International Monetary Fund.

———(2001). *Assistance to Post-Conflict Countries and the HIPC Framework.* Washington, DC: World Bank.

Jayachandran, Seema, and Michael Kremer (2004). "Odious Debt." California Center for Population Research On-Line Working Paper Series, November 1.

Joint Assessment Mission (1999). "East Timor, Building a Nation: A Framework for Reconstruction and Development." Macro-Economics Background Paper. Available at http://pascal.iseg.utl.pt/~cesa/dtcjammamacroecon.pdf.

Jolliffe, J. (1978). *East Timor: Nationalism and Colonialism.* Queensland, Australia: University of Queensland Press.

Jonas, Susanne (2000). *Of Centaurs and Doves: Guatemala's Peace Process.* Boulder, CO: Westview Press.

Kanbur, Ravi (2000). "Aid, Conditionality, and Debt in Africa." In *Foreign Aid and Development: Lessons Learnt and Directions for the Future*, ed. Finn Tarp. London: Routledge, 409–422.

Kanbur, Ravi, and Anthony J. Venables, eds. (2005). *Spatial Inequality and Development.* Oxford: Oxford University Press.

Kapiriri, L., O. F. Norheim, and K. Heggenhougen (2003). "Public Participation in Health Planning and Priority Setting at the District Level in Uganda." *Health Policy and Planning* 18, no. 2: 205–213.

Kapoor, Kapil (1995). "Restructuring Uganda's Debt: The Commercial Debt Buy-back Operation." World Bank, Policy Research Working Paper, no. 1409, Washington, DC.

Kasekende, Louis A., and Michael Atingi-Ego (1999). "Uganda's Experience with Aid." *Journal of African Economies* 8, no. 4: 617–649.

Khadr, Ali (1999). "Fiscal Management." In *Development Under Adversity: The Palestinian Economy in Transition*, ed. Ishac Diwan and Radwan A. Shaban. Washington, DC: World Bank, 110–135.

Khalfan, Ashfaq, Jeff King, and Bryan Thomas (2003). "Advancing the Odious Debt Doctrine." Working Paper, Centre for International Sustainable Development Law, Montreal.

Khattry, Barsha, and J. Mohan Rao (2002). "Fiscal Faux Pas? An Analysis of the Revenue Implications of Trade Liberalization." *World Development* 30, no. 8: 1431–1444.

Kremer, Michael, and Seema Jayachandran (2003). "Odious Debt: When Dictators Borrow, Who Repays the Loan?" *Brookings Review* 21, no. 2: 32–35.

Kumar, Maitra Utpal et al. (2004). *Evolution of the Treasury Sector Pre-UNTAET, in Timor-Leste—A Strategy for Building the Foundation of Governance for Peace and Stability.* Dili, Timor-Leste: United Nations Mission of Support for East Timor, Public Information Office.

Larios, Jose (2000). "How the Tax Burden Is Distributed by Class of Tax Income in Guatemala." Fiscal Pact Preparatory Commission, Guatemala City.

"Law No. (1) of 1998 for Investment Promotion in Palestine." Available at http://www.pnic.gov.ps/english/law/law9.html.

Lawson, David, Andy McKay, and John Okidi (2005). "Poverty Persistence and Transition in Uganda: A Combined Qualitative and Quantitative Analysis." Working Paper 004, Economic and Social Research Council, Global Poverty Research Group, London.

Le Billon, Philippe (2000). "The Political Ecology of Transition in Cambodia 1989–1999: War, Peace and Forest Exploitation." *Development and Change* 31: 785–805.

———(2003). "Buying Peace or Fuelling War: The Role of Corruption in Armed Conflicts." *Journal of International Development* 15: 413–426.

Lopes, Jorge (2004). "Customs Services in a Strategy for Building the Foundation of Governance for Peace and Stability." Dili, Timor-Leste: UNMISET, Public information Office.

MacFarlane, Neil, and Yuen Foong Khong (2006). *Human Security and the UN: A Critical History.* Bloomington: Indiana University Press.

Mann, Arthur (2002a). "Guatemala: Los costos administrativos de la tributación y de impuestos de bajo rendimiento." DevTech Systems, unpublished study prepared for the Project on Promotion of a Solid and Simple Tax System, financed by the US Agency for International Development.

————(2002b). "La incidencia del sistema tributario en el año 2001." DevTech Systems, unpublished study prepared for the Project on Promotion of a Solid and Simple Tax System, financed by the US Agency for International Development.

Mann, Arthur, and Robert Burke (2002). "El gasto tributario en Guatemala." DevTech Systems, unpublished study prepared for the Project on Promotion of a Solid and Simple Tax System, financed by the US Agency for International Development.

Matovu, John Mary, and Frances Stewart (2001). "Uganda: The Social and Economic Costs of Conflict." In *War and Underdevelopment*, vol. 2, ed. Frances Stewart and Valpy Fitzgerald. Oxford: Oxford University Press, 240–303.

McKinley, Terry (2006). "Economic Policies and Poverty Reduction in Asia and the Pacific: Alternatives to Neoliberalism." In *Human Development in the Era of Globalization*, ed. James K. Boyce, Stephen Cullenberg, Prasanta K. Pattsanaik, and Robert Pollin. Cheltenham, UK: Edward Elgar, 344–360.

McNamara, Robert (1968). *The Essence of Security.* New York: Harper and Row.

Menzies, Gordon Douglas (2004). "Debt-Relief Policy Tradeoffs for Conflict-affected Countries," University of Technology, Sydney.

Michailof, Serge, Markus Kostner, and Devictor Xavier (2002). *Post-Conflict Recovery in Africa—An Agenda for the Africa Region.* Washington, DC: World Bank.

Mijumbi, Peter (2001). "Uganda's External Debt and the HIPC Initiative." Paper presented at the WIDER Conference on Debt Relief, Helsinki, Finland, August 17–18.

Ministry of Finance (Uganda), Planning and Economic Development (1992). "Background to the Budget, 1992–1993," Kampala, June.

————(2003). The Public Finance and Accountability Act (No 6). *Uganda Gazette* 96, no. 23, May.

————(2005). "Budget Speech, Financial Year 2005/06," Kampala, June 8.

Mitra-Datta, Jayati (2001). *Uganda: Policy, Participation, and People.* Washington, DC: World Bank.

Moe, Ye Naing, and Ngep Navin (2002). *Light of the Voters—The Model for the Change in Power Is Already Up and Running.* New York: Independent Journalists Foundation. Available at http://www.ijf-cij.org/folder_file_for_cambodia/3htm.

Morris, Benny (2002). "Camp David and After: An Exchange (An Interview with Ehud Barak)." *New York Review of Books*, June 13.

Moss, Todd, Gunilla Pettersson, and Nicolas van de Walle (2005). "An Aid-Institutions Paradox? A Review Essay on Aid Dependency and State Building in Sub-Saharan Africa." Mario Einaudi Center for International Studies, Working Paper no. 11-05, Cornell University, November. Available at http://www.einaudi.cornell.edu/files/workingpaper/11-2005.pdf.

Mulford, David, and Michael Monderer (2003). "Iraqi Debt, Like War, Divides the West." *Financial Times* (London), June 22.

Mutibwa, Phares (1992). *Uganda Since Independence: A Story of Unfulfilled Hopes.* Trenton, NJ: Africa World Press.

Nannyonjo, Justine (2001). "The HIPC Debt Relief Initiative: Uganda's Social Sector Reforms and Outcomes." UNU/WIDER Discussion Paper no. 2001/138, Helsinki.

————(2005). "Conflicts, Poverty, and Human Development in Northern Uganda." *The Round Table* 94, no. 381: 473–488.

Nasr, Mohamed N. (2004). "Monopolies and the PNA." In *State Formation in Palestine*, ed. Mushtaq H. Khan et al. London: RoutledgeCurzon.

Ndikumana, Léonce (1998). "Institutional Failure and Ethnic Conflicts in Burundi." *African Studies Review* 41, no. 1: 29–47.

————(2000). "Towards a Solution to Violence in Burundi: A Case for Political and Economic Liberalization." *Journal of Modern African Studies* 38, no. 3: 431–459.

————(2004). "Additionality of Debt Relief and Debt Forgiveness and Implications for Future Development Financing." *International Review of Economics and Finance* 13, no. 3: 325–340.

Ndikumana, Léonce, and James K. Boyce (1998). "Congo's Odious Debt: External Borrowing and Capital Flight in Zaire." *Development and Change* 29, no. 2: 195–217.

Ndikumana, Léonce, and Kisangani Emizet (2005). "The Economics of Civil War: The Case of the Democratic Republic of Congo." In *Understanding Civil War: Evidence and Analysis*, ed. Nicholas Sambanis. Washington, DC: World Bank, 63–88.

Neutral and Impartial Committee for Free and Fair Elections in Cambodia (2002). "Cambodian Commune Council Election Report 2001–02." Available at http://www.ngoforum.org.kh/Working_Group_Issues/Civilsociety/nicfec_report.html# Decentralization.

Newitt, M. (1995). *A History of Mozambique.* London: C. Hurst and Co.

Ngaruko, F., and J. D. Nkurunziza (2000). "An Economic Interpretation of Conflict in Burundi." *Journal of African Economies* 9, no. 3: 370–409.

NGO Forum (2002). "Proceedings of Karamoja Strategic Planning Workshop," Kampala, Uganda, May 17.

Nicol, B. (1978). *Timor: The Still-born Nation.* Victoria, Australia: Visa Widescope.

Nkusu, Mwanza (2004). "Financing Uganda's Poverty Reduction Strategy: Is Aid Causing More Pain than Gain?" IMF Working Paper 170, Washington, DC.

Obidegwu, Chukwuma (2003). "Rwanda: The Search for Post-Conflict Socio-Economic Change, 1995–2001." World Bank, Africa Region Working Paper Series no. 59, Washington, DC.

O'Connell, D. P. (1967). *State Succession in Municipal Law and International Law. Internal Relations: Volume I.* Cambridge: Cambridge University Press.

Okidi, John A., Sarah Ssewanyana, Lawrence Bategeka, and Fred Muhumuza (2004). "Operationalizing Pro-poor Growth: A Country Case Study on Uganda." Paper sponsored by the AFD, BMZ, DFID, and the World Bank Program on Operationalizing Pro-Poor Growth, Economic Policy Research Centre, Kampala, October.

Okurut, Francis N., Jonathan A. O. Odwee, and Asaf Adebua (2002). "Determinants of Regional Poverty in Uganda." AERC Research Paper 122, Nairobi, Kenya.

Østby, Gundrun (2004). "Do Horizontal Inequalities Matter for Civil Conflict?" International Peace Research Institute, Oslo. Available at http://www.polarizationand conflict.org/bcn04/7%D8stby_Horiz.pdf.

Ovesen, J., I. Trankell, and J. Ojendal (1995). *When Every Household Is an Island: Social Organization and Power Structures in Rural Cambodia.* Phnom Penh, Cambodia: Swedish International Development Agency.

"PA Recruiting 5,000 Police Officers for Gaza Pullout" (2005). *Ha'aretz* (English edition), May 28.

Palestinian Center for Policy and Survey Research (2004). *Public Opinion Poll no. 11,* March 14–17. Available at http://www.pcpsr.org/survey/polls/2004/p11a.html.

Palestinian Central Bureau of Statistics (2005). "PCBS's Main Findings of Satisfaction of the Living Conditions in Palestinian Territory, 2004." July 16. Available at http://www.palestine-pmc.com/details.asp?cat=2&id=994.

Palestinian Investment Promotion Agency (n.d.). "Taxation." Available at http://www.pipa.gov.ps/taxation.asp.

Palestinian Ministry of Finance (2005). "Palestinian National Authority: Fiscal Developments in 2002–2005," and 2005 budget press release, March 16. Available at http://www.mof.gov.ps.

Paris Club (2006). "Afghanistan," Press release, July 19. Available at http://www
.clubdeparis.org/en/news/page_detail_news.php?FICHIER=com1153385428.

Pearson, L. (2005). "Canada's Debt Relief Initiative: Helping the Poorest." Available
at http://sen.parl.gc.ca/lpearson/htmfiles/hill/17_htm_files/canada_debt.htm (ac-
cessed December 21, 2005).

Picciotto, Robert, Charles Alao, Eka Ikpe, Martin Kimani, and Roger Slade (2005).
"Striking a New Balance: Donor Policy Coherence and Development Cooperation
in Difficult Environments." Background paper commissioned by the Learning and
Advisory Process on Difficult Partnerships of the Development Assistance Committee of the OECD. Available at http://www.oecd.org/dataoecd/31/62/34252747
.pdf.

Pires, Emilia (2004). "Planning and External Assistance Management in Timor-
Leste—A Strategy for Building the Foundation of Governance for Peace and Sta-
bility." United Nations Mission of support for Timor-Leste, Public Information
Office, Dili.

———(2005). "To What Extent Is the Active Involvement of Politicians in the Tech-
nical Formulation of the Budget Contributing to Low Budget Execution in East
Timor?" MS diss., Faculty of Economics (Development Management), London
School of Economics.

Pressman, Jeremy (2003). "Visions in Collision: What Really Happened at Camp
David and Taba?" *International Security* 28, no. 2 (Fall): 5–43.

"Protocol on Economic Relations Between the Government of Israel and the PLO"
(1994). Paris, April 29, 1994. Available at http://www.palestinecenter.org/cpap/
documents/economic.html.

Prud'homme, Remy, and P. Smoke (2000). "Fiscal Decentralization in Cambodia."
Prepared for the United Nations Department of Social and Economic Affairs and
the Ministry of Economy and Finance, Phnom Penh.

Quartet (2006a). "Quartet Statement," June 17. Available at http://www.un.org/news/
dh/infocus/middle_east/quartet-17jun2006.htm.

———(2006b). "Statement by Middle East Quartet," January 30. Available at http://
www.un.org/News/Press/docs/2006/sg2104.doc.htm.

Ranck, S. R. (1977). "Recent Rural-Urban Migration to Dili, Portuguese East Timor."
MA thesis, Department of Geography, Macquarie University.

Reinikka, Ritva, and Jakob Svensson (2002). "Coping with Poor Public Capital." *Journal of Development Economics* 69: 51–69.

———(2004). "Local Capture: Evidence from a Central Government Transfer Program in Uganda." *Quarterly Journal of Economics* 119, no. 2: 679–705.

Republic of Uganda (2004a). "Annual Health Sector Performance Report FY
2003/04," Kampala, October.

———(2004b). "The National Policy for Internally Displaced Persons." Office of the
Prime Minister, Department of Disaster Preparedness and Refugees, August.

Rohde, David, and Carlotta Gall (2005). "Delays Hurting U.S. Rebuilding in
Afghanistan." *New York Times,* November 7.

Romeo, L. (2000). *The Seila Program and Decentralized Planning in Cambodia.* New
York: Institute of Public Administration, New York University.

Rose-Ackerman, Susan (1999). *Corruption and Government: Causes, Consequences,
and Reform.* Cambridge: Cambridge University Press.

Ross, Dennis (2004). *The Missing Peace: The Inside Story of the Fight for Middle East
Peace.* New York: Farrar, Straus, and Giroux.

Royal Government of Cambodia (2001a). "Governance Action Plan." Phnom Penh.

————(2001b). "Proceedings of Workshops on Fiscal Decentralization and Background Papers." Ministry of Economy and Finance, Phnom Penh.

————(2002). "Poverty Reduction Strategy Paper." Council for Social.Development, Phnom Penh.

————(2004). "National Workshop on Strengthening Commune Revenues." Ministry of Economy and Finance, Phnom Penh.

————(2005). "Strategic Framework for Decentralization and Deconcentration Reforms." Phnom Penh.

Rubin, Barnett R. (2005). "Constructing Sovereignty for Security." *Survival* 47, no. 2: 93–106.

Sachs, Jeffrey D., ed. (1989). *Developing Country Debt and the World Economy.* Chicago: University of Chicago Press.

Sack, Alexander (1929). "La Succession Aux Dettes Publiques D'Etat." *Receuil des Cours* 23.

Saldanha, João Mariano De Sousa (1994). *The Political Economy of East Timor Development.* Jakarta, Indonesia: Pustaka Sinar Harapan.

Sam Rainsy Party (2002). "Who Is the Big Loser at the Commune Election?" Phnom Penh, Cambodia.

Sanford, Jonathan E. (2004). "IDA Grants and HIPC Debt Cancellation: Their Effectiveness and Impact on IDA Resources." *World Development* 32, no. 9: 1579–1607

Schenone, Osvaldo, and Carlos de la Torre (2003)."Guatemala: Fortalecimiento de la estructura tributaria." Association for Research and Social Studies (ASIES), Guatemala City.

Sedra, Mark, and Peter Middlebrook (2005). "Beyond Bonn: Revisioning the International Compact for Afghanistan." *Foreign Policy in Focus* 9, no. 24 (November). Available at http://www.fpif.org/fpifzines/pr/2924.

Sewell, David (2001). *Governance and the Business Environment in the West Bank/Gaza.* N.p.: World Bank.

Smith, Dan (2004). *Towards a Strategic Framework for Peacebuilding: Getting Their Act Together.* Overview Report of the Joint Utstein Study of Peacebuilding. Oslo, Norway: International Peace Research Institute. Available at http://www.dep.no/filarkiv/210673/rapp104.pdf.

Smoke, Paul (2003). "Decentralization and Deconcentration in Cambodia: Integrated Fiduciary Assessment/Public Expenditure Review Background Paper." World Bank, Washington, DC.

State Department (2003). *A Performance-Based Roadmap to a Permanent Two-State Solution to the Israeli-Palestinian Conflict.* Available at http://www.state.gov/r/pa/prs/ps/2003/20062.htm.

Stedman, Stephen J. (1997). "Spoiler Problems in Peace Processes." *International Security* 22, no. 2: 5–53.

————(2002). "Introduction." In *Ending Civil Wars: The Implementation of Peace Agreements,* ed. Stephen J. Stedman, Donald Rothchild, and Elizabeth M. Cousens. Boulder, CO: Lynne Rienner Publishers, 1–40.

Stedman, Stephen J., Donald S. Rothchild, and Elizabeth M. Cousens, eds. (2002). *Ending Civil Wars: The Implementation of Peace Agreements.* Boulder, CO: Lynne Rienner Publishers.

Stephens, Joe, and David B. Ottaway (2005). "A Rebuilding Plan Full of Cracks." *Washington Post,* November 19.

Stewart, Frances (2000). "Crisis Prevention: Tackling Horizontal Inequalities." *Oxford Development Studies* 28, no. 3: 245–262.

———(2002). "Root Causes of Violent Conflict in Developing Countries." *British Medical Journal* 324 (February 9): 342–345.

Sun, Yan (2004). "External Debt Sustainability in HIPC Completion Point Countries." IMF Working Paper WP/04/160, Washington, DC.

Swedish International Development Agency [SIDA] (2006). *Manual for Conflict Analysis.* Stockholm, Sweden: SIDA. Available at http://www.sida.se/shared/jsp/download.jsp?f=SIDA4334en_Web.pdf&a=3351.

Swishers, Clayton (2004). *The Truth About Camp David.* New York: Nation Books.

Tanzi, Vito, and Howell H. Zee (2000). "Tax Policy for Emerging Markets: Developing Countries." IMF Working Paper 00/35, Washington, DC.

Taylor, John (1994). "A Brief History of East Timor." *New Internationalist,* no. 253 (March).

Thatcher, P. L. (1988). "The Role of Women in East Timorese Society." Honors thesis, Monash University, Melbourne.

———(1993). "The Timor-Born in Exile in Australia." Master's thesis, Anthropology, Monash University, Melbourne.

———(2000). Lecture at University of Technology, Victoria, Australia, November 5.

Therkildsen, Ole (2004). "Autonomous Tax Administration in Sub-Saharan Africa: The Case of the Uganda Revenue Authority." *Forum for Development Studies* 31, no. 1: 59–88.

Transparency International [TI] (2004). *Transparency International Corruption Perceptions Index 2004.* Berlin: TI.

Turner, M. (2002). "Whatever Happened to Deconcentration? Recent Initiatives in Cambodia." *Public Administration and Development* 22, no. 3: 353–364.

Uganda Bureau of Statistics [UBOS] (2003). *Uganda National Household Survey 2002/2003.* Report on the Social Economic Survey. Entebbe: UBOS.

———(2004). *Statistical Abstract.* Entebbe: UBOS.

Uganda Revenue Authority (2004). "Taxation and Investment in Uganda: Structure and Trend." Presentation by Christopher Kiwanuka Kaweesa to the Business Forum for Investment Opportunities in Uganda, London, UK, May.

UK Foreign and Commonwealth Office (2005). "G8 Gleneagles. 2005 Summit Statement on the Middle East Peace Process." Available at http://www.fco.gov.uk/Files/kfile/PostG8_Gleneagles_MEPP.pdf.

United Nations Department of Peacekeeping Operations (2003). *Handbook on United Nations Multidimensional Peacekeeping Operations* (UN DPKO Peacekeeping Best Practices Unit, December 2003), chap. 15. Available at http://pbpu.unlb.org/pbpu/handbook/START-Handbook.html.

United Nations Development Programme [UNDP] (2003). *Human Development Report 2003.* Geneva: United Nations.

———(2004). *Human Development Report 2004.* New York: UNDP.

United Nations Development Group and World Bank (2005). *An Operational Note on Transitional Results Matrices: Using Results-Based Frameworks in Fragile States.* Washington, DC: United Nations Development Group and World Bank. Available at http://siteresources.worldbank.org/INTLICUS/Resources/UNDG_WB_TRMs.pdf.

United Nations Office for Coordination of Humanitarian Affairs [UNOCHA] (2005a). "Financial Tracking Service FTS," Table 3: Uganda 2005, Kampala, May 27.

———(2005b). *Humanitarian Update Uganda,* vol. 7, issue 4. Geneva: UNOCHA.

———(2005c). *Consolidated Appeal for Uganda 2005.* Geneva: UNOCHA.

United Nations Security Council (2001). *Report of the Panel of Experts on the Illegal Exploitation of Natural Resources and Other Forms of Wealth of the Democratic Republic of the Congo.* New York: United Nations.

United Nations Special Representative of the Secretary General for Human Rights in Cambodia (2002). "Commune Council Elections 2002." United Nations, Phnom Penh.

US Agency for International Development [USAID] (2002). "Addressing Pastoralist Conflict in the Karamoja Cluster of Kenya, Uganda, and Sudan." Greater Horn of Africa Building Project, Washington, DC, March.

———(2005). "West Bank and Gaza Program Budget." February 24, 2005. Available at http://www.usaid.gov/wbg/budget.htm.

US Agency for International Development, Office of Conflict Management and Mitigation (2005). *Conducting a Conflict Assessment: A Framework for Strategy and Program Development.* Washington, DC: USAID. Available at http://www.usaid.gov/our_work/cross-cutting_programs/conflict/publications/docs/CMM_ConflAssessFrmwrk_May_05.pdf.

US Department of State, Office of Research (2006). "Opinion Analysis: Hamas and Fateh Neck and Neck as Palestinian Elections Draw Near." M-05-06, January 19. Available at http://www.fas.org/irp/agency/inr/hamas.pdf.

Vaz, F. J. (1964). *Moeda de Timor.* Lisbon: Banco Nacional Ultramarino.

White House (2002). "President Bush Calls for New Palestinian Leadership." June 24. Available at http://www.whitehouse.gov/news/releases/2002/06/20020624-3.html.

World Bank (1998). *Aid Effectiveness: What Works? What Doesn't? Why?* Oxford: Oxford University Press.

———(1999a). *Aid and Reform in Africa.* Development Research Group. Washington, DC: World Bank.

———(1999b). *Cambodia Public Expenditure Review.* Washington, DC: World Bank.

———(1999c). *West Bank and Gaza: Strengthening Public Sector Management.* Washington, DC: World Bank.

———(2000). *Aid Effectiveness in the West Bank and Gaza.* Washington, DC: World Bank.

———(2001). *Uganda: Policy, Participation, People.* Washington, DC: World Bank.

———(2002a). "The Conflict Analysis Framework." Conflict Prevention and Reconstruction Unit, Social Development Department Dissemination Note no. 5. Available at http://Inweb18.worldbank.org/ESSD/sdvext.nsf/67ByDocName/TheConflictAnalysisFrameworkCAFIdentifyingConflict-relatedObstaclestoDevelopment/$FILE/CPR+5+final+legal.pdf.

———(2002b). "Guatemala Integrated Financial Management III—Technical Assistance Project." Washington, DC.

———(2002c). *The Republic of Uganda Public Expenditure Review, Report on the Progress and Challenges of Budget Reforms, no 24882-UG.* Washington, DC: World Bank.

———(2003a). *Cambodia Integrated Fiduciary Assessment and Public Expenditure Review.* Washington, DC: World Bank.

———(2003b). *Poverty in Guatemala.* Washington, DC: World Bank.

———(2004a). *Cambodia at the Crossroads.* Phnom Penh, Cambodia: World Bank.

———(2004b). *Disengagement, the Palestinian Economy, and the Settlements.* World Bank, Washington, DC, June 23. Available at http://lnweb18.worldbank.org/mna/mena.nsf/Attachments/Disengagement+Paper/$File/Disengagement+Paper.pdf.

———(2004c). *Four Years—Intifada, Closures, and Palestinian Economic Crisis: An Assessment.* Washington, DC: World Bank.

————(2004d). *Global Development Finance 2004.* Washington DC: World Bank.

————(2004e). *Stagnation or Revival? Israeli Disengagement and Palestinian Economic Prospects—Overview.* World Bank. Available at http://siteresources.world bank.org/INTWESTBANKGAZA/Resources/WBG-Overview-e.pdf.

————(2004f). *West Bank and Gaza: Country Financial Accountability Assessment.* Washington, DC: World Bank.

————(2004g), *World Development Indicators 2004.* Washington DC: World Bank.

————(2005a). *Afghanistan: Managing Public Finances for Development.* Vol. 1: *Main Report.* Report no. 34582-AF, December 22. Washington, DC: World Bank. Available at http://siteresources.worldbank.org/AFGHANISTANEXTN/Resources/305984-1137783774207/afghanistan_pfm.pdf.

————(2005b). *Afghanistan: Managing Public Finances for Development.* Vol. 5: *Improving Public Finance Management in the Security Sector.* Report no. 34582-AF, December 22. Washington, DC: World Bank. Available at http://www-wds .worldbank.org/servlet/WDSContentServer/WDSP/IB/2006/01/11/000160016_20060111123047/Rendered/PDF/345821vol051AF.pdf.

————(2005c). "Public Financial Management Reform Trust Fund Status Report," Washington, DC: World Bank.

————(2005d). *Reaching the Poor: Public Expenditure Tracking Survey in Primary Education.* Washington, DC: World Bank.

————(2005e). *World Bank Conditionality Review: Conditionality and Policy Based Lending Trends.* Paris: World Bank, February 4. Available at http://siteresources .worldbank.org/PROJECTS/Resources/ConditionalityTrendsPresentation12705 .pdf.

————(2005f). *World Development Indicators 2005* (CD-ROM). Washington, DC: World Bank.

————(2006a). *Cambodia: Halving Poverty by 2015? Poverty Assessment 2006.* Washington, DC: World Bank.

————(2006b). "The Impending Palestinian Fiscal Crisis: Potential Remedies," May 7. Available at http://siteresources.worldbank.org/INTWESTBANKGAZA/Resources/PalestinianFiscalCrisis,PotentialRemediesMay7.pdf.

———— (2007). *World Development Report 2007.* Washington, DC: World Bank.

World Bank, Operations Evaluation Department (1999). "Aid Coordination and Postconflict Reconstruction: The West Bank and Gaza Experience." *Précis* 185 (Spring).

World Bank and International Monetary Fund (2005). *Global Monitoring Report 2005: Millennium Development Goals: From Consensus to Momentum.* Washington, DC: World Bank and International Monetary Fund. Available at http://site resources.worldbank.org/GLOBALMONITORINGEXT/Resources/complete.pdf.

World Food Program (2005). "Emergency Report no. 22," May 27. Available at http://www.wfp.org.

The Contributors

Patricia Alvarez-Plata is a research associate at the German Institute for Economic Research (DIW Berlin). She is currently pursuing a doctorate in economics at the Free University of Berlin.

James K. Boyce directs the program on development, peacebuilding, and the environment at the Political Economy Research Institute and teaches economics at the University of Massachusetts, Amherst. He is the author of *Investing in Peace: Aid and Conditionality After Civil Wars* (2002) and editor of *Economic Policy for Building Peace: The Lessons of El Salvador* (Lynne Rienner Publishers, 1996). He received his doctorate in economics from Oxford University.

Tilman Brück is acting head of the Department of International Economics at the German Institute for Economic Research (DIW Berlin). He is cofounder and codirector of the Household in Conflict Network and research fellow at the Institute for the Study of Labor (IZA). He received his doctorate in economics from Oxford University.

Rex Brynen is professor of political science at McGill University and has served as a consultant to the Canadian government, United Nations, and World Bank. His books include *Palestinian Refugees: Challenges of Repatriation and Development* (2007, coedited with Roula el-Rifai); *Persistent Permeability? Regionalism, Localism, and Globalization in the Middle East* (2004, coedited with Bassel Salloukh); *A Very Political Economy: Peacebuilding and Foreign Aid in the West Bank and Gaza* (2000); and *Political Liberalization and Democratization in the Arab World* (Lynne Rienner Publishers, 1995 and 1998, coedited with Bahgat Korany and Paul Noble).

323

Warren Coats is the senior monetary policy adviser to the Central Bank of Iraq and an International Monetary Fund consultant on monetary policy to the Central Bank of Afghanistan. Before retiring from the IMF in 2003 after twenty-six years of service, he led IMF technical assistance missions to the central banks of a number of countries, including Bosnia and Herzegovina, Croatia, Kosovo, and Serbia.

Michael Francino is an international consultant specializing in public finance. He served as cabinet member for finance in Timor-Leste's transitional government and has held advisory posts in several postconflict countries.

Ashraf Ghani is the chancellor of Kabul University. He served as finance minister of Afghanistan from June 2002 to December 2004; chief adviser to President Karzai from February to June 2002; and a special adviser to the Special Representative of the Secretary-General of the UN from October 2001 to February 2002. He previously served at the World Bank and on the faculties of Kabul University; the University of Aarhus; the University of California, Berkeley; and Johns Hopkins University. He holds a PhD in anthropology from Columbia University.

Clare Lockhart is a fellow at the Overseas Development Institute in London. From 2002 to 2005 she served as adviser to the Ministry of Finance in Afghanistan. She is a Member of the Bar of England and Wales, where she practiced public and commercial law.

Baqer Massoud served in the Afghanistan Ministry of Finance under Ashraf Ghani.

Justine Nannyonjo is a senior research fellow at the Economic Policy Research Centre at Makerere University in Kampala; prior to that position she worked at the Bank of Uganda's Research Department as head of the Statistics Division. She holds a PhD in development macroeconomics from the University of Gothenburg in Sweden.

Léonce Ndikumana is director of research in macroeconomics at the UN Economic Commission on Africa in Addis Ababa; associate professor of economics at the University of Massachusetts, Amherst; and president of the African Finance and Economics Association. He received a PhD in economics from Washington University in St. Louis.

Nargis Nehan served in the Afghanistan Ministry of Finance under Ashraf Ghani.

Madalene O'Donnell is on the staff of the UN Department of Peacekeeping Operations. Previously, she coordinated the program on postwar statebuilding at New York University's Center on International Cooperation; she has also worked on public-sector reform at the World Bank and served as anticorruption adviser at the US Agency for International Development.

Emilia Pires is an international consultant specializing in aid management, currently working with the World Bank in West Bank and Gaza. She was formerly secretary of the Planning Commission, Timor-Leste, and was responsible for the first Timor-Leste National Development Plan. She holds a master's degree in development management from the London School of Economics and Political Science.

Pablo Rodas-Martini is the director of Central America in the World Economy of the XXI Century and a columnist for *El Periódico* of Guatemala. He has collaborated in the UNDP's *Human Development Reports*, Transparency International's *Global Report on Corruption*, and the Center for Public Integrity's *Global Integrity Report*. He holds a PhD in economics from the University of London.

Paul Smoke is associate professor and director of international programs at the Robert F. Wagner Graduate School of Public Service at New York University. He is coeditor of *Decentralization in Asia and Latin America: Towards a Comparative Interdisciplinary Perspective* (2006) and author of *Fiscal Decentralization in Developing Countries* (2001) and of *Local Government Finance in Developing Countries: The Case of Kenya* (1994). He received his doctorate from the Massachusetts Institute of Technology.

Robert R. Taliercio Jr. is the World Bank's senior country economist for Cambodia. He has also worked extensively in Latin America and Asia. Prior to joining the World Bank in 2000, he was a lecturer in the public finance group at the Harvard Institute for International Development. He holds a PhD in public policy from Harvard University.

Index

Abbas, Mahmud, 189–190, 194, 195, 205, 206

Accelerated District Development program (ADD), 65, 72

Accountability: Afghanistan, 153–154, 156–159, 166, 177, 178, 180, 181; Cambodia, 59, 64–67, 72, 76; Guatemala, 112–113; overview of countries, 4, 5(table); Palestinian Authority, 192–193, 203; and statebuilding, 153–154; Timor-Leste, 146

Acholi people, 17(map), 18(table), 19–23, 20(table), 48

ADB. *See* Asian Development Bank

ADD. *See* Accelerated District Development program

Afghan militia forces (AMF), 180–181

Afghan National Army, 180, 290

Afghanistan, 12–13, 153–183, 235–240, 294–295; accountability, 5(table), 153–154, 156–159, 166, 177, 178, 180, 181; banking and currency (*see* Afghanistan, currency and banking system); budget allocation and expenditure management (*see* Afghanistan, expenditure management); corruption, 165, 166, 168, 172, 181; economic indicators (*see* Afghanistan, economic indicators); foreign aid (*see* Afghanistan, external assistance); government credibility and delivery of

services, 160; government legitimacy and control of public finance, 169, 272; historical context, 3, 155–156, 235–236; Human Development Index (HDI), 5(table); impact of neighboring countries, 3; Islamic theory of governance, 169; lack of agreement on final status, 3; narcotics trade, 3, 172, 174–175, 238, 278; and odious debts, 292; public perceptions of accountability and government effectiveness, 4, 5(table); taxation (*see* Afghanistan, revenue mobilization); and transparency, 166

Afghanistan, currency and banking system: banking system, 162–165, 175, 221–222, 224, 236, 239–240, 242; currency, 236–238; currency and banking reform, 155, 162–165, 214–215; currency exchange mechanism, 163–165, 219, 237–238; dollarization, 236, 237; *hawala* dealers, 163, 164, 224, 236, 238, 240; monetary policy, 238–239; payment system, 237–240

Afghanistan, economic indicators: domestic revenue/external assistance, 4, 5(table), 6; exchange rate, 162–163, 170, 239; GDP/capita, 5(table); inflation, 5(table); revenue/GDP, 4, 5(table), 6, 272

Afghanistan, expenditure management, 175–180, 272; and

327

About the Book

In the aftermath of violent conflict, how do the economic challenges of state-building intersect with the political challenges of peacebuilding? How can the international community help lay the fiscal foundations for a sustainable state and a durable peace? *Peace and the Public Purse* examines these questions, lifting the curtain that often has separated economic policy from peace implementation.

Drawing on recent experiences in Afghanistan, Bosnia and Herzegovina, Cambodia, Timor-Leste, Guatemala, Palestine, and Uganda, the authors bring to life a key dimension of how both peace and states are built.

James K. Boyce is professor of economics at the University of Massachusetts, Amherst, where he directs the program on peacebuilding at the Political Economy Research Institute. He is author of *Investing in Peace: Aid and Conditionality After Civil Wars* and editor of *Economic Policy for Building Peace: The Lessons of El Salvador.*

Madalene O'Donnell is on the staff of the UN Department of Peacekeeping Operations. Previously, she coordinated the program on postwar statebuilding at New York University's Center on International Cooperation; she has also worked on public-sector reform at the World Bank and served as anticorruption adviser at the US Agency for International Development.

Center on International Cooperation
Studies in Multilateralism